Fiscal Policy without a State in EMU?

Fiscal Policy without a State in EMU?

Germany, the Stability and Growth Pact and Policy Coordination

Jani Kaarlejärvi

palgrave
macmillan

First published 2007 by
PALGRAVE MACMILLAN
Houndmills, Basingstoke, Hampshire RG21 6XS and
175 Fifth Avenue, New York, N.Y. 10010
Companies and representatives throughout the world

PALGRAVE MACMILLAN is the global academic imprint of the Palgrave Macmillan division of St. Martin's Press, LLC and of Palgrave Macmillan Ltd. Macmillan® is a registered trademark in the United States, United Kingdom and other countries. Palgrave is a registered trademark in the European Union and other countries.

ISBN 13: 978–0–230–54275–4 hardback
ISBN 10: 0–230–54275–1 hardback

This book is printed on paper suitable for recycling and made from fully managed and sustained forest sources. Logging, pulping and manufacturing processes are expected to conform to the environmental regulations of the country of origin.

A catalogue record for this book is available from the British Library.

A catalogue record for this book is available from the Library of Congress.

10 9 8 7 6 5 4 3 2 1
16 15 14 13 12 11 10 09 08 07

Printed and bound in Great Britain by
Antony Rowe Ltd, Chippenham and Eastbourne

Contents

List of Figures and Tables

Figures

Tables

Acknowledgements

This book is based on my doctoral dissertation reviewed in the University of Sheffield in Britain. I am really happy to say that the choice of the topic could have not been more interesting. In fact, this was the primary reason why I have managed to work so effectively with my own strict timetable. The empirical and theoretical timing and contribution of the research to the understanding of the system of fiscal policy coordination could not either have been more appropriate because the Stability Pact lived its own fascinating life with major downturns and upturns throughout this whole research process from 2002 to 2005. To present and analyse the continually changing dynamic of the Stability Pact in the EMU environment with its entire complex political, economic, institutional and legal dimensions has been a major work but a highly rewarding one.

Although this project has been entirely my own, it has still required cooperation and networking with leading academics and experts in this research field: EU/EMU studies. I would like to thank Prof. Andrew Gamble at the Department of Politics in the University of Sheffield for making our cooperation work so effectively. I am also grateful for the facilities and the encouraging environment for academic research that I experienced at the Max-Planck Institute in Cologne in Germany in 2004.

I have also benefited greatly from thought-provoking suggestions from and discussions with Prof. Pertti Ahonen (University of Tampere), Prof. Paul De Grauwe (University of Leuven), Prof. Knud Erik Jørgensen (University of A[o]rhus), Prof. Veli Karhu (University of Tampere), Dr Susan Marton (University of Gothenburg), Mrs Virginia Mattila (University of Tampere), Prof. Vivien Schmidt (University of Boston) and Prof. Amy Verdun (University of Victoria).

I also want to thank those EMU experts in the European Central Bank, the European Commission, the German Bundesbank, the German Bundesländer, the German Federal Ministry of Finance and leading German research institutions with whom I was in close cooperation during the research process for their cooperation and information.

Most sections of the book have been presented at a number of leading international and European conferences and workshops on EU/EMU studies, and the study has benefited from the comments and views evinced on those occasions:

1 The European International Relations Summer School on *The EU Facing Eastern Enlargement* in Jena, Germany and in Prague, Czech Republic in July 2002;

2 The Comparative Summer School on *Economic Analysis of Illegal Activities* in Oslo, Norway in August 2002;
3 The International Conference on *Multilevel and Federal Governance* in Victoria, Canada in October 2002;
4 The European Summer School on *Theories and Research Design in the Field of EU Studies* in A[o]rhus, Denmark in August 2003;
5 The European Economic Workshop on *EMU: Current State and Future Prospects* in Rethymno, Greece in August 2003;
6 The ECPR Conference on *Winners and Losers of EU Decision Making* in Marburg, Germany in September 2003;
7 The EUROFRAME Conference on *Economic Policy Issues in the European Union* in Paris, France in June 2004;
8 The ECPR Conference on *Implications of a Wider Europe: Politics, Institutions and Diversity* in Bologna, Italy in June 2004;
9 The UACES *Research Conference* in Birmingham, UK in September 2004;
10 The Research Seminar on *The Fiscal Authority of the Member States in EMU* at the Department of Economic History in Gothenburg, Sweden in February 2005; and
11 The Research Conference on *Is There a Fiscal Policy without a State in EMU?* at the Centre For Public Sector Research in Gothenburg, Sweden in February 2005.

The importance of my family in Finland: priceless.

Introduction

This study focuses on one of the most topical issues on the European political and economic agenda: fiscal policy coordination in Economic and Monetary Union (EMU) and the required adjustments to national fiscal policies by EMU Member States. It presents a single coherent case study of German fiscal policy with the creation of the Stability and Growth Pact (or the Stability Pact) in 1995–1997 and with the implementation of the Stability Pact since 1997. Both the theoretical and empirical contributions of the study are significant. *Theoretically*, this study shows that in the process of Europeanisation, national interests have had a major impact on the formation (uploading) of fiscal policy coordination. It also shows how European fiscal policy coordination has affected national fiscal policies and policy implementation (downloading) in EMU, and how changes in national interests have finally launched the reform process of the original Stability Pact (reuploading), a new phase of Europeanisation. *Empirically*, this study demonstrates how the EMU process, originating in the Maastricht Treaty, created a new role for national economic policy with the transfer of monetary authority to an independent European Central Bank. In these circumstances, the second element of economic policy, fiscal policy (including budgetary policy, public finances, taxation and employment policy) has become a significant instrument in effectively adapting national economies to cyclical global and European environments. However, the credibility of fiscal policy coordination under the Stability Pact has, to say the least, been controversial in EMU.

Through the main question of *how and to what extent the formation of the Stability and Growth Pact has affected the implementation of German national fiscal policy in EMU*, the study analyses the German economy under the first and second Schröder governments (1998–2005). The empirical material on the German economy in EMU shows that if it is analysed only through the formal rules of the Stability Pact, Germany has undeniably broken the fiscal rules since 2002. However, the formal rules for assessing the national economy ignore a crucial understanding of the development of the German economy over this period because Germany has sought to promote fiscal stabilisation through major reforms even though they have not yet been fully effective. However, as Germany, like certain other EMU Member States, continually faced major problems with the Stability Pact, the original fiscal rules were finally amended at the Ecofin Council meeting on 20 March 2005. In short, this extensive analysis of the German economy raises four central findings on European fiscal policy coordination. *Firstly*, the fiscal rules of the Stability Pact and fiscal policy coordination in EMU are as essential as ever in the economic environment of mounting national debt and deficit stocks. *Secondly*, Member States have to renew and strengthen their political and economic commitments to the common objectives of fiscal policy coordination. *Thirdly*, the developments in Member States should be assessed from a country-specific approach under the excessive deficit procedure of the Stability Pact. *Finally*, as shown in this study, the making of a common European fiscal policy through increasing fiscal policy coordination briskly and in a similar way to the common monetary policy has experienced serious difficulties and thus, it is possible to argue that at the moment, there is not yet a common fiscal policy without a state in EMU.

Part I

Germany, the Stability and Growth Pact and Policy Coordination on the Political and Economic Agenda in Europe

1
The Europeanisation of Fiscal Policy Coordination

1.1 Europeanisation and European economic integration

Fiscal policy in Economic and Monetary Union (EMU) and its successful coordination are largely unsolved issues. That is why this study provides an understanding of the institutional dynamic of European fiscal policy coordination. It focuses on fiscal policy coordination, the implementation of the Stability and Growth Pact (SGP) in Germany and German national adjustments. Fiscal policy coordination in this study refers to the political and economic power of the institutions of the European Union (EU) to set formal and informal fiscal constraints for the national economies of the Member States within which they have to implement their national fiscal policies.[1] National adjustments mean those domestic economic, institutional, political and cultural mechanisms of national policy-making through which the Member States have tried to adjust their national economies to increasing fiscal policy coordination.

The fundamental objective of fiscal policy coordination among national economies in EMU is to contribute to price stability and a successfully functioning EMU (monetary dominance). Fiscal policy coordination is expected to reduce and eliminate the impact of poor (overly expansive or restrictive) national fiscal policies on the stability of the single-currency area, the Euro area, and thus to create an economically favourable environment for stability and growth. For this purpose, Member States have agreed to establish more and more formal and informal coordination models and procedures, for example the Stability and Growth Pact, that have, in practice, considerably constrained the traditional fiscal authority of the Member States and increased that of the common EU institutions. As most recent experience of the Stability Pact shows, the institutional system of fiscal policy coordination has, however, pointed to significant limitations: the making of a common European fiscal policy is still clearly an unfinished process. Therefore, the aim of this research is to develop an empirical analysis regarding the Europeanisation of fiscal policy coordination and the institutional capacity of the EU institutions for effective fiscal policy coordination by drawing on the increasing knowledge of the complex relationship between EU institutions and national adjustments in EMU: *how and to what extent does the increasing fiscal policy coordination "Europeanise" the national economies of the EMU Member States?*

As some EU Member States, such as Britain, Denmark and Sweden, did not participate in the latest phase of economic integration by joining EMU in 1999, the politico-economic situation in the EMU and non-EMU Member States is significantly different at the moment: the EMU Member States, such as Germany and France, have the common monetary policy with its economic (monetary and fiscal) constraints, whereas the non-EMU Member States, such as Britain, face EMU's economic spill-overs as informal constraints for their national monetary and fiscal policies due to strong European economic interdependencies.[2] Thus, establishing and implementing a truly common economic policy in Europe in the long term, which includes both monetary and fiscal affairs, appears an exceptionally challenging subject. Monetary and fiscal policy coordination is an extremely interesting subject on the European agenda in striving for coordination within the existing EU institutions. Due to the increasing interdependence of the European national economies, economic policy coordination is required not only among the EMU Member States but throughout the economic area of the EU. The increasing significance of fiscal policy coordination for national fiscal authority stems from the fact that although Member States themselves have established the common objectives for coordination in the EU and EMU, the implementation of fiscal policy coordination has set major limitations for national economic policy-making. For example, Germany as the promoter (the pace-setter and the key EMU player) of the economic integration process and as the biggest and the most powerful European economy, amounting to about one-third of the whole EU economy, has experienced the most difficulties in fully meeting all the criteria and objectives that have been set under fiscal policy coordination in EMU.[3] Due to the unforeseen national and European as well as economic and political developments, Germany has clearly broken the fiscal rules for deficit and debt in the 21st century although it was Germany that outlined (uploaded) the strict fiscal rules for the common monetary policy in the mid-1990s. Thus, through the case study of the German economy under European fiscal policy coordination, the broad politico-economic contribution of this research, which lies at the heart of the political (political science) as well as economic (EMU studies) debate, is: *how and to what extent does European fiscal policy coordination affect national economic policy-making in EMU? And how have national economies responded to this?*

Europeanisation and European integration

This introductory chapter develops two interconnected arguments, political and economic, of European economic integration and its impact on national economic policy-making (Europeanisation) for the study of the institutional dynamic of European fiscal policy coordination in EMU; both arguments will be taken further in the empirical part of the research. From the point of view of political science, the current phase of European political and economic integration is an ambiguous and challenging process, and it relates to the study of EU institutions, policy coordination and national adjustments in a unique way.[4] There has been an accelerated integration process, highlighted by the establishment of the EU[5] in 1993 and the start of the third stage of EMU in 1999, soon after the collapse of the Soviet Union and German reunification in Europe. The direct and indirect impact of the EU and EMU on European political and economic order, statehood, economy and all individual EU citizens is unparalleled.[6] Although the EU Member States together agreed to delegate authority to a new collective and regional organisation, the European Union, the meaning, importance and implications of the EU for the Member States have exceeded predictions. On the other hand, some predictions have not yet been fulfilled. Due to the interconnected politico-economic environment, the EU has gradually become a complex community affecting and guiding all major policy areas, but simultaneously, its fundamental authority is still defined by the Member States. This characterises the current era in Europe in a unique way: interdependence in all policy areas in which actors and agencies are interrelated. The significance of European integration also stems from the fact that its direct and indirect impact is felt primarily within one continent and that European integration has created new, complex, formal and informal coordination and governance structures in its every stage. Currently, supranational treaties and directives are the strongest element of the existing political and economic system of the European Union.

Academically, this entire European political and economic process has been included in the concept of Europeanisation. According to Radaelli, Europeanisation refers to "processes of (a) construction, (b) diffusion, and (c) institutionalisation of formal and informal rules, procedures, policy paradigms, styles, 'ways of doing things' and shared beliefs and norms which are first defined and consolidated in the making of EU decisions and then incorporated in the logic of domestic discourse, identities, political structures and public choices".[7] Europeanisation, with all its implications for the European nation-states, national politics, economy and citizens, provides a current and comprehensive definition of Europe where European, national, regional and local actions are very much interrelated. Europeanisation, which should be seen as a top-down process, aims in loose theoretical terms to describe the current nature and outcomes of European integration.[8] Among scholars in EU studies, the concept of Europeanisation is a widely debated subject but is sometimes confused with the process of European integration. However, European integration and Europeanisation are not entirely different themes. European integration, which started immediately after the Second World War, should be seen as a gradual, bottom-up process that has resulted in a politically and economically collective organisation, the European Union, whereas Europeanisation includes the implications of this process for its Member States.

Already before Europeanisation, there have been a lot of different concepts, definitions and "-isations" applied to European integration. Although not all "-isations" should always be seen as purely competing concepts but partly as overlapping, the advantage of Europeanisation compared to earlier terms, for example globalisation, liberalisation and regionalisation, is, according to Ladrech, its specific focus on national levels, Member States, which arbitrate both formally and informally the effects of the European integration process.[9] In general, globalisation has been seen to affect the traditional sovereignty of nation-states in governing their national policies independently but global institutions have emerged to try to control the globalisation process and the liberalisation of world trade, in particular in the field of finance. In this politico-economic framework, regionalisation, in Rosamond's view, puts in an appearance as "various economic arrangements among groups of geographically proximate countries".[10] However, Schmidt argues that "countries' responses to Europeanisation have brought changes in policies, practices and politics even greater than those related to globalisation".[11] Europeanisation together with regionalisation and institutionalisation can also be seen as a counterforce, or as a response, to globalisation and liberalisation because within Europeanisation, European countries have established their own institutions and policy-making processes to control the Internal Market on the one hand, and to retain the major role of the nation-states in Europe on the other.

Europeanisation as a two-way process

The problem of the concept of Europeanisation, however, in understanding the current state of policy-making in the EU is that it primarily focuses either on the formation of common policy areas (the bottom-up process) or national policy implementation (the top-down process). Robert Ladrech, when analysing French national politics within the then European Community at the beginning of the 1990s, defined Europeanisation for the very first time as "an incremental process reorienting the direction and shape of politics to the degree that EC political and economic dynamics become part of the organisational logic of national politics and policy-making".[12]

Ladrech's interpretation aptly characterised the then nation-state-led process that at that time yielded totally new common policy areas and major institutional changes in European integration. However, understanding the fundamental nature of the European Union today cannot be done thoroughly by focusing solely on the formation of common institutions and policy areas or the national policy implementation process alone, but by combining the bottom-up and top-down processes; Europeanisation as a two-way process.

The most recent academic literature specifically devoted to the process of Europeanisation has been increasingly interested in the intimate relationship between these two bottom-up and top-down processes. Although the topic has been politically and economically debated, Knill and Lehmkuhl still argue that the developments in the role of national policy-making have not been thoroughly investigated in the context of the current European integration. Their starting point is to draw out the main mechanisms of Europeanisation through which the European integration process has been transferred directly and indirectly to national policy-making. Knill and Lehmkuhl identify three main European mechanisms: "European policies might be: a) very prescriptive and demand that Member States adopt specified measures in order to comply with EU requirements; b) confined to changing domestic opportunity structures; or c) in their weakest form, without any direct institutional impact at all since their primary aim is to change domestic beliefs and expectations."[13] Thus, their approach to Europeanisation already recognises the fact that it is not the bottom-up process or the top-down process alone that affects EU institutions and national policy-making in the European Union but the complex relationship between these two processes.

Most interestingly from the point of view of this research, it is Risse, Green Cowles and Caporaso who adopt a specific "three-step approach" through which they analyse how European integration affects national policy strategies and policy-making processes. Their approach effectively combines both the bottom-up (European integration) as well as the top-down (Europeanisation) processes for the study of the relationship between EU institutions and national policy-making. Firstly, their approach regards Europeanisation as a powerful set of European coordination systems, which, in practice, formalise supranational rules, regulations and common policy objectives. They argue that Europeanisation as a top-down process causes significant adaptation pressures to carry out national adjustments to effectively adapt common policy objectives in Member States. Basically, these national adaptation pressures refer to "the extent to which domestic institutions would have to change in order to comply with European rules and policies".[14] Secondly, the degree of national adaptation pressures is a result of policy "fit" (policy compatibility or the goodness of "fit") or "misfit" (adaptation problem) between the objectives of the EU and those of the Member States. Thirdly, these national adaptation "fits" and "misfits" occur because according to Risse, Green Cowles and Caporaso, there are different "institutional and cultural conditions that facilitate or prohibit flexible responses to adaptation pressures" in the Member States.[15]

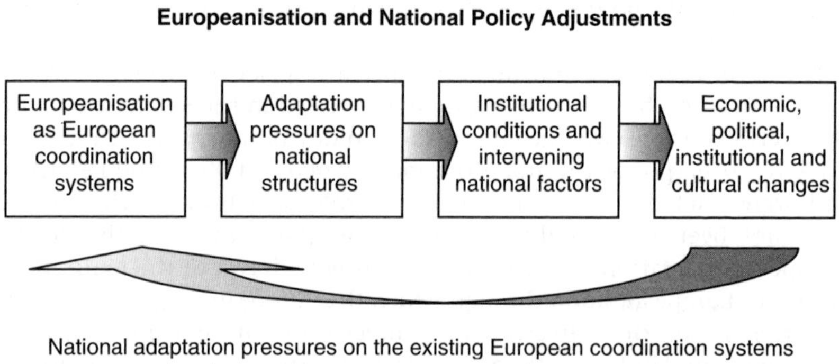

Figure 1.1 The three-step approach from the formation of European coordination systems via adaptation pressures to changes in national policy-making.[16]

Although Risse, Green Cowles and Caporaso take the role of adaptational, institutional and cultural conditions into account in their analysis of the process of Europeanisation, what they do not emphasise sufficiently is the fact that during the implementation process, European and national interests may be reformed directly affecting the effectiveness of the adaptation of common policy objectives in Member States. Thus, the core theoretical and empirical intension of this research is directed to the role of national factors that in the end define the extent to which common policy objectives create national adaptation "fits" and "misfits" in the implementation process (downloading) and the extent to which the concrete experience (success and/or failure) from national implementation finally reforms the existing European coordination systems (reuploading). As an analytical result, this three-step approach focuses on the relationship between European coordination systems, national adaptation pressures and national policy adjustments as modified and specified for this research in Figure 1.1. This complex relationship thus draws together both the bottom-up (European integration) and top-down (Europeanisation) dimensions in the European Union.[17]

Europeanisation and European institutionalism

Based on Scharpf's (1997) and (2000b), Risse, Green Cowles and Caporaso's (2001), Schmidt's (2001), Buller and Gamble's (2002), Howell's (2002), Schmidt's (2002), Dyson's (2003a), Heipertz and Verdun's (2003a), and

Börzel and Sedelmeier's (2006) analyses, one of the strongest forms of current European research relates to the study of the relationship between EU institutions and national policy adjustments. Where the formation of common EU institutions is defined as an uploading process in which national interests are integrated into common policy areas and objectives, a downloading process refers to the national implementation of the common policy objectives within common EU institutions; the bottom-up and top-down processes of Europeanisation. From this perspective, as Buller and Gamble argue, the bottom-up process is characterised by "the importance of purposeful choices" because new institutional systems at the European level are "designed for reasons".[18] In the following top-down process, according to Anderson, "institutions influence what actors do (or do not do) by allocating power to some actors but not others, structuring the content and sequence of policy-making, and providing opportunities for, and constraints on, the state as its officials seek societal support for their policy choices".[19] Similarly, Börzel regards European integration as an institutional process that has set significant authority limitations for national policy-making. Therefore, she takes the view that Europeanisation is a two-way process in which bottom-up "emphasises the evolution of European institutions as a set of new norms, rules and practices", whereas top-down "refers to the impact of these new institutions on the political structure and processes of the Member States".[20] Analysed critically, the two-way process can also be seen as a gradual but continual pathway towards European institutionalisation, which would create even more powerful common institutions, wider and deeper common policy areas and stronger policy coordination than in the European Union today, a European harmonisation process.[21]

The timing element of Europeanisation

European integration can be seen as a path-dependent process that has an impact on national policy-making over time. Buller and Gamble thus introduce the timing of Europeanisation as a new explanatory factor for the study of the impact of institution formation and policy evolution on national policy-making (Figure 1.2).[22] Timing as a temporal dimension is an essential variable when analysing the implementation (downloading) phase of previously established (uploaded) common policy objectives in Member States.[23] Timing, for Buller and Gamble, refers to a concrete two-way process "where domestic actors in one country at one point in time (t1) encouraged the process of European integration (t2) which then impacted back on the domestic politics of that same country (t3)".[24] According to them, "governments who have been or are in the process of experimenting with policies also being introduced at the European level, will find it easier to adapt to such European pressure as and when it materialises".[25] If studies focused only on European and national processes

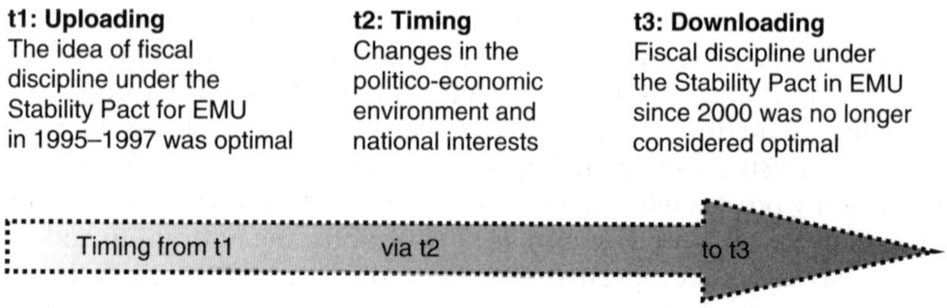

Figure 1.2 Timing in the uploading and downloading of the Stability Pact.

between t2 and t3 and not at all on the comparison between t1 and t3, Buller and Gamble correctly deduce that there would be a considerable risk of "neglecting important causal mechanisms further back down the temporal chain".[26] Therefore, Bache argues that "only by understanding what is being downloaded from the EU in relation to what is being and has been uploaded from Member States, and contextualising this dynamic in relation to broader international processes and independent domestic sources of change can we understand of the process of Europeanisation".[27]

In agreement with Buller, Gamble and Bache, this research contends that the timing element is a crucial factor when analysing the differences between the uploading and downloading processes in European fiscal policy coordination domestically and at the European level: common coordination systems are expected to have a major impact on national policy-making. In fiscal policy coordination, the optimal outcome of increasing coordination would be a situation where, despite possible adaptation and coordination problems, the established EU institutions would function effectively and Member States would achieve common policy objectives (debt and deficit rules) from t1 to t3 (a win-win situation). However, the present problems in the implementation phase of the fiscal rules of the Stability Pact clearly imply the possibility that the changes in the internal and external environment in t2 have notably affected the interests of some large Member States, such as Germany and France, for common policy objectives, which have, in turn, caused a change, a major reduction, in the level of national commitments and a lack of adequate national adjustments to fully comply with the common objectives of fiscal policy coordination. As the main result from the declining national commitments, EU institutions are no longer successfully coordinating national fiscal policies in t3 (a lose-lose situation). To thoroughly examine the primary reasons for the problems in the implementation phase of fiscal policy coordination in the German economy, this research benefits greatly from the temporal dimension in this process-tracing.

Europeanisation and national adjustments in fiscal policy coordination

Although Europeanisation is not the first "process" to which European countries have had to adjust their national policies, Schmidt finds that EU Member States have dealt with the need for national adjustments very differently.[28] For example, convergence in European economic policy has not occurred as fast as was thought because Member States have continued to respond in different ways and to varying degrees to common monetary and fiscal objectives and increasing economic policy coordination. Thus, according to Jupille and Caporaso, most recent research on the Europeanisation of national policies "attempts to explain variations in domestic institutions by appealing to institutional and economic changes at the European level".[29] Dyson, however, emphasises that it is very challenging to differentiate between the adjustment pressures from Europeanisation, liberalisation and globalisation, and the actual needs for policy adjustments in Member States. European economic integration, together with EMU and the Stability Pact, has already had a major impact on national monetary and fiscal authority and national adjustment processes. Thus, Dyson regards the current state of European economic integration as "a complex dynamic interaction between top-down and bottom-up effects".[30] Since it has been the Member States that have established common EU institutions and policy objectives for increasing economic policy coordination in the EU, national economic and political interests and adjustment processes, and in particular those of traditionally powerful Member States Germany and France, have played a major role in both the uploading and downloading processes.[31]

Yet, there have been significant differences in uploading and downloading processes between Member States in fiscal policy, for example between Germany and Britain. Where Britain has had no major role in uploading fiscal policy coordination nor has it been fully subjected to its downloading impact, the practice in Germany has been the opposite.[32] On the one hand, the uploading process (bottom-up) in European fiscal policy coordination has been characterised by the leading role of Germany as the key pace-setter and uploader in the formation of the Stability Pact in 1995–1997. It was Germany and German national interests that most significantly contributed to the objectives of the Stability Pact for the EMU era, which brought strict fiscal policy coordination and a substantial sanction procedure for breaking the common fiscal rules.[33] On the other hand, Germany has also been increasingly subjected to European fiscal policy coordination and economic monitoring in the downloading phase (top-down) in EMU and thus, German economic policy-making has been considerably influenced by the common institutional systems; a fact that has caused one of the main problems in the German economy in 2002–2005.[34] In the formation process of the Stability Pact in 1995–1997, the German government assumed that implementing national fiscal policy under the fiscal rules in EMU would not require any major national adjustments or cause any major national difficulties because the German government had played the key role in uploading its national interests into the common coordination system. It was assumed that the more the Member State contributes to the formation process of totally new coordination objectives in European fiscal policy, the less adaptation pressures, "misfits", it should have when implementing them.

However, as discussed here from the point of view of political science, the formation of fiscal policy coordination has created major adaptation challenges for Germany and its national economic policy-making in EMU. What is also of great significance here is that the existing knowledge of the process of Europeanisation does not include a full understanding of *what, if anything, happens in European and national policy-making if substantial national "misfits" occur in the implementation phase of the common policy objectives*. The literature on Europeanisation has correctly pointed out that Member States may face adaptation "fits" and "misfits" in policy implementation but the essential question of what happens in the implementation phase if Member States face severe adaptation problems remains unclear. If severe "misfits" occur in the implementation phase at the national level, do Member States just totally freeze the implementation process? Or, will they only partially implement the common policy objectives? Or, will they perhaps try to reform existing common objectives to better comply with changed national interests to reduce national adaptation "misfits", that is reuploading?[35] Therefore, with this as background, Hypothesis One can now be formulated:

> **Hypothesis One** The greater role a Member State has had in the formation (uploading) of the common institutional system for European fiscal policy coordination (the Stability Pact), the fewer national economic and other adaptation problems it has when implementing (downloading) the common fiscal objectives.

1.2 EMU and fiscal policy coordination

Institutionalising fiscal policy coordination in EMU

The thorough analysis of uploading and downloading processes in European fiscal policy coordination cannot be based only on the political perspective alone. Even though the fundamental policy-making process in the formation of the Stability Pact has been distinctly political, the driving force behind increasing fiscal policy coordination in EMU has been economic: stability, employment and growth. The significance of the economic perspective for the uploading and downloading processes stems from the fact that European fiscal policy coordination has a notable and concrete impact on national economies and national economic policy-making and *vice versa*. As will be shown next, the institutional study of fiscal policy coordination should be based on both a theoretical approach and an analytical framework that can adequately combine the political and economic elements of European fiscal policy coordination. In the current stage of European integration, one cannot be understood without the other.

From the standpoint of economics (EMU studies), EMU was established with the aim of achieving economic stability and growth for the whole of Europe. After the start of EMU on 1 January 1999, monetary authority totally shifted from the EMU Member States to the federal European Central Bank (ECB).[36] During the three stages of EMU, there was an extensive social and academic debate about the economic requirements for the success of EMU. The main themes included, for example, EMU as an optimum currency area, monetary stability in participating national economies and the credibility of the common monetary policy. The primary focus was thus directed towards monetary questions and how monetary stability could promote the success of EMU. However, concentrating only upon the common monetary policy ignores another significant economic reality: the importance of national fiscal policies in improving price stability and safeguarding economic growth in EMU. In other words, the close relationship between the common monetary policy and national fiscal policies in EMU was partly forgotten. For the Chief Economist of the ECB, Otmar Issing, "while the single monetary policy is oriented towards a union-wide objective, namely the maintenance of price stability, the other policy areas – involving fiscal and wage policies – largely remain the competence of national governments and other national actors".[37]

Currently, there is one common monetary policy among 12 EMU Member States, 13 different monetary policies and 25 different fiscal policies among 25 EU Member States within the system of European economic policy coordination. In these highly complex circumstances, the main challenge for the success of EMU lies in coordinating monetary and fiscal objectives effectively between different EU institutions and Member States. Buti, Roeger and in't Veld argue that, fundamentally, "conflicts between monetary and fiscal policies arise when the central bank's objective function differs from that of fiscal authorities".[38] It would be very interesting to study how credible and successful EMU could be with a common monetary policy but no common fiscal policy in the long term. If Europe really wants a successful EMU, there should be institutionally organised and effective coordination models between monetary and fiscal policies for the common good, stability and growth.[39] In practice, fiscal policy coordination in the EU is based on the fiscal rules of the Maastricht Treaty and those of the Stability Pact on which EU politicians agreed at the Dublin European Council in December 1996.[40] The objective of the fiscal rules is firstly, to act as preconditions for joining EMU and secondly, to strengthen economic stability in EMU. However, the formal fiscal policy coordination is only defined by the three percent of Gross Domestic Product (GDP) deficit rule and the 60 percent of GDP debt rule, the exceeding of which may result in the implementation of the supranational sanction mechanism. To achieve and maintain required fiscal stability in EMU, Member States have thus decided to use more strict supranational restrictions than national flexible incentives: more stick than carrot. The driving force of fiscal policy coordination has been a strong political conviction that the more coordination and stricter rules there are in EMU, the less asymmetry and the fewer implementation problems there will be between national economies. It is this asymmetry that creates a critical link between the political and economic perspectives of Europeanisation because Member States have sought a political solution (institutional fiscal policy coordination) to economic objectives (stability and growth) in EMU. To capture the current state of fiscal policy coordination, Hypothesis Two is now formed:

> **Hypothesis Two** The more institutionalised fiscal policy coordination is at the European level, the fewer adjustment problems will occur in fiscal policy implementation in a Member State and the less the Member State will try politically and economically to reform and reinterpret the common rules (reuploading).

The question of asymmetric fiscal policies and asymmetric policy adjustments is crucial and characterises the current state of fiscal policy coordination in EMU.[41] In principle, the ultimate objective of the debt-to-GDP and deficit-to-GDP criteria is to eliminate asymmetric national fiscal policy actions. The requirement of symmetric fiscal policies stems from the fact that the stability and credibility of the common monetary policy may be jeopardised by completely uncoordinated and asymmetric fiscal policies and policy responses in EMU.[42] In the worst-case scenario, this kind of asymmetric national fiscal behaviour could, according to the ECB, cause "an upward drift in public spending and deficit ratios that can put the sustainability of public finances at risk".[43] In reality, despite the strict rules of the Stability Pact, there still exists sizeable asymmetry between national fiscal policies in EMU. Member States have succeeded in bringing down high debt levels to some extent but with the deficit ratio some large EMU Member States have had persistent problems. For example, the Commission has launched the monitoring and reporting mechanism of the Stability Pact against Germany and France but, ironically, it has been Germany that has had most difficulties with the Stability Pact in 2002–2005. As the strict and clear fiscal rules have not secured and strengthened symmetric national fiscal policy-making, the fiscal policy coordination under the Stability Pact has not been as effective as was planned. Instead of improving fiscal stability and hastening fiscal convergence, recent economic developments in Germany and France have resulted in increasing asymmetry between national fiscal policies in EMU: economic developments have proceeded from symmetric and counter-cyclical actions towards asymmetric, expansive and pro-cyclical national fiscal policies.

Fiscal policy coordination in practice

Politically, the powerful sanction mechanism of the Stability Pact, the excessive deficit procedure, has still not been implemented although Germany and France have clearly exceeded the deficit and debt limits. Analysed critically, the decision of the Ecofin Council on 25 November 2003 not to penalise Germany and France for breaking the deficit rule for the third time in succession destroyed or at least froze the credibility of fiscal policy coordination in EMU. The Ecofin Council and the Brussels European Council finally tried to restore the lost credibility by reforming the original rules of the Stability Pact of 1997 in their meetings on 20 and 22–23 March 2005.[44] Where the Commission has done its supranational duty and monitored and reported the developments in both countries to the Ecofin Council, it has been the Ecofin Council that has persistently decided not to apply the sanction mechanism.[45] Economically, what is significant here is that there were 12 different national fiscal policies among EMU Member States prior to EMU, and there are still 12 different national fiscal policies in EMU Member States in the EMU era. What has changed in European economic policy is that monetary authority has been shifted from Member States to the independent ECB. However, the success of EMU in the long term is not only dependent on the common monetary policy but also effectively executed national fiscal policies. For the success of EMU, eliminating asymmetric national fiscal policies and asymmetric fiscal behaviour through effective European fiscal policy coordination is thus crucial. In agreement with this argument, the ECB has also taken the view that "well-designed institutions that create incentives to pursue stability and sustainability-oriented policies are essential in achieving such objectives".[46]

There are a large number of institutions in the EU and EMU that aim to contribute towards national fiscal policy convergence and to reduce asymmetry between them. Institutionally, the broad system of economic policy coordination is governed by the concrete political cooperation between the main EU bodies: the European Council of Ministers, the European Central Bank, the Commission and the European Parliament. In practice, the European Council of Ministers for Financial Affairs (the Ecofin Council), the Commissioner for Economic and Financial Affairs (Directorates General II), the Governing Council of the ECB, the Economic and Monetary Affairs Committee of the European Parliament, the Monetary Policy Committee (MPC), the Economic and Financial Committee (EFC), the Economic Policy Committee (EPC), and the Euro-12 group as economic actors constitute the coordination system of the European Union and EMU.[47] However, there is no common and responsible body where decisions concerning both monetary and fiscal affairs could be made simultaneously in the EU and EMU. This being so, economic, monetary and fiscal, policy co-ordination and the politico-economic future of EMU become even more challenging. As Virén puts it, "policy coordination is subjected to all possible problems of political economy".[48]

Currently, there is economic evidence of fiscal policy coordination within the Stability Pact in EMU. During the first month of its existence, the dramatic fall in the Euro exchange rate against the US dollar caused a new wave of social and academic debate about the credibility of EMU. Coordinating monetary and fiscal policies in EMU had not proved to be a watertight system after all. However, the effectiveness of EMU to provide and maintain stabilised and predictable exchange, interest and inflation rates has gradually improved in the 21st century.[49] The most recent attention in the European economy has thus focused not only on monetary policy but also fiscal policy coordination and its credible and successful practice to achieve the common economic objectives in the Euro area. In practice, the political and economic topicality of European fiscal policy coordination arises from the situation that Germany exceeded the three percent of GDP deficit limit in 2002–2006 and France in 2002–2004, but the Ecofin Council has not yet invoked the excessive deficit procedure; a fact that has meant a substantial setback for the political and economic credibility of the Stability Pact, fiscal policy coordination and national fiscal discipline in the EMU era.[50]

As there is a serious lack of an institutional system in the EU and EMU that could coordinate both monetary and fiscal policies simultaneously and effectively, the present state of European economic policy coordination is under considerable challenge. If a successful monetary and fiscal policy requires more and more coordination, there arises another related question in the EU and EMU: what would this mean for the economic authority of the Member States?[51] *Could there be a common European fiscal policy without a state in EMU?* It is a real question of economic authority when one examines the current system of European economic policy coordination where 12 EMU Member States have a common monetary policy in EMU and where there exist 13 different national monetary policies and 25 different national fiscal policies in the EU; this is an incomplete and ineffective institutional system for economic policy coordination within which severe political, economic, institutional and legal conflicts have occurred and may occur in the future. What is also critical in the future is how the EU Enlargement will affect the effectiveness of economic policy coordination. How could European economic policy coordination possibly operate optimally after the EU Enlargement, when there was not effective and successful policy coordination between only 15 Member States in the European Union prior to May 2004?

1.3 Outline of the book

This research presents a single coherent case study of German fiscal policy with the creation of the Stability and Growth Pact in 1995–1997 and with the implementation of the Stability and Growth Pact since 1997.[52] The main question is: *how and to what extent has the formation of the Stability and Growth Pact affected the implementation of German national fiscal policy in EMU?* As recognised in this chapter, there is an obvious need for the study of the institutional system of fiscal policy coordination. However, there is a major contradiction in EMU stemming from the fact that economic policy-making in Member States has direct and indirect effects (spill-overs) on both the EMU and the non-EMU Member States' national economies. Member States are not only increasingly dependent on the fiscal policies of the other Member States but also on the common monetary policy of the ECB. Thus, all Member States, whether in EMU or not, are equally responsible for the concrete implementation and achievement of common European economic objectives.

Theoretically, this study shows that in the process of Europeanisation, national interests have had a major impact on the formation of European fiscal policy coordination (uploading). It also shows how fiscal policy co-ordination has affected national fiscal policies and policy implementation (downloading), and how changes in national interests have finally launched the reform process of the original fiscal rules of the Stability Pact (reuploading); a new phase of Europeanisation. Empirically, this study demonstrates how the EMU process, originating in the Maastricht Treaty, created a new role for national economic policy as monetary authority has been transferred to an independent ECB systems. In these circumstances, the second element of economic policy, fiscal policy (including budgetary policy, public finances, taxation, structural and labour policy) has become a significant instrument in effectively adapting national economies to cyclical global and European environments. However, the credibility of fiscal policy coordination under the Stability Pact has, to say the least, been controversial in EMU. This argument is based on the critical fiscal developments in Member States and the concrete policy limitations set by the Maastricht convergence criteria (1992), the Stability and Growth Pact (1996), the Luxemburg process (1997) introducing the European employment strategy, the Cardiff process (1998) setting structural and labour policy reforms, the Vienna strategy (1998) confirming coordination, the Cologne process (1999) establishing the European macroeconomic dialogue, and the Lisbon strategy (2000) adopting economic reforms, which all serve to confine national economies and economic policy-making in EMU.[53]

A single case study method is applied as the main instrument to analyse the two-way process between the formation process (uploading) of fiscal policy coordination and its national implementation (downloading) in the

German economy. The case of Germany demonstrates how fiscal policy coordination has affected national economic policy-making and policy adjustments in Germany. The case study examines changes and tendencies in the German economy over time from the uploading process to the downloading process of the Stability Pact and beyond (reuploading) in the course of the development of EMU; this is done both descriptively and conceptually. A case study method enables the researcher to understand how fiscal policy coordination has affected the German economy, how and to what extent the German economy has had to respond to it, and how the experience from German economic policy-making has in turn affected fiscal policy coordination. In addition to analysing German economic policy and national adjustments, this research also considers German experience in relation to the experience of other large Member States, such as Britain, France and the EU in general.

A combination of qualitative and quantitative research methods is used in this research. The research material consists of literature, quantitative data and qualitative documents and key interviews. Firstly, literature on EU institutions, fiscal policy coordination and national adjustments is exceedingly crucial due to the academic nature and theoretical contribution of this research. A major part of the literature consists of academic journals. Secondly, primary data consists of policy documents and data related to economic policy-making and implementation in Germany, EMU and the EU. The economic databases of the German government, the German Bundesbank, the European Central Bank and the Commission are utilised when analysing quantitative data on policy coordination, fiscal convergence and national policy responses. Thirdly, there are also a large number of key interviews, altogether 20 conducted, to compile latest knowledge of and experience from the system of fiscal policy coordination and its current problems and future challenges in EMU. The method employed is a semi-structured interview with open-ended questions, thus allowing the researcher and the interviewees to cover some specific themes and topics in more detail and in more depth than in a structured interview. The interviews in this study were conducted personally, face-to-face, making it possible to analyse the insider information of interviewees as well as their experience. The targets of these 20 interviews were leading officials and public servants in the German Federal Ministry of Finance and the German Bundesbank, representatives of the Bundesländer, officials in the European Commission and the European Central Bank and leading German academics, all of whom have been involved with the German economy and fiscal policy coordination at the national and European levels.

The first of the three research areas, "Germany, the Stability and Growth Pact and Policy Coordination on the Political and Economic Agenda in Europe" includes Chapter 1. It analyses the Europeanisation of fiscal policy coordination from various perspectives and argues for the social relevance and academic topicality of the study of fiscal policy coordination. Although there is some knowledge of the relationship between EU institutions and national adjustments among EMU scholars, the chapter claims that there is still a lack of understanding of the extent to which EU institutions, once established, affect national economic policy-making in EMU and *vice versa*.

The research area two, "Fiscal Policy Coordination under the Stability and Growth Pact in Economic and Monetary Union", consists of four chapters. Chapter 2 provides the political, economic, institutional and legal foundations of European fiscal policy coordination and examines the role of existing EU institutions in economic policy agenda-setting and fiscal policy coordination. The implementation of national fiscal policy under the terms of the Maastricht Treaty and the Stability Pact has in particular faced major challenges in Germany. The analysis is concerned with the questions of why and how national fiscal policies are coordinated in EMU and how effective the fiscal rules and institutional fiscal policy coordination have been in practice.

By analysing developments in the German economy and German national politics Chapter 3 traces the question of under what economic and political circumstances Germany introduced the idea of the Stability Pact. The main focus is to study the main trends in German economic policy from right after German reunification to the start of the Stability Pact in 1997 and how Germany planned to prepare for fiscal policy coordination in EMU. The analysis of the German fiscal pathway to EMU focuses not only on economic factors but also political, institutional and cultural dimensions when examining German national interests in having strict fiscal policy coordination: what policy elements did Germany (the Bundesbank, the government and other social stakeholders) want to upload into the Stability Pact in 1995–1997?

In line with the analysis of the formation process in Chapter 3, Chapter 4 goes on to analyse the implementation phase of the Stability Pact under Schröder's first government 1998–2002: why did Germany have severe problems in implementing the Stability Pact? The chapter examines to what extent Germany succeeded and failed in responding to the rules of the Stability Pact. Although the German economy had a high growth period 1998–2000, the sudden and sharp downturn after 2000 resulted in major problems not only in budgetary policy but also in public finances, monetary policy and labour policy, causing the breaking of the fiscal rules in 2001 and 2002.

Chapter 5 focuses on German fiscal policy during Schröder's second government 2003–2005. Although the critical financial reality escalated in the German economy in 2001–2002 and although Germany was subjected to increasing European economic monitoring, the Ecofin Council permitted Germany major national fiscal flexibility. The chapter's primary contention is that due to the major economic and political problems,

Germany started the political process of revising the interpretation of the fiscal rules within the EU institutions in 2003–2005 by reuploading its new and changed interests into the original Stability Pact of 1997; a new phase of Europeanisation. Finally, the Ecofin Council reformed the interpretation of the original fiscal rules on 20 March 2005.

The final research area, "Germany, the Stability and Growth Pact and Policy Coordination: Institutional Capacity for Effective Fiscal Policy Co-ordination in EMU" consists of two chapters. Based on the empirical findings from the case study of the German economy, Chapter 6 assesses the present and future state of fiscal policy coordination. The institutional system of the Stability Pact is reviewed through 20 key interviews with leading European, national and regional experts conducted in June and July 2004. The chapter analyses in particular the extent to which the difficulties in the German economy under European fiscal policy coordination in 2002–2004 affected the overall functioning of the Stability and Growth Pact in EMU.

While Chapter 6 deals more with empirical findings and concrete policy recommendations, Chapter 7 provides a summary of the most crucial theoretical findings based on this research on "Fiscal Policy without a State in EMU?" clearly providing weighty theoretical feedback and a contribution to Europeanisation theory-building. By defining a new concept of re-uploading, it explains in great detail what the real added-value in the Europeanisation of fiscal policy coordination is and which of the three "-loading" phases (uploading, downloading and reuploading) matter most in the present European fiscal policy coordination. In addition, the chapter deliberates to what extent it is still possible, if at all, to discuss traditional national fiscal authority under increasing fiscal policy coordination in EMU: is there already a common European fiscal policy without a state in EMU? Or, do national interests and national economic policy-making still play a key role in European economic policy after all?

Part II

Fiscal Policy Coordination under the Stability and Growth Pact in Economic and Monetary Union

2
The Institutional System of Fiscal Policy Coordination

2.1 Theory of institutional fiscal policy coordination

Rationales for fiscal policy coordination in EMU

Rationales for fiscal policy coordination in EMU are one of the most challenging topics on the current European economic agenda. This current relevance stems from the fact that although it was Germany that required the strict and formal system of fiscal policy coordination for EMU, this chapter will finally show that, surprisingly, it has been Germany that has had the most difficulties in complying with the common rules for national fiscal policies in EMU. The making of a common European fiscal policy through the institutional system of fiscal policy coordination has thus pointed to significant limitations. This chapter will analyse *the political, economic, institutional and legal foundations of European fiscal policy coordination* and examine *the extent to which this foundation in practice constrains national fiscal policy in EMU.*

The starting point for analysing the theoretical and practical aspects of fiscal policy coordination is the fact that monetary instruments, exchange rate, and interest and credit rate policies are no longer available to boost exports and accelerate growth in EMU Member States since the establishment of the ECB in 1999. As the primary objective of fiscal policy coordination is to secure fiscal discipline for monetary stability in EMU, the Stability and Growth Pact requires Member States to keep national budgetary policies within the three percent deficit and the 60 percent debt criteria. The key argument of the traditional Keynesian macroeconomic model and the optimum currency area theory for fiscal policy coordination is that by stabilising the fiscal elements of national economic policies in a monetary union it is possible to contribute to long-term economic stability and growth. For other economists, however, such as Artis and Winkler, the fundamental problem of economic policy coordination relates to "national and aggregate European fiscal policies and the common monetary policy, rather than across national fiscal authorities alone".[1] In practical terms, monetary and fiscal policies of participating economies have to be consistent in EMU because major debt and deficit stocks could undermine the ECB's main objective: price stability. The purpose of monetary and fiscal policy coordination in EMU is thus to eliminate economic problems and prevent them from escalating through coordinated policy actions to deal with any economic shocks, whether symmetric or asymmetric.[2]

Regarding effective national economic policy-making, economists have debated whether increasing fiscal policy coordination has only advantages or whether it also causes some disadvantages in EMU. The main disadvantage of EMU for participating Member States has been the shift of ultimate monetary authority from national control to European authority: the fact that monetary policy instruments are no longer at national governments' disposal has meant completely new requirements for national fiscal policy instruments, adjustments and flexibility. The political and economic impact of this disadvantage depends primarily on what alternative mechanisms and instruments there are available to secure effective adjustments to symmetric and asymmetric shocks in Member States in EMU. Fiscal policy instruments have a major role in the event of an asymmetric demand-side, country-specific shock, whereas symmetric shocks are most effectively eliminated collectively in the Euro area by the monetary supply-side instruments of the ECB. If an economic shock, whether demand-side or supply-side, has a substantial impact on the whole Euro area, close policy coordination also occurs as an effective policy measure. In perfectly flexible markets, national adjustments would not be required because production factors would stabilise the impact of asymmetric shocks automatically and instantaneously. However, the current EMU area is not considered perfectly flexible by the optimal currency area theory and thus, the function and movement of production factors, such as labour and capital factors, cannot stabilise national economies across and within countries automatically and instantaneously.[3]

Some economists, such as Breuss and Weber, define an ideal Euro area to be an economic area in which "the single monetary policy would, given the primary objective of preserving price stability, be able to provide a common response to aggregate economic development, whereas decentralised budgetary policies and other national economic policy instruments would be available for responding to country-specific circumstances".[4] In current European economic circumstances, it is the fiscal policy that has the primary responsibility for providing required flexibility for national economic policy-making in EMU Member States. Ideally, "in the case of a full cooperation, where the 12 EMU countries coordinate their fiscal policy with the monetary policy of the ECB the welfare gains obtained are very large for Euroland as a whole".[5] However, there is no "full cooperation" between fiscal and monetary policies in EMU at the moment, and the development of effective economic, fiscal and monetary, and policy coordination models is not progressing without problems. Coordinating fiscal and monetary policies in EMU, which is defined as European policy mix, is therefore still one of the main challenges in the whole EMU system.

Many economists such as Gros and Thygesen have argued strongly for effective European policy mix in EMU, by which they mean a policy-making process in which fiscal and monetary policies are coordinated simultaneously. Firstly, European policy mix is required because fiscal policy as a powerful economic instrument affects national demand and it has direct and indirect spill-overs to demands in other Member States. According to Robson, "coordination of policy becomes an issue whenever spillover effects of domestic fiscal policies on partner countries are significant and are not taken into account by member countries".[6] Secondly, European policy mix is required because fiscal policy has an impact on the common monetary policy through several economic channels. For example, excessive budgetary policy causes an increase in interest rates and thus it slows down growth in the Euro area, which in turn has to be compensated by actively implemented monetary instruments. These developments could, without any economic policy coordination at all, lead to the politically difficult situation in which a Member State would have to "explain to its electorate that it has to increase taxes and/or reduce expenditure because demand is too strong in other parts of the EU".[7] Finally, Gros and Thygesen arrive at the critical conclusion that "the real obstacle to effective fiscal policy coordination, under any circumstances, is the fact that fiscal policy is determined mostly by short-term domestic political considerations".[8] This is echoed by Eichengreen. To prevent bad, uncoordinated and short-term economic policy-making in EMU, such as expansive national fiscal policies together with a restrictive common monetary policy, he argues for close economic policy coordination and European policy mix by suggesting, "it is desirable that national fiscal policies are coordinated, and monetary and fiscal policies are harmonised".[9]

The economic literature on economic policy coordination in EMU has sought to deal with these spill-over effects through two primary interconnected economic policies: a) to eliminate fiscal spill-overs from a Member State to other Member States, and b) to stabilise inflationary pressures.[10] Fiscal spill-overs are a major reason for coordinating the ECB's monetary objectives and the fiscal policies of Member States in EMU. Due to the increasing deficit and debt stocks in EMU Member States, however, it is currently the common monetary policy that has the main responsibility for stabilising the impact of expansive fiscal policies. Economists have analysed how the way that Member States use fiscal instruments has come to define the concrete models of coordination for eliminating macroeconomic problems, such as beggar-thy-neighbour, free-rider and bail-out situations. Firstly, negative fiscal spill-overs, which result from running an expansionary fiscal policy in a Member State compared to other participating EMU

Member States, are interpreted as a beggar-thy-neighbour situation. Secondly, if a Member State systematically utilises positive fiscal spill-overs deriving from other EMU Member States, economic policy coordination should instantly try to eliminate this free-rider possibility. In the third situation, according to Begg *et al.*, "a government could run up its debt to an unsustainable level and then extract a transfer of resources from other countries through a bail-out operation".[11] The politico-economic situation of bail-out in EMU stems from the fact that Member States have positive incentives to implement expansive fiscal policies with major debt and deficit stocks because they believe that there always exists the ECB's ultimate financial support in EMU if required in the event of a financial crisis. For example, in a situation with no coordination at all, Buti argues that Member States would not consider that they could significantly benefit from the spill-overs of a fiscal expansion in other Member States;[12] a belief that would reduce the likelihood of unfavourable national fiscal behaviour in EMU.[13]

As regards inflation, economists have noted how the ECB can monetarise the increase in national public debts and allow much higher inflation rates in EMU than would be optimal and desirable for European economic stability and growth as a whole.[14] Chari and Kehoe, for example, in the context of monetary union, stress the importance of the relationship between the debt and deficit rules for national fiscal policies and the objectives of the common monetary authority, low and stable inflation and interest rates. They argue that the desirability of national debt and deficit constraints in EMU depends on the extent of the ECB's commitment. If the ECB cannot commit to its own monetary objectives, "there is a free-rider problem in fiscal policy, and debt constraints may be desirable".[15] This lesson is derived from the fact that public debts in participating national economies can partially be monetarised in the future by the ECB, but Member States may still ignore "the costs this induced inflation imposes on other Member States".[16] According to Eichengreen, Member States may be reluctant and incompetent to anticipate the impact of increasing public borrowing on interest rates in EMU but the main problem, according to him, is that "excessive borrowing in one country will drive up the level of interest rates monetary union wide".[17] If Member States still continue to issue more and more public debt in EMU, the situation results in a politico-economic crisis with a free-rider problem and major economic inefficiency in the whole EMU area. As the two main solutions to eliminate this fiscal-policy-caused monetary problem, Chari and Kehoe suggest either imposing fiscal constraints on Member States or strengthening the ECB's commitment to its primary objectives.

Institutional design, adjustments and risks in theory

In order to achieve these coordination objectives a number of formal and informal institutions within the European Union have been established.

According to Beetsma, Debrun and Klaassen, "in the context of the European Union, the issue of policy coordination is often addressed in institutional terms, the question being whether decisions about a given policy instrument should be taken at the central level (the Union level) or be decentralised (at the national, regional or local levels)".[18] The main institutional difference which characterises monetary and fiscal policies in EMU is the fact that monetary policy is already institutionalised (harmonised), whereas coordination in fiscal policy is still based on a softer, less institutionalised and more flexible intergovernmentalist approach. Where the common monetary policy has its formal institutional system (EMU, the European System of Central Banks (ESCB) and the ECB), fiscal policy is defined by soft regulating institutions (for example the Stability Pact and the open method of coordination). Formal monetary institutions are regarded as *ex ante* coordination models because they aim at converging and harmonising the whole implementation process of common objectives strictly and directly. Beetsma, Debrun and Klaassen argue that *ex ante* coordination models operate "through formal agreements recognised by the parties as international obligations (pacts, treaties, regulations or any compelling norm of international or supranational law)".[19] This community method together with formal institutions in monetary policy is based on the ECB's Treaty-based mandate and its independent institutional structure in which the Governing Council has the highest decision-making power. In fiscal policy, there are also important institutions, but their role is seen more as informal due to the lack of an institutionalised and Treaty-based structure in the European Union. The main purpose of fiscal policy coordination is to ensure a stabilised economic environment for the common monetary policy and therefore, it is defined as *ex post* coordination. However, Beetsma, Debrun and Klaassen argue that *ex post* coordination in fiscal policy is "ad-hoc and takes place on the basis of the current state of affairs".[20] Where institutions in monetary policy have acted as preconditions for the European monetary stability, institutions in fiscal policy try to safeguard the broad economic environment for the operational success of EMU.

Undoubtedly, national adjustments also play a major role in fiscal policy coordination within this existing *ex ante* and *ex post* institutional design. The importance of national adjustments stems from the fact that monetary policy instruments can no longer be used to stabilise national economies over the economic cycle in EMU. Eichengreen argues that "a European country which ties its monetary hand behind its back should keep its fiscal hand free. Having abandoned the exchange rate and an independent national monetary policy as instruments of adjustment, it is essential that it retains its fiscal flexibility".[21] In these circumstances, the main challenge is to find an optimal policy solution to the extent to which Member States respond and make national adjustments to increasing fiscal policy coordination in the EMU context. Buti and Sapir's starting point to analyse national policy responses and macroeconomic adjustments within EU institutions is the fact that the ECB executes the centralised monetary instruments primarily for symmetric economic shocks in EMU, whereas it is the decentralised national fiscal policies that are effective in responding to asymmetric, country-specific economic shocks. Thus, national adjustments have the key role in stabilising national economies in the event of asymmetric shocks in the EMU era. According to Buti and Sapir, effective national fiscal stabilisation requires in the event of a major economic crisis that, firstly, national fiscal policies have a certain degree of flexibility and secondly, that the objectives and instruments of national fiscal policies are coordinated at the European level.[22] Following their reasoning, to achieve national fiscal flexibility and the effective system of European fiscal policy coordination simultaneously poses a distinctly ambiguous challenge for national adjustments and EU institutions.

It is also the case, as Winkler shows, that the likelihood of joining EMU and effective national adjustments have become inextricably linked. If a Member State has made effective national adjustments in a determination to achieve a high level of economic convergence, this has increased the probability of joining EMU right from the start in 1999. On the other hand, a high likelihood of participating in EMU has contributed to national budgetary stability, inflation and interest rates and other policy adjustments. However, Winkler ironically argues that "if EMU is the solution to domestic credibility problems, requiring candidates to solve their credibility problems before joining appears paradoxical".[23] Economic data on budgetary deficits in EMU Member States in 1970–1995 illustrates that to comply with the strict three percent deficit criterion most Member States have had to make substantial adjustments. Based on Gros and Thygesen's economic study, only seven Member States, such as Finland, France and Germany, had an average budgetary deficit below the required three percent ratio in 1970–1995. Gros and Thygesen thus arrive at the critical conclusion that "it is beyond doubt that the trend in fiscal policy must change radically under EMU".[24] Furthermore, they ask "whether member countries need just to bring the average deficit below three percent of GDP or whether they also have to make their budgets more stable".[25] They also show that budgetary deficit ratios have deteriorated over the three percent ceiling a number of times over the last 25 years but in the current economic circumstances, this kind of significant variation in national budgetary policies, if repeated, would cause unpredictable risks and challenges to the whole EMU system.

Although fiscal policy coordination in EMU has many advantages from an economic perspective, there are also several risks and challenges involved. Firstly, European economic policy can currently be defined as a policy mix in which the European Central Bank executes the common monetary policy with the price stability target and Member States are responsible for national budgets, redistribution and wage policies under the guidelines of the Maastricht Treaty, the Stability Pact, the broad economic policy guidelines and the so-called European processes.[26] Beetsma, Debrun and Klaassen are convinced that the primary reason for current problems in economic policy coordination in EMU stems from the fact that the institutional system of coordination consists of too many and too powerful political and economic actors and competing national and European interests and therefore, "the risk of a poorly coordinated policy mix is potentially greater than in the usual situation in which there is one central bank and only one government".[27]

Secondly, another risk that Beetsma, Debrun and Klaassen also identify relates to differences in monetary and fiscal policy coordination. Traditionally, both economic policy areas together have had the leading role in eliminating problems in national economies and counterbalancing national economic cycles. Whereas monetary policy is considered fairly straightforward and easy to coordinate and monitor at the European level, fiscal policy has experienced major problems in coordination and monitoring since 2001. Beetsma, Debrun and Klaassen emphasise the complexity of and variation in fiscal affairs (budgetary policy, taxation and labour policy) and the diversity in the fiscal interests of Member States and that of EU institutions. For example, they point out the challenge of analysing public expenditure in Member States, which, in practice, has different implications depending on whether it relates to public consumption or investments.[28] In these circumstances, fiscal policy appears much more difficult and challenging to coordinate in EMU than monetary policy when also taking into account variations across national economies and policy-making processes.[29]

A third risk is that the close relationship between European fiscal policy coordination and national adjustments and commitments is not sufficiently emphasised in the current EMU debate. According to Virén, the need for strict fiscal policy coordination and national political and economic commitments should "both be accepted and effectively enforced at the national level". Otherwise, "it is not hard to imagine which kind of political problems that could arise and in this light it seems that discretionary policy coordination can only succeed in very special cases".[30] This critical position towards inadequate national adjustments and commitments is also clearly presented by Cobham, who believes that failure to secure national commitments to common economic objectives leads the debate to the fundamental question of whether to allow more national flexibility in European economic policy or whether to strengthen the role of common institutions in coordination and monitoring in EMU. According to Cobham, "the former remains difficult and inevitably relies on a large measure of discretion, while the latter continues to be seen as involving a significant loss of national sovereignty and therefore continues to be resisted".[31]

A fourth risk is that as Buti, Franco and Ongena argue, fiscal discipline as defined in the Stability Pact and fiscal flexibility are not mutually exclusive but complementary aspects of economic policy coordination. According to them, "once EU countries have attained a budgetary position of 'close to balance or in surplus' and are operating at 'cruising speed' under the Pact, there will be sufficient room for their automatic stabilisers to operate fully".[32] Analysed more realistically, the fact that some large Member States, such as Germany and France, have had major fiscal problems in EMU points, according to Buti and Sapir, "to the need for a sufficiently rapid convergence by EMU members towards the medium-term fiscal target in order to avoid excessive deficits in the event of a cyclical downturn".[33] The primary problem in budgetary deficits stems from the fact that at the beginning of the EMU era, in 1999, many national economies were not at the medium-term balance, but many of them were about to reach fiscal balance due to the unfinished fiscal convergence in the late 1990s. Thus, national economies have had to continue working towards fiscal balance through major adjustments in the EMU era, under increasing economic policy coordination and under the loss of monetary policy instruments: a fact that has not yet allowed optimal conditions for effective national adjustments and successful economic policy coordination in EMU.

2.2 Formal rules of fiscal policy coordination

Forms of economic policy coordination

In EMU fiscal policy coordination should not be understood as a separate coordination system but as an integral part of the broad system of European economic policy coordination, which in practice varies from information exchange to collective decisions and independent institutions across different economic policy areas. According to the Commission, "the degree and the mechanisms for coordination differ according to how convincing the economic rationale for coordination is in the particular policy area".[34] For example, the wide range of instruments in fiscal policy coordination consists of European legislation, strict European rules, decisions, sanctions, financial incentives, agreed targets and benchmarks. For the Commission, these coordination instruments "have often been added on an ad hoc basis without necessarily taking the wider picture fully into account" and therefore, "the present framework has arguably become complex and more difficult to understand and explain".[35] As shown in Table 2.1, there is a variety of coordination models depending on the competence level (exclusive EU competence, shared competence or exclusive national competence), and micro policy areas (value added tax, competition and environmental policies and labour markets), as well as macro policy areas (monetary and fiscal policies) in EMU. Firstly, monetary policy in the Euro area is defined as the "single policy" (exclusive EU competence)

Table 2.1 Forms of economic policy coordination in EMU.[36]

	Policies	Forms of Coordination	Modes of Coordination	Actors Involved	Procedures
Single Policy	**Monetary policy**	**Single policy**	**Single Institution**	**ECB**	
	Exchange rate	**Single policy**	**Coordination in the Ecofin Council**	**Ecofin Council, ECB, Euro-12 group, Commission**	
	Competition policy	**Single policy**	**Implementation by the Commission**	**Member States, Commission, Ecofin Council**	
Close Coordination	Budgetary policy	Treaty rules, peer view, commonly agreed rules and objectives, information exchange	Coordination in the Ecofin Council	Member States, Commission, Ecofin Council, Euro-12 group	Excessive Deficit Procedure, Stability and Growth Pact, Broad Economic Policy Guidelines
	Structural policies, Internal Market	Rules, directives joint decisions, Council peer view	Coordination in the Ecofin Council	Member States, Commission, Ecofin Council	
Weak Coordination	Policy mix	Dialogue, information exchange	Joint fora	ECB, Commission, Ecofin Council, Euro-12 group, Social partners	
	Budgetary policy (quality of public finances)	Commonly agreed objectives	Coordination in the Ecofin Council	Member States, Commission, Ecofin Council, Euro-12 group	Stability and Growth Pact, Broad Economic Policy Guidelines

Table 2.1 Forms of economic policy coordination in EMU.[36] – *continued*

	Policies	Forms of Coordination	Modes of Coordination	Actors Involved	Procedures
Single Policy	**Monetary policy**	**Single policy**	**Single Institution**	**ECB**	
	Exchange rate	**Single policy**	**Coordination in the Ecofin Council**	**Ecofin Council, ECB, Euro-12 group, Commission**	
	Competition policy	**Single policy**	**Implementation by the Commission**	**Member States, Commission, Ecofin Council**	
	Wage developments	Dialogue, information exchange	Joint fora	Social partners, Commission, Ecofin Council	Broad Economic Policy Guidelines, Macroeconomic dialogue (Cologne)
	Labour market policies	Information exchange, discussion of best practices, peer view, guidelines	Coordination in the Ecofin Council	Member States, Commission, Ecofin Council, Social partners	Broad Economic Policy Guidelines, Employment Guidelines (Luxemburg)
	Product and capital market policies	Information exchange, discussion of best practices, peer view, guidelines	Coordination in the Ecofin Council	Member States, Commission, Ecofin Council	Broad Economic Policy Guidelines, Economic reform reports (Cardiff)
	External representation, communication	Agreement on a common understanding	Joint fora	ECB, Euro-12 group, Commission	

among EMU Member States sharing not only the same policy and policy instruments but also the same institutions (the ECB and the Euro-12 group). Secondly, "close coordination" (shared competence) refers to coordination that is primarily based on the authority of Member States in close cooperation with common institutions. However, close coordination simultaneously contains some common rules and some shared objectives for national policy implementation, such as the Stability Pact acts in fiscal policy. Thirdly, in some policy areas policy coordination is characterised by "weak coordination" (exclusive national competence) together with coordination processes (Luxemburg, Cardiff and Cologne) and strategies (Vienna and Lisbon) and models from information exchange to peer pressure under the exclusive national competence.

Binding rules of fiscal policy coordination

The Maastricht Treaty of 1992 introduced specific preconditions, the convergence criteria for the third and final stage of EMU, the membership in the single-currency area. Although the criteria are fundamentally based on monetary policy, they are also an integral part of the system of fiscal policy coordination because they establish two core criteria for national fiscal policies: public debt and budgetary deficit criteria. Formally, the convergence criteria are defined by Articles 102a–109m of the Maastricht Treaty and the Protocols of the Maastricht Treaty No. 5 and No. 6, as follows:

1 Public debt must not exceed 60 percent ratio to GDP.[37] However, exceeding the debt ratio is acceptable if the ratio has declined substantially and continuously, and it has reached a level that comes close to the reference value; or, alternatively, the excess over the reference value is only exceptional and temporary, and the ratio remains close to the reference value.[38]
2 Member States must avoid excessive budgetary deficits.[39] The planned or actual budgetary deficit must not exceed 3 percent of GDP.[40] However, the ratio of budgetary deficit can exceed the reference value, unless the ratio is sufficiently diminishing and approaching the reference value at a satisfactory pace.[41]
3 Member States have to support all actions towards the achievement of a high degree of price stability.[42] The criterion means that a Member State has a price performance that is sustainable and an average rate of inflation, observed over a period of one year before the examination, that does not exceed by more than 1.5 percentage points that of, at most, the three best performing Member States.[43]
4 Member States must proceed towards the durability of convergence in the terms of the long-term interest-rate levels.[44] The criterion means that, observed over a period of one year before the examination, a Member State has had an average nominal long-term interest rate that

does not exceed by more than 2 percentage points that of, at most, the three best performing Member States.[45]

5 The currency of the Member State has been observed within the normal fluctuation margins provided for by the Exchange Rate Mechanism (ERM) of the European Monetary System, for at least two years, without devaluing against the currency of any other Member State.[46] The criterion means that the Member State has respected the margins provided for by the ERM without severe tensions for at least the last two years before the examination. The Member State must not devalue its currency's bilateral central rate against any other Member State's currency on its own initiative for the same period.[47]

Apart from the five core criteria, the Maastricht Treaty also defines the Broad Economic Policy Guidelines (BEPG) for converging national fiscal policies in the EU. Firstly, Article 98 requires that "Member States shall conduct their economic policies with a view to contributing to the achievement of the objectives of the Community in the context of the broad guidelines". Secondly, Article 99 establishes clear convergence and coordination obligations for national fiscal policies by stipulating that "Member States shall regard their economic policies as a matter of common concern and shall coordinate them within the Council". Thirdly, Member States are also required to implement national fiscal policies strictly under the broad economic policy guidelines. Finally, the Maastricht Treaty introduces a supranational sanction procedure on excessive budgetary deficits in EMU. If national economic policy-making is not "consistent with the broad guidelines", or it "risks jeopardising the proper functioning of Economic and Monetary Union", the Ecofin Council may make "the necessary recommendations to the Member State", or it may "decide to make its recommendations public".[48]

However, the fiscal rules of the Maastricht Treaty proved to be insufficient to provide the required fiscal discipline for the EMU era because the Treaty defined only two general fiscal rules: the deficit and debt rules. These two fiscal rules were considered inadequate to stabilise national economies without any further specification in the implementation of the rules and without any further reforms in common coordination procedures. To specify the fiscal rules of the Maastricht Treaty and to ensure fiscal stability in the third stage of EMU more effectively, the heads of states and governments agreed to establish a Stability and Growth Pact in the Dublin European Council of December 1996, and the final decision on the Stability Pact was made in the Amsterdam European Council in June 1997.[49] In practice, the Stability Pact specified the implementation of the sanction procedure of the excessive budgetary deficit and the sanction mechanism, which concretised the institutional procedure for breaking the fiscal rules more precisely than was originally defined in the Maastricht Treaty, became a part of fiscal policy coordination. To safeguard national fiscal discipline in EMU, the Member

States thus decided to use more formal restrictions (rules) than national political and economic incentives (discretion) – more stick than carrot.

In the final decision on the Stability Pact, the Amsterdam European Council emphasised "the importance of safeguarding sound government finances as a means to strengthening the conditions for price stability and for strong sustainable growth" and therefore, "it is necessary to ensure that national budgetary policies support stability oriented monetary policies".[50] According to the European Council, Member States have three main obligations under the rules of the Stability Pact: they have to a) "respect the medium-term budgetary objective of position close to balance or in surplus", b) "commit themselves to take the corrective budgetary action to meet the objectives of their stability and convergence programmes", and c) "correct excessive deficits as quickly as possible after their emergence".[51] Although the Commission ensures the timely and effective functioning of the Stability Pact, it is the Ecofin Council that has the supreme and final decision-making role in the issue regarding the implementation of the Stability Pact. According to the Stability Pact, the Ecofin Council "is invited always to impose sanctions if a participating Member State fails to take the necessary steps to bring the excessive deficit situation to an end", and it has to "state in writing the reasons which justify a decision not to act on a Commission recommendation".[52] However, what has to be emphasised here is that before any sanctions under the Stability Pact can be imposed, Article 99 of the Maastricht Treaty stipulates that the Ecofin Council has first to decide on the existence of an excessive budgetary deficit in a Member State.

There are three primary regulations and procedures in European fiscal policy coordination through which the objectives of fiscal policy coordination are targeted: a) the broad economic policy guidelines (Article 99 of the Maastricht Treaty), b) the multilateral surveillance of national budgetary policies (the Stability Pact), and c) the excessive deficit procedure (the Stability Pact). Firstly, the broad economic policy guidelines as defined by Article 99 of the Maastricht Treaty aim at strengthening economic stability together with the multilateral surveillance procedure and the excessive deficit procedure. The objective of the broad economic policy guidelines, which have been implemented in the European Union since 1993, is to support economic growth through economically stable circumstances, such as sound budgetary policy, sustainable public finances, predictable inflation rates, and high employment and productivity rates. For these purposes, the Ecofin Council annually adopts broad economic policy guidelines with country-specific recommendations within which every Member State, whether in EMU or not, is required to implement its national economic objectives and instruments under the multilateral surveillance of the Commission.[53]

Secondly, the Council Regulation on the Strengthening of the Surveillance of Budgetary Positions specifies the rules on multilateral surveillance in fiscal policy coordination. According to the regulation, all EMU Member States have to submit their national stability programmes to the Council and the Commission and non-EMU Member States have to submit their national convergence programmes. These programmes are needed "for the purpose of multilateral surveillance", "to prevent, at an early stage, the occurrence of excessive general government deficit", and "to promote coordination of economic policies".[54] Both stability and convergence programmes have to clearly present "the medium-term objective for the budgetary position of close to balance or in surplus and the adjustment path towards this objective".[55] This Council regulation in particular emphasises that the information given to EU institutions on national economic developments must be reliable and updated "on an annual basis and shall cover, as well as the current and preceding year, at least the following three years".[56]

Thirdly, the excessive deficit procedure is made up of three single regulations: a) the Regulation on the Application of the Protocol on the Excessive Deficit Procedure; b) the Regulation on Speeding up and Clarifying the Implementation of the Excessive Deficit Procedure; and c) the Regulation on References to ESA 95 (Commission 2002a), which only specifies previous economic definitions. The Regulation on the Application of the Protocol on the Excessive Deficit Procedure defines budgetary deficit (or surplus) as the net borrowing (or net lending) of national government, which includes central government, local government and social security funds. Public debt refers to "the total gross debt at nominal value outstanding at the end of the year of the sector of general government".[57] In particular, this regulation imposes an obligation for economic reporting by requiring Member States to "report to the Commission their planned and actual government deficits and levels of government debt twice a year, the first time before 1 March of the current year (year n) and the second time before 1 September of year n".[58] The regulation thus specifies the deficit and debt definitions of the Maastricht Treaty and sets the exact deadlines for national economic reporting to the Commission.

The Regulation on Speeding up and Clarifying the Implementation of the Excessive Deficit Procedure further defines the implementation of excessive deficit procedure. Despite the aim of strict fiscal discipline in EMU, this regulation allows Member States to exceed the fiscal limits in some specific, exceptional and temporary, circumstances. The regulation specifies that the excess of deficit over the rule is considered exceptional and temporary when it results from "an unusual event outside the control of the Member State concerned and has a major impact on the financial position of the general government", or when it results from "a severe economic downturn".[59] Budgetary deficit is considered exceptional "only if there is an annual fall of real GDP of at least 2 percent", and temporary if deficit should "fall below the reference value following the end of the unusual event or the severe economic downturn".[60] By defining exceptional and temporary circumstances the Stability Pact thus clearly allows national fiscal flexibility in a downturn.

In addition, the regulation defines supranational sanctions to be applied by the Ecofin Council to Member States that fail to meet the deficit rule. For example, the Ecofin Council may require a non-interest-bearing deposit which consists of fixed and variable components up to the annual limit of 0.5 percent of GDP. Eventually, the Ecofin Council may also impose fines of an appropriate size.[61]

2.3 Institutional procedures in fiscal policy coordination

Institutional system of fiscal policy coordination

Currently, fiscal policy coordination involves close cooperation in various economic policy areas and through different processes between EU institutions and between EMU and non-EMU Member States. Although it is the EMU Member States that share the same monetary policy objectives and the same currency, the non-EMU Member States are still expected to take part in coordinating national budgetary, and structural and labour policies. The Resolution of the European Council on Economic Policy Coordination has in particular expressed the importance of strengthening dialogue over political and economic objectives and coordination models between EMU and non-EMU Member States and between EU institutions and Member States.[62] Even though the basis of fiscal policy coordination lies at the heart of the Maastricht Treaty and the Stability Pact, there are also other major coordination procedures closely related to fiscal affairs, such as the European employment strategy (the Luxemburg process), national economic and structural reforms (the Cardiff process), the macroeconomic dialogue (the Cologne process) and growth and competitiveness (the Lisbon strategy) (Table 2.1).

In practice, the Ecofin Council and the Commission are the main formal institutions in European fiscal policy coordination. However, it is noteworthy that although there is a large number of different political and economic actors in the EU and EMU, there is no common and responsible institution where decisions regarding both monetary and fiscal affairs could be made simultaneously. The Commission is responsible for preparing, executing, monitoring and reporting fiscal policy in the EU and it is seen as a federal institution that functions as the key actor and promoter in fiscal policy agenda-setting. However, it is the Ecofin Council that has the highest decision-making authority in fiscal policy under the Stability Pact. The Ecofin Council's main task is to coordinate fiscal policies "for all EU Member States and not strictly those of the Euro area".[63] The Ecofin Council as a counterbalance to the Commission thus ensures that national economic interests are taken into account when collective decisions in fiscal policy are made. This is the basis for the power struggle between the Ecofin Council and the Commission that has characterised most recent developments in fiscal policy coordination.[64] There are also more informal institutions that contribute to the effectiveness of fiscal policy coordination. For example, the Finance

Ministers of the EMU Member States have constituted the Euro-12 group, which operates in monetary and fiscal policy without an official decision-making role within the EU system. In Scharrer's opinion, "although cooperation between monetary and fiscal policy should be the order of the day, the ministers in the Euro-12 group tend to see their role primarily as a counterweight to a central bank that has done its job well so far". He also adds that "instead of focusing on their own tasks of fiscal stabilisation and encouraging growth, they are thinking out loud about dictating an inflation target to the ECB".[65] Alongside the Euro-12 group, the Economic and Financial Committee and the Economic Policy Committee focus on (in)formally balancing economic, monetary and fiscal interests and objectives between EU institutions and EMU and non-EMU Member States.

Broad economic policy guidelines

The main challenge of formal and informal institutions relates to coordinating European and national economic interests effectively. There are three main institutional procedures with specific procedural "steps" in the EU and EMU within which EU institutions and Member States coordinate fiscal policy: a) the broad economic policy guidelines (general economic objectives), b) the procedure of stability and convergence programmes (fiscal policy and national budgets), and c) the excessive deficit procedure (sanctions for breaking the fiscal rules). Coordination within these three procedures constitutes the concrete system of European fiscal policy coordination.[66] The procedure of the broad economic policy guidelines, as defined in the Maastricht Treaty, has two main objectives. Firstly, it provides a medium-term coordination procedure between national economies in the EU and secondly, it functions as an *ex ante* coordination framework with strong peer pressure for an effective European policy mix. Through the broad economic policy guidelines Member States and the EU aim at adopting "an economic policy which is based on the close coordination of Member States' economic policies, on the internal market and on the definition of common objectives".[67] Coordination within the broad economic policy guidelines is based on Article 99 of the Maastricht Treaty, which stipulates that "Member States shall regard their economic policies as a matter of common concern and shall coordinate them within the Council". Contrary to the Stability Pact, coordination under the guidelines does not include any direct supranational sanctions; rather, the role of the broad economic policy guidelines can be interpreted more as a widely shared political consensus on European and national economic developments in the medium term.

The broad economic policy guidelines, such as those for the period 2005–2008, are drafted by the Commission (Figure 2.1). The Commission assesses national economies and coming economic developments as a preliminary task, and the main focus of the assessment is directed to national budgetary policies. Based on the recommendation of the Commission, the Ecofin Council plays a key role in coordinating national economic interests

1. The Ecofin Council formulates a draft by a qualified majority on a recommendation from the Commission for the broad economic policy guidelines and reports it to the European Council.
2. The European Council discusses a conclusion on the broad economic policy guidelines.
3. The Ecofin Council adopts by a qualified majority a recommendation for the guidelines and it informs the European Parliament.
4. The Ecofin Council monitors economic developments in each Member State on the basis of the reports submitted by the Commission (multilateral surveillance).
5. The report of the Commission is based on the stability and convergence programmes submitted by the Member States of the EU and EMU (multilateral surveillance).
6. The Ecofin Council may by a qualified majority on a recommendation from the Commission make the necessary recommendations to the Member State (multilateral surveillance).
7. The Ecofin Council may by a qualified majority on a proposal from the Commission decide to make its recommendations public (multilateral surveillance).
8. The President of the Ecofin Council and the Commission report to the European Parliament on the results of multilateral surveillance.

Figure 2.1 Broad economic policy guidelines and multilateral surveillance.[68]

before the European Council officially accepts the recommendations. The final version of the broad economic policy guidelines of the Ecofin Council includes country-specific economic recommendations for each Member State. The Ecofin Council has two main institutions to assist it with the formulation of the recommendations: the Economic and Financial Committee (EFC) and the Economic Policy Committee (EPC) to both of which the Member States, the Commission and the European Central Bank each appoint two representatives. The EFC is responsible for delivering opinions at the request of the Ecofin Council or the Commission, or on its own initiative, and reviewing the economic and financial developments in Member States.[69] The EPC also supports the Ecofin Council in coordinating economic objectives between the EU and the Member States but it in particular focuses on "the long-term sustainability of public finances" and "the functioning of goods, capital, services and labour markets".[70] The EPC also supports the work of the EFC and provides "the framework within which the macroeconomic dialogue involving representatives of the Committee (including the ECB), the EFC, the Employment Committee, the Commission and social partners shall take place at technical level".[71] It is the European Council in June every year that officially decides the content for the broad economic policy guidelines to be concretely adopted by the Ecofin Council. Although the Ecofin Council has the power to monitor and apply this multilateral economic surveillance, it has only two soft instruments at its disposal. Firstly, if a Member State fails to comply with the policy guidelines, the Ecofin Council may issue necessary recommendations. Secondly, with a qualified majority the Ecofin Council may also make its policy recommendations public.

Stability and convergence programmes

To strengthen this multilateral surveillance and fiscal policy coordination in the EU, all Member States have been required to submit their national economic programmes to the Commission and the Ecofin Council on a yearly basis from March 1999.[72] In the procedure of stability and convergence programmes EMU Member States have to submit stability programmes and non-EMU Member States submit convergence programmes (Figure 2.2). Both programmes, whether a Member State is in EMU or not, should include information about medium-term budgetary objectives, anticipated economic developments and national actions to achieve the country-specific objectives of the broad economic policy guidelines and the common economic rules.[73] Based on the assessments of the Commission and the Economic and Financial Committee, the Ecofin Council examines if national economic objectives and developments, as outlined in the programmes, provide "for a safety margin to ensure the avoidance of an excessive deficit", if programmes are "realistic", if programmes contribute to "the closer coordination of economic policies", if national measures are "sufficient", and if national economic policies are "consistent with the broad economic policy guidelines".[74]

1. EMU Member States submit stability programmes and non-EMU Member States submit convergence programmes to the Commission and the Ecofin Council.

2. The Commission and the Economic and Financial Committee evaluate the programmes.

3. The Ecofin Council examines the programmes within the framework of multilateral surveillance.

4. The Ecofin Council, on a recommendation from the Commission and after consulting the Economic and Financial Committee, delivers its opinion on the programmes.

5. The Ecofin Council invites a Member State in question to make adjustments.

6. Adjustments are assessed by the Economic and Financial Committee, the Commission and the Ecofin Council.

7. The Ecofin Council can give warnings and recommendations to make further national adjustments.

Figure 2.2 Procedure of stability and convergence programmes.[75]

The Ecofin Council, on a recommendation from the Commission and after consulting the Economic and Financial Committee, delivers its opinion on the national economic programmes. If the common European economic policy objectives and the national programmes are not consistent, the Ecofin Council may "invite the Member State concerned to adjust its programme".[76] After the required national adjustments, national programmes are reassessed by the Economic and Financial Committee, the Commission and the Ecofin Council. Based on the multilateral surveillance of the broad economic policy guidelines, the Ecofin Council does not only monitor the implementation of the national economic programmes to be in line with the country-specific recommendations but may also exert meaningful supranational peer pressure on Member States. If the economic development in the Member State "is persisting or worsening", the Ecofin Council may also make a recommendation to take "prompt corrective measures" and eventually, it may also make its recommendations public.[77] More concretely, if there is "significant divergence of the budgetary position from the medium-term budgetary objective, or the adjustment path towards it" in a Member State, the Ecofin Council may issue an early warning and a recommendation to the Member State in question. It is worth emphasising that it is the Articles 6 and 10 of the Council Regulation 1466/97 that legally, institutionally and politically allow the Ecofin Council to issue an early warning to an EMU Member State, on the basis of a recommendation from the Commission, even before the deficit criterion is officially broken.[78] In practice, the early warning mechanism has played a major role in European economic monitoring processes over the German economy under the Stability Pact in 2002–2004.

Excessive deficit procedure

The excessive deficit procedure is originally based on the Maastricht Treaty according to which "Member States shall avoid excessive government deficits".[79] To avoid the sanction mechanism of the excessive deficit procedure Member States have to pursue the sort of national fiscal policies that do not exceed the 3.0 percent deficit and 60.0 percent debt limits in EMU. The Commission is responsible for monitoring and reporting economic developments in Member States and in particular, whether deficit and debt limits are exceeded. However, it also has to be pointed out that breaking the fiscal rules does not automatically result in the implementation of the excessive deficit procedure. The interpretation that an excessive deficit really exists in a Member State, which is not exceptional and temporary, always requires both a Commission recommendation and an Ecofin Council decision. As Stark correctly interprets the institutional procedure, "the Commission and the Council, however, are not obliged to submit either a recommendation or a decision".[80] The deficit limit may be exceeded if "the ratio has declined substantially and continuously and reached a level that comes close to the reference value", and if "the excess over the reference value is only exceptional and temporary and the ratio remains close to the reference value".[81] Regarding the debt limit, the sanction procedure may also be avoided if the debt ratio "is sufficiently diminishing and approaching the reference value at a satisfactory pace".[82] Economic problems in a Member State to meet one or both of the fiscal rules, or a view of the Commission that there is a risk of exceeding one or both of the rules in the near future will result in a Commission report to the Ecofin Council (Figure 2.3).[83]

After considering the recommendation of the Commission, the Ecofin Council may decide with a qualified majority whether an excessive deficit really exists in a Member State. If such an excessive deficit exists, the Ecofin Council makes recommendations to the Member State to bring the economic situation to an end within a given time. If the Member State fails to implement the recommendations, the Ecofin Council may decide to give notice to the Member State to take further measures within a new time limit. The Ecofin Council may also require the Member State to submit a report of planned and implemented national adjustments. As long as the Member State fails to comply with the given recommendations and the deadline, the Ecofin Council may apply a number of different policy measures, such as: a) the Member State has to publish information specified by the Ecofin Council before it can issue bonds and securities; b) the Ecofin Council invites the European Investment Bank to reconsider its lending policy towards the Member State; c) the Ecofin Council requires the Member State to make a non-interest-bearing deposit with the EU until the

1. The Commission monitors national economic developments.
2. Exceeding the fiscal rules results in a report formulated by the Commission.
3. The Economic and Financial Committee gives an opinion on the report of the Commission.
4. The Commission gives a report to the Ecofin Council.
5. The Ecofin Council decides on the possible existence of budgetary deficit.
6. The Ecofin Council makes recommendations to be implemented within given time.
7. The Ecofin Council decides to give a notice to the Member State.
8. As long as the Member State fails to comply with the recommendations, the Ecofin Council can apply a number of measures.
9. The Ecofin Council informs the European Parliament of made decisions.

Figure 2.3 Sanction procedure within the excessive deficit procedure.[84]

excessive deficit has been corrected; and finally, d) the Ecofin Council may impose concrete fines of an appropriate size. However, the Ecofin Council is responsible for informing the European Parliament of decisions made and measures taken against the Member State.

In these matters, the Ecofin Council acts on a recommendation from the Commission with a majority of two-thirds of the votes of its members excluding the votes of the Member State concerned. However, Cabral makes a legally correct point that the Ecofin Council is not required to make any decisions if the Member State has taken necessary measures; rather, the Ecofin Council acts "if no effective action was taken by the Member State concerned".[85] On the other hand, what is equally critical concerning European fiscal policy coordination is the fact that all actions in the European Union are subject to the European Court of Justice. In fact, the Treaty of Nice has strengthened the supranational authority of the European Court of Justice in all appeals in the policy areas in the European Union. For example in fiscal policy coordination, according to the Treaty of Nice, any EU institution, such as the Commission, or a Member State, has the right to bring the decision of the Ecofin Council to implement or not to implement the excessive deficit procedure of the Stability Pact to the Court of First Instance. Interestingly, the Commission brought the failure of the Ecofin Council to act under the excessive deficit procedure before the European Court of Justice in January 2004.[86]

2.4 Adaptation pressures of the Stability Pact in EMU

Implementing the institutional system of fiscal policy coordination

The Stability Pact, together with the excessive deficit procedure, is a powerful policy mechanism to promote stabilisation between national economies by requiring Member States to take European and national volatile economic cycles into account in their national economic policy-making. However, the more different models and instruments of macroeconomic coordination Member States and EU institutions have introduced, whether "softer" or "harder", the greater the additional challenges that have occurred in concrete policy coordination. Since close economic policy coordination between the Commission and the Ecofin Council has been extended also to involve, for example the European Central Bank, the Economic and Financial Committee and the Euro-12 group, the implementation of this multi-level coordination system has resulted in substantial coordination problems. According to Issing, "attempts that extend beyond the informal exchange of views and information give rise to the risk of confusing the specific roles, mandates and responsibilities of the policies in question".[87] Not surprisingly, problems in the national implementation of the Stability Pact have put great ammunition into the hands not only of EMU-sceptics but also of EMU-promoters.

In practice, the mechanisms of fiscal policy coordination have been implemented several times, albeit with varying success since the sudden decline of the European economy in 2001.[88] Firstly, the Ecofin Council implemented the peer view of the broad economic policy guidelines in line with the Stability Pact to the case of Ireland for the very first time in February 2001. The question of Ireland was not about an excessive budgetary deficit but a domestically overheated economy, which, in the Commission's view, could have jeopardised the broad economic policy guidelines of Ireland and those of the whole Euro area. The Ecofin Council considered that the surplus of 4.7 percent of GDP in 2001 could significantly increase inflationary pressures and eventually endanger national fiscal stability in Ireland. The Ecofin Council argued that Ireland should have more effectively implemented a national policy mix between monetary and fiscal policy instruments. The Ecofin Council and the Commission were also dissatisfied with the fact that Ireland had not made economic adjustments to ensure fiscal stability based on the Ecofin Council's warnings in 2000. The Ecofin Council concluded: "Irish fiscal policy in 2001 is not consistent with the broad guidelines of the economic policies as regards budgetary policy." As the result, the Ecofin Council made a recommendation under Article 99 of the Maastricht Treaty to Ireland to eliminate this economic inconsistency (pro-cyclical national fiscal policy) in February 2001.[89]

Secondly, due to the occurrence of an excessive deficit, the Commission made a recommendation to the Ecofin Council to issue an early warning to Portugal in January 2002.[90] However, the Ecofin Council decided not to issue an early warning, but it was convinced of the commitment of the Portuguese government to secure its national fiscal stability and to make the required adjustments not to break the deficit rule. Portugal assured the Ecofin Council that it would take measures to achieve a stable fiscal position by 2004. Under these commitments, the Ecofin Council considered in February 2002 that Portugal "has effectively responded to the concerns expressed in the Commission's recommendation and therefore, the recommendation is not put to a vote and the procedure is closed".[91] However, Portugal did not manage to reduce its deficit and moreover, its public debt was also about to reach the 60 percent limit. Eventually, Portugal was the first EMU Member State to exceed the deficit limit in 2002. Based on the recommendation of the Commission,[92] the Ecofin Council implemented the excessive deficit procedure with the view "to bringing an end to the situation of an excessive government deficit" in November 2002.[93] According to the Ecofin Council, Portugal had to take all necessary measures to reduce deficit within the deadline of 31 December 2002. The Ecofin Council also required Portugal to ensure that "the government deficit in 2003 is further reduced clearly below three percent of GDP and that the government debt ratio is kept below the 60 percent of GDP reference value".[94]

Thirdly, the Commission recommended in January 2002 that the Ecofin Council should issue an early warning to Germany due to its increasing deficit. The Ecofin Council, together with the Commission, was concerned about the substantial increase in the deficit from 1.5 percent in 2000 to 2.6 percent of GDP in 2001. However, in its statement of February 2002, the Ecofin Council was satisfied with the undertakings of the German government to closely monitor developments in the national deficit and to take the necessary measures to bring national budget back to medium-term balance. As Germany promised to the Ecofin Council to reach the balanced budgetary position by 2004, the Ecofin Council did not put the Commission's recommendation into action.[95] However, the Commission submitted a new report to the Ecofin Council in November 2002, which indicated that the deficit was at 3.8 percent of GDP, and the public debt had increased from 59.5 percent in 2001 to 60.9 percent of GDP in 2002.[96] Based on this new information, the Commission made a new recommendation to the Ecofin Council to decide whether an excessive deficit existed in Germany. The Ecofin Council finally concluded in January 2003 that "an excessive deficit exists in Germany" and that Germany has to "put an end to the present excessive deficit situation as rapidly as possible".[97] These measures should include the reduction of the deficit and debt ratios, the implementation of structural and tax reforms, strengthening economic growth and the improvement of national economic coordination by 21 May 2003.

Due to ineffective national actions, the Commission proceeded with the excessive deficit procedure against Germany in November 2003. The Commission was still concerned about the increasing deficit that had reached more than 4.0 percent of GDP in October 2003, and it required the German government to put an end to the excessive deficit situation "as rapidly as possible and at the latest by 2005".[98] The Ecofin Council in its meeting on 25 November 2003 finally took a vote on the recommendation of the Commission to apply the sanction procedure of the Stability Pact to Germany. Although small Member States, such as Austria, Belgium, Denmark, Finland, Greece, the Netherlands, Spain and Sweden voted for the recommendation of the Commission, there was not a qualified majority for adopting the decision of sanctions because of large Member States.[99] However, the Ecofin Council required the German government to report on the national progress made in fulfilling its economic commitments on a regular basis. Even though the Ecofin Council agreed "to hold the excessive deficit procedure for Germany in abeyance for the time being", it still "stands ready to take a decision under Article 104" if "Germany fails to act in accordance with the commitments".[100]

Fourthly, the Commission also recommended in May 2003 that the Ecofin Council should make a recommendation to France to take measures to reduce its deficit. The deficit of France had reached 3.1 percent of GDP in 2002, and the Commission estimated that the deficit could reach 3.7 percent in 2003. According to the Commission, required measures should be taken before 3 October 2003.[101] The Ecofin Council recommended in June 2003 that France eliminate the deficit problem by 2004 at the latest.[102] Although France made some meaningful national adjustments, such as reforms in public expenditure and pensions, it in general failed to carry out measures as effectively as was required by the Ecofin Council in June 2003. In the recommendation for the Ecofin Council's decision, the Commission considered that the economic improvements in France "will not be sufficient to ensure that the cumulative improvement in the cyclically-adjusted balance in 2003–2004 brings the nominal deficit below three percent in 2004". In addition, debt could "increase from 59.0 percent of GDP in 2002 to 61.4 percent of GDP in 2003".[103] The Commission took further actions and formulated a recommendation to the Ecofin Council in October 2003 stating that "France took no effective action in response to the Ecofin Council's recommendations last June", and "the French government should put an end to the present excessive deficit situation as rapidly as possible and by 2005 at the latest".[104] Based on the recommendation, the Ecofin Council in its meeting of 25 November 2003 voted on whether the recommendation should be put into action. As in the case of Germany, although small Member States voted for the recommendation, there was not a qualified majority for adopting the sanctions due to the votes of the large Member States.[105] However, the Ecofin Council concluded that it would "stand ready to take a decision" if France fails to reach the fiscal rules by 2005.[106]

Criticism of fiscal policy coordination under the Stability Pact

As discussed above, the institutional system of fiscal policy coordination has succeeded in monitoring the economic developments in the Member States, but the effectiveness of institutional coordination and the concrete national implementation of fiscal policy coordination have been questionable; and they both are still in progress. In practice, it has been the implementation of the fiscal rules of the Stability Pact that has faced the most serious problems since 2002. Surprisingly, it has been Germany among other EMU Member States that has had the most difficulties in complying with the common rules and regulations, because it was the German national interests on which the strict fiscal policy coordination in the EMU era was based. The original idea of coordinating national fiscal policies in EMU was presented in 1995 by the then German Finance Minister, Theo Waigel, who argued that fiscal policy coordination together with the strict monitoring role of the Commission was required for ensuring economic stability and the success of the single currency in EMU.[107] Even though the Stability Pact has strengthened fiscal policy coordination between national economies in EMU, such as by introducing the excessive deficit procedure and requiring national economic programmes on a yearly basis, the concrete European and national implementation of the Stability Pact has still pointed to significant limitations and given rise to criticism.

Firstly, the case of Ireland has illustrated that fiscal policy coordination involves not only deficit and debt coordination but also more extensive economic policy coordination by stabilising national overly weighty upward and downward pressures. Regarding the cases of Portugal, Germany and France, the institutional coordination system has successfully monitored national economic developments and started the supranational reporting procedure when there had been the first signals of possible budgetary problems in those Member States. However, the precise problem of the Stability Pact has resulted from the ineffective national implementation of the recommendations from this monitoring and reporting. Despite the fact that all these three Member States have made commitments to take required national adjustments, the German and French governments have still persistently struggled with the deficit criterion. According to Schuknecht, these implementation problems occur because "it is not totally clear precisely what the policy response is intended to be". He also argues that "it is also unclear as to whether, under such circumstances, the established horizon for full convergence with the target would be observed or whether it would be allowed to slide forward".[108] For De Grauwe, the main reason for the implementation problems stems from the fact that "the economic rationale of the Stability Pact is weak".[109] This means that only numerical and political rules for budgetary policy, which have no basis in economic theory, cannot guarantee long-term stability and growth in EMU.

If policy responses and institutional procedures in EMU are not clear to all leading EMU experts, it seems that it is likewise not clear to all EU institutions how the system of fiscal policy coordination should be governed. The formal relationship between the Ecofin Council and the Commission in fiscal policy coordination has not functioned successfully, as the cases of Germany and France clearly illustrate. The Commission has done its duty in monitoring and reporting on developments in deficit and debt ratios in these two Member States to the Ecofin Council, but the Ecofin Council has still persistently decided not to apply the excessive deficit procedure to them. To solve this recurring problem in implementation, the Commission has raised a critical question of the fundamental objectives of the Stability Pact. After the Ecofin Council's decision not to apply the sanction mechanism to Germany and France for the third time in succession on 25 November 2003, the Commission has advised the Ecofin Council about the EC law and the terms of the Maastricht Treaty and the Stability Pact. The Commission also took legal actions against the Ecofin Council and brought the institutional failure to act before the European Court of Justice under Article 232 of the Treaty of Nice in January 2004.[110] This action of the Commission finally brought out a striking power struggle over institutional responsibilities and duties in European fiscal policy coordination. As Jonung interprets the state of fiscal policy coordination: "Policy-making and institution building are trial-and-error processes."[111]

Secondly, the main aim of the Stability Pact has been to further fiscal convergence through formal and numerical rules. Although the formal rules oblige Member States to attain their budgetary policies in balance or close to the rules, the main debate on the rationale for fiscal rules, according to Gros and Thygesen, is concerned with "how the systemic stability of EMU can justify interference in national budgetary policies, especially when public debt or deficits threaten to become unsustainable".[112] This interference causes several politico-economic implications, such as the question of national fiscal flexibility within the strict rule-based coordination, the level of national commitments in unpredictable economic developments and the role of European policy mix in EMU. Despite the major impact of the fiscal rules on national economies, fiscal convergence should, in Buti, Franco and Ongena's view, "be continued in the coming years and further adjustments will be necessary to comply with the obligations of the Stability and Growth Pact".[113] However, although excessive deficit and debt ratios may endanger monetary discipline through an increasing risk of high interest and inflation rates, strict criteria for national economic policy-making may also limit national capability for responding to economic shocks and other downward pressures in EMU.

It has been argued by a number of economists, for example Artis, Buiter, El-Agraa and De Grauwe, that the rationale for numerical monetary and fiscal criteria in EMU has been more political than economic. Artis claims that the only rationale for the deficit rule was a political aim to set "a tough but achievable target which was adequate to stem the threat of insolvency".[114] As it was the Member States that agreed on the political interpretation of the Maastricht criteria for the third and final stage of EMU, they naturally achieved all those criteria exceptionally or very well except that of the budgetary deficit. Theoretically, it is questionable how and to what extent numerical limitations are able to stabilise and converge European economic policies without any other supporting national adjustments (institutional, structural and economic adjustments). As Buiter summarises: "Those who proposed and defended the three percent deficit ceiling of the SGP readily admit that they would have been happy with any number, as long as it was low."[115] More than being economically justifiable, El-Agraa argues that the three percent deficit rule just happened to be the average level in the Member States at that time.[116] When analysing the other criteria theoretically, it is impossible to justify economically on what basis 2.0 percent inflation or 60.0 percent public debt targets could ensure more successfully the stable economic environment in EMU than for example 3.0 percent inflation and 70.0 percent public debt limits. Like

El-Agraa, De Grauwe is also highly sceptical about the economic nature of the formal criteria and he argues that most of the rules "have always been unconvincing, and remain so".[117] He is convinced that the success of the Stability Pact is not dependent on the numerical level of the formal fiscal rules but the national economic and political behaviour within the fiscal rules in EMU. Therefore, he cannot understand "what difference does it make for the French budget deficit to be 1.8 or 2.6 percent of Gross Domestic Product?" In his words, "the nitpicking numerology is out of place" because "it has absolutely no bearing for the risk of a future debt default".[118]

Thirdly, the main criticism of the Stability Pact has also been directed at national fiscal flexibility under the required fiscal discipline because national economies should have some flexible fiscal instruments at their disposal in the context of the common monetary policy. This requirement arises from the fact that the one-size monetary policy in the EMU area does not necessarily respond optimally to all participating Member States, whether large or small, for example in the event of asymmetric economic shocks. According to Brunila, Buti and in't Veld, "the policy assignment and institutional arrangements of EMU are based on a widespread consensus that monetary policy should take care of stabilisation in the event of symmetric shocks while the smoothing asymmetric shocks and diverging cyclical conditions falls to national fiscal policy as the single monetary policy responds only to area-wide price developments".[119] For this reason, Willett argues that EU institutions should compensate for the loss of national fiscal flexibility because EMU excludes "the option of counter-cyclical monetary policy in the participating countries".[120] In the event of a country-specific shock, the effective alternative to respond to the shock would be to apply national fiscal instruments (budgetary, structural and labour policies). Increasing policy coordination, however, constrains national economic policy-making more and more and could cause severe economic problems in the future. For Artis and Winkler, "whatever the rationale for the Maastricht criteria and the Stability Pact there is a potential price to be paid for satisfying their rigid numerical limits. This price comes in the form of lost flexibility in the use of active fiscal policy of in the operation of the built-in automatic stabilisers of national budgets and has been the major source of criticism of the fiscal criteria."[121]

Although the Stability Pact includes national flexibility to some extent, such as allowing a temporary and exceptional overshoot of deficit and debt criteria, country-specific shocks could still challenge such overshoots. Allsopp argues that the Stability Pact has the same problem of the common monetary policy by arguing that "the SGP goes too far by imposing the same one-size-fits-all rule on each member country".[122] However, Buti, Eijffinger and Franco believe that national flexibility is secured in the event of asymmetric shocks because "the Pact does not curb governments' incentives to increase expenditure or cut revenue in favourable cyclical periods".[123] Beetsma is also convinced that the Stability Pact enables fiscal flexibility in Member States because "the time that elapses from the observation of an excessive deficit until the payment of a fine is at least two years, which should be enough to overcome a normal recession".[124] Currently, national fiscal flexibility under the rules of the Stability Pact has two equally critical dimensions. On the one hand, the Commission and the European Court of Justice have argued that the Ecofin Council has allowed far too much national fiscal flexibility in Germany and France under the common fiscal rules. On the other hand, severe national economic problems and increasing fiscal policy coordination have started to jeopardise national fiscal discipline, and these two large Member States are clearly moving away from stable national fiscal policy and sustainable public finances in EMU.

Fourthly, the declining national fiscal discipline has also challenged the effectiveness of European policy mix in EMU. As fiscal discipline or the lack thereof in Member States affects the common monetary policy, the effective national implementation of the Stability Pact could strengthen the credibility of the monetary policy of the ECB in the financial market. In practice, European policy mix has aimed at reducing tensions between fiscal and monetary policy objectives by ensuring a stable economic environment for the common monetary policy. If Member States ran large deficits and debts, the ECB could allow a more inflationary monetary policy to eliminate the economic impact of the expansive national budgetary policy. Expansive national fiscal policies together with the tight common monetary policy could otherwise "place additional burden on the Euro exchange rate".[125] The effectiveness of European policy mix in coordinating these complex tensions between fiscal and monetary objectives is dependent significantly on national commitments and institutional cooperation in EMU. This "actual European policy game", as it is called by Bibow, is based on the monetary independence of the ECB and multi-level fiscal authority between EU institutions and Member States.[126] This divided system of economic policy coordination has caused the main problems for effective European policy mix. For example, for Issing, there are no convincing arguments for *ex ante* economic policy coordination through European policy mix because the concrete problem in coordination relates to information available. Timely relevant information is only available on general economic developments across most European economies. However, identifying economic shocks and in particular the nature of shocks *ex ante* faces the problem of specific information. As Issing summarises: "As a result, attempts to coordinate policy actions seem particularly prone to the well-known recognition and decision lags of policy-making, rendering the timely agreement on the appropriate joint actions in practice almost impossible."[127] Member States have nevertheless succeeded in introducing some supporting coordination models *ex ante* between the common monetary policy and national fiscal policies. For example, although the Euro-12 group, which has been chaired by Jean-Claude Juncker since January 2005, meets one day before the Ecofin Council to coordinate the fiscal and monetary objectives of the EMU Member States, it is still an informal actor without a formal decision-making role in the EU.

Fifthly and finally, the fact that the Stability Pact does not coordinate public finances along with national budgetary policies has been regarded as undermining its credibility in the long term. Buti and Giudice stress that national public finances have a very close relationship in stabilising national fiscal policies in EMU. For example, "maintaining a broadly balanced budget may deter the adoption of fundamental pension reforms, which enhance discipline in the longer run, but are costly in the short run". Such decisions in public finances would "leave the burden of adjustment on other budgetary items over the coming years".[128] According to Gros and Thygesen, "the discussion about the rationale for fiscal rules has shown that they should be designed in such a way that they reduce the likelihood of a financial crisis that can arise when financial markets have doubts that a government is able to service its debt".[129] To coordinate public finances in EMU the economic literature suggests that there could be the so-called golden rule of public finance included in the Stability Pact. According to the golden rule, national public borrowing would only be allowed to finance public investments but not normal, current public expenditure such as public services. The effective implementation of the golden rule would require the introduction of a dual national budget within the Stability Pact in which current expenditure (including consumption) and capital expenditure (including investments) would be separated.

However, Buiter argues that "the distinction between current and capital expenditures is fraught with ambiguities" because it risks "inducing a misplaced sense of complacency about the accumulation of public investment-related public debt".[130] In Britain, the golden rule is defined so that "over the economic cycle the government will borrow to invest and not to fund current expenditure", and "public debt as a proportion of national income will be held over the economic cycle at a stable and prudent level".[131] The golden rule should be seen only as an instrument to pave the way for fiscal stabilisation because it does not provide any permanent solution to national fiscal problems. National economies could continue to execute expansionary fiscal policies under the golden rule in a downturn because borrowing for public investments would not cause the breaking of the deficit rule as defined in the Stability Pact. However, Balassone and Franco claim that the role of the golden rule in the Stability Pact should be "evaluated with regard to its consistency with the objectives of EMU's fiscal rules and to its impact upon the effectiveness of the surveillance procedure set to safeguard their enforcement".[132]

Institutional fiscal policy coordination still in progress in EMU

Despite the effort to establish an effective system for fiscal policy coordination in EMU, the concrete problems in institutional coordination and national commitments have caused national fiscal discipline to deteriorate significantly. However, the politico-economic literature and concrete developments suggest that EMU requires fiscal policy coordination and that effective fiscal policy coordination under the Stability Pact requires better institutional coordination and stronger national commitments than before. The importance of institutional coordination and national commitments for the credibility of the Stability Pact arises from the situation where the system of fiscal policy coordination only sets common requirements and sanctions but it is the Member States that still have the authority to decide on the nature of concrete policy actions. According to Willett, "one of the greatest problems in designing institutions to constrain pressures on monetary and fiscal policies is that it is much easier to maintain sound economic policies once a stable situation has been achieved than to get to this point from a position of substantial disequilibrium".[133] To achieve national economic equilibrium more effectively, new formal and informal coordination models, for example the Euro-12 group, have been introduced in the EU and EMU. The main aim of formal and informal coordination models should be to secure both fiscal discipline and national flexibility. As Artis and Winkler summarise this discipline-flexibility situation in the Stability Pact: "While there is some reason to doubt the effectiveness of the technical provisions of the Stability Pact in guaranteeing the desired discipline and flexibility in practice, the mere fact that Member States have agreed to subject national budget policies to a concerted European joint discipline is of great significance."[134] Following Artis and Winkler's reasoning, this research will next empirically show how and to what extent European fiscal policy coordination and the case of the German economy under the Stability Pact link to this "great significance".

3
The German Dynamics of Uploading the Stability Pact

3.1 German fiscal challenges in the post-reunification era

German reunification and challenges in national adjustments

Although the Stability Pact has introduced a specific coordination system for national fiscal policies, it is still an open question how it will manage to secure required national commitments and adjustments in EMU. Germany, regarded as the leading European economy since the establishment of the European Monetary System (EMS) in the late 1970s, has continually struggled with its budgetary policy under the fiscal rules of the Stability Pact. Mounting adaptation problems in the German economy have prompted a wide European debate on reforming the fiscal rules of the Stability Pact to allow more national flexibility in economic policy-making in downturns in EMU. The fundamental problem in German fiscal policy stems from the fact that in the EMU circumstances, national monetary adjustments to economic decline are no longer a policy option and simultaneously, adjustments in national fiscal policy are subjected to increasing fiscal policy coordination. In practice, the German economy has moved from being the early pace-setter of EMU to an economy that has most serious problems in adjusting to increasing fiscal policy coordination in the EMU era. The German pathway to EMU has been straightforward (with strong continuity) but stabilising its national budgetary policy under the Stability Pact as a crucial single step in EMU has proved to be a major challenge (causing marked discontinuity). Before comprehending the current state of the implementation of the Stability Pact in Germany and its future prospects in Europe, it is essential to analyse under what national circumstances Germany first launched proposals for a Stability Pact in 1995–1997. How did Germany seek to shape the Stability Pact to ensure the best possible national adaptation "fit" with its national economy for the EMU era? In other words, *how did it seek to upload its interests to ensure "fit" with national policies and practices in the downloading phase of European fiscal policy objectives*? This chapter will demonstrate that although the German government tried to seek national adaptation "fits" in strict fiscal policy coordination for EMU, the process, however, resulted in an increasing number of national adaptation "misfits" under the Stability Pact in EMU. Acting both as the key pace-setter and uploader in the formation (uploading) process of fiscal policy coordination for EMU did not prevent Germany from experiencing serious problems in the concrete national implementation (downloading) process of the Stability Pact in EMU.

German economic developments in the pre-Maastricht era can be seen as one of the key explanatory factors for its macroeconomic instability problems in the late 1990s and in the 21st century. The German adjustment process towards EMU has been characterised by three main periods: a) from German reunification in 1990 to the establishment of the Stability Pact in 1997 (uploading), b) from 1998 to 2002 (downloading), and c) from 2003 to 2005 (reuploading). The starting point of this economic analysis of the formation of the Stability Pact is on 3 October 1990 when the Unification Treaty of the German Democratic Republic and the Federal Republic of Germany created a unified Germany: the Federal Republic of Germany. German reunification together with the currency union of 1 July 1990 caused not only major national challenges but also significant external pressures to German policy strategies regarding, for example, the start of the Internal Market, the creation of the EU, the establishment of EMU and the introduction of the Stability Pact. The significance of German reunification for the negotiations of the Maastricht Treaty and the whole European political and economic integration at that time raised, according to Tsoukalis, a considerable "need to reaffirm the country's commitment to European integration in the wake of reunification".[1] This simultaneous dual integration was crucial not only for Germany but also for the EU as a whole.

These internal and external challenges resulted from economic, political, institutional and cultural changes at the national level, which affected directly and indirectly Germany and Germany's role in European political and economic integration. Economically, reunification created new and partly unpredicted problems for fiscal policy (debt and deficit levels), which also had a major impact on national monetary stability (exchange and inflation rates). When the West German economy and its open-economy principles were applied directly to the existing East German structures, the East German economy faced a more competitive and productive West German economy resulting in the collapse of the East German economy.[2] The reunification process caused a substantial economic shock to the whole German economy over 15 years ago, which still has a major effect on national economic stability in EMU. This has also been recognised in a recent analysis on the economics of reunification in which Streeck and Trampusch argue that non-wage labour costs have significantly risen since the 1970s causing severe unemployment in Germany.[3] Germany has thus had to continue implementing major reforms in labour, social and budgetary policy. Politically and institutionally, the reunification process was also led by a very challenging objective to adjust East Germany to the political and institutional structures of West Germany. The implementation of this objective brought out new and challenging societal issues such as the future relationship between the federal government, the Bundesbank, Old and New Länder, trade unions and other social partners in a unified Germany.[4] After reunification unified Germany also had to deal with concrete and difficult problems of creating a unified capital market area, privatising state-owned companies, reducing unemployment, making wage adjustments, maintaining national competitiveness, increasing economic productivity and supporting economic growth. For example, both Germanies enjoyed relatively low unemployment rates and high economic growth rates prior to reunification, which, however, developed into a severe unemployment crisis, threatening stagnation in the unified Germany by the beginning of the 21st century.

Reunification also challenged German culture for effective national cooperation. As the fundamental objective of Germany was to maintain its leading role in the European integration process after reunification, the importance of national cooperation over collective national policy objectives increased. In practice, reunification required strong commitments from both West and East Germany (Old and New Länder) to ongoing European political and economic integration. In economic policy, national cooperation was required for making a common economic strategy in the EMU negotiations on the one hand, and for making effective and adequate national adjustments and compensations for the coming EMU conditions on the other. The impact of the start of the Stability Pact along with the EMU era on national policy-making culture, however, was partly unpredictable: European economic constraints for national policy-making caused major issues over the direction and interests of the national economic strategy.

Public debt before and after German reunification

Germany's pathway towards medium-term budgetary stability, as required by the Maastricht Treaty and the Stability Pact, has not been a self-evident process. Historically, problems in this pathway were caused in particular by the strong economic legacy of two oil crises and the EMS problems. According to Scharpf, "while the external macroeconomic shocks of the 1970s and 1980s had affected all industrialised economies more or less in the same way, the changes of the international economic environment that came to a head in the 1990s manifested themselves as very different challenges in different countries, depending on the structural characteristics of their economies and even more so on the policy legacies that had shaped national employment systems and welfare states".[5] When analysing the most recent historical "legacies" of the German economy it is possible to trace the main developments in national economic position that have created the current economic environment. The analysis of the economic developments in Germany as the leading EMU economy is crucial because, according to Eichengreen and Wyplosz, this pathway shows if EMU Member States have "attained a budgetary position that on average is in balance or even in surplus, thereby leaving scope for customary levels of automatic fiscal stabilisation to be provided in recession without triggering penalties under the Stability Pact".[6]

Figure 3.1 shows public debt of Germany comparatively from the reunification process in 1989 to the start of the Stability Pact in 1997. In this period, the debt as percentage of GDP progressively increased in Germany, France and the European Union area as a whole, whereas Britain managed to slow down the pace of the increase. Regarding the EU area, the major increase in public debt can be explained, for example, by the enlargement of the EU in 1981 (Greece) and 1986 (Portugal and Spain) and the major instability problems in the EMS in 1992–1993. The debt in the EU area increased on average from 57.1 percent in 1989 to 74.5 percent in 1997, jumping a striking 30.5 percentage points in nine years. The increase in debt was clearly slower in Germany, France and Britain than in the EU area although the debt ratio was also rising in these three countries. Although the debt of Germany was only 39.9 percent in 1989, it surpassed the formal 60 percent limit at the start of the Stability Pact, being 60.9 percent in 1997. In France the debt also escalated almost 20 percent-

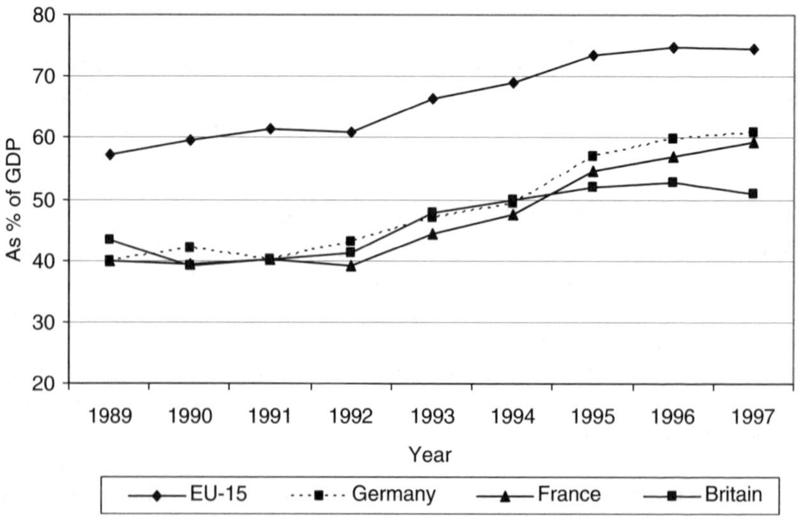

Figure 3.1 Public debt 1989–1997.[7]

age points from 39.9 percent in 1989 to the same high 60 percent level (59.2%) with Germany in 1997. By contrast in Britain, the debt ratio rose sizeably from 43.2 percent in 1989 to the level of 52.6 percent of GDP in 1996 but thereafter it decreased to 50.9 percent in 1997; the lowest debt ratio among these three biggest European economies in 1997 (Figures 4.4 and 5.4).

The reunification process was a crucial as well as a detrimental development for the public debt ratio of Germany. Firstly, there were a number of specific funds with a total of 380 billion Euros that funded the costs of the reunification and controlled the indebtedness of East Germany.[8] Secondly, the debts of these funds were partly included in the unified German budget in 1995, which explains the significant jump in the public debt from 49.4 percent (841.1 billion Euros) in 1994 to 57.1 percent of GDP (1010.4 billion Euros) in 1995 (Figure 3.8). Surprisingly, the budgetary deficit of the unified Germany grew only from 2.6 percent in 1994 to 3.5 percent of GDP in 1995. Due to this inheritance of the major East German debt, the unified Germany could have requested a flexible interpretation of the debt and deficit rules of the Maastricht Treaty to allow its entry to EMU in 1999 if Germany had not otherwise met the criteria for the final stage of EMU. As Owen Smith has pointed out, in those circumstances "this exception would probably be permitted under EMU's fiscal harmonisation rules".[9]

Budgetary deficit in transition

Budgetary deficit also spread notably in Germany and Europe, which, however, recovered by 1997. As the trends in Figure 3.2 suggest, the deficit of Germany seemingly stood at a lower level than in France, Britain and

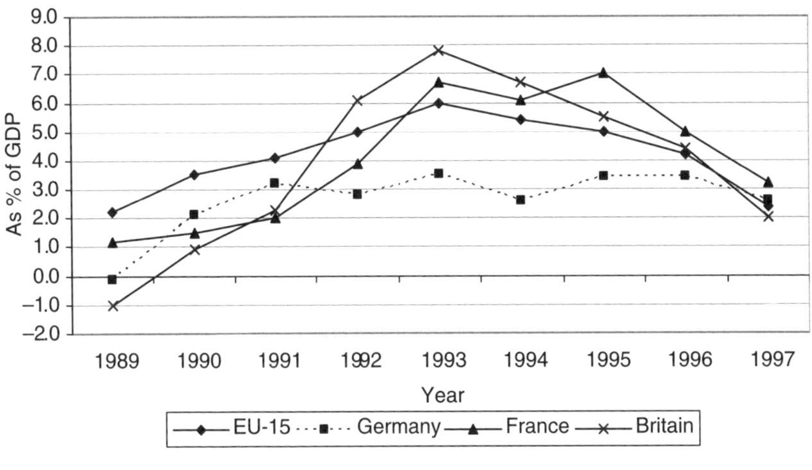

Figure 3.2 Budgetary deficit 1989–1997.[10]

the EU area after 1992. Although the deficit in the EU on average increased at the beginning of the 1990s, it nevertheless fell back to its 1989 level in 1997. In 1989 the deficit in the EU area was 2.2 percent of GDP and continued to grow to 6.0 percent in 1993. After 1993 the deficit, however, decreased as rapidly as it had grown so that in 1997 the average deficit in the EU dropped to a mere 2.4 percent. Germany had a slight surplus of 0.1 percent of GDP in 1989, which turned into a consistent deficit in the 1990s. After the deficit fell to a ratio of 3.2 percent in 1991, it remained about 3.0 percent. When the Stability Pact came into being in 1997 the deficit of Germany was 2.6 percent of GDP. Developments in the deficit in France and Britain were not entirely similar to those in Germany. The deficit of Britain jumped from a surplus of 1.0 percent in 1989 to a serious deficit of 7.8 percent in 1993. However, the deficit recovered from 1993 to only 2.0 percent by 1997. In France the deficit also jumped to a decidedly high level in the 1990s. Although the deficit was only 1.2 percent in 1989, it increased to as much as 7.0 percent in 1995. When approaching the start of the Stability Pact the deficit of France had fallen back to a more acceptable ratio of 3.2 percent of GDP in 1997.

When analysing the main trends of public debt (Figure 3.1) and budgetary deficit (Figure 3.2) in Germany and the EU in 1989–1997, it is possible to note that the debt level grew steadily but the deficit ratio was much more volatile. For example, in Germany, the deficit faced major uncertainties eventually ending up with about the same ratio in 1997 with the year of 1990. By the start of the Stability Pact in 1997 Germany had the highest debt ratio and France had the highest deficit ratio among these three biggest European economies. However, it was Britain that had controlled its budgetary policy most effectively because Britain had both the lowest debt and deficit ratios in terms of GDP in 1997. Barrell and Weale explain the considerable increase in the public debt throughout the EU area as the differences in economic cycles and national adjustments. According to them, most European countries were afraid of major spending cuts and increased tax burden during the downturn in the early 1990s because this might have slowed down the overall national economic growth even more than did the increasing debt and deficit stocks. Therefore, European countries did not want to react immediately and appropriately to growing debt and deficit stocks.[11] Significant differences in debt and deficit ratios between Germany, France, Britain and the rest of the EU, in practice, resulted from a number of national devaluations in the early 1990s and differences in growth rates and economic cycles. For example, the deficit-to-GDP ratio was 3.6 percent in Belgium, 7.4 percent in Greece and 7.1 percent in Italy in 1996, whereas the debt-to-GDP ratio was 130.2 percent in Belgium, 111.3 percent in Greece and 122.1 percent in Italy in 1996; a fact that markedly increased the average debt and deficit ratios of the EU area.

Public finances in the federal government and the Bundesländer

A brief politico-institutional overview of German economic policy-making reveals that Germany's economic policy is implemented at different national levels from the federal government via the Bundesländer to the municipal levels. In German federalism, it is the regional Bundesländer apart from the federal government that have a major role in achieving national economic objectives. Due to their economic and political autonomy, the Bundesländer play a key role in allocating and redistributing the federal budget. However, the economic autonomy of the Bundesländer makes it more difficult for the federal government to set common national economic objectives and to achieve an overall national fiscal stability throughout the country, at the regional and federal levels simultaneously.[12] As effective national cooperation in economic policy is increasingly important for implementing the national economy as an integral part of the whole EMU system, the traditional relationship between the federal government and the Bundesländer should be subjected to a thorough political and economic analysis.

Given that there was a significant increase in the debt and deficit ratios after reunification in 1990, it is also crucial to study in detail the extent to which reunification affected the German position in public finances as a whole. Figure 3.3 with the distinction of Old and New Länder identifies the fiscal volume of German economic problems more specifically. In the five-year period 1993–1997, the financial position of the Old and the New Länder was serious but it clearly moved towards financial stabilisation. The deficit of the New Länder diminished from over 2000 million Euros to less than 800 million Euros over the period. The deficit of the New Länder was 2300 million Euros in 1993 and 2700 million Euros in 1994,

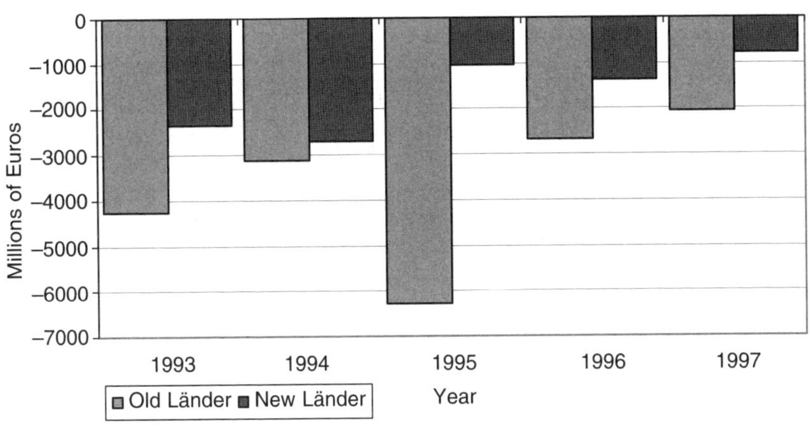

Figure 3.3 The financial position of Old and New Länder 1993–1997.[13]

but it decreased sizeably by 1997 resulting in only 797 million Euros. As the Old Länder are bigger in economic terms and in population than the New Länder, the deficit of the Old Länder has also been at a much higher level. Although the deficit of the Old Länder increased from 4200 million Euros in 1993 to 6300 million Euros in 1995, it dropped to 2000 million Euros by 1997.

As Figure 3.4 shows, the most striking result of these financially critical developments has been in trends in public spending, public revenue and economic growth in Germany in the period 1989–1997. A stabilised financial position together with consistent economic growth has been regarded as the cornerstone for the existence of the whole German welfare state since the 1980s. However, problems in the national economy have affected the nature of the welfare state in a substantial way. Public spending in Germany exceeded public revenue over the whole nine-year period and the national economy simultaneously had to struggle with diminishing or even negative annual growth rates. Although the increase in the public spending reached its ceiling and started to fall since the mid-1990s, the financial gap, budgetary deficit, between public spending and revenue, however, widened. Public spending in Germany jumped from 148 billion Euros in 1989 to 194 billion in 1990 due to German reunification. Public spending expanded further to 241 billion in 1994 but thereafter it fell to 226 billion by 1997. Public revenue increased from 138 billion in 1989 to 215 billion Euros in 1994 but then, revenue fell from 212 billion in 1995 to 194 billion in 1997. Thus, the gap between public spending and public revenue widened from 10 billion in 1989 to 26 billion Euros in 1994 and from 25.9 billion in 1995 to 32.4 billion Euros in 1997. On the other hand,

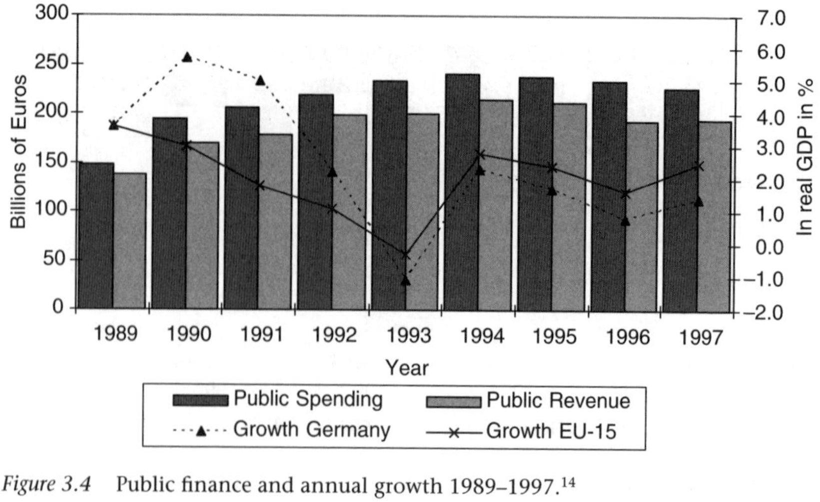

Figure 3.4 Public finance and annual growth 1989–1997.[14]

what is most striking here is the fact that Germany managed to maintain even this kind of financial stability through the whole 1990s although German reunification had such a significant impact on the public debt, the budgetary deficit and the public finances. The economic impact of German reunification on national economic stability might have been expected to be much larger; *a fact that seems to be totally forgotten, undervalued or even ignored in the European political and economic debate on the current state of German fiscal stability in EMU.*

The crisis in the public finances exacerbated in Germany because annual economic growth did not manage to bridge the negative gap in the budget and thus the financial gap widened after the beginning of the 1990s. Germany experienced high growth rates during the first years of reunification and annual growth was 3.6 percent in 1989 and almost doubled to 5.7 percent in 1990. The growth in the EU area, however, declined from 3.6 percent in 1989 to a negative growth rate of 0.3 percent in 1993 because of a major recession in the EMS countries 1992–1993. The growth rate in Germany diminished more slowly than in the EU area but it also turned into a negative rate of 1.1 percent in 1993. There was a recovery in the German economy and it grew 2.3 percent in 1994, after which the growth hardly reached the level of 1.0 percent (0.8% in 1996 and 1.4% in 1997). The growth in the EU area recovered faster and to a higher level after 1994 than in Germany by reaching a rate of 2.5 percent in 1997. What is noteworthy is that low growth rates did not compensate for the financial impact of the striking increase in debt, deficit and spending in Germany in the mid-1990s.

3.2 Stabilisation and/or room for national fiscal flexibility

The Bundesbank and monetary discipline

German national strategies to stabilise the post-reunification economy and maintain economic stability through European fiscal policy coordination can be analysed through three main national politico-economic actors, their objectives, interests and interaction: a) the Bundesbank, b) the federal government and c) the Bundesländer and trade unions (and other social stakeholders). This analytical position stems from the concrete policy-making culture in Germany, which has focused on three main elements of national economic policy: monetary policy (the Bundesbank), fiscal policy (the federal government and the Bundesländer) and wage and labour policy (trade unions). As Scharpf summarises: "In Germany, coordination between monetary policy, fiscal policy and wage policy was traditionally based on nothing more demanding than the mechanisms of 'mutual adjustment'."[15] In reality, one cannot separate the negotiations of EMU (monetary policy) and the formation of the Stability Pact (fiscal policy) in the German national political and economic strategy. The introduction of the Stability

Pact has to be seen in the broad framework of European economic policy because for Germany, the Stability Pact was only a mechanism for the operational success of EMU. How national politico-economic actors acted to achieve this coordination mechanism in fiscal policy for the EMU era and what elements of coordination they wanted to include (upload) in the system of fiscal policy coordination arise as crucial questions for understanding the present position of Germany under the Stability Pact. According to Ardy's interpretation, the ECB ensures the priority of monetary policy in EMU, whereas the Stability Pact "helps to limit the possibility of a leadership battle between the monetary and fiscal policy, which can be costly, as shown by the contradictory policy pursued by the German government and the Bundesbank after German unification".[16]

Firstly, the Bundesbank has played a major role not only in the formation of EMU and the Stability Pact but also in German macroeconomic leadership. The Bundesbank has historically cooperated closely with the other main national actor, the federal government, in achieving Germany's current economic position in Europe. However, cooperation between these two main national actors has not always been unproblematic: monetary policy and fiscal policy as individual policy areas have sometimes required policy measures that have excluded the measures and objectives of the other policy area. On the one hand, Stern argues that the Bundesbank and the federal government are "obliged by law to coordinate in terms of respecting the aims of both statutes".[17] On the other hand, Heisenberg claims that "the history of European monetary cooperation is fraught with conflict between the Bundesbank and the federal government over the international dimension of monetary policy".[18] Aligning monetary and fiscal policy objectives and national cooperation over them has become even more crucial and more challenging when implementing national fiscal policy as a part of the single-currency area under increasing European economic, fiscal and monetary policy coordination.

The process by which the Bundesbank took over the responsibility for the monetary policy of East Germany affected its role in the European monetary environment in two significant ways. In economic terms, the integration of the German currencies caused interest rate and price stability problems for the Bundesbank in a unified Germany. The Bundesbank criticised the currency ratio of 1:1 between the East and West German Mark, which it considered to directly jeopardise the traditional West German monetary discipline; a fact that finally forced the Bundesbank to increase its interest rates to secure monetary stability resulting in declining growth rates in the unified Germany (Figure 3.5). Through the expanded German economic area, the overall uncertainties in the East German economy were spread over the monetary area of the Bundesbank.[19] In political terms, the political power of the Bundesbank increased sizeably in European monetary policy due to the reunification; the 1990s can thus be characterised as the domination era of the Bundesbank and the strong D-Mark (*Deutschmark*).

Reunification was a watershed for the current monetary position of Germany, as the trends in the monetary instruments of the Bundesbank show (Figures 3.5, 3.6 and 3.7). As reunification caused major costs in fiscal policy, as discussed above, the Bundesbank had to implement an active monetary policy through its two main instruments: interest rate and exchange rate policies. For example, the crisis of the EMS also explains why the Bundesbank had to run a restrictive monetary policy to prevent the economic crisis from escalating further in 1990–1992 but turned to a more expansive monetary policy again in 1993.[20] As seen in Figure 3.5, the long-term interest rate in Germany progressively declined to a low and stable level until 1997. In Germany, the interest rates declined from 8.9 percent in 1990 to as low as 5.7 percent in 1997. There was also a similar trend in France (from 10.0% to 5.6%), Britain (from 10.2% to 7.1%) and the EU area on average (from 9.9% to 6.2%) over the period 1989–1997. Along with the economic recovery after the 1992–1993 EMS crisis, national central banks further eased their interest rate policies so that the trends in the long-term interest rates became more favourable to economic growth in the EU area, but Britain still had the highest interest rates due to some country-specific developments. What is significant here is that the long-term interest rate in Germany was at a much lower level than elsewhere in Europe before the mid-1990s. Due to the strong and continual European economic convergence in the 1990s, interest rates approached each other so that the rates were almost at the same level in Britain, France, Germany and the EU area as a whole in 1997.

Together with long-term interest rates, exchange rate policy also affected German monetary stability and economic policy strategy. One of the main economic shocks to the exchange rate policy came from the EMS crisis in 1992–1993 although it was the D-Mark that had the key role as the monetary anchor of the EMS. Stability and confidence problems in the EMS forced its member countries to widen the actual limit of currency fluctuation from 2.5 percent to as much as 15 percent around the ECU's average value. Nevertheless, as seen in Figure 3.6, the Bundesbank maintained a relatively stable exchange rate policy during the whole period 1989–1997. For example, the D-Mark (DEM) appreciated against the US dollar from 1993 (1.65 DM) to 1995 (1.43 DM) and depreciated from 1996 (1.50 DM) to 1997 (1.84 DM). Where the appreciation of the D-Mark slowed down national economic growth, the depreciation in turn had a positive effect on exports, economic activity and growth (Figure 3.4). In general, the D-Mark appreciated against the US dollar by over 180 percent in the period 1950–1996, corresponding with the depreciation of 65 percent of the US dollar against

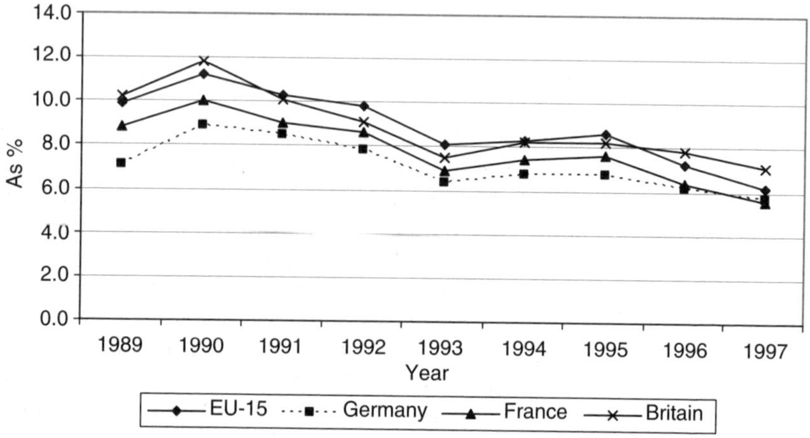

Figure 3.5 Long-term interest rate 1989–1997.[21]

the D-Mark.[22] The German exchange rate trend was relatively stable from 1989 to 1997 when taking into account the major problems in other European currencies within the EMS. For example, due to the severe exchange rate problems, the membership of the British pound (GBP) in the EMS was only one year and 11 months from October 1990 to September 1992, and the French franc (FRF) was very volatile throughout the 1990s. Major uncertainties and volatilities in most European currencies nearly resulted in the collapse of the whole EMS in the mid-1990s despite the widening of the currency bands within the Exchange Rate Mechanism. However, the considerable effort of national governments to control these critical trends clearly contributed to the emergence of a stable monetary environment for exports and imports in the late 1990s.

The third main responsibility of the Bundesbank has been to maintain price stability, which means contributing to low inflation and supporting consistent economic growth. Similarly to the developments in the long-term interest rates, there was a strong trend towards convergence in inflation in Europe over the period 1990–1997. As Figure 3.7 shows, the average inflation rate in the EU area declined from 5.4 percent in 1990 to only 1.9 percent in 1997. With the similar trend, France also experienced a major lowering in inflation from 3.4 percent in 1990 to 1.1 percent in 1997. In the wake of reunification and the EMS crisis, the inflation rate in Germany expanded from 2.7 percent in 1990 to 5.1 percent in 1992 but the Bundesbank succeeded in reducing the inflation after 1992 so that inflation in Germany reached the same level (1.9%) with the EU area in 1997. Thus, it can be argued that the Bundesbank succeeded in its task of maintaining price stability through strict monetary discipline. On the other hand, it can also be argued that a low trend in the inflation rate had been achieved not

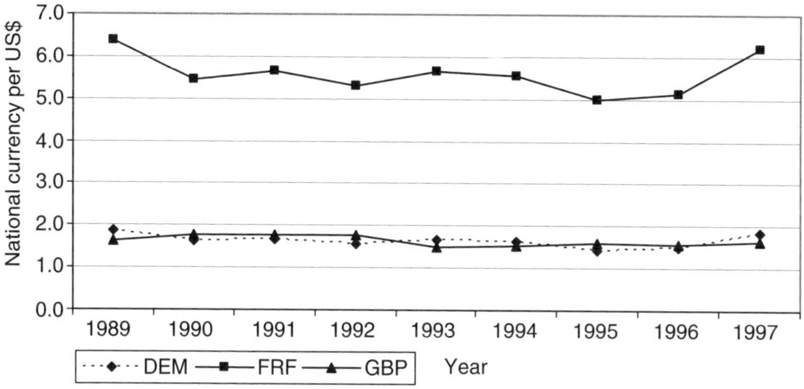

Figure 3.6 Exchange rate 1989–1997.[23]

only because of the Bundesbank alone but also because of poor economic performance and low economic growth in Germany: the low annual growth rate partly explains the similar declining trends in inflation in France, Britain and the EU as well. Although high inflation was persistent in Britain, the inflation rate in Britain fell even more rapidly than elsewhere in Europe from 8.1 percent to 2.6 percent. One of the main reasons for the fact that the inflation of Britain was still at a higher level than in Germany, France and the EU in 1997 was the fact that Britain, in the context of its own economic policy, was not seeking to achieve the EMU conditions for price stability (as a result of its problems in the EMS) and thus, Britain did not take economic convergence towards the low inflation objective of EMU as the first priority in its national monetary policy.

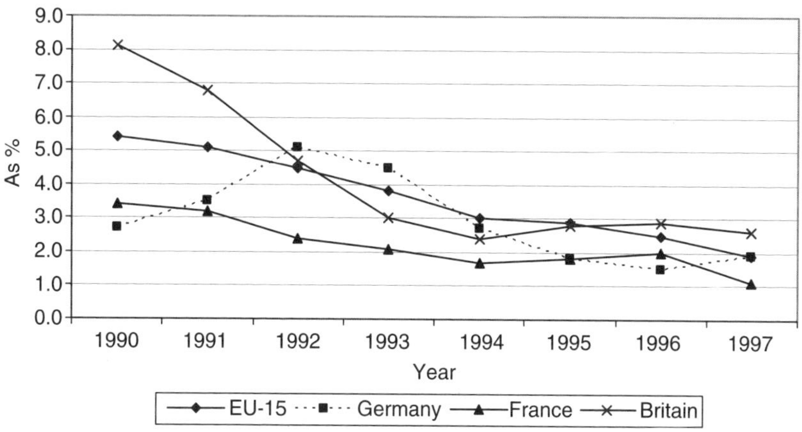

Figure 3.7 Inflation rate 1990–1997.[24]

Given this unstable but clearly improving monetary environment in the mid-1990s, the fundamental reason why the Bundesbank wanted to have fiscal policy coordination between European national economies and why it supported the idea of a Stability Pact was its own strategy and interests towards maintaining monetary discipline and anti-inflation policy in EMU since 1999.[25] These objectives can be seen in the context of the traditional German economic policy. The Bundesbank wanted to ensure price stability and the independence of monetary authority as the first priority in the EMU circumstances. However, the main disappointment of the Bundesbank was that due to the supranational authority of the European Central Bank, the Bundesbank had to give up its independent role in ensuring the external value of the D-Mark and also its policy of maintaining the D-Mark as the leading reserve currency in Europe. The Bundesbank was also worried about the ECB's "one-size-fits-all" monetary policy, which would be specified as the monetary policy for the whole EMU area and not for the German national economy primarily. The Bundesbank feared that this aggregate monetary policy would not always be the most optimal policy for German economic interests.

Apart from price stability, the Bundesbank was also concerned about major problems in budgetary policies in some Member States joining EMU. The Bundesbank was worried about Portugal, Italy, Greece and Belgium and that the fiscal problems in those countries could expand further in the coming Euro area and cause long-lasting monetary and fiscal instability and low growth spill-overs. For example, public debt in 1996 was 130.2 percent of GDP in Belgium, 111.3 percent in Greece, 122.1 percent in Italy, 62.9 percent in Portugal and 72.1 percent in the EU area as a whole.[26] It was in the Bundesbank's interests for Member States to coordinate national fiscal policies in EMU to prevent overly expansive budgetary policies. It was considered that the elimination of the free-rider problem of public debt would be possible only through strict fiscal rules in EMU. In the worst-case scenario of the Bundesbank, non-coordination might increase the likelihood of excessive debt and deficit stocks, which could in turn endanger the price stability and exchange rate targets of the ECB. As a result of this, the Euro could become a less stable currency than the D-Mark was. For the Bundesbank, the Maastricht convergence criteria for national fiscal policies were not clear enough for ensuring this kind of economic stability in EMU. The President of the Bundesbank, Hans Tietmeyer, took the view that when EU Member States entered to EMU there would be an increase in pressure to implement an expansive fiscal policy as an adjustment measure to the loss of national monetary policy; a possibility that was not stated clearly enough in the Maastricht Treaty.[27] The Bundesbank thus supported Finance Minister Waigel's idea of the Stability Pact for more specific rules for national fiscal policies and national fiscal discipline for EMU. In Heipertz and Verdun's view, the Bundesbank "liked the idea of further legislation because it went some way towards addressing its concerns about a lack of stability-orientation in EMU".[28] For the Bundesbank, fiscal policy coordination under the Stability Pact was one of the key elements of a successful EMU.

The federal government and fiscal discipline

Chancellor Kohl's government played a key role in the formation of the Stability Pact together with the Bundesbank. Kohl was in office in Germany for 16 years, from 1982 to 1990, and oversaw reunification. Kohl, as one the leading figures in European politics, will be remembered as a politician committed to both German reunification and European political and economic integration. However, the dual integration, German reunification and European integration, proved to be much more expensive than expected both in economic and political terms; a price that Schröder's second government is still paying in the 21st century. According to von Hagen *et al.*, "in Germany, the ailing of the Kohl government, the difficulties created by the way this government had handled German reunification, and, perhaps also, the lack of enthusiasm for monetary union in the German public, which would have made maintaining a higher degree of fiscal discipline for the sake of the Maastricht criteria politically easier, caused a considerable slippage in the quality of its budget process".[29]

When analysing the economic interests of the German government, it has to be pointed out that the formation of EMU and the introduction of fiscal policy coordination under the Stability Pact were closely related in Chancellor Kohl's (CDU) national politics. Kohl had to fight hard for national acceptance of the EMU project and the Stability Pact even though he had a strong political coalition behind him.[30] Kohl's economic objectives were clear and straightforward and he and his main ministers spoke for Finance Minister Waigel's proposal for coordinating national budgetary policies in the EMU era. For example, the Minister of Economics, Günter Rexrodt, regarded the three percent ceiling for budgetary deficits as a very good long-term solution for Germany because he predicted that Germany would not have any difficulties in achieving a stable 2.0–2.5 deficit level of GDP in 1996 and 1997.[31] However, the main opposition party, SPD, and the then party leader, Oskar Lafontaine, strongly and publicly criticised Kohl's intentions towards strict fiscal rules in EMU. According to Lafontaine, EMU and the Stability Pact, as the Chancellor and the Finance Minister had proposed, ignored the great importance of economic growth and employment policy along with the proposed unrealistic monetary and budgetary aims. In Lafontaine's view, economic stability could not be achieved through focusing only on strict monetary and budgetary policy in EMU. Achieving long-term economic stability in EMU would require more extensive economic policy coordination including clear growth and employment targets and sufficiently national economic flexibility to achieve them. Therefore, the main opposition party SPD regarded the objectives of the Stability Pact as "unfeasible".[32]

These political tensions and uncertainties about the government's economic strategy also pervaded to public opinion. A major part of public opinion was against EMU and the Euro and the German public thought that the establishment of EMU with the single currency would affect the economy, employment and growth highly negatively. The Germans believed that they, rather than the French or British, would have to pay the ultimate economic price for having a European monetary union. Public opinion on the single currency Euro and EMU was very sceptical and only 14 percent of the people in the Old Länder were in favour of the Euro, whereas in the New Länder the figure was only 11 percent in 1995. By contrast, both the Old (59%) and the New (58%) Länder were clearly against the Euro.[33] In this national political environment, Kohl and Waigel regarded the Stability Pact with strict national fiscal discipline in EMU as crucial to the government's public policy on European economic integration. The government wanted to include explicit fiscal rules with strict supranational monitoring in the Maastricht Treaty because the breaking of the fiscal rules (running excessive fiscal policy) in some Member States (for example Mediterranean countries) would otherwise become far too attractive and cause the free-rider problem in EMU: a situation that could make the economic fears of the German public a reality. If a significant economic shock were to occur in a Member State in EMU, without effective policy coordination, the impact of the shock would spread rapidly to other Member States (including Germany). Kohl and Waigel presented the aims of fiscal policy coordination to the public as if it greatly supported Germany's national economic interests in EMU. Thus, it could be argued that without the strict fiscal rules it would have been very difficult or even impossible for the government to convince the public of the economic and political advantages of EMU.[34]

Similarly to the Bundesbank's view, the German government also considered that the fiscal rules of the Maastricht Treaty would not sufficiently ensure fiscal stability in EMU and therefore, the Finance Minister, Theo Waigel, made a proposal for an additional and supplementary set of fiscal rules for EMU in September 1995.[35] Waigel argued that an effective and successful EMU would require institutionalised fiscal policy coordination along with the common monetary policy. In his opinion, "it is crucial that the countries taking part in the last stage of the monetary union will establish an additional safeguard for budgetary discipline".[36] Waigel officially presented his proposal for a Stability Pact in the *Bundestag* in Bonn in November 1995. He argued that in normal economic circumstances the annual budgetary deficit of GDP should not be more than one percent in EMU. Such an EMU Member State would otherwise face an "automatic" and "massive" sanction mechanism.[37] At the Dublin European Council in December 1996, the heads of the states agreed on the content and objectives of the Stability and Growth Pact but not in the exact form originally presented by Waigel. The Stability and Growth Pact defined the fiscal rules for deficit and debt more specifically than in the Maastricht Treaty and set concrete sanctions but without any automatic sanction mechanism. In addition, based on a French initiative (the Chirac Memorandum), the Dublin European Council incorporated a common growth and employment strategy into Waigel's original Stability Pact. France wanted to secure through the Dublin European Council that the strict fiscal policy guidelines supported by the German government would be in line with a "macroeconomic strategy for economic growth and employment";[38] the fundamental growth objective of France finally transformed the original Stability Pact into the Stability and Growth Pact.

There were several crucial policy elements in relation to the government's interests and objectives towards the Stability Pact. From the European perspective, Kohl's primary objective was to secure the formation of a European political union (the EU) through the Maastricht Treaty and it was Waigel who concentrated more on the economic stability of EMU. However, the Maastricht negotiations over the EMU system and the common fiscal rules subsequently combined the interests of both powerful German politicians and that was why *Die Zeit* named them, Kohl and Waigel, as *"das Duo Kohl/Waigel"*.[39] Their main economic attention was eventually directed towards the EMU criteria and the effort of other Member States to achieve the required degree of economic convergence to be able to join the final stage of EMU. Germany promoted the view that all convergence criteria should be fulfilled completely and without any exceptions before joining EMU in 1999. Kohl and Waigel were concerned in particular about public debt in some EU Member States, such as Greece, Belgium and Italy, in the mid-1990s (Figure 3.1) and they feared that without strict criteria poor budgetary policies in these countries could jeopardise the objectives of EMU and those of the German economy in the EMU era (monetary discipline); a development that could have caused increasing and persistent resistance against the Euro and EMU in the German public.

From the national perspective, Kohl and Waigel's effort to introduce the Stability Pact for EMU was also interpreted as a political intention to settle Germany's own increasing national problems in fiscal policy.[40] Although Germany politically checked that all EU Member States entering to EMU would fulfil all the economic preconditions prior to 1999, the German economy itself also had major problems in meeting the debt and deficit rules simultaneously. As shown in Figure 3.8, the public debt and budgetary deficit of Germany experienced a strong upward pressure from 1990 to 1997. For example, the deficit increased by a striking 70.1 percent from

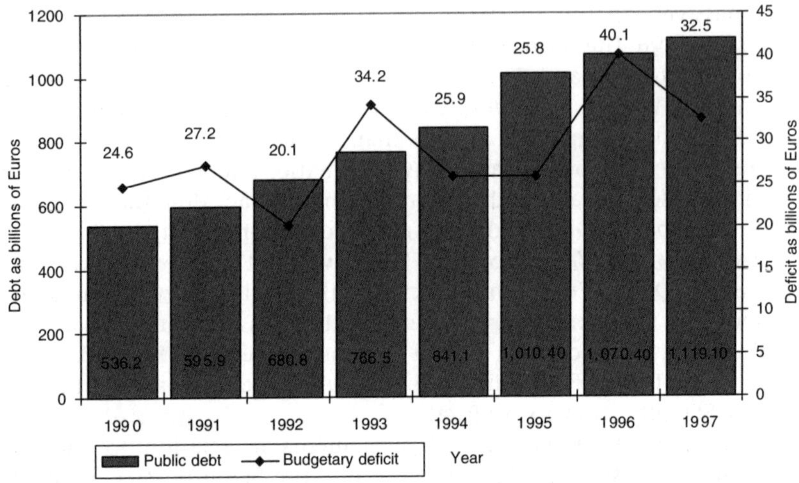

Figure 3.8 Public debt and budgetary deficit in Germany 1990–1997.[41]

20.1 billion in 1992 to 34.2 billion Euros in 1993. In addition to the year 1993, the deficit also jumped up to 40.1 billion in 1996, as much as 55.4 percent up from 25.8 billion Euros in 1995. The debt also increased from 536.2 billion in 1990 to as much as 1119.1 billion in 1997, up 109 percent in eight years. This dramatic increase in national debt and deficit stocks acted as a direct incentive for strict budgetary discipline in Germany in the mid-1990s.

For both European and national political and economic reasons, Finance Minister Waigel argued that the German government could not create any impression prior to the start of the third stage of EMU that could mean a relaxation of the economic criteria for the entry to EMU. In reality, Waigel proposed an even stricter fiscal rule of a mere one percent ceiling of GDP for national budgetary deficits with automatic sanctions than was originally agreed in the Maastricht Treaty in 1992.[42] However, the dramatic policy failure of the German government was to underestimate how increasingly constrained fiscal policy simultaneously with the loss of the monetary authority would affect German national economic policy-making in EMU, budgetary and labour policies, public finances and economic stability and growth just as the opposition and the public had feared. According to Scharpf's interpretation, "while fiscal constraints are tightening, high unemployment and the greater inequality of primary incomes are increasing the demands on the social-security and equalising functions of the welfare state".[43] This was one of the fundamental reasons why the Bundesländer and trade unions wanted to take an active role in the national political and economic debate over the introduction of EMU, the Euro and the Stability Pact.

The Bundesländer and trade unions and room for national flexibility

The Bundesländer and trade unions also had a role in debating the relationship between national fiscal flexibility and the need for fiscal discipline in EMU.[44] Waigel's proposal for increasing fiscal policy coordination under the Stability Pact came in for a lot of criticism in German society. *Die Zeit* reported that "domestically no one understands what the bureaucratic structure of the Stability Pact has to do with the stability of the Euro".[45] "Soft" Eurosceptics in the Bundesländer and "hard" Eurosceptics in trade unions agreed with the government and the Bundesbank that during a high economic cycle the fiscal rules could be achieved without any major national adjustments.[46] However, what the Eurosceptics did not understand in the government's plan was how these binding fiscal rules could be achieved in the event of a major downturn. In the Eurosceptics' opinion, in a downturn these rules would become much more difficult to achieve and they would require a more restrictive fiscal policy and more negative national adjustments, such as cuts in public spending, than would otherwise be the optimal policy for the German national economy. In these circumstances, the Bundesländer, municipalities and trade unions would have preferred pro-cyclical fiscal policy implemented by the government. They thus considered it crucial to continue to allow national budgetary flexibility in a downturn under the rules of the Stability Pact in EMU. In Huffschmid's view, "in Germany, too, opposition grows against the policy of income and welfare cuts and comprehensive downsizing, legitimised by allegedly European imperatives".[47] This public suspicion forced Kohl's government to try to convince the public that EMU, together with European fiscal policy coordination, would ultimately lead to long-term political and economic advantages in Germany.

The Bundesländer also feared that they would lose some of their traditional economic independence and autonomy due to the binding rules and the sanction mechanism of the Stability Pact in EMU. One of the main critics of the government's economic policy, who also promoted the economic autonomy of the Bundesländer in the formation of the Stability Pact, was the then Prime Minister of Lower Saxony (the present Chancellor), Gerhard Schröder (SPD). Both the Old and the New Länder had been accustomed to extensive public revenue coming from the federal government in the 1990s but now, the Stability Pact and EMU would require stricter national fiscal discipline than after reunification. In order to fully comply with the Stability Pact it would require major cuts in public finances and investments to the Bundesländer even though Germany faced relatively low economic growth rates at the same time in the mid-1990s. Any problems in public finances would directly cause cuts in public services or an increase in the tax burden, in particular in the New Länder, where economic developments were still heavily dependent on federal finance.

The trade unions shared many of the fears and doubts of the Bundesländer on EMU and the increasing need for fiscal discipline in Member States. The significant role of the trade unions in national economic policy-making stemmed from the reunification process because labour policy and employment were one of the main channels, together with budgetary and monetary channels, through which the economic impact of reunification transformed into concrete economic challenges in Germany in the 1990s.[48] The main doubt of the trade unions with the EMU system was that an excessively restrictive fiscal policy together with the common monetary policy would bring down the whole German national labour market if there was not enough national economic flexibility to counteract economic downturns and other unfavourable developments. For the trade unions, increasing uncertainties over national employment and wages policies could also cause instability in interest rates and reduce investments and growth and thus hasten the snowball effect in the national economy. For example, high unemployment rates after reunification had a direct negative impact on public faith in Kohl's government's ability to combat unemployment, and faith in the government's labour policy significantly decreased from 1994 to 1997. In the Old Länder 30 percent of the public trusted the employment policy of Kohl's party (CDU) in 1994, whereas this figure was only 19 percent in 1997. In the New Länder the trend was even more striking as faith in labour policy fell from 18 percent in 1994 to only 6 percent in 1997.[49]

Figure 3.9 presents the trends on labour productivity, real unit costs and unemployment rate in Germany from 1991 to 1997. For the trade unions, these three indicators of national labour policy were closely related and they clearly illustrated the start of declining economic performance in the

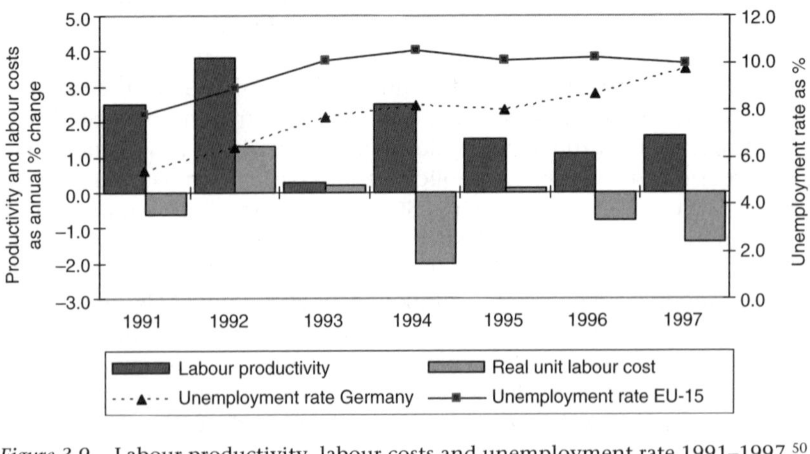

Figure 3.9 Labour productivity, labour costs and unemployment rate 1991–1997.[50]

mid-1990s. On the one hand, when Streeck analysed the competitiveness of Germany on the world market on the basis of national labour policy during the reunification period, he arrived at the conclusion that "West Germany was internationally the most successful of the major economies".[51] On the other hand, Hemerijck and Schludi argued that "the shift to monetarism and restrictive fiscal policy in the 1980s and 1990s undermined the capacity of national policy-makers to use macroeconomic policy instruments to achieve full employment".[52] Labour productivity as an explanatory factor of national employment policy did not develop as positively as the government would have wished because productivity faced a strong downward trend after a high increase in 1992 (3.8%), falling to only 0.3 percent in 1993. Productivity recovered well after the EMS crisis in 1994 but it stood at just above one percent until 1997.[53] As productivity growth faced problems, German collective labour agreements, which played a major role in wage policy, also had to control the increase in real unit labour costs. Controlling the increase in costs was essential for competitiveness because if the real unit labour costs increased, then wage costs for companies would grow simultaneously and competitiveness and the ability to employ would decline. In Germany, the labour costs rose in 1992 (1.3%), 1993 (0.2%) and 1995 (0.1%), whereas the costs declined in 1991 (0.6%), 1994 (2.0%), 1996 (0.8%) and 1997 (1.4%). Streeck explains these low or even negative real unit labour costs by traditionally strong national economic cooperation. In his view, "German collective bargaining together with the institutionalised monetarism of the Bundesbank has always been remarkably good at keeping unit labour costs under control".[54]

According to Streeck and Hassel, this impact of the budgetary and financial crisis on unemployment and *vice versa* was possible because still in the mid-1990s "centralised collective bargaining continued to produce both high wages and an egalitarian wage structure".[55] The unemployment crisis in the 1990s can thus be understood in the context of labour costs, productivity, employment and competitiveness. Firstly, although the increase in labour costs was relatively well under control, labour productivity simultaneously diminished, which lowered competitiveness. Secondly, unemployment in Germany showed a progressive upward trend but still remained at a lower level than in the EU area as a whole. The unemployment rate increased from 5.4 percent in 1991 to 9.7 percent in 1997 in Germany and from 7.8 percent in 1991 to 10.0 percent in 1997 in the EU area. Thirdly, although the unemployment crisis was clearly linked to the overall economic developments and the performance of the German economy after reunification, Streeck considered that increasing unemployment "might have come even without unification" but "it could also have been caused by unification alone".[56] Manow and Seils when focusing on the economic trends in the German economy found that "German unification and every slump since the early 1970s triggered...a higher level of unemployment, a lower level of total employment, and steadily increasing non-wage labour costs, which adversely affected long-term job growth in the low-productivity service sector";[57] concrete fears due to which the Bundesländer and trade unions spoke for allowing national fiscal flexibility in EMU.

3.3 Designing and securing national fiscal stability in EMU

The need for national adjustments and national economic coordination

Along with pushing through the Stability Pact in Dublin in December 1996, Germany also had to make national adjustments to meet the fiscal rules and supranational monitoring in 1996 and 1997. After the Dublin European Council, Chancellor Kohl and Finance Minister Waigel were convinced that, firstly, Germany would meet all the criteria for EMU and secondly, it would be Germany that would benefit most from the increased fiscal discipline and policy coordination in EMU. The government's faith in the performance of the national economy under the Stability Pact was based on the belief that Germany would make national adjustments sufficiently and efficiently before the implementation of the Stability Pact and the start of the EMU era. However, the fiscal pathway of Germany under the Stability Pact in practice required major political efforts and adjustments; the national pathway which culminated in the introduction of the so-called Saving Programme 1996.[58] The programme, which was a crucial national adjustment to ensure fiscal discipline, was a result of the downturn of the national economy. However, the reforms in the programme did not prove to be effective enough in stabilising the economy and consequently, the government had to make more adjustments and more explicit policy actions in 1997 and 1998. The main argument of Kohl's government for increasing national reforms and policy coordination was that both the federal government and the Bundesländer had benefited from the expansion of social policy and social security and thus, both partners should now be responsible for carrying the economic burden. The government realised that the increase in the public debt in the 1990s had to be slowed and the current course of the economy could no longer continue in the direction of ever increasing borrowing. However, the German Council of Economic Experts argued that the favourable economic environment of the mid-1990s for major national reforms had faded away and Germany had already lost a major part of its momentum. According to the Council, "the economic development in Germany has sizeably lost its momentum in 1995" and "the economic cycle for Germany does not seem more favourable at all".[59]

In the first attempt to make the system of national economic coordination function effectively between the federal government and the

Bundesländer, Kohl's government developed and reformed national institutional economic cooperation.[60] Since 1 January 1970 the Law on Budgetary Procedures (*Haushaltsgrundsätzegesetz*) had controlled and monitored the politico-institutional process of the federal budget and in line with the German Constitution, the law had further defined economic responsibilities between the federal government and the Bundesländer. According to the law, the federal government and the Bundesländer were obliged to implement economic policy under the guidelines of the annual federal budget.[61] Both were also required to submit a five-year economic plan for public finances.[62] Institutionally, the Law on Budgetary Procedures established the Financial Planning Council (*Finanzplanungsrat*), which consisted of representatives of the Federal Minister of Finance, the Federal Minister of Economics, the Ministers of Finance of the Bundesländer and four representatives of interest groups.[63] The foremost duty of the Financial Planning Council was to coordinate planning in budgetary policy and public finances between the federal government, the Bundesländer and the municipalities.[64] The Financial Planning Council thus acted as an essential coordinating institution throughout the economy of the federal republic.

The developments in the German fiscal and monetary environment, as analysed in Sections 3.1 and 3.2 of this chapter, caused a substantial increase in the overall public debt from 536.2 billion Euros in 1990 to as much as 1119.1 billion Euros in 1997 (Figure 3.8); a critical development that the government's policy actions now planned to change. However, the government could not deal with the increasing debt and deficit stocks alone and therefore, Finance Minister Waigel wanted the Bundesländer to take greater and more equal responsibility for securing Germany's fiscal position for the EMU era. For Waigel, this responsibility meant rapid reforms in the system of national economic coordination and in the structure of the public finances. As a concrete policy objective, the federal government and the Bundesländer were expected to reduce the debt and deficit ratios equally.[65] However, the Bundesländer and trade unions strongly objected to the government's austerity measures. According to them, European economic integration already placed highly restrictive constraints on national fiscal policy and any additional limits set by the government would make it even harder to maintain stability, growth and employment within the common rules in EMU. The chairman of the trade union IG Metall, Klaus Zwickel, called the plan for reforming public finances and cutting spending "a conspiracy against employment and social equality".[66] For Zwickel, massive cuts and reforms in public spending would endanger social equality and employment, and the equality problem would also cause a widening gap in finance between the Old and New Länder.[67] Regardless of strong criticism and protest from the Bundesländer and trade unions, Kohl and Waigel pushed through new reforms in September 1996 and a major part of the public reforms came into effect in

October 1996. Kohl's Saving Programme 1996 consisted of three main policy programmes for securing German national fiscal stability under the Stability Pact in EMU: a) the Annual Economic Report 1996 (*Jahreswirtschaftsbericht 1996*), b) the National Stability Pact (*der nationale Stabilitätspakt*), and c) the Action Plan for Investment and Employment (*Aktionsprogramm für Investitionen und Arbeitsplätze*).

Designing sustainable public finances in 1996

The Annual Economic Report 1996 tried to tackle national economic problems with the instruments of social policy and social security although the German Council of Economic Experts warned that major reforms in social policy would directly affect "the core principle of the welfare state – the solidarity principle".[68] The government was concerned about the economic developments because debt, deficit, unemployment and low growth caused increasing pressures on public spending while tax revenue saw a simultaneous downward trend. For the government, social security as one of the biggest expenditure targets could not be left outside the reform plan and the government in particular weakened the social benefit for workers. Before, continuation of payments to sick workers (*Lohnfortzahlung im Krankheitsfall*) had been 100 percent of salary. Now, this sick-leave payment was cut from 100 percent to 80 percent for the first time in the history of Germany's welfare state. Simultaneously with the sick pay reform, there was a public pension reform, which was directed at both retirement age and retirement pay. As a result, the retirement age for women was set to rise from 60 years to 63 years from 1997 and for men from 63 to 65 years.[69] Thus, the government presented and implemented a concrete social programme for securing sustainable public finances.

Secondly, the government introduced a National Stability Pact that reformed national economic coordination and the structure of the public finances and in particular that of public spending. The objective of the National Stability Pact was to strengthen economic coordination between the federal government, the Bundesländer and the municipalities. The government believed that it could stabilise the critical increase in the debt and deficit stocks through more intensive national economic coordination between the government and the Bundesländer. Although the first idea for a National Stability Pact was presented already in 1994, a specified proposal did not come until April and June 1996. The government proposed in April 1996 that the precise target in diminishing public debt should be 25.5 billion Euros by 2000. According to this plan, the Bundesländer would be equally responsible for a half of this debt target, 12.75 billion. However, due to the other simultaneous economic reforms, the Bundesländer feared that their total saving balance would be more than 18.9 billion instead of 12.75 billion Euros.[70] They considered that constraining regional economies more than the rules in the Maastricht Treaty and the Stability Pact required would inevitably result in overly-restricted national and regional economic policy-making. Therefore, the Bundesländer insisted at the meeting of the Financial Planning Council in June 1996 that the planned economic burden for the Bundesländer should be renegotiated and reduced to the same level as the government's saving target.

Thirdly, the government introduced the Action Plan for Investment and Employment in January 1996, which was based on a broad government plan, Alliance for Jobs (*Bündnis für Arbeit und zur Standortsicherung*), for restructuring government-labour relations. The Alliance for Jobs included reforms in social policy and social security and collective bargaining system between the government and trade unions (both employers and employees) to combat unemployment more effectively and with new instruments.[71] It was the Action Plan for Investment and Employment with its fifty-point programme through which the government concretised the Alliance for Jobs: by increasing investments and contributing to creating new jobs the government planned to boost economic growth.[72] The government was politically ready to compel unemployed persons to do more to find work. From the mid-1990s, Germany had started to suffer from ineffective labour policy, which was caused by, for example increasing unemployment and decreasing productivity, and thus, high wages and labour inflexibility had started to require a thorough reform of national labour policy.[73] This was why the government executed some radical changes in social policy and unemployment benefits. For example, the government cut by half unemployment benefit for the first week of unemployment and in addition, the maximum period of time for unemployment benefit was limited to five years. Although the government prepared for the marked increase in unemployment by 300,000 to a total of 3.9 million in 1996, it was still optimistic that the Action Plan would cut the unemployment rate by half to two million by 2000.[74]

The government's labour policies met with a lot of criticism. The trade unions in particular protested against the labour reforms, cuts in unemployment benefits and the weakening of social security. For them, these changes struck at the fundamental right of citizens: to secure income and a living for an individual in the event of unemployment.[75] Finally, when the Daimler-Benz Group, one of the biggest employers in Germany, announced its intention to apply the new 80 percent level of sick-pay for its workers, 80,000 people in June 1996 and then 100,000 people in October 1996 publicly demonstrated against the government's saving policy.[76] Although there was a need for reforming the public finances in Germany, the government's actions did not receive any support from the opposition or trade unions. The National Stability Pact and the cuts in public spending caused major political issues between the government, the opposition and trade unions, and it was the government's social and employment reforms, the declining economy and trade unions that finally contributed to Kohl's

(CDU) defeat and Schröder's (SPD) victory in the September 1998 elections. As Streeck and Hassel understood: "The rift between the government and unions, as documented by a large union protest rally in May 1996, was not healed until the election in September 1998."[77]

European guidelines for German national economic reforms I

At the European level, EU Member States were increasingly concerned about how Germany and some other Member States could tackle high unemployment together with decreasing economic growth. Therefore, Member States decided to further European economic policy coordination to support growth, employment and stability through the so-called European processes, that is European Council agreements on common policy actions, within the procedure of the broad economic policy guidelines. The main Council agreements extended to economic policy areas from the common employment strategy (the Luxemburg process), and structural and labour reforms (the Cardiff process) to confirming further economic coordination (the Vienna strategy). These processes were planned to act as a "soft" coordination framework by introducing new policy actions and new coordination models between national governments, such as joint fora, peer review and discussions of best practices (benchmarking); soft policy coordination was seen as a new set of supranational policy guidelines for national economic policy-making along with the formal, "hard" rules and coordination procedures.[78]

In the Luxemburg European Council of November 1997, Member States agreed to have more coordination between national labour policies as part of broad macroeconomic strategies in Europe. The Council argued that "Union-wide employment guidelines" should be "incorporated into national employment action plans drawn up by the Member States in a multiannual perspective".[79] Given the problems in the German unemployment policy, this Luxemburg process introducing a common European employment strategy brought a new and challenging commitment to the German government to reassess its capability to cut down increasing unemployment. In line with this coordination in labour policy, the European Council meeting in Cardiff in June 1998 was also crucial for European economic policy coordination. The Cardiff process required Member States to develop the functioning of product and capital markets and it urged further national economic reforms "to promote growth, prosperity, jobs and social inclusion".[80] Finally, the Vienna European Council in December 1998 presented the Vienna strategy for Europe, a major part of which strengthened economic policy coordination and which was concerned with concrete coordination challenges relating to EMU. The Council stressed that "economic policies in the EMU must be based on close coordination involving all actors including European social partners".[81] The Council also wanted to intensify economic policy coordination in taxation policy and structural reforms and to develop further the employment strategy of the Luxemburg process. Although these new responsibilities aimed at more effective co-ordination between national economies (micro level), the importance of the Luxemburg and Cardiff processes and the Vienna strategy should be seen from a broad European, EMU perspective (macro level). By requiring structural and labour reforms and by improving the functioning of capital and product markets, Member States wanted to contribute to the effectiveness of the Internal Market and EMU as a whole. According to Dierx, Ilzkovitz and Sekkat, structural reforms in national economies have a major impact on "a balanced policy-mix between macroeconomic and microeconomic policies by reducing the burden on macroeconomic policies in the event of shocks".[82]

Improving growth before the parliamentary elections of 1998

The Annual Economic Report 1997 of the German government noted that the reforms of 1996 had not been working as fast and effectively as planned and that more measures were required. The Minister of Economics, Günter Rexrodt, had to admit that despite the measures, unemployment had risen to over four million people and economic growth continued to face problems. According to Rexrodt, "the failure in the creation of competitive jobs associated with high unemployment is the great challenge in national economic policy".[83] The Annual Economic Report 1997, which was named as "Reforms for Employment" (*Reformen für Beschäftigung*), set a new ten-target Programme for Growth and Employment (*Programm für Wachstum und Beschäftigung*). The basis of the programme was to create a positive trend in the national economy given the costs of reunification and the increasing European economic policy coordination. As concrete objectives, the government targeted a 2.5 percent GDP growth in 1997 (1.4% in 1996) and keeping the unemployment rate below 11.0 percent (10.4% in 1996). This high growth expectation was also anticipated to reduce budgetary deficit from 3.9 percent (39.9 billion Euros) in 1996 to 2.9 percent (32.5 billion Euros) in 1997.[84]

The first element of the Programme for Growth and Employment tackled the declining national economy and, like the Annual Economic Report 1996, the Annual Economic Report 1997 introduced further cuts in public spending and social security benefits. Secondly, the government improved the economic environment for growth by financing public investments in current production as well as technology and innovation. Thirdly and more significantly, the government strengthened its labour policy, which basically meant the decentralisation of power in labour policy measures and the responsibility from the federal government to the regional and local levels, new training and education opportunities and programmes for unemployed. As the Annual Economic Report 1997 stated: "For the German government, it is the fight against unemployment that is the first priority in the economic policy from now on."[85] Regardless of these policy actions and the assumed high 2.5 percent growth rate, Rexrodt was still prepared for the fact that unemployment could rise to as many as 4.2 million people in 1997.

The last annual economic report before the parliamentary elections of 1998 was based on a very positive view on the national economy and it expected a clear boost in growth and employment.[86] However, with 4.8 million registered as unemployed in 1998, the government was required to continue executing reforms in the society; a policy that was the priority in the Annual Economic Report 1998 named as "Promoting an Upward Trend – Creating Jobs" (*Den Aufschwung voranbringen – Arbeitsplätze schaffen*). Despite the declining employment trend, the government had managed to create 1.5 million new jobs in the service sector in the period 1991–1997.[87] In the report the government set a high 2.5 percent growth target, which would still result in an 11 percent unemployment rate and a 2.8 percent deficit rate (28.8 billion Euros) in 1998. In addition, the government believed in the National Employment Action Plan (*Reformen für Investitionen und Arbeitsplätze*) that reforms in public spending, social security and labour policy would create a stabilised and more favourable environment for better growth and employment.[88] Due to the beginning of the strong upswing in the German economy, the government also decided to lower the size of the public sector in 1998, which would require a clear decline in the overall tax burden on employees and employers as well as cutting public services and social policy, all of which were expected to be fully compensated by improving growth and employment from 1998.[89]

3.4 Securing German national "fits" 1995–1997

Fiscal discipline for the EMU era on the German national agenda

In Sections 3.1, 3.2 and 3.3 of this chapter, the uploading process of securing national adaptation "fits" in Germany in 1995–1997 was analysed through the framework of German national interests, strategies and objectives which have acted as the economic, political, institutional and cooperational basis for Germany's introduction of the system of European fiscal policy coordination (Figure 3.10). As subsequently realised, developments after reunification in Germany were not only economic or fiscal but more profoundly politically and socially related; the economic impact of reunification had a major influence on the socio-political environment as well. According to Dyson and Featherstone, "the EMU negotiations reveal how EMU strategy was born out of a specific German cognitive context and then fed back into that context once it was confronted with changing political and economic realities".[90] Similarly to the EMU process, the formation of the Stability Pact also appeared as a highly complex German-led process when putting the German national realities into the context of

European economic and political developments. Although the fiscal rules of the Stability Pact were simple, the main challenge arose from the fact that the implementation (downloading) of the Stability Pact after 1997 (t2) did no longer meet and correspond to all those German interests and politico-economic circumstances that existed when the Stability Pact was formed in the mid-1990s (t1) (Figure 1.2): the difference between national adaptation "fit" and "misfit". Where monetary policy was a "fit" in Germany, German national fiscal policy faced major adaptation "misfits" in EMU. As von Hagen and Strauch summarised the basis of this implementation problem in Germany: "On the European front, the Kohl government spent every effort to insist on tight fiscal policies and on hardening the fiscal constraints embedded in the Maastricht Treaty. Domestically, in contrast, the same government showed a growing disregard for sound fiscal policies and for the rules set by the existing budgetary institutions."[91]

Basically, there were three main German rationales for the idea of having a Stability Pact in EMU. Firstly, the German government considered that fiscal discipline under the Stability Pact could more effectively eliminate excessive national fiscal policies with the free-rider possibility (the deficit bias) in EMU than the original rules of the Maastricht Treaty. As Heipertz and Verdun summarized: "between 1995–1997 there were sound economic and political reasons to create a set of rules that would put limits on budgetary deficits".[92] Secondly, the government needed the Stability Pact and the strict fiscal rules of the Stability Pact for promoting the EMU membership and the single currency for the highly sceptical German people. The Stability Pact thus acted as an instrumental security for German economic and political interests in EMU. Thirdly, introducing strict fiscal rules at the European level also promoted the German government's national objectives in implementing additional saving and reform measures domestically (Figure 3.8). Reunification, together with low growth and high unemployment, increased the political pressure on expanding public spending but in the low-growth circumstances, the high public spending caused the emergence of major debt and deficit stocks. The fourth German rationale for the strict fiscal rules was distrust in whether other Member States, such as Greece and Italy, would really adopt a strong national stability culture in EMU. For these purposes, the German government considered that it would be crucial to strengthen "stability-oriented monetary policy and national

- ➢ Fiscal discipline for the EMU era on the national and European agenda
- ➢ Monetary policy as a "fit" and fiscal policy as a "misfit"
- ➢ Ineffective national cooperation over the common economic strategy
- ➢ Insufficient national adjustments for the Stability Pact in EMU
- ➢ Securing national adaptation "fits" resulted in an increasing number of "misfits"

Figure 3.10 Summary: Securing German national "fits" 1995–1997.

budgetary discipline".[93] It was Finance Minister Waigel who proposed the Stability Pact for EMU in 1995, which, according to him, would only specify the already existing rules of the Maastricht Treaty, not setting any additional economic requirements for Member States. As Waigel argued: "We do not need any changes in the Maastricht Treaty but we need a common agreement in which participating Member States commit themselves to maintain stability."[94] However, public opinion in Germany was against the kind of EMU and fiscal policy coordination that would require further cutting in public spending and unemployment, health and social services.[95]

It seems that in the politico-economic environment in the mid-1990s, it was thought highly unlikely that Germany would have any major fiscal difficulties ("misfits") in complying with the rules of the Stability Pact in EMU. This positive outlook can be discovered in Table 3.1, which shows that Kohl's government expected to have a progressive reduction in public net borrowing from 1995. In 1995, when the idea of the strict fiscal rules was introduced, the government planned to lower the deficit to as little as 14.8 billion Euros by 1999. This highly positive prospect was based on the belief that "from 1995 the German economy has experienced a clear expansion trend".[96] However, the government had to rescale the deficit target to a significantly lower level from the Economic Plan 1995–1999 to the Economic Plan 1996–2000 due to emerged economic uncertainties. In the last Economic Plan 1998–2002 of Kohl's government, the target was to cut the deficit at 23.1 billion Euros by 2002 but in reality, the deficit in 2002 was 31.8 billion Euros. The government still stated in August 1998 that "Member States have the responsibility for bringing down the budgetary deficit to a large extent in economically good times":[97] a fundamental national target for and in the EMU era, which did, however, dramatically fail to be executed by the German government itself.

Although there were favourable fiscal developments in the EU prior to the Stability Pact in the 1990s (fiscal convergence), in some Member States, such as in Germany, the debt and deficit stocks had not been brought down effectively and permanently. As the most significant finding, Germany did not reach a medium-term budgetary balance before joining EMU in 1999, which caused the lack of room for national fiscal flexibility in the post-Pact and the post-EMU eras. In addition, national economic coordination did not reach the level either that could have contributed to finding a nation-wide consensus over the required national adjustments to stabilise the national economy for the EMU era. Reflecting these politico-economic developments in Germany, the scope and timing of national adjustments turned out to be ineffective. This summarises the legacy of the Kohl era (–1998) for the Schröder era (1998–): declining economic growth, increasing unemployment, malfunctioning national coordination and ineffective adjustments.

Table 3.1 Expected budgetary balance in Germany 1995–2002.[98]

billion Euros	1995	1996	1997	1998	1999	2000	2001	2002
Economic Plan 1995–1999								
Budgetary deficit	25.0	30.5	25.3	20.1	14.8			
Economic Plan 1996–2000								
Budgetary deficit		30.6	28.8	28.6	28.3	24.9		
Economic Plan 1997–2001								
Budgetary deficit			36.3	29.5	29.4	27.2	23.9	
Economic Plan 1998–2002								
Budgetary deficit				28.8	28.7	27.8	26.8	23.1

National economic coordination and increasing adaptation "misfits"

In addition to the economic developments, the political, institutional and cultural underpinnings necessary for national economic cooperation did not function effectively post-reunification, but were to develop to more intensive forms of cooperation through the 1990s. In Germany, national cooperation included at least three levels (the federal government, the Bundesländer and the municipalities) not to mention the Bundesbank and powerful trade unions. Political and institutional structures were not in practice ready to tackle such severe problems in a unified Germany leading, for example, to increasing unemployment and declining growth. Manow and Seils argued that "the failure of proper coordination among fiscal, monetary and wage policy resulted in a labour market catastrophe for eastern Germany and a dramatic decline in employment in the west".[99] Germany had clear national political and economic issues between the then government (CDU/CSU) and the main opposition party (SPD), the Bundesbank (monetary policy), the Bundesländer (Old versus New Länder), and trade unions (labour and wage policy). For example, the establishment of EMU together with the increasing fiscal policy coordination under the Stability Pact divided national debate over strict fiscal stabilisation and national fiscal flexibility. The Bundesbank together with the government spoke for fiscal discipline, whereas the Bundesländer and trade unions were afraid of the impact of the common monetary policy and the strict fiscal rules on the German economy and employment. Following Schmidt's reasoning, by analysing these cultural developments in national economic cooperation and policy-making it has been possible to gain "insights into the reasons for success or failure of policy reform which go beyond explanations in terms of interests and/or institutions alone".[100]

In practice, national cooperation between the government and the Bundesbank was most intensive in formulating the monetary and fiscal rules for European economic policy coordination, that is EMU and the Stability Pact. The government wanted to regain some of the leading role in overall economic policy from the Bundesbank, which was considered to have too much power in the economy due to its independent monetary and macroeconomic role (and dominance). As an implication of this power competition, it was the government that took the formal initiative over the Bundesbank and presented a political outline for the Stability Pact for stabilising national fiscal policies in EMU. On the other hand, Finance Minister Waigel clearly wanted to "tie in" the Bundesbank into the formation process of the Stability Pact as closely as possible because that way the Bundesbank "would not be able to act as an external critic".[101] By linking the Bundesbank with the formation of the Stability Pact, the German government also had additional political support and economic power to defend itself and give reasons to the German public, other EU Member States and Eurosceptics for why over 60 percent public debt and 3 percent budgetary deficit ratios of GDP in a Member State could endanger the overall economic objectives of Economic and Monetary Union.

Economic planning and coordination between the federal government and the Bundesländer, based on the Law on Budgetary Procedures and the role of the Financial Planning Council, has been active for 35 years now. However, as discussed thoroughly in the analysis, national coordination models for contributing to economic stability and growth did not prove to be "an effective instrument", which could have strengthened "fiscal discipline" and which could have secured the aim of the federal budget to be "without new public debt in 2006".[102] As Germany finally met all the fiscal criteria for EMU in 1998, there were no more European or national incentives for the German government to develop any further national economic coordination under the National Stability Pact and thus, the National Stability Pact was officially forgotten in national economic policy-making. According to von Hagen and Strauch's interpretation, "while former Chancellor Kohl and his government were trying to impose tighter budgeting institutions on its European partners, they let Germany's own fiscal institutions slip. As a result, Germany's post-Maastricht (and post-Kohl) fiscal institutions are much weaker than before, and Germany's fiscal policy outlook is a liability rather than a stronghold of stability for the EMU".[103] Due to the increasing problems ("misfits") in national fiscal policy in the EMU era, the idea of having a National Stability Pact in Germany was, however, revived by Chancellor Schröder and reintroduced into German politics alongside major reforms in spring 2002; economic and structural reforms were introduced not because of national voluntary discretion but because of declining national economy and increasing European economic monitoring.

It appears that when outlining the scope and extent of national adjustments for the Stability Pact and EMU the German government had too much faith in growth and its capability to solve all the problems in the national economy. After the period 1990–1997, the economy had a high growth period 1998–2000, which, however, rapidly developed towards prolonged stagnation (no growth or growth less than one percent a year) after 2001. Originally, Germany believed that by supporting economic stability in EMU, it could also eliminate national low-growth developments.[104] The government did not have enough capability to solve all national economic problems, improve national economic coordination and incorporate the objectives of all political actors with the government's reform plans that would indeed have been a crucial requirement when taking into account the performance of the German economy in EMU. When approaching the implementation of the Stability Pact, the government began to realise that fiscal stabilisation was not cost-free in EMU after all and that national economic policy-making, national adjustments and national economic coordination should have focused more on creating "more flexibility for the economy and the government".[105] Strengthening fiscal stabilisation in EMU, together with spending and tax cuts turned out to be politically and economically very painful for the government. Dyson considered that it was the dual role of Germany, to act as a "pace-setter" as well as an "uploader", which caused the failure in implementing the Stability Pact. In Dyson's view, "Germany was a 'pace-setter' in 'uploading' its policy interests in monetary and fiscal policies. But in both areas Germany had to cope with unanticipated consequences: a pro- rather than anti-cyclical monetary policy and serious problems in meeting its fiscal commitments."[106] As a result, Helmut Kohl (CDU) faced increasing national criticism, which culminated in his defeat to Gerhard Schröder (SPD) in the elections in September 1998. This chapter has not focused on the process of negotiating the Stability Pact but on a different question – the nature of the national economic and political developments which formed the context for Germany's acceptance of the idea of a Stability Pact for EMU. It has clearly shown that the fundamental idea of securing adaptation "fits" through the strict rules of the Stability Pact, in fact, acted as the starting point for increasing national problems, "misfits", in German fiscal policy in EMU.

4
Downloading the Stability Pact in Germany

4.1 Political changes and refocusing fiscal policy

A new government, the same challenges

The primary politico-economic debate on the implementation (downloading) of the Stability Pact has focused on the quantitative analysis of the extent to which national economies have met the numerical convergence criteria for achieving economic stability in EMU. However, much less attention has been directed to the qualitative analysis of whether national economies have adequately made adjustments to safeguard this stability. Given the European and national processes around the formation (uploading) of the Stability Pact, this empirical research proceeds to an evaluation of the impact of the implementation of the Stability Pact in Germany in 1998–2002. In this chapter, a study is made of *how and to what extent the German economy has faced and responded to the need for national adjustments under the Stability Pact in EMU.* Buti and Sapir have also highlighted the importance of the study of the national implementation of common economic policy objectives. In their opinion, "there is increasing support for the view that budgetary institutions are important determinants of fiscal performance. Even though inadequate institutions *per se* may not create deficits, they tend to delay the necessary budgetary adjustments following adverse shocks. Measures which change institutional budgetary processes have a direct impact on the rules and practices according to which budgets are drawn up, adopted and implemented."[1] The present problems of Germany in implementing the Stability Pact should not be underestimated because the economy plays a leading role in EMU, equalling one-third of the whole EU economy. In retrospect, it is both surprising and dramatic that Germany has faced the most difficulties in achieving fiscal stability under the Stability Pact, because it was German national interests on which strict fiscal policy coordination was based in EMU.

A major change in national politics was caused by the German parliamentary elections on 27 September 1998 that ended the long era of

Chancellor Kohl and the Christian Democratic Union's (CDU) domination of German politics and gave the Social Democratic Party (SPD) its biggest victory since 1972.[2] The SPD earned its victory by criticising the economic and social circumstances in the German welfare state that were caused by the poor performance and management of the national economy under Chancellor Kohl's governments.[3] Indeed, the legacy of Chancellor Kohl and Finance Minister Waigel to the economic policy of Chancellor Schröder and Finance Minister Lafontaine was far from satisfactory: declining economic growth and mounting debt and deficit stocks together with high unemployment. The red-green majority government (SPD and Alliance 90/The Greens with 351 out of 666 seats) was formed on the basis of the election result by which the SPD had 40.9 percent, CDU/CSU 35.1 percent and the Greens 6.7 percent of the votes. The SPD's Chancellor Candidate, Gerhard Schröder, took over the new centre-left coalition and in his government (1998–2002), the SPD party leader, Oskar Lafontaine, was appointed Minister of Finance.

The first federal budget of Schröder's government was considered crucial for the political and economic success of the whole new government.[4] In addition to the critical national economic realities, the new challenge of the German government came from EMU because monetary policy shifted from national governments and national central banks to the ECB in 1999: how could the impact of the loss of national monetary policy be compensated by using only fiscal instruments under increasing policy coordination in EMU? As the stability culture at the end of the Kohl-Waigel era was not taken seriously, adopted and incorporated into the concrete policy measures sufficiently, the primary challenge of the Schröder-Lafontaine era was to create a new stability culture through major national reforms and adjustments in the EMU era (Table 4.1). Therefore, the relationship between a) the policy actions of the new government to stabilise the national economy in late 1998 and 1999, b) increasing economic policy coordination for strengthening employment, stability and growth, and c) the range, scope and effectiveness of national adjustments in 2000–2002 are next under investigation.

Policy actions and refocusing fiscal policy in 1999

In the Annual Economic Report 1999, the government specified the policy targets of the coalition parties for 1999.[5] Where Finance Minister Waigel in Kohl's government was concerned about fiscal discipline for EMU, Finance Minister Lafontaine in Schröder's government considered that "the most essential objective of the government is to cut down the far too high unemployment rate".[6] Lafontaine's first budget in 1999 was the first after Germany had become a part of EMU. The government recognised this policy change, and it presented both supply- and demand-side actions to give the final fiscal boost to the national economy for the start of the EMU

Table 4.1 National adjustments and European economic policy coordination in Schröder's first government 1998–2002.

Timing / Measures	National policy reforms and adjustments in the German national economy	European economic policy coordination and European economic monitoring
Late 1998–1999: Beginning of the high growth period 1998–2000 Refocusing national fiscal policy Adjusting to the impact of EMU	Annual Economic Report 1999 Alliance for Jobs, Training and Competitiveness Major Tax Reform 1999 Annual Economic Report 2000	German Stability Programme in January 1999 ECB Annual Report 1999 Economic and Monetary Union 1999 Agenda 2000 Broad economic policy guidelines 1999 Cologne process Lisbon strategy German Stability Programme in December 1999
2000: High growth Stabilising economy Optimistic European peer pressure	Annual Economic Report 2000 Future Programme 2000 Tax Reform 2000 Guiding Principles of the National Fiscal Policy	Broad economic policy guidelines 2000 Public Finances in EMU 2000 German Stability Programme 2000
2001: Investment plans Declining growth Financial problems	Annual Economic Report 2001 Future Investment Programme	Broad economic policy guidelines 2001 Public Finances in EMU 2001 German Stability Programme 2001
2002: Financial crisis Facing European economic monitoring Improving national economic coordination	Annual Economic Report 2002 National Stability Pact Financial Planning Council	Public Finances in EMU 2002 Broad economic policy guidelines 2002 Commission's recommendation in January 2002 No voting in the Ecofin Council in February 2002

era. The Annual Economic Report 1999 was called "The New Way to Increasing Employment" (*Neue Wege zu mehr Beschäftigung*), and it took the stability-and-growth objective as its first priority because the ECB started to implement the common monetary policy in the Euro area in January 1999. Although the government targeted a high GDP growth of 2.5–3.0 percent, the unemployment rate was still expected to rise to 11.5 percent and public net borrowing would be as much as 28.9 billion Euros in 1999.

According to the German Council of Economic Experts, the German government had two major problems to solve: improving employment and securing sustainable public finances.[7] The Annual Economic Report presented a combination of reforms in labour and taxation policy as concrete measures for dealing with these challenges. Firstly, the Alliance for Jobs, Training and Competitiveness (*Bündnis für Arbeit, Ausbildung und Wettbewerbsfähigkeit*) was planned to combat unemployment, create new training opportunities for unemployed youth and reform the management and dialogue between social partners in labour policy.[8] The government publicly urged different social partners (federal, regional and local levels, trade unions and employers' associations) to develop a close and productive dialogue to work together in a coordinated way for more effective labour policy. The government thus supported an idea of a regular three-way dialogue (*das Dreier-Gespräch*) within the Alliance for Jobs. The target was to bring down youth and long-term unemployment by developing education and training systems, and Schröder's government had already launched a plan for improving youth employment (*Programm zur Qualifizierung und Beschäftigung*) right after the 1998 victory aiming at a reduction of a total of 100,000 young people unemployed.[9]

Secondly, the government reduced labour costs for employees and employers by reforming corporate and personal income taxation as the main instrument for improving employment. The Tax Reform 1999 (*Steuerreform 1999*) was planned to be implemented in three steps in 1999, 2000 and 2002. In the first phase from January 1999, the basic tax rate level (*Eingangssteuersatz*) was reduced from 25.9 to 23.9 percent, and 1.0 percent less to 22.9 percent in the second phase from January 2000. In the third phase from January 2002, the government planned to make further commitments to lower the basic tax rate to only 19.9 percent. The maximum rate for corporate tax profits (*gewerbliche Einkünfte*) was also lowered from 47 to 45 percent in 1999, and then from 45 to 43 percent in January 2000. The tax reform of 1999 would thus alleviate the tax burden of German society, citizens and companies by 27.6 billion Euros by 2002 and 7.7 billion Euros compared to 1998.[10]

Lafontaine also submitted Germany's first national stability programme to the Ecofin Council and the Commission one month after the December 1998 deadline in January 1999.[11] The stability programme was to ensure that national economic policy was implemented within common economic policy guidelines in EMU. In the first German Stability Programme, the government committed itself to cut the public spending ratio from 49 percent in 1997 to 45 percent of GDP in 2002. It also had a strongly held belief that "the medium-term objective set out in the Stability and Growth Pact will be met in the year 2002 at a deficit ratio of about one percent".[12] The government was convinced that European macroeconomic coordination was a crucial mechanism to achieve "constant, adequate economic growth as a high level of employment and against a background of stability".[13] However, these debt and deficit objectives appeared to be far too ambiguous when noting that the objectives were set in the high growth period 1998–2000 and that the growth dramatically and suddenly halted after 2000.

Due to the lack of clear and effective measures in the Annual Economic Report 1999 and the Stability Programme 1999 for ensuring stable fiscal policy, Finance Minister Lafontaine took a lot of criticism from European and national levels as well as from his own party. At the European level, the ECB and the Commission argued that the objectives of the German government to maintain fiscal stability under the fiscal rules were unrealistic. The presented policy measures were not concrete enough and might not safeguard the medium-term balance of the German fiscal policy. In its very first annual report, issued in April 1999, the ECB criticised the large EMU Member States, Germany and France, because they had allowed a major increase in public debt ratios without active policy reactions. According to the ECB, "government debt ratios in the Euro area on average remain at a very high level, thereby substantially limiting the budgetary room for manoeuvre in many Member States".[14] The ECB was also worried about the direction of national budgetary policies and the effectiveness of planned national adjustments. According to the ECB, "some programmes built on the notion that the structure of the adjustment should be regarded as a priority, the magnitude of the necessary correction being less important".[15] By contrast, the ECB argued that reducing debt and deficit stocks and implementing long-term reforms should be the same policy to stabilise the economy throughout the EMU area. In the ECB's view, "some countries seem to believe that attempts to address structural issues could, at times, justify a more relaxed timetable for completing consolidation".[16] More concretely, Commissioner for Economic Affairs, Yves-Thibault de Silguy, claimed that Germany's Stability Programme in 1999 was purely political and took a far too "minimal position" towards bringing the high debt ratio down under the Stability Pact.[17]

At the national level, there was an increasing public opinion that the fiscal rules for national economic stability were too tight and the government's plans constrained the national budgetary policy even more instead of focusing on growth and employment.[18] Lafontaine also shared this critical view with the public because he considered that the Stability Pact set a far too inflexible coordination system for Member States in a downturn. In February 1999, Lafontaine argued that the fundamental objectives of the Stability Pact should be revised towards a more growth-supporting system of coordination.[19] He was in favour of improving national economic growth through an active and expansive fiscal policy: a policy that is used to stabilise the national economy over the economic cycle. By contrast, European fiscal policy coordination aimed, in his view, at bringing down the debt and deficit stocks at the price of declining growth and employment. Lafontaine argued that the growth together with the employment target, as formulated in the Coalition Agreement of 1998, should be the priority of the German government in the existing economic circumstances where Germany had more than four million unemployed. However, Chancellor Schröder argued that "the EU economy has to be as planned and implemented with the same discipline as national economies".[20] If national fiscal policies were not strictly implemented under the Stability Pact, achieving stability and growth in EMU would be unrealistic. Schröder thus renewed his commitment to the Stability Pact and EMU and withdrew his political support from Lafontaine simultaneously. Lafontaine resigned as the Finance Minister and SPD party leader on 11 March 1999 and next day Schröder named Hans Eichel (SPD) as the new Finance Minister. Schröder took over the party and Eichel became his key minister.[21]

Schröder's political nomination to replace Lafontaine with Eichel meant a significant refocus in the German fiscal policy and a new and strong national commitment to the common European economic policy objectives: the attainment of national fiscal balance by reducing debt and deficit ratios would be the first priority throughout the EMU area. Eichel's economic policy was in practice based on strict fiscal discipline because he considered that the debt and deficit stocks should not expand any more. This strict fiscal policy was also included in his first Annual Economic Report in 2000, which planned to cut the budgetary deficit by 15.3 billion Euros in 2000 through a major saving programme. Where the formation of the Stability Pact for the EMU era was based on the Kohl-Waigel alliance in 1995–1997, it became obvious that the success of the implementation of the Stability Pact in Germany would depend on Schröder-Eichel cooperation.[22] The renewed political commitment to a major reduction in the public debt and budgetary deficit gave a good starting point not only for the whole Stability Pact but also for the future of Schröder's red-green government.[23]

European guidelines for German national economic reforms II

German national policy actions for stability and growth were closely related to the developments within the European Union in the late 1990s. The German economy was not only constrained by national policy-making alone but also policy-making at the EU level. The EU imposed a number of new constraints on national policy-making to which the German government had to respond domestically, for example EMU with the Stability Pact, Agenda 2000, and the Cologne, Helsinki and Lisbon Council decisions. The start of EMU in January 1999, which basically meant the completion of the Internal Market (introduced in the Single European Act in 1985), caused new economic challenges. Despite the previous establishment of the Internal Market in 1992 and of EMU in the Maastricht Treaty in 1992, the impact of EMU on national economic policy was still partly unanticipated because the third stage of EMU was also followed by other policy changes from economic policy coordination (Cologne, Helsinki and Lisbon) to the European financial structure (Agenda 2000). As monetary authority shifted from national central banks to the ECB, it was the national fiscal policy that had to be able to play the leading role in responding to changes in the national economic cycle. This key role of fiscal policy appeared highly demanding when considering that some countries, such as Germany, did not achieve budgetary balance prior to EMU. In fact, Germany's budgetary position was far from optimal at the start of EMU.

Regarding the concrete monetary targets of the ECB, the first policy issue dealt with the election of the first President of the ECB. The election process was considered to concretise the coming monetary strategy in the Euro area because preferring more German price stability-led monetary policy or more French fiscal-led monetary policy would have a different impact on national economic strategies. The political debate over this first concrete Euro dilemma, which tested the historical Franco-German alliance, had started in Germany already in 1997.[24] Germany's candidate was the President of the Bundesbank, Hans Tietmeyer, whereas the French government advocated the President of the French Central Bank, Jean-Claude Trichet. Tietmeyer was considered a person who would contribute to the creation of an independent ECB and monetary discipline in EMU (*Stabilitätsgemeinschaft*), whereas Trichet was regarded to be more in favour of supporting economic growth over the cycle and economic cooperation between the ECB and national governments (*gouvernement économique*).[25] Trichet's very close cooperation with the French government was eventually believed to undermine his and the ECB's independence in EMU. Wim Duisenberg, who was well-known for promoting strict monetary discipline in the Dutch Central Bank, was Germany's second candidate after France turned down Tietmeyer's election.[26] As a political compromise in May 1998, Duisenberg started as the first President of the ECB to be replaced after the first four years by the Frenchman Trichet.[27] Thus, the ECB was assumed to focus first on monetary discipline while later it would run a growth-oriented monetary policy.

Apart from the common monetary strategy, there were also a number of other economic policy guidelines, coordination procedures and policy changes in the EU that had an impact on national economic policy-making. The critical developments in national economies forced Member States to reform the relationship between political objectives and economic burdens in the EU. The financial stability of the EU required a major cut in spending and an improvement in effectiveness for allocating common resources. Finally, the Berlin European Council in March 1999 introduced

Agenda 2000, which was a financial response to intensifying and widening European integration, the coming enlargement process and its economic challenges: the new responsibilities of the EU would significantly increase the financial burden of the Member States. Agenda 2000 reformed European agricultural policy and the use of European structural funds and, more importantly, it adopted a totally new financial structure in the EU for the period 2000–2006. The increasing pressure on EU's spending together with the declining economic outlook in Member States required stronger budgetary discipline than before. In these financial circumstances, the Council concluded that there was "the need to ensure that the Union has sufficient resources at its disposal to ensure the orderly development of its policies for the benefit of its citizens and to cope effectively with the process of enlargement".[28]

Based on Article 99 of the Maastricht Treaty, the Commission and the Ecofin Council set the broad economic policy guidelines in EMU for the very first time in 1999. In its recommendation to the Ecofin Council in March 1999, the Commission proposed that national commitments "regarding budgetary policies, wage developments and structural policies are essential to ensure that monetary policy has adequate room for manoeuvre in the light of prevailing economic conditions".[29] According to the country-specific recommendations, Germany should focus more on "the tight control of expenditure", "the target of the governmental deficit of two percent of GDP", and "active labour market measures".[30] The Ecofin Council agreed with the Commission in its final decision on the recommendations in July 1999, but it wanted to emphasise that in the third stage of EMU, "the durable success of economic and monetary union will demand discipline from all policy actors, a deepened and adequate coordination of economic policies and a continuous and fruitful dialogue between the Council and the ECB".[31]

The Cologne European Council in June 1999 restructured and intensified macroeconomic dialogue between EU institutions and Member States for the success of EMU in line with the broad economic policy guidelines of 1999. By this macroeconomic dialogue the Council referred to economic cooperation between the Ecofin Council, the Commission, the European Central Bank and the Member States. The European Council argued that economic policy coordination should focus on the requirement of securing national fiscal stability in EMU and therefore, it emphasised "the need for strict application of the provisions of the Stability and Growth Pact".[32] This Cologne process clearly stated again, in line with the decisions of the Luxemburg, Cardiff and Vienna European Councils, that the EU believed that it was essential to establish close economic policy coordination between the common monetary policy and national budgetary and employment policies in EMU. The Cologne European Council took the view that "the key to sustainable non-inflationary growth and increased employment lies in a properly coordinated mix of macroeconomic policies geared towards growth and stability and comprehensive structural reforms".[33] In addition, the Helsinki European Council in December 1999 highlighted the importance of sustainable public finances in Member States for future fiscal developments in the EU. By this the Council meant demographic changes that would require effective budgetary actions on "ageing and increased efficiency in the public and private sectors to manage the economic burden of such changes".[34] Moreover, the Lisbon European Council in March 2000 formulated a new objective for the EU to promote economic and structural reforms for a more effective European employment and growth policy. This Lisbon strategy made employment and competitiveness to be the first priorities of the EU. According to the challenging political declaration, the EU will become "the most competitive and dynamic knowledge-based economy in the world, capable of sustainable economic growth with more and better jobs".[35]

4.2 Policy adjustments and the financial reality

Stabilising public finances at speed in 2000

Given the German fiscal position under the Stability Pact and increasing economic policy coordination within the EU, the real importance of effective national adjustments for economic stability was realised in its true meaning in Germany only in 1999; not before, not afterwards. If German national adjustments had not been sufficient before, now Schröder's government and Finance Minister Eichel started to implement a very restrictive economic policy towards expanding public spending and debt and deficit stocks. In his notable speech *"Finanzpolitik für das nächste Jahrzehnt"* on the coming German economic policy at the Humboldt University in November 2000, Eichel asserted that "national fiscal policy cannot be based on issuing new public debt year after year". Eichel also took as the first priority that "saving is essential" and that "we have to consolidate the public finances and reduce the public expenditure burden".[36]

In December 1999, the Finance Ministry had to revise the German Stability Programme due to the financial impact of the Tax Reform 2000 and the start of EMU. Surprisingly, the Ministry of Finance revised the stabilisation objectives upwards, not downwards, although EMU together with other economic developments had caused increasing external pressures in the national economy. The underlying forecast of the German economy remained at the same level compared to the Stability Programme in January 1999 except that the government expected to have a major increase in GDP growth from 1.5 to 2.5 percent in 2000. Based on the impact of the high growth, the government speeded up its original plan to reduce the debt and deficit ratios. Although the debt of Germany could increase up to

61 percent in 1999, it would be reduced to 58 percent by 2003. More significantly, the deficit target of 1.0 percent, as outlined in the Stability Programme in January 1999, would already be achieved one year ahead in 2001. It was expected that the diminishing deficit would have a positive impact on national fiscal flexibility under the Stability Pact: "Adequate scope will thus be created below three percent deficit ceiling for the automatic stabilisers to take effect."[37]

The Annual Economic Report 2000, entitled "Creating Jobs – Achieving Future Competitiveness" (*Arbeitsplätze schaffen – Zukunftsfähigkeit gewinnen*), also made clear commitments to European economic objectives. Compared to Lafontaine's growth-supporting approach in 1998–1999, Eichel included a strict anti-debt policy in his first annual budget in 2000. Eichel's extensive savings plan meant a major cut in public spending and a totally new tax reform to safeguard financial stability. The German Council of Economic Experts believed that cutting public spending and reforming taxation would have a very positive and much needed impact on the public finances and not only on the debt and deficit stocks but also on growth.[38] The Bundesbank was also satisfied with the saving policy that aimed at reducing public debt, which would also reduce interest costs and thus stabilise interest rates and other monetary policy instruments. The President of the Bundesbank, Hans Tietmeyer, also assumed that a reduction in debt would mean additional economic flexibility for the national economy under the Stability Pact.[39] On the other hand, bringing down taxes rapidly, without any other sources of revenue, could jeopardise the whole structure of the public finances, increase private consumption too much and thus risk inflation.

Eichel also set out the first outline of the coming Future Programme 2000 (*Zukunftsprogramme 2000*) by announcing that the main aim was to reduce the financial burden of the public sector by 15.3 billion Euros in 2000. This would decrease the size of the public spending by a total of 7.4 percent.[40] The government also strengthened its commitment to reduce public debt so that the net borrowing would diminish by 15.3 billion in 2001, 20.4 billion in 2002 and a further 25.5 billion Euros in 2003. According to the programme, without these massive reduction measures the net borrowing would otherwise be as much as 76.5 billion Euros in the coming four years 2000–2003.[41] The main objective of the Future Programme 2000 was that the national economy would not require any public net borrowing after 2003. In addition, the government again renewed its tax reform originally introduced in 1999. Now, the extensive Tax Reform 2000 (*Steuerreform 2000*) specified the government's timetable to reduce taxes in three separate phases in 2001, 2003 and 2005. Most significantly, the basic tax rate level (*Eingangssteuersatz*) would fall from 23.9 percent via 19.9 and 17 to 15 percent and corporation tax (*Körperschaftsteuersatz*) would be reduced to 25 percent by 2005.[42]

By the beginning of the 21st century and half way through Schröder's first government in power, the government considered that through a clear and sound economic strategy, it would be possible to strengthen the effectiveness of the policy actions. Thus, the government introduced the Guiding Principles of the National Fiscal Policy 2000–2012 (*Finanzpolitische Leitplanken*) in November 2000. The strategy consisted of seven principles aimed at improving Germany's economic position in European and international competition by bringing down the high debt and deficit stocks and by strengthening employment and growth. The future economic policy was set to be based on two main objectives: firstly, to reduce public debt and treat different generations in economic and social policy equally, and secondly to contribute to employment and growth through reforming taxation and expenditure. The government also planned to improve national economic coordination between the federal government, the Bundesländer and the municipalities to better respond to the challenges derived from increasing European economic policy coordination. Firstly, the government urged that the Bundesländer and the municipalities should take more responsibility for the national economy through the Financial Planning Council. Secondly, the government argued that the implementation of the Stability Pact required more effective cooperation in the EU. Thirdly, the government also argued that the guiding idea of subsidiarity in European fiscal policy coordination should be implemented "as much as necessary and as less as possible".[43] The main objective of the seven guiding principles was to target an economic policy in the coming years that would provide a "realistic", "long-term", "future-oriented", "transparent", "self-control" and "credible" framework for the German national policy-making as a part of European economic integration.[44]

The Old Länder and municipalities, however, considered that saving too much and bringing down public spending as intensively as the government planned in the Future Programme and the Tax Reform 2000 did not improve their economic stability. By contrast, the major reforms without any financial compensation could cause the collapse of the regional and local economies. The Chairman of the German Conference of Towns, Hajo Hoffmann, feared that the Future Programme 2000 would result in a 2.1 billion Euros additional economic burden on the Bundesländer and the municipalities.[45] Similarly, the President of the German Association of Towns and Municipalities, Heribert Thallmair, argued that the decrease in public taxation would cause as much as 1.28 billion Euros extra financial burden for regional and local levels only in 2001. Thallmair thought that the regional and local economies could not bear the full burden of increasing public responsibilities and thus, the government should compensate for the economic impact on them by allocating additional financial support.[46]

By contrast, some New Länder defended the Future Programme 2000 and the Tax Reform 2000. For example, Sachsen-Anhalt and Mecklenburg-Vorpommern argued that without these major reforms in public spending, the government could not commit financially to the further reconstruction of the former East Germany in the future.[47] Eichel agreed with the New Länder that without reforming the national economy the government would have serious problems in supporting reforms in the former East Germany. Eichel also reminded the German electorate and sceptics that it was the CDU/CSU coalition, now in opposition, that produced the massive stock of as much as 765 million Euros public debt in the first place. Thus, the sceptics and the opposition should focus more on presenting alternative and effective policy actions of their own instead of attacking the reforms of the current red-green government.[48] Schröder also found that there was a real and urgent need for major reforms in public finances and the financial reality was that Germany had "no easy and comfortable way out of this".[49]

Optimistic European peer pressure on the German economy

While the broad economic policy guidelines in 1999 required Germany to tighten its policy on the public finances and labour policy, the broad economic policy guidelines in 2000 took a much more optimistic view of the German economy. In the country-specific recommendations presented to the Ecofin Council in April 2000, the Commission stated that Germany had successfully complied with the deficit rule but the public debt had not achieved the same downward trend. The Commission was, however, concerned about the very minimal reduction in the budgetary deficit from 1.1 percent to only 1.0 percent of GDP in 2000 despite the impact of the high growth in 2000. The Commission regarded this decline as very "modest" because the government had planned and implemented major reforms in taxation and public expenditure. Finally, the Ecofin Council recommended that the focus of the German government should be directed more intensively to the public debt and that the additional revenue from the auction of UMTS mobile phone licences "should be used fully for debt reduction".[50]

The Commission's first Public Finances in EMU 2000 analysed the developments in the German economy and elsewhere in EMU. The primary idea of this very first report was to outline an overall assessment on the financial developments in the Euro area that could be transformed into "Member States' budgetary performance" and thus support national economic policy-making.[51] The Commission in particular raised the critical question of the trends in public debt and public expenditure in the Euro area. According to the Commission, although there had been notable convergence in fiscal policy during the first few years of EMU, the debt and the size of the public sector had remained large. As the main reason for this trend, the Commission found that there had been "uncontrolled rise in the stock of public debt" and the size of the public sector in the national economy had resulted from "expanding social transfers and rising interest payments".[52] The Commission also thought that the German government's saving policy had been effective in introducing new tax and social reforms in 1999 but in 2000 it would be highly unlikely that the reforms would have a positive impact on the debt and deficit ratios due to the expected major shortfall in the tax revenue.[53]

In the German Stability Programme 2000, the government presented economic reforms, the Future Programme 2000 and the Tax Reform 2000 to the Ecofin Council and the Commission. The programme also voiced a highly optimistic belief that these actions would be sufficient to further fiscal convergence in Germany. The government also made a commitment to use the additional revenue, 50.7 billion Euros, which it received from the UMTS auction in 2000, directly and to its full extent to the reduction of the public debt.[54] Due to the UMTS revenue and high growth, the government speeded up its plan to reduce the debt ratio, which was to be brought below the 60 percent ceiling already in 2001, resulting in a 54.5 percent level in 2004. The government also renewed its objective to cut the deficit to only 1.0 percent by 2002, and it estimated that the public sector would no longer require any net borrowing in 2006.

Introducing future-oriented adjustments in 2001

The German government's reform policy encountered harsh criticism primarily from the opposition CDU and CSU parties because they considered that the economic policy did not sufficiently improve national employment and growth in EMU. In particular, the substantial fall of the exchange rate of the Euro against the US dollar caused rampant disbelief in the effectiveness of national economic and structural reforms to revive employment and growth.[55] The falling Euro basically implied for the German and European economies that the Euro area was not functioning effectively, and further national and European reforms should be accomplished (Figure 4.2). In the Annual Economic Report 2001 "Continuing Reforms – Strengthening Growth" (*Reformkursen fortsetzen – Wachstumsdynamik stärken*), the government furthered the future-oriented reforms that were already introduced in 2000. Eichel was financially able to continue his saving policy in the last D-Mark-based annual budget because growth was expected to be as high as 2.5–3.0 percent of GDP. High growth was expected to create space for the budget, and the government introduced future-oriented investments for employment and growth. For the German Council of Economic Experts, employment, along with fiscal stability, was "the most difficult and persistent breach of the economic policy".[56] However, Eichel argued that "the current public debt of 1.5 billion DM [765 million Euros] cannot be eliminated in one night" and thus, the economic strategy should focus on growth through job creation and the better functioning of the labour market.[57]

Although a major part of the Tax Reform 2000 for supporting economic growth came into effect in 2000, including the reduction of private and corporate income taxes, a new Future Investment Programme (*Zukunfts-Investitionsprogramm*) planned to annually allocate as much as 2.04 billion Euros for production, 306 million for research and education, and 1.48 billion to improve transport infrastructure from 2001 to 2003. The government also took action in social policy because the demographic challenge, population ageing and decreasing birth rates, would markedly affect the financial basis of the budget in the future. To prepare for the coming financial challenges in social and health policy, reforms included a pension reform, improving compulsory health insurance (*Gesetzliche Krankenversicherung*) and modifying nursing care insurance (*Pflegeversicherung*).[58] The government also had the UMTS revenue of 50.7 billion Euros, which was used for cutting net borrowing to be only 23 billion Euros; the lowest level of budgetary deficit since the early 1990s (19.7 billion Euros in 1992).

After monitoring the developments in the German economy, the Commission stated in its recommendations for the broad economic policy guidelines to the Ecofin Council in April 2001 that due to the economic reforms and the UMTS revenue, the budgetary deficit of Germany "should fall gradually to zero by the year 2004".[59] However, the Commission argued that national economic reforms had not taken adequately into account the financial impact of population ageing and thus, "long-term budgetary risks remain".[60] The Ecofin Council required in the final country-specific guidelines in June 2001 that the German government should ensure "the long-term sustainability of government finances" by implementing new social, pension and health care reforms; in other words, stabilise the national economy by cutting public expenditure. The Council also urged Germany to improve "the coordination of budgetary policy among the various levels of government by strengthening the role of the *Finanzplanungsrat* and eventually, in the framework of a National Stability Pact".[61]

The Commission's second Public Finances in EMU 2001 analysed more thoroughly the financial trends in EMU than the first report in 2000. Now, the assessment allowed the findings of the European economic surveillance to be used as concrete national policy guidelines. In fact, the Commission argued that "budgetary surveillance at the EU level needs to evolve if it is to support Member States in pursuing ambitious reform agendas that do not jeopardise the commitment to fiscal discipline".[62] Based on this surveillance, the Commission considered that Germany's budgetary position had improved during the high growth year 2000 although much of the positive progress in debt and deficit owed to the UMTS revenue. It also believed that this reduction in debt "will lead to clear savings in interest payments in coming years".[63] However, the Commission took the critical view that the

2.75 percent growth for 2001 as estimated in the German Stability Programme 2000 would be far too optimistic. Due to the lower growth expectation of the Commission for 2001, the Commission expected that in 2001 Germany would not "fully comply with the requirements of the Stability and Growth Pact of a medium-term position of close to balance or in surplus".[64]

Strengthening national fiscal policy coordination I

The German government planned to make it more efficient to coordinate national budgetary objectives between the federal and regional levels (Solidarity Pact I).[65] For this purpose, Eichel presented a concrete plan to reform the institutional system of national economic coordination and the responsibilities of the Financial Planning Council under the Law on Budgetary Procedures, which was previously reformed in December 1997. The government considered the smooth functioning of the Financial Planning Council a crucial element for achieving national fiscal balance in EMU and the plan was to more effectively commit all governmental levels to the Stability Pact. In reality, one of the main incentives to reform national economic coordination came from the Commission that specifically monitored Germany's declining economy and increasing debt and deficit stocks. According to the reformed Law on Budgetary Procedures in 2001, the Financial Planning Council, which meets twice a year, was made responsible for maintaining national budgetary policy within the Stability Pact.[66] For the very first time, the Financial Planning Council was responsible for budgetary policy, economic planning and management to be in line with the common European fiscal rules. However, the amended law in 2001 did not include any sanction mechanism or monitoring procedure to secure the full national fulfilment of this new economic responsibility. Due to the political decision, the implementation of the law and the new responsibility of the Financial Planning Council were, however, postponed until 2005.[67]

In the German Stability Programme 2001, the government noted that the uncertainties emerging in the European economy had a major impact on the national fiscal policy. The government argued that the deficit and debt criteria would be achieved in 2002 but within "an additional safety margin in relation to the medium-term stability target".[68] Although the government regarded it as a priority to comply with the Stability Pact, it still emphasised that the national economy would grow only 0.75 percent in 2001; an estimate that was at a markedly lower level than the growth expectation in the Stability Programme 2000. The deficit ratio was expected to stand at 2.0–2.5 percent of GDP and the debt ratio would be at 60 percent in 2001. Commissioner Pedro Solbes took the critical view that "Germany has to work hard to achieve the objectives of the National Stability Programme".[69] What had in practice prevented the German national economy from reverting to the financially critical state of the mid-1990s was the economic flexibility produced by the major Tax Reform 2000. According to the Stability Programme 2001, "it has prevented an even more marked weakening of growth".[70]

Facing European economic monitoring I

Although the German government still had an optimistic view of the national economy in 2001, a sudden European-wide downturn forced the government to totally reschedule its investment plans and the economic strategy in 2002. The economic slowdown caused the government to postpone its sizeable investment plans, which were introduced in the high growth year 2000. Implementing those investment programmes would have been, according to Schröder, "a big mistake" for the public finances.[71] It would also have been too great a political risk for Schröder to implement the programmes and thus jeopardise the hard work of his government in cutting the size of public debt and budgetary deficit in the coming election year of 2002. Due to the election year, the government did not want to freeze the phases of the Tax Reform 2000, which proceeded as planned despite the uncertain economic outlook. However, dwindling tax revenues together with decreasing growth threatened to turn the public finances back to the state of the mid-1990s (Figures 4.6 and 4.7); a trend that was feared by the opposition parties CDU and CSU.[72] The German Council of Economic Experts was also worried about the coming national budgetary developments because according to their estimates, the deficit of Germany could rapidly expand up to 3.7 percent of GDP in 2002.[73]

Therefore, the Annual Economic Report 2002, which was named as "Awaiting a New Upturn – Continuing a Reliable Economic and Fiscal Policy" (*Vor einem neuen Aufschwung – verlässliche Wirtschafts- und Finanzpolitik*), focused on reviving growth. The government calculated that in 2002 the economy could save some one billion Euros less than was previously estimated. The government thus moved from a massive saving policy to an expansionary fiscal policy before the critical financial reality in 2002.[74] The need for new economic and labour reforms in the election year stemmed from the fact that growth was only 0.75 percent of GDP, the unemployment rate stood at 9.5 percent and net borrowing was 55 billion Euros. Firstly, the government tried to develop further the Alliance for Jobs, Training and Competitiveness (originally set up in 1999) as a promising programme within which the government and trade unions and employers' associations could work for increasing flexibility in part-time work, improving training systems for unskilled workers and the long-term unemployed.[75] Secondly, the government was concerned about financial instability between the Old and New Länder because modernising the structure of the public finances had been successful but not sufficient to secure overall national fiscal stability. According to the government, structural developments in East Germany had taken "longer than was expected" and thus, it introduced another solidarity programme, Solidarity Pact II, to strengthen reconstruction by allocating 105 billion Euros to the New Länder from 2004 to 2019.[76]

The critical financial reality eventually struck the German government at the beginning of 2002. Despite the latest national effort to stabilise the economy (Solidarity Pacts I and II), the economic slowdown caused difficulties in eliminating the increase in the debt and deficit stocks in 2001 and 2002. These difficulties were so critical from the point of view of the Stability Pact and the broad economic policy guidelines that the Commission had to perform its duty in monitoring and reporting on some large EMU Member States, such as Germany and France. The Commission recommended in January 2002 that the Ecofin Council should issue Germany an early warning under the Stability Pact and thus, the Commission voiced its serious concern about increasing deficit and debt ratios in Germany. That was why, according to Commissioner Solbes, "the Commission implemented the early-warning mechanism".[77] This announcement did not come as an economic surprise, but the political surprise was that it was Germany against which the Commission made the recommendation for an early warning. Given that it was Germany (Kohl and Waigel) which introduced the Stability Pact for the EMU era in 1995–1997, it was a political fiasco in German national politics that Eichel in Schröder's government was to break the formal Treaty-based deficit rule. The CDU party and opposition leader (current CDU Chancellor Candidate), Angela Merkel, considered the threat of the early warning a "political scandal" and purely a result of the incapability of Schröder's government for economic planning and management.[78]

However, large Member States did not want to implement the sanction procedure in the Ecofin Council, whereas small Member States (for example Finland and the Netherlands) insisted on the strict interpretation of the Stability Pact. The Ecofin Council rejected the Commission's recommendation because the German government made a renewed commitment to comply with the fiscal rules. Although the Ecofin Council did not execute the recommendation, it decided to closely monitor the German economy and the implementation of further national reforms. Before the decision of the Ecofin Council, the Commissioner for Budget Policy, Michaele Schreyer, warned the EU Finance Ministers against using the veto to block the procedure, which would cause, according to her, a substantial setback in the credibility of the Stability Pact.[79] Similarly, the Chief Economist of the ECB, Otmar Issing, argued that "if the Commission does not execute the warning of the Stability Pact, what should it then do?"[80] However, the British Chancellor, Gordon Brown, took a more flexibility-oriented view arguing that "this matter should not be left in the hands of the European Commission".[81] Economically, Britain, France, Italy and Spain as large EMU

Member States considered that Germany's economic difficulties were not so severe that the warning should be issued and thus, the majority in the Ecofin Council decided not to issue the warning. This process, however, gave the first clear signals to the EU institutions that some EMU Member States had economic difficulties in complying with the strict rules of the Stability Pact in a downturn. Politically, this decision implied that when large Member States other than Germany would face similar problems and approach the ceiling of the deficit criterion, the early warning could also be left without being executed. Institutionally, this event started the institutional power struggle in fiscal policy coordination between the Commission's monitoring duty and the role of the Ecofin Council in the political interpretation of the rules as the supreme decision-making body.

Despite the decision of the Ecofin Council, the Commission continued the debate on the critical national economic developments in its third Public Finances in EMU 2002. The Commission shared the opinion of the Ecofin Council that the slowdown in 2001 was much more serious than anticipated. For Germany, this deterioration meant a shift from a temporary budgetary surplus in 2000 to a major deficit in 2001. The Commission argued that the federal government, the Bundesländer and the municipalities should respect fiscal discipline in national economic policy-making to more effectively and rapidly stabilise the national economy in the low-growth circumstances under the Stability Pact. The Commission emphasised again that "additional measures will have to be implemented in line with the agreements on expenditures reached between *Bund* and *Länder* in the special *Finanzplanungsrat* of 21 March 2002".[82] According to the Commission, "due to the important tax relief of the 2005 income tax reform, the non-achievement of the close-to-balance position in 2004 would normally imply that a balanced budget would be difficult to attain even in 2006".[83]

Strengthening national fiscal policy coordination II

Domestically, the Commission's recommendation of an early warning, even though it was not implemented by the Ecofin Council, had a direct impact on German national economic policy-making. The German government was forced to refocus its economic policy on complying more effectively with the fiscal rules of the Stability Pact. Finance Minister Eichel took the early-warning threat seriously and even in the parliamentary election year 2002, with Chancellor Schröder's support, he heeded the recommendations and strengthened the government's saving policy. Eichel also argued that the Bundesländer and the municipalities should be more committed to achieving national budgetary stability through reducing debt and deficit ratios together with the federal government. To implement the national fiscal policy in line with the Stability Pact, Eichel considered that they should take "a more active role in supporting the effort of the federal government". However, this political view was widely criticised by the Bundesländer Bavaria (CSU), Hessen (CDU) and even SPD-led Lower Saxony.[84]

As a policy response to European economic monitoring, the Financial Planning Council introduced a new National Stability Pact to ensure German budgetary stability under the Stability Pact on 21 March 2002.[85] Through a specific five-point programme for more effective national fiscal planning, the Financial Planning Council stated for the very first time that all national levels, the federal government, the Bundesländer and the municipalities were committed to reduce deficits and cut public expenditure. Firstly, the Financial Planning Council emphasised the importance of the German fiscal stability for the whole Stability Pact in EMU. Secondly, Article 51a of the Law on Budgetary Procedures (the responsibility to comply with the Stability Pact) was put into effect before the end of the term of Schröder's first government in September 2002 instead of the original plan of 2005. Thirdly and more significantly for national economic coordination, the federal government, the Bundesländer and the municipalities agreed to lower the budgetary deficit collectively. This was a major political decision having a direct impact on the structure of national economic coordination and the traditional economic autonomy of the Bundesländer. Fourthly, the Financial Planning Council agreed on the allocation of the budgetary deficit in a ratio of 55 to 45 where 55 percent of the overall deficit is allocated to the Bundesländer and the municipalities, and 45 percent of the deficit belongs to the federal government and the social security funds. Finally, as a concrete strategy, the federal government, the Bundesländer and the municipalities agreed to reduce the public spending by 0.5 percent of GDP annually in 2003 and 2004.

Strikingly, what was not agreed in the National Stability Pact in March 2002 was, firstly, through which concrete measures these challenging but essential economic objectives could be achieved. The existing economic conditions in Germany did not allow any additional manoeuvring for national economic policy-making. Therefore, achieving these economic objectives in the two years allowed was decidedly unrealistic because the government had already introduced major demand- and supply-side reforms before the National Stability Pact without the final stabilisation effect. Secondly, the decision of the Financial Planning Council did not set any sanction rules or mechanisms regarding how to respond domestically to breaking the economic objectives of the National Stability Pact. In fact, the implementation of the National Stability Pact was only based on soft national peer pressure and further political discussions and decisions. Therefore, the new objectives of the National Stability Pact and the modified role of the Financial Planning Council seemed to be directed only towards ensuring short-term fiscal balance and the fulfilment of the fiscal rules of the Stability Pact under the Commission's economic monitoring rather than improving national economic coordination and ensuring national fiscal stability in the long term.[86]

In the proposed broad economic policy guidelines for Germany in April 2002, the Commission stated that despite the effort of the German government, the budgetary deficit of Germany had reached 2.7 percent of GDP in 2001 and the economic outlook for 2002 could push the budgetary deficit clearly above the 3.0 percent criterion. The Commission conceded that the German government had improved national economic coordination within the Financial Planning Council as was recommended by the Ecofin Council in June 2001. The Financial Planning Council had also reconfirmed its political and economic commitments to comply with the debt and deficit rules of the Stability Pact in March 2002. However, in the final country-specific recommendations in June 2002, the Ecofin Council argued that in Germany, "the highest priority should be to increase and make full use of growth potential".[87] According to the Ecofin Council, "this should be supported by policies to increase the employment rate, notably by reforming the benefit schemes in order to make work pay".[88] As a response to the criticism of the Germany's economic policy, Finance Minister Eichel declared that the reduction of debt and deficit ratios and improving growth and employment would continue to be at heart of the German economic policy. Eichel also emphasised that in 2006, for the first time since 1970, Germany would be in an economic situation in which no public net borrowing would be needed. Despite the restrictive fiscal policy in recent years, the German government had not only finished previously launched economic and structural reforms but had also introduced and implemented completely new reforms for ensuring national fiscal stability in 1998–2002.[89]

4.3 Unforeseen changes in the German economic environment

Changes in the trends in the German economic environment

In economic terms, where German reunification was the starting point for the declining fiscal position in the early and mid-1990s, the German economy was subjected not to only one fundamental factor but also to a number of factors at the beginning of the EMU era. The economic realities in Schröder's first government in 1998–2002 did not enable Germany to pursue a sustainable economic policy but the changes in the environment had a major impact on national economic policy-making and economic stability. The extent of the economic problems at the beginning of the 21st century was not anticipated in the formation of the Stability Pact in 1995–1997. In fact, the observation in this empirical research suggests that the implementation of the Stability Pact in EMU was considered to be primarily painless and cost-free in the German public debate and thus, it was not expected to require any major national adjustments. However, economists had clearly demonstrated through the historical macroeconomic evidence on budgetary policies prior to EMU that the strict three percent deficit ratio would be very difficult to achieve and maintain in EMU.[90]

There were a number of economic factors that caused problems for the German government in complying with the fiscal rules of the Stability Pact after the high growth period 1998–2000. Most significantly, the slowdown in the world market in the US, Japan, Latin America and Russia together with unpredictable trends in the price of oil negatively affected German exports and growth. The outbreak of foot-and-mouth disease in Britain in February 2001 and the terrorist attacks in the US in September 2001 also caused significant uncertainties in the global economy acting as counterfactors for exports, growth and financial stability in the European economy. This deteriorating outlook directly affected the export-oriented German economy because historically, it had been exports that had acted as promoter for the German upswing. Figure 4.1 illustrates the impact of net exports and domestic demand on the real GDP growth in Germany in 1998–2002. From the start of EMU in 1999 to the launch of the Euro in 2002, the contribution of the net exports in Germany showed a strong upward trend, whereas domestic demand developed the opposite way. The sharp increase in net exports happened because the fall of the Euro against the US dollar created a favourable environment for German exports (Figure 4.2). The negative contribution of net exports to the growth in 1998 and 1999 was compensated by an increase in domestic demand, which helped to boost growth in Germany from 1998 to 2000 (Figure 4.6).

Due to the downturn and the falling pace of the expansion in domestic demand since 2000, the government had to postpone its major investment plans in 2002; a fact that hastened the decline in domestic demand.

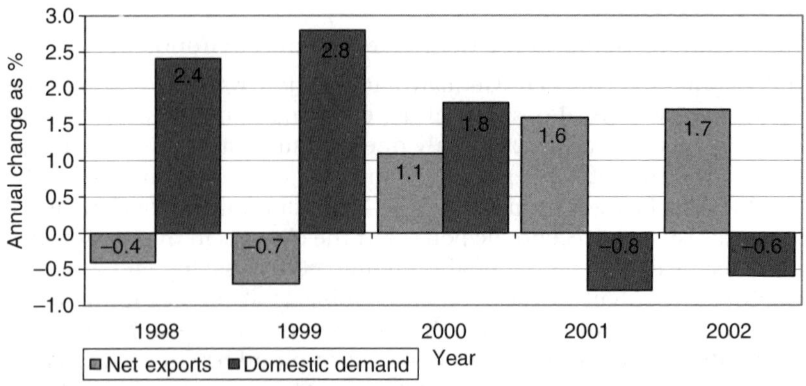

Figure 4.1 Contribution to real domestic GDP in Germany 1998–2002.[91]

Domestic demand and net exports in turn compensated for the negative development of the other in this period. Net exports played a key role in accelerating the growth in 2000, whereas domestic demand was crucial in compensating for the changes in exports in 1998 and 1999. The changes in exports and demand also caused the emergence of the widening output gap.[92] Reflecting the compositions of the net exports and the domestic demand, the output gap in percentage of the potential GDP was 0.7 in 1998 and 0.1 in 1999, whereas there were two consecutive years in 2000 (1.3%) and 2001 (0.8%) when the high economic growth kept the output above the potential GDP. However, the downturn created a new output gap of 0.3 percent again in 2002.[93]

Early challenges in the common monetary policy

The unfavourable trends in the German economic environment also affected monetary policy. What characterised the first few years of EMU was the development of the exchange rate of the Euro (Figure 4.2). Despite or because of high expectations towards the single currency, the Euro faced a testing period of credibility in the financial markets from 1999 to 2002. The Euro, which was assumed to perform very well right from the beginning of EMU, was planned to become a hard currency performing the role traditionally played by the D-Mark in Germany and thus, it was quoted as a much stronger currency than the US dollar with the exchange rate of 1.18 USD (1.1789 USD) in January 1999. By contrast, the early trends in the external value of the Euro were far from successful. By the end of the fourth quarter of 1999, the Euro had fallen and it was rated to be equal to the US dollar. The Euro continued to sink to 0.9 USD in the third quarter of 2000, which was thought to be the lowest possible quote against the US dollar. The downward pressure, however, pushed the Euro as low as 0.83 USD (0.8252 USD) on 26 October 2000, which is the lowest parity against the US dollar since the introduction of the Euro. The Euro thus fell 29.7 percent in 22 months from January 1999 to October 2000. The Euro finally started to appreciate in the first quarter of 2002 to be almost equal to the dollar (0.999 USD) by the end of 2002. Similarly to the dollar, the pound first appreciated against the Euro but at a lower level than the US dollar from 1999 to 2001 but thereafter the pound also depreciated. According to the ECB, the pound "was probably supported by the strength of the US dollar, given the close historical dollar-sterling link and the strength of the US economy".[94]

It is worth noting that the depreciation of the Euro caused both economic and political problems, and not only exchange rate but also interest rate problems. EMU politicians were concerned about the impact of the depreciating Euro because European economies had based their economic strategies on the fundamental Bundesbank tradition that "a strong national economy means a strong national currency". The President of the ECB,

Wim Duisenberg, argued that the fall of the Euro could jeopardise the effectiveness of the monetary objectives in EMU. He also considered the high likelihood of monetary intervention to support the external value of the Euro by the ECB "when that is required and advisable".[95] Duisenberg, however, was not in favour of the idea that the bilateral parity between the Euro and the US dollar would be one-to-one either; a development that would slow down exports and growth in EMU. Despite optimistic expectations, the EMU economies simultaneously faced declining growth rates and falling exchange rates. A major part of the fall of the Euro can be explained by the ECB's lack of credibility on world markets. The success of the process by which the ECB took over the role of the Bundesbank required earning its own credibility to sustain monetary discipline and growth in EMU. On the other hand, it is hard to believe that the problems with the Euro were exclusively related to psychological and image questions; rather, the problems resulted from a combination of declining growth and normal starting problems in introducing a totally new monetary authority (institution) in the economy.

The trends in the exchange rate of the Euro had a close relationship to the interest rate policy in EMU (Figure 4.3). The long-term interest rates experienced notable convergence in the period 1998–2002 and in particular in the second half of this period. Although the long-term interest rates in Britain were above the rates of the Euro area in 1998 and 1999, the interest rates became nearly equal after 2000. Thus, the interest rate differential pertaining between Germany and Britain prior to EMU (Figure 3.5) narrowed and eliminated in the EMU era primarily because of greater economic stability, better economic outlook, a more favourable inflation trend

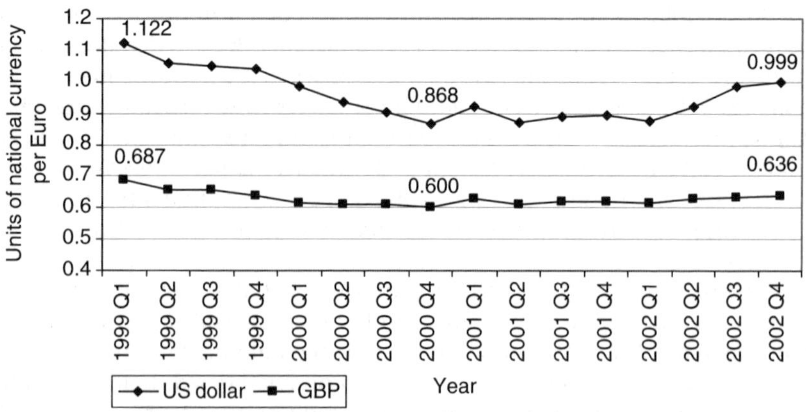

Figure 4.2 Exchange rate of the Euro 1999–2002.[96]

in Britain than the Euro area.[97] Interest rates progressively declined from 1998, and the rates dropped to their lowest level in the Euro area for about 50 years being at 4.0 percent at the beginning of 1999. Developments in short-term interest rates were even more striking because they reached their lowest level of 2.6 percent in May 1999. The ECB explained this difference in short-term and long-term interest rates by the belief of the market that growth, terrorism and the oil price "did not initially prompt a reappraisal of long-term growth prospects for the Euro area economy".[98] Thus, the long-term interest rates acted as a stabiliser of future expectations more than the volatile short-term interest rates. Low interest rates also reflected the strong belief of the market that risks to rapidly increasing inflation were low and under the control and monitoring of the monetary authorities.

The close relationship between the Euro and interest and inflation rates related to trends in the economic environment and their impact on national economies. Basically, the falling Euro increased European exports to the US after 1999, which together with the simultaneous loosening of interest rates increased economic activity and created inflationary pressures in EMU. Instead of only lowering interest rates for faster growth, the ECB decided to implement its interest rate policy actively but restrictively from mid-1999 to mid-2001.[99] Although the high growth year 2000 transformed into a fast and major downturn in 2001, the interest rates of the ECB remained high from late 2000 to early 2001, causing an additional negative impact on the declining economy; a fact which prompted a lot of criticism towards the monetary policy of the ECB. Instead of keeping interest rates high in late 2000 and early 2001, the immediate policy choice of the ECB should have been to lower the interest rates faster than it did. Thus, the ECB would have effectively supported the growth and that way it would also have contributed to stable interest and inflation rates and the Euro. Large Member States, such as Germany and France, would have wanted that the ECB to respond to the downturn faster and thus improve national economic flexibility in a downturn. However, the ECB did not lower its interest rates until the escalation of the economic crisis in 2001. This was how the independent monetary policy of the ECB and the economic requirements of the Member States created the first significant conflict of interests in EMU.

On the other hand, too low interest rates also caused a conflict of interests between the ECB and some small national economies in EMU. Small EMU Member States, such as Ireland and Finland, experienced high growing GDP rates in 2000 and 2001, whereas large Member States faced a substantial downturn after 2000. The boosted economies of Ireland and Finland would have required restrictive national fiscal policy as well as the restrictive monetary policy of the ECB to keep the developments under the objectives of the broad economic policy guidelines after early 2001. However, the "one-size-fits-all" monetary policy of the ECB finally chose to support the overall growth in the Euro area and Germany and France from mid-2001, whereas the economic needs of these two small EMU economies would have required a more restrictive monetary policy with higher interest rates. Eventually, the overheated national economy with national procyclical policy measures in Ireland resulted in the "crisis of Ireland" in which the Irish economy no longer complied with the broad economic policy guidelines. As a result, the Ecofin Council issued a warning to the Irish government to slow down its growth in 2001 by using restrictive fiscal policy (instead of restrictive monetary policy). Thus, one of the few economies in EMU to sustain strong growth since 2000 was issued a warning about pursuing too expansive (positive) a fiscal policy.

Price stability was also under strong pressures in the Euro area from 1998 to 2002 (Figure 4.3). Taking into account the fact that the labour cost factor of inflation (Figure 4.10) remained stable in this period, the volatility of the annual inflation was primarily caused by the changes in oil and food prices. The increase in the price of oil resulted from the terrorist attacks of 2001, whereas mad cow disease had a direct impact on the upward trend in the world market price of food. For example, the price of oil rose rapidly from 17.1 Euros per barrel in 1999 to as much as 31.0 Euros in 2001.[100] Simultaneously, the depreciated Euro contributed to a temporary but major increase in growth in Germany and the Euro area from 1999 to 2000, raising domestic sources of inflation as well. Although inflation in the Euro area was clearly below the upper limit of 2.0 percent of the ECB in 1998 and 1999 (1.1%), it jumped to 2.3 percent in 2000, thus growing as much as 1.2 percentage points from 1999 to 2000. After the jump in 2000, the inflation rate did not have a fast and continual normalisation; rather, the

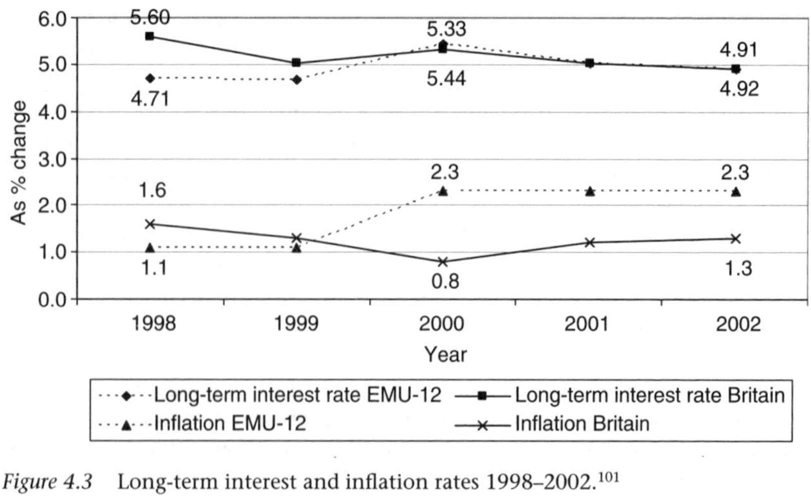

Figure 4.3 Long-term interest and inflation rates 1998–2002.[101]

rate stabilised at a high 2.3 percent level. Reflecting this empirical trend, the impact of the falling Euro, the shocks in the oil and food prices, the deterioration of the economic outlook as well as the new (corporate and consumer) costs of the changeover of national currencies to the Euro in 2002 helped to maintain the high inflation rate in EMU.

The degree of dispersion of the inflation rate remained notable between the Euro area and Britain. The dispersion cannot entirely be explained by the lack of economic coordination because although Britain's monetary policy was not subject to the objectives of EMU, the Bank of England was still consulted about the European inflation target. Britain's monetary policy benefited greatly from the decision of British Chancellor Brown to reform the role of the Bank of England making it independent of the government in the setting of interest rates; a fact that helped the Bank of England to fight inflation more effectively.[102] Fundamentally, where the ECB targeted price stability to be strictly below 2.0 percent (measured as HICP), the Bank of England set a broader and more flexible inflation target of 2.5 percent (measured as CPI). Despite the looser definition of price stability in the Bank of England, the trend in inflation was much more favourable in Britain than the Euro area. The inflation in Britain fell from 1998 to 2000, but reflecting the pressures from the increase in the oil and food prices, there was also a sizeable increase in inflation in Britain since 2000. Yet, the inflation rate in Britain was well below the inflation in the Euro area. In practice, the appreciation of the pound against the Euro caused a small increase in import prices in Britain resulting in low pressure on inflation.[103]

Deteriorating budgetary policy in Germany

Where the budgetary developments prior to EMU were positive, fast and progressive, the budgetary convergence in the EMU era was much slower and less significant. The concrete strategies and policy actions of national governments to bring down debt and deficit stocks were considered too moderate and political by the ECB. According to the ECB, reforms in national budgetary policies were too "unambitious in the light of the favourable forecasts for real growth and interest rates".[104] Where the debt-to-GDP ratio continued to decline from the 1990s, the deficit-to-GDP ratio faced a substantial setback and deteriorated in 2001 and 2002 for the first time since 1993. Firstly, public debts fell but more slowly in the Euro area from 1998 to 2002 compared to the achievements prior to EMU (Figure 4.4). In 1998 the debt ratio was 73.9 percent of GDP in the Euro area, and declined to 69.2 percent in 2002, 4.7 percentage points down from 1998. This decrease in the debt in the Euro area occurred partly because Member States with originally large debt stocks, such as Belgium, Greece and Italy, had a major reduction in debt.[105] A striking feature was that where both France and Germany struggled with the debt rule, Britain had no difficulties in meeting the 60 percent of GDP criterion. Where France hardly managed to reach the debt limit in 1998–2002, the debt of Germany was persistently above 60 percent but dipping to 59.4 percent in 2001. The debt of Germany fell only marginally from 60.9 percent in 1998 to 60.8 percent in 2002.

Secondly, where the trend in the debt was rather similar in all the three largest European economies, the developments in budgetary deficit were very volatile and dissimilar (Figure 4.5). Following the major improvement in the deficit in Britain, France, Germany and the Euro area 1998–2000, the deficit stocks increased again in the wake of the economic problems of 2001.[106] In EMU, the deficit ratio of GDP on average deteriorated along with the overall economic outlook since 2001, resulting in the same 2.3 percent deficit level in 2002 than in 1998. Outside EMU, the previous surplus of the British economy fell into a major deficit so that the deficit-to-GDP ratio was 2.1 in 2002. The trend in the budgetary balance of Britain 1998–2001, however, suggested that the adaptation of the golden rule in 1998 was effective in controlling the budgetary developments and the public spending in different stages of the economic cycle.[107] However, not even the golden rule could prevent the British budgetary policy from facing similar economic and financial difficulties to the EMU economies from 2002.

In Germany, the budgetary balance deteriorated at the end of the period 1998–2002. The major surplus of 2000 resulted from the UMTS revenue of 50.7 billion Euros and in fact, this revenue had a large impact on the budget of 2000. If the impact of the UMTS revenue on the deficit in 2000

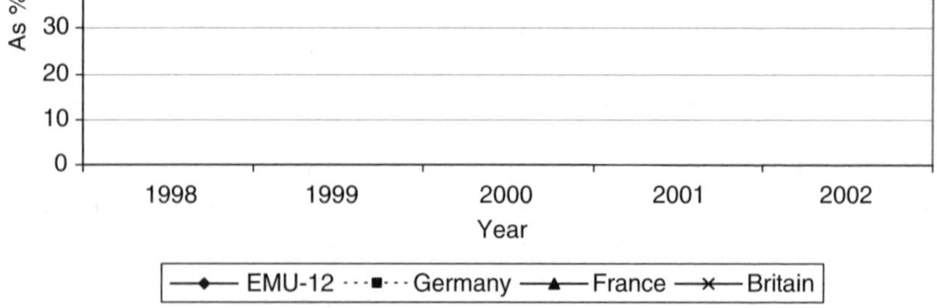

Figure 4.4 Public debt 1998–2002.[108]

had been excluded, the deficit would have been 1.0 percent in 2000.[109] Analysed critically, the German economy without the upward boost from the UMTS revenue and the major tax relief in 2000 would have been in a very critical condition in 2001 and 2002. Although the government made a commitment to stabilise the budget in its stability programmes 1999–2002, the budgetary balance still continued to deteriorate. Thus, Finance Minister Eichel wanted the Bundesländer and the municipalities to play a stronger role in the effort of the government in reducing the increasing debt and deficit ratios. However, according to the economic evidence, the contribution of the Bundesländer and the municipalities to the deficit of Germany was not as significant as might have been expected. In fact, the Bundesländer and the municipalities produced only 0.2 percentage points of the overall German budgetary deficit in 2000, 1.0 percentage points in 2001 and 0.5 percentage points in 2002.[110]

Reflecting on the trends in the debt and deficit levels in Germany, there are three fundamental reasons why debt and deficit ratios did not experience a positive trend despite the high growth period 1998–2000 and the major national reforms. Firstly, the declining growth from 2000 did not support the government's effort to reduce deficit and debt as effectively as the high growth period 1998–2000 did. Secondly, the Tax Reform 2000 and the Future Programme 2000 were left without compensation measures for the public revenue causing increasing financial problems and a major shortfall in tax revenue (Figure 4.7). Thirdly, the deteriorating of the budgetary position can also be explained by the malfunctioning of national automatic stabilisers in the downturn from 2000. This happened because the German fiscal policy prior to EMU did not create any additional room for the automatic stabilisers to work under the fiscal rules of the Stability

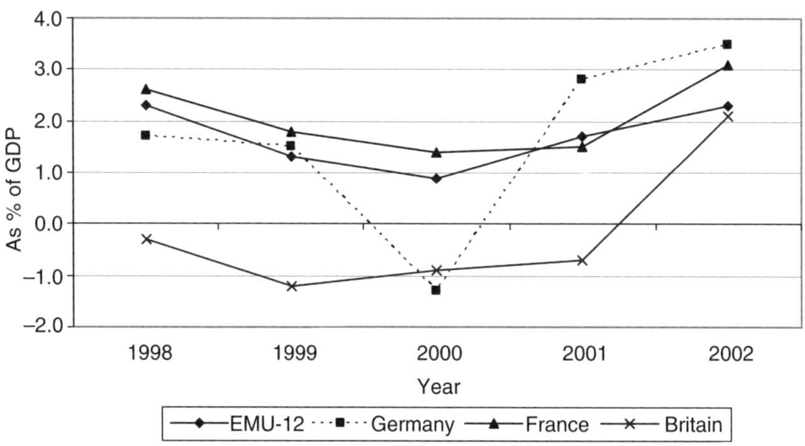

Figure 4.5 Budgetary deficit 1998–2002.[111]

Pact in EMU. According to the ECB, it is thus essential that first, a Member State achieves a medium-term budgetary balance and then it should "let automatic stabilisers operate symmetrically over the cycle, thus contributing to macroeconomic stability".[112] However, this would be a question of national willingness to make additional (and more costly) discretionary adjustments over the economic cycle possibly for the benefit of other Member States as well (due to the spill-overs and the free-rider dilemma in EMU). For these reasons, major adjustments in Germany had not been translated into a decline in the deficit ratio as it was translated into a clear slowdown in the increase in debt. The ECB was concerned with this trend that suggested that national adjustments had only affected the debt ratio rather than affecting the deficit ratio simultaneously. According to the ECB, the overall adjustments, directed to both debt and deficit, had left "the deficit unaffected but have had an impact on debt".[113]

A widening gap in the public finances

It is also essential to link trends in the monetary and fiscal environments with trends in German public finances in the EMU era; only thus can the current state of fiscal policy be put into an adequate and meaningful perspective. The basis of the public finances consists of stable public spending over the economic cycle in the federal government and the Bundesländer, progressive economic growth and stable tax revenue (Figures 4.6, 4.7 and 4.8). Firstly, public spending had an upward trend in the period 1998–2002 although the government managed to stabilise the increase in the spending temporarily in 1999–2001 (Figure 4.6). After having a declining trend in 1995, 1996 and 1997 (Figure 3.4), spending grew again as of 1998. Although the government introduced the reduction of spending in the public sector through major reforms in taxation and public services, the spending still increased from 224 billion in 1998 to 253 billion Euros in 2002. The trend in the public revenue followed the spending but at a significantly lower level. However, where the spending started to rapidly increase in 2002, the public revenue deteriorated from 221 billion in 2001 to 215 billion Euros in 2002. Simultaneously, the deficit, which had diminished from 28.9 billion in 1998 to 22.9 billion Euros in 2001, jumped to 37.3 billion in 2002. Despite the government's efforts to cut the financial burden of the public sector, the public spending ratio strikingly remained at about the same level from 1998 to 2002. The public spending ratio was 48.8 percent of GDP in 1998 and 48.5 percent in 2002, only 0.3 percentage points down from 1998 (Figure 4.7). Regardless of the major tax reforms, the increasing use of unemployed and other social benefits kept the public spending ratio very high in Germany.

Secondly, as Figure 4.6 shows, the economic cycle from 1998 to 2000 contributed to the emergence of a period of a very high growth rate not only in Germany but also in the European Union in 2000. The pace of the growth was already relatively good in 1998 and 1999 and the German GDP

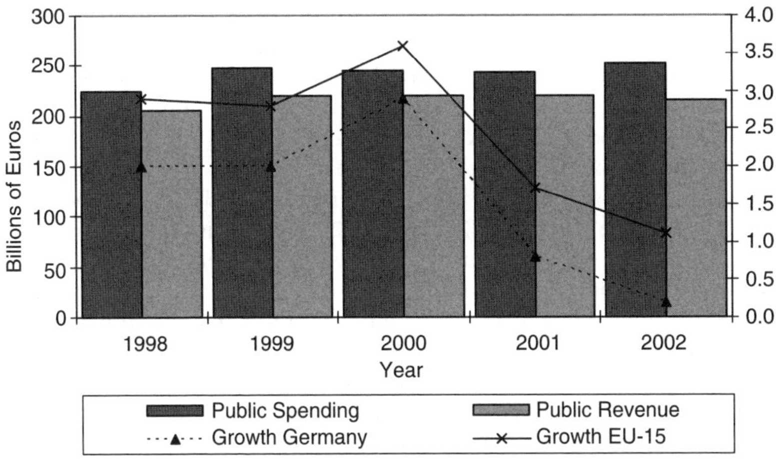

Figure 4.6 Public finance and annual growth 1998–2002.[114]

grew 2.0 percent in both years, whereas the EU area experienced even faster GDP growth rates of 2.9 percent in 1998 and 2.8 percent in 1999. The boost in 2000 resulted in 2.9 percent growth in Germany and 3.6 percent in the EU area, being one of the highest figures since the early 1990s. However, the growth faced major uncertainties in late 2000 causing a strong downward pressure on the European and German economies and since 2000, the forecasts for the growth were continually revised downwards. The German economy grew 0.8 percent in 2001 and only 0.2 percent in 2002, whereas the EU area had 1.7 and 1.1 percent growth rates. The growth declined together with the trend in domestic demand in Germany and the simultaneous upward trend in net exports did not manage to compensate for the major fall of the domestic demand. It was the domestic demand that boosted the growth in Germany in 1998–2000, and it was the domestic demand again that, on the other hand, had a negative impact on the decline in the growth in Germany in 2001 and 2002.

One of the primary objectives of the German government was to cut the size of public expenditure to better comply with the Stability Pact and coming fiscal challenges, such as population ageing. For this purpose, the government introduced a number of economic and social reforms of which the Tax Reform 2000 and the Future Programme 2000 were the most essential. However, as Figure 4.7 shows, the size of public expenditure in terms of GDP did not diminish as expected. Public expenditure remained at a persistently high level of about 48 percent of GDP although the instant financial impact of the first phase of the Tax Reform 2000 reduced expenditure to 45.7 percent in 2000. Together with the high expenditure ratio, tax revenue declined after a peak in 2000. Along with the implementation of the Tax Reform 2000 the tax revenue declined to 193.8 billion in 2001 and further down to 190.7 billion Euros in 2002. Surprisingly, although the amount of public tax revenue declined, the overall tax burden of GDP did not decline but remained high and even increased in 2002. The tax burden was 43.1 percent of GDP in 1998 and increased to 43.9 percent in 1999 and 2000. Although the tax burden fell to 42.3 percent in 2001, it still increased to 42.6 percent again in 2002.[115] It is worth noting that firstly, a tax reduction of a total of 8.1 billion Euros from 2000 to 2002 caused major financial pressure on public finances. Secondly, low growth and high unemployment did not create any additional financial room for national economic policy-making; rather, they both further constrained public finances. Thirdly, the increased use of social transfers, pension payments and unemployment benefits simultaneously kept the economic burden of the budget very high. For example, social transfers in terms of GDP declined slightly from 30.1 percent in 1998, via 30.0 percent in 1999 to 29.8 percent in 2000. However, the social transfers increased from 2001 so that the social transfers of GDP were 30.6 percent in 2002, 0.7 percentage points up from 29.9 in 2001.[116]

This increase in the size of social transfers in Germany in 2002 can be explained by the increase in the use of unemployment benefits, health and social security benefits, and the introduction of extended social and family benefits in 2001 and 2002; factors that also contributed to the crisis of public finance. Based on this knowledge of public finance, it is possible to understand why the German government faced a lot of criticism in introducing its reforms on social and labour policy: Germans have been used to extensive social services and benefits. When social transfers equal almost one-third of annual GDP and they are about to be cut, any reduction of the

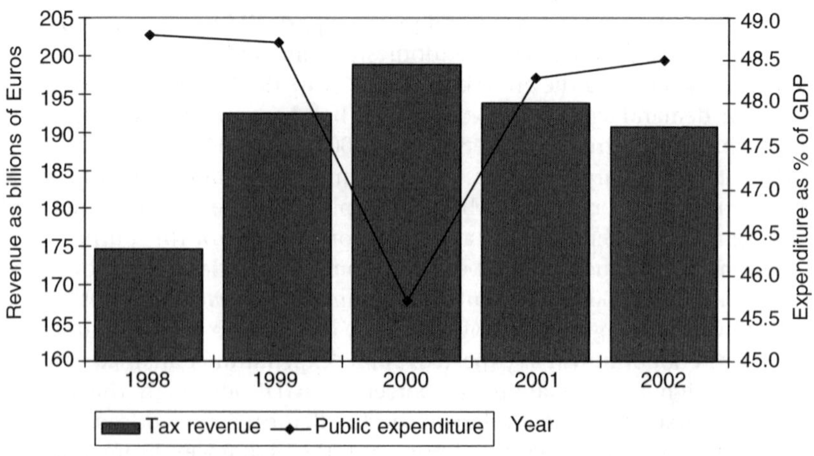

Figure 4.7 Tax revenue and public expenditure in Germany 1998–2002.[117]

range or scope of such transfers affects most of the population and the interest and pressure groups. In practice, the main problem in reforming social benefits is that most of them are based on existing laws, the changing of which usually requires a lot of time and wide political consensus: a consensus that can be hard to achieve in the cuts in public services, social benefits and social security. *The Economist* aptly argues that "cutting subsidies can be harder than raising taxes, particularly in Germany".[118]

Thirdly and finally, the financial position of the Bundesländer also reflected the overall declining trend in the German economy, as Figure 4.8 shows. After being extremely negative in 1993–1997 (Figure 3.3), the financial position of the Bundesländer improved in 1998. Where the Old Länder experienced three consecutive years of financial surplus in 1998, 1999 and 2000, the New Länder only achieved a positive level in the high growth year 2000. What these empirical findings suggest is that the severe problems in the federal public finances also affected the financial position of the Bundesländer. However, the downturn since 2000 seems to have had less impact on the economically stronger Old Länder than the New Länder although the government emphasised the political and economic importance of the continual reconstruction of East Germany for the whole national economy in the Coalition Agreement in 1998. What was most critical is the fact that low or even close to zero growth rates did not support the simultaneous reforms in the financial structure at all. By contrast, the major reduction in the tax burden and the tax revenue had a major impact on the financial position of the federal and regional economies; a fact that emphasises the need for sustainable public finances in EMU. These developments in budgetary position and public finances

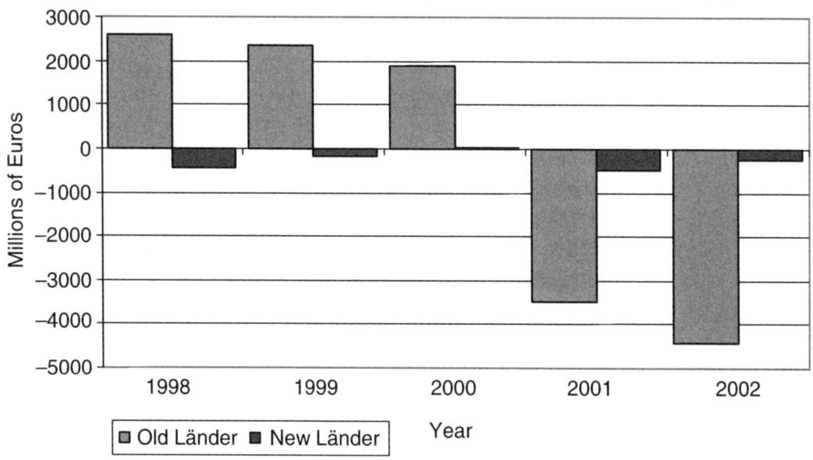

Figure 4.8 The financial position of Old and New Länder 1998–2002.[119]

inhibited the ability of national automatic stabilisers to perform, causing a national incapability to delay the sharp economic decline from late 2000.

Sluggish trends in labour policy and employment

Consistent with the slowdown in the Euro area as analysed through the monetary, fiscal and financial trends, labour policy and employment also encountered difficulties in Germany. On the one hand, the unstable macroeconomic environment did not support labour policy, employment, productivity, wages and labour costs domestically (Figures 4.9 and 4.10). On the other hand, the poor performance of the German labour market also increased pressures elsewhere in the national economy, monetary and fiscal policies. In the Euro area, boosting the economy by using an expansionary fiscal policy moved beyond the control of national governments from 1999: pro-cyclical demand and supply measures for contributing to growth and employment were no longer a policy option under the Stability Pact in EMU.[120] If the growth was not sufficiently effective to improve employment, then increasing productivity could have compensated for the low growth in the labour market. However, the productivity growth in Germany was not at that required level from 1998 to 2002, as shown in Figure 4.9. The empirical evidence suggests that the labour productivity growth followed the same declining trend with the economic activity in Germany and the Euro area.

Neither were the macroeconomic trends favourable to the employment rate in Germany and the Euro area after 2000. The fast growth in 1998–2000 did not affect the employment trend although the unemployment rate slightly declined in Germany and the Euro area from 1998 to 2001. Although the differential between the unemployment rates in the Euro area and Germany was eliminated by 2002, the unemployment rate of the Euro area diminished more than that of Germany. The unemployment rate in the Euro area was 10.2 percent in 1998, whereas the corresponding figure in Germany was 9.2. The unemployment rate in the Euro area declined sharply to 8.0 percent in 2001, but thereafter it increased to 8.4 percent in 2002. The reduction of the unemployment rate in Germany was slower resulting in 7.8 percent both in 2000 and 2001, and it also increased to 8.6 percent in 2002. It is noteworthy that there was a major variation in unemployment between the Old and New Länder. Where the unemployment rate declined from 9.4 percent (2.91 million) in 1998 to 7.6 percent (2.49 million) in 2002 in the Old Länder, the unemployment rate remained very high 18.2 percent (1.38 million) in 1998 and 17.7 percent (1.56 million) in 2002 in the New Länder.[121]

The ECB explained the difference in the unemployment rate between Germany and the Euro area primarily by the number of jobseekers. The overall trust in the high growth contributed to the fact that people sought jobs more actively in the Euro area than in some large Member States.

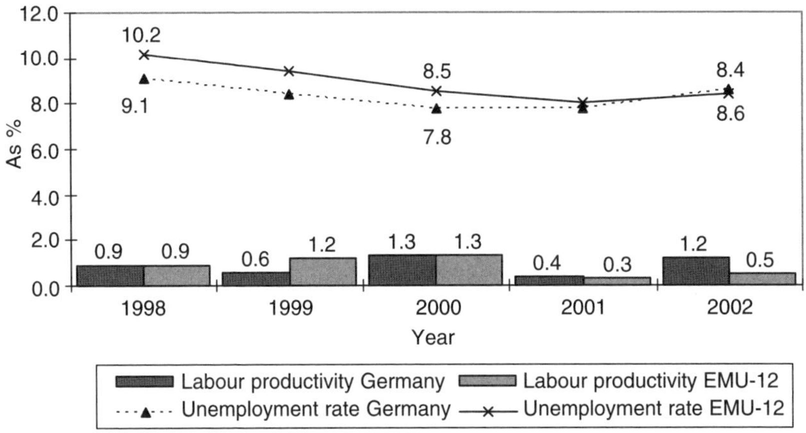

Figure 4.9 Labour productivity and unemployment rate 1998–2002.[122]

Thus, the unemployment rate in the Euro area as a whole was much higher than in some large European economies, such as in Germany and Britain. According to the ECB, "apart from the trend in population growth, the perception of better employment prospects may have encouraged inactive people to enter or to return to the labour market".[123] However, the fact that Germany experienced persistent unemployment remained an interesting question because the government took a number of demand- and supply-side measures focusing on the improvement of the national labour market. On the demand side, the reforms dealt with cutting tax on private income, reducing social benefits for the unemployed and improving training and

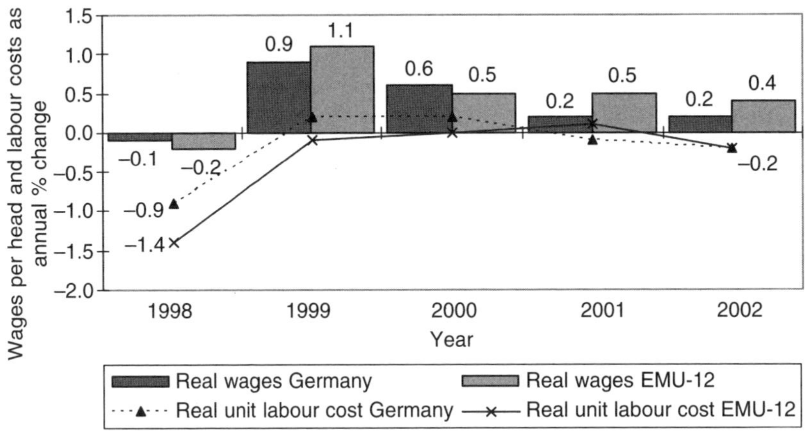

Figure 4.10 Real wages and real unit labour costs 1998–2002.[124]

education opportunities. Simultaneously on the supply side, the government reduced taxes and other social costs on employing workforce. As the government introduced major reforms in the labour policy, the impact on unemployment would have been expected to be more significant from 1998 to 2002. The empirical evidence suggests that the major slowdown simply maintained unemployment high in Germany.

In line with the trends in the unemployment rate, real unit labour costs were slightly negative before the high growth year 2000 both in Germany and the Euro area (Figure 4.10). While the labour costs were clearly reduced in Germany and the Euro area in 1998, they increased slightly in 1999 and 2000. However, after the peak in GDP growth in 2000, labour costs in Germany and the Euro area declined by 0.2 percent in 2002. According to the Bundesbank, this negative wage drift occurred in Germany because of the major employment reforms of the government and due to "the sharp increase in low-paid part-time workers, which in purely mathematical terms, meant a reduction in aggregate average earnings".[125] Real wages showed a trend similar to the labour costs from 1998 to 2002. As a practical guideline, the increase in real wages should not exceed the increase in productivity: a situation that could otherwise cause a decline in competitiveness and employment. After increasing by 0.9 percent year-on-year in Germany in 1999 and 1.1 percent in the Euro area, there was a progressive downturn in the growth in real wages until 2002. In short, these findings in labour policy (productivity, employment, wages and costs factors) clearly indicate that the unfavourable economic environment in Germany and the Euro area in 1998–2002 had a negative impact on employment and *vice versa*. Although the slowdown in the economic expansion explained a lot, the sluggish trends in employment in Germany also owed much to the existing structural rigidities in the national labour market, and the need for structural reforms became more and more apparent: a policy focus on structural, labour and economic reforms was put on the primary political agenda in Germany in 2003 and 2004 by Chancellor Schröder. In short, the critically developed labour factors implied that the fundamental reason for the declining German economy and loosening budgetary position in EMU was not only the changes in the economic cycle but also significant structural problems in the national economy.

4.4 Dealing with German national "misfits" 1998–2002

Refocusing German national fiscal policy in EMU

Sections 4.1, 4.2 and 4.3 of this chapter analysed in detail how and to what extent the German government dealt with the increasing ("misfits") need for national adjustments under the Stability Pact in EMU in 1998–2002 (Figure 4.11). In the wake of the politico-economic legacy of the Kohl era, the political change in the government from CDU/CSU to SPD/The Greens raised high expectations for a totally new policy towards national economic problems and more effective policy actions. Despite major reforms (Table 4.1), the impact of reunification, the Euro membership, low GDP and productivity growth rates, high unemployment, slowness of the ECB to respond to the downturn, and the increasing economic policy coordination maintained strong uncertainties in the German economy. The unexpectedly sharp decline from 2000 totally froze economic activity. Where global growth was 4.5 percent in 2001, 2.5 percent in 2001 and 3.0 percent in 2002, the corresponding figures in Germany were 3.0 percent, 0.6 percent and 0.2 percent. The almost zero pace of expansion after 2000 was a clear signal of a cyclical downturn that would have required measures to be prepared in the high growth period 1998–2000 and to compensate its impact on the German economy 2001–2002. For these reasons, *The Economist* argued that "Germany is both the continent's biggest economic giant and over the past few years its worst performer".[126]

As shown in this chapter, there was a major refocus on strict fiscal discipline in German economic policy 1998–2002. Whereas Waigel was a stability-oriented politician in Kohl's governments, Lafontaine took a more growth-supporting view on the economy in Schröder's government. However, Schröder believed that instead of growth-orientation, a stability-orientation should be the strategy in EMU and thus, Lafontaine was replaced by a new Finance Minister, Eichel, soon after the election in March 1999. Consistent with the government's commitments to fiscal discipline, Eichel adopted a strict stability-oriented policy with major saving plans. As the German government stated: "The government will in particular contribute to strengthening economic cooperation and coordination in order to safeguard the stability-orientation in the monetary union."[127] However, the legacy of Kohl's governments appeared to be so strong that the new government was forced to take somewhat similar measures to somewhat similar problems: low growth and high unemployment. The new government did not find a more effective perspective for identifying a long-term solution to the declining economy. In this vein, Schröder's government continued the same pathway in economic policy as that

- Refocusing national fiscal policy in EMU
- Improving the functioning of national automatic stabilisers
- Strengthening national economic coordination
- Suddenly declining economic outlook since 2000
- First signals from strict European economic monitoring
- Increasing national pressure from adaptation "misfits"
- Financial reality over fiscal policy coordination in EMU

Figure 4.11 Summary: Dealing with German national "misfits" 1998–2002.

determined by Kohl's governments. What the new government did was to make a major commitment to reforming the structure of public finances and cutting debt and deficit stocks, thus improving fiscal stability and economic growth. This was the primary policy shift from Kohl (CDU) to Schröder (SPD), and this characterised the politico-economic legacy of Schröder's government in 1998–2002.

Declining national economy and striking financial reality

Increasing uncertainties characterised the economic outlook in Germany and the Euro area 1998–2002. Since 2001, it became obvious that the downturn was far from a short-term phenomenon but a combination of long-lasting and critical problems in the German macroeconomic environment causing major monetary and fiscal problems. Firstly, the monetary policy in EMU faced low interest rates but volatile exchange and inflation rates in 1998–2002. The Euro was expected to become as important a reserve currency as the US dollar had been on the financial market. However, the falling Euro from 1999 to 2001 implied the perception on the financial market that the common monetary policy of the ECB and the outlook of the Euro area as a whole were not credible enough. According to the Bundesbank, as a clear signal of this mistrust, "the US dollar continued to fly high even after conditions in the Euro area had distinctively improved, whereas the first 'skid marks' were emerging in the United States".[128]

Consistent with this mistrust, the "one-size-fits-all" monetary policy was not effective in practice either. For example, during a high growth year 2000, the small EMU Member States, Ireland and Finland, required higher interest rates than was the then policy of the ECB, whereas the rest of the Euro area had low growth rates and a need for low interest rates. The ECB chose the latter policy with the overall growth, which contributed to the "crisis of Ireland". Instead of supporting Ireland in its effort to maintain high national growth when large Member States faced problems, the Ecofin Council in 2001 warned Ireland about its economic policy. However, the interest rate policy of the ECB was anything but favourable for Germany and France after all. Although growth suddenly fell in the Euro area after 2000, the ECB adjusted its interest rates very slowly to this changed environment. The high interest rate policy appeared very questionable when taking into account that the frozen growth in 2001 further reduced already low inflation pressures. Therefore, it could be argued that, in fact, the slowness of the ECB to lower its interest rates right after the high growth year 2000 did not support the overall growth in the Euro area at all, as the ECB had planned to do; or rather, the slowness in response instead caused further deterioration in the prospects of the national economies.

Neither were the developments in the exchange rate of the Euro anticipated during the first years of EMU because the Euro against the US dollar sharply declined from 1999. The falling Euro raised concerns about the future of the Euro area and the impact of the "soft" Euro on the European economy as a whole. The depreciation did not only have an effect on exports but also import prices, interest and inflation rates. However, the appreciation of the Euro in mid-2002 started to stabilise the pressures on interest and inflation rates. While the Euro appreciated 7.0 percent against the pound in 2002, the Euro had a major appreciation of 19.0 percent against the US dollar. Although the exports of the Euro area benefited from the depreciated Euro in the early years, the national economies were simultaneously negatively affected by increasing uncertainties over future economic activity. The Euro area had a number of new economic, political and institutional challenges, the impact of which reflected the overall outlook and the external value of the Euro. Therefore, unstable national economies in EMU did not contribute to the credibility of the Euro area right from the beginning.[129] Similarly to the trends in the Euro, inflation in the Euro area also faced challenges. In fact, the high growth and the external shock of oil and food prices caused a major increase in the year-on-year inflation from 1.1 percent in 1999 to 2.3 percent in 2000. Although the objective of the ECB was to maintain inflation as measured by HICP within 2.0 percent, the ECB was forced to announce that the price stability exceeded its inflation target in the Euro area in 2000. For the very first time, price stability was not in line with the monetary strategy of the ECB, although simultaneously, the Bank of England managed to keep the inflation rate in Britain at a low level. Thus, the British government argued that its monetary policy framework "has dealt successfully with unforeseen shocks".[130]

As an essential question, the volatile Euro recalled to people's minds the strong likelihood that the German government might have economically set far too high an exchange rate for the D-Mark in the Euro meeting of the Ecofin Council in 1998 at which the EU Finance Ministers decided the national parities against the Euro for EMU membership. For German national growth and employment, it would have been more favourable to choose a low and suitable D-Mark parity against the Euro. In terms of the US dollar, the D-Mark significantly strengthened from the rate of 1.88 DM in 1989 to 1.43 DM in 1995. When approaching EMU membership, the D-Mark, however, fell against the US dollar from 1.51 DM in 1996 to 1.75 DM in 1998;[131] the year when the EU Finance Ministers agreed on the irreversible national exchange rates against the Euro. The fact that Germany has had consistently low growth rates with declining employment prospects in EMU can partly be explained by the final and high exchange rate against the Euro in 1998 (1.95583 DM): a figure that seems not to have been realised until now. When reflecting on this fact in regard to the case of Britain in the European Monetary System in the early 1990s, both countries valued their currencies far too high. Contrary to the case of Britain, Germany does not have the same policy options at its disposal now in EMU, that is to depreciate the national currency to lower interest rates domestically and to depart from the single-currency system of EMU.

Secondly, developments in budgetary policy, public finances and labour policy were also critical. Although the debt-to-GDP ratio fell slightly in the Euro area and Britain from 1998 to 2002, the public debt of Germany and France stood at a very high 60 percent level. Despite the major efforts of the German government to bring down the debt and deficit stocks, the budgetary position resulted in a situation where the debt ratio stood at 60 percent and the deficit continued to increase above the 3.0 percent ceiling. All in all, the empirical evidence clearly indicated that the pitfalls of relaxing fiscal policies in some Member States, in particular in Germany and France, were real and that some Member States were moving away from the sustainable debt and deficit ratios in EMU. Most strikingly, although the declining outlook affected the whole Euro area and not only Germany, still some other Member States simultaneously managed to keep their fiscal convergence in progress. For example, the deficit declined from 0.7 percent of GDP in 1998 to 0.0 percent in 2002 in Belgium, from 2.5 percent in 1998 to 1.5 percent in 2002 in Greece and from 3.1 percent in 1998 to 2.4 percent in 2002 in Italy. Similarly, the public debt of GDP diminished from 119.6 percent in 1998 to 105.8 percent in 2002 in Belgium, from 105.8 percent in 1998 to 104.7 percent in 2002 in Greece and from 116.7 percent in 1998 to 108.0 percent in 2002 in Italy.[132] When looking back at the history of the growth in Germany it was possible to note that the year 2000 was one of the best years in terms of GDP growth since the 1980s. The fall of the Euro, high exports and domestic demand, and low interest and inflation rates boosted growth in Germany and EMU. However, very low or even close to zero growth in Germany in 2001 and 2002 did not compensate for the increasing deficit after 2001. The high GDP ratio of public expenditure together with declining tax revenue also caused financial pressures in Germany. In the environment of slow growth and declining revenue, the size of social transfers, about 30 percent of GDP, was intolerable for public finance, and new, radical reforms were required in the economy. According to the ECB, "these developments draw particular attention to the need for continued efforts in implementing labour market reforms and gearing wage developments towards supporting employment growth...and to better mitigate the effect of cyclical downturns".[133]

Increasing economic monitoring and national fiscal flexibility

The lack of effective national adjustments to European fiscal policy coordination under the Stability Pact was recognised in Germany and the Euro area at the latest when the Commission made a recommendation to the Ecofin Council to issue an early warning to Germany on an increasing deficit ratio in January 2002. As Germany had worked to stabilise the national economy, the crisis in public finance in early 2002 appeared suddenly. The recommendation from the Commission could be seen more as a political than as an economic process because the deficit of Germany had not yet exceeded the three percent limit in January 2002: the Commission wanted to direct more attention to the developments in fiscal policy not only in Germany but throughout EMU.[134] However, Germany with some other Member States, such as Britain and France, was not satisfied with the recommendation for four primary reasons. Firstly, the monitoring role of the Commission was considered too proactive; acting too much in advance to prevent the breaking of the rules in a downturn where a Member State implemented its fiscal policy normally and with normal variation in the budget. Secondly, the recommendation gave a strong signal to the EU and EMU that some Member States (Germany and France) had major problems in pursuing national fiscal policies in line with the economic common rules in a downturn. Thirdly, some Member States were still ready to be less than compliant with the Stability Pact although the rules and coordination models were set by the Member States themselves. As the Finnish Finance Minister, Sauli Niinistö, put it: "Three is always three and in particular when it is minus three."[135] Fourthly, the recommendation of the Commission was a major political embarrassment for the German government because it was Germany that had insisted on having a strict fiscal discipline in EMU and a strict monitoring and reporting responsibility for the Commission in 1995–1997. According to von Hagen and Strauch, "one might argue that the rules of EMU will force Germany to attack its fiscal problems. But it seems doubtful that the constraints of the Stability Pact will be enforced by the EMU, if the very country that imposed them shows itself unwilling or unable to respect them".[136]

Germany's primary problem with the Stability Pact stemmed from the fact that it was a result of the negotiations and economic interests and objectives in the mid-1990s, whereas its implementation took place within increasing coordination under a new national government and in the changed economic environment not until in the 21st century (the timing element). Not only did the actions of the government play a key role, but also the broad economic environment played a role in creating (un)favourable circumstances for the planned national reforms. As Allsopp argued: "Given that the Pact can be seen as imposing the double duty of medium-term fiscal restraint and short-term fiscal stabilisation on each country, it was always quite likely that stresses and strains would emerge, especially if growth in the Euro area were weak."[137] To put the situation in a broader context, just when Germany was criticised for exceeding the deficit criterion, the Ecofin Council accepted Greece as a member of EMU as of 2001. At that time Greece had a massive debt ratio of 104.0 percent of GDP while the Treaty-based limit was 60.0 percent. Furthermore, the US economy had a record high deficit of 5.0 percent in 2002. While the increase in the economic activity and growth in Germany was much higher than expected in 2000, the extent of the economic downturn in 2001 also caused a massive surprise. The adjustment problems in this period appeared to be even more essential when taking into account that the German budgetary policy was not stabilised prior to EMU although the macroeconomic developments would have allowed this. In other words, Germany did not complete fiscal stabilisation in good times 1998–2000; a fact that has a considerable impact on German fiscal stability in EMU.

Towards the end of Schröder's first government, the German government began to realise that the fiscal constraints, even though they aimed at ensuring the stabilised economic environment in EMU, required major national adjustments. Germany had responded to the need for national adjustments but the adjustments had not been effective.[138] The government recognised that European economic policy coordination "constrains national economic policy-making" although it simultaneously "strengthens European interdependence".[139] In these circumstances, the government raised a critical question of the fundamental meaning of coordination in EMU: "The economic policy coordination, however, has its limitations that lay there where national accountability and national calls for action become a blur. The common policy actions cannot act as a compensation for national responsibilities in the areas where subsidiarity exists. Thus, economic policy coordination also has its limitations."[140] What the government argued here was basically that despite the aims of broad economic policy coordination, Member States should have more independence and flexibility in their economic policy-making under the common rules. In this vein, in the German government's view, the situation in which the Ecofin Council decided not to issue an early warning to Germany "did not, in fact, weaken the Pact; but rather, it qualitatively improved it" by allowing flexibility in national economic policy-making in hard times.[141]

5
Reuploading Fiscal Policy Coordination in EMU

5.1 Adjusting to European economic authority and monitoring

German fiscal policy after the parliamentary elections of 2002

Until now, it has been taken for granted that once common objectives and coordination models in fiscal policy have been enacted in the EU (uploading), the common fiscal policy objectives are implemented equally across Member States (downloading). German Finance Minister Hans Eichel still argued in December 2001 that *"wir werden den Stabilitätspakt auf Punkt und Komma einhalten. Da müsste schon der Himmel einstürzen. Aber dann stürzt er nicht nur über Deutschland ein, sondern auch über Europa und der Welt"*.[1] However, the unforeseen and serious problems that Germany faced in the implementation phase of the Stability Pact after 2002 resulted in a political situation in which, instead of fully ensuring their execution, Germany tried to reform the common fiscal policy objectives once formulated by Germany itself. Through the process of reuploading the German government actively lobbied in the Ecofin Council to reform the political interpretation of the rules of the Stability Pact, as will be argued in this chapter. Thus, reuploading, as defined in this research, refers to a process by which a Member State uses the common EU institutions and political procedures to reshape the collectively agreed policy responsibilities which were set in t1 to better suit the national interest of that specific Member State after the failed implementation phase in t3 (Figures 1.1 and 1.2).

In fiscal policy coordination this process means that Germany has argued that the rationale of the fiscal rules is still valid in EMU but the original rules no longer comply with the existing developments in the German economy and thus, it has acted to change the interpretation of the Stability Pact in 2003–2005, a new bottom-up process to reupload changed national interests. Although Germany started to reshape the fiscal rules of the Stability Pact since its first major budgetary problems, the European Court of Justice still retained the institutional system of the Stability Pact through its judgment on the excessive deficit procedure in July 2004. However, the Ecofin Council and the Brussels European Council finally amended the original rules of the Stability Pact of 1997 on 20 and 22–23 March 2005. Therefore, the main question that arises is: *due to what politico-economic developments has the German government contributed to the reinterpretation of the fiscal rules of the Stability Pact?* This reuploading process of Europeanisation is analysed through three primary developments: a) the problems of Germany to adjust to European economic authority and monitoring in late 2002, b) increasing European economic monitoring in 2003, and c) the softening of the fiscal rules since 2004 (Table 5.1).

In autumn 2002, it seemed somewhat unlikely that there would be Schröder's second government to follow in Germany because the SPD-led government had not succeeded in maintaining growth and improving employment in the national economy. However, international political developments in Iraq, the fear of war in the Middle East and a domestic environmental catastrophe in East Germany in autumn 2002 caused unanticipated uncertainties over national security, and the prospects for the European market deteriorated still further. Internationally, Germany did not agree to join the coalition forces led by the US against the Iraq government and through this political decision Chancellor Schröder increased the feeling of national security in Germany. Domestically, the public also considered that Schröder responded to the dramatic flood in East Germany quickly and sufficiently and the government allocated enough financial support to the flood area (the River Elbe) in August 2002 just a few weeks before the election in September. Despite this favourable publicity for Schröder before the parliamentary elections, the SPD party leader nearly lost his position as Chancellor to the CDU Chancellor Candidate, Edmund Stoiber, in the elections of 22 September 2002. In the close result, SPD received 251 seats (38.5%) and the Greens 55 seats (8.6%), whereas CDU/CSU had 248 seats (38.5%) out of a total of 603 seats in the *Bundestag*. Based on the same red-green coalition as the first one, Schröder formed his second government for 2003–2006.

In the new Coalition Agreement 2003–2006 in October 2002, the SPD and the Greens agreed to continue the work for economic, structural and social reforms. They in particular agreed to implement the reforms of the Hartz Commission in the labour market, ensure the financial basis of public services and balance the national economy.[2] The Annual Economic Report 2003 was the first annual budget to be formulated under the new ministry, the Ministry for Economics and Employment, and under the new Minister of Economics, Wolfgang Clement, in January 2003. The report was called "Alliance for Modernisation – Promoting Reforms Collectively" (*Allianz für Erneuerung – Reformen gemeinsam voranbringen*) and it started with a major argument that "right from the beginning of 2003 Germany introduces the crucial economic and budgetary turning point".[3] The beginning for this

Table 5.1 National adjustments and European economic policy coordination in Schröder's second government 2002–2005.

Timing / Measures	National policy reforms and adjustments in the German national economy	European economic policy coordination and European economic monitoring
Late 2002: Declining growth Unstable public finances Adjusting to increasing economic monitoring	Annual Economic Report 2003 Hartz Commission Rürup Commission Financial Planning Council	German Stability Programme 2002 Commission's recommendation in November No voting in the Ecofin Council Commission's New Communication in November 2002
2003: Freezing the fiscal rules of the Stability Pact First signals of improving national economy	Annual Economic Report 2004 Agenda 2010	Public Finances in EMU 2003 Broad economic policy guidelines 2003–2005 Commission's recommendation in November 2003 Voting in the Ecofin Council German Stability Programme 2003
2004: National criticism of major reform policy Recovering growth Improving public finances	Annual Economic Report 2005 Financial Planning Council Agenda 2010	Commission's appeal to the European Court of Justice in January 2004 Public Finances in EMU 2004 ECJ's decision in July 2004 Commission's New Communication in September 2004 Shared view in the Ecofin Council in September and November 2004
2005: Meeting the fiscal rules Towards stabilisation	Agenda 2010	Reforming the original fiscal rules of the Stability Pact of 1997 at the Ecofin Council meeting in March 2005

"turning point" was not, however, optimal because the economy was expected to grow by only 1.1 percent and unemployment was expected to rise from 9.8 percent in 2002 to 10.0 percent in 2003.[4] Although the German Council of Economic Experts criticised the national economic policy for not taking clear actions in labour policy and not ensuring a stable fiscal position in 2002, the Council considered in 2003 that major adjustments had contributed to the direction that "is more positive than a year ago".[5] However, reforming public finances (tax cuts) had reduced the already limited financial room and thus, it had constrained automatic stabilisers more than would otherwise have been the case. The Council expressed its concern about the dramatic trend in public finance and argued that if the government continued to reform public finance in the uncertain economic environment, it would be likely that the deficit ratio would jump higher than 3.6 percent in 2004.[6] The government responded to the Council by stating that actions in taxation and growth had "a crucial impact not only on the reduction of high unemployment but also on the consolidation of the national economic policy".[7] However, at this point, Finance Minister Eichel started to consider that although EMU required fiscal discipline, it should still be possible for national governments "to adjust the national economic policy to the economic cycle".[8] The President of the Bundesbank, Welteke, was sceptical about Eichel's idea of challenging national fiscal discipline under the Stability Pact by allowing expansive budgetary policy, calling it "very dangerous" and "undermining credibility".[9] Welteke's opinion was that Germany should keep its commitments to fiscal discipline and respect the Stability Pact even though the economic cycle was not currently favourable to its own national interests.

Schröder's first government set up a commission of 15 experts from a wide range of society to make proposals for improving the functioning of the labour market. Although the priority in the Hartz reforms was given to the functioning of the labour market, they were also planned to have an impact on public finances and fiscal policy through better employment in the economy. In August 2002, a month before the elections, the government accepted the plan of the Hartz Commission, "Modern Services in the Labour Market" (*Moderne Dienstleistungen am Arbeitsmarkt*), which introduced actions to modernise the labour market. Schröder's second government declared its intention to implement the proposals in full because it considered that reforming the labour market "could give an impulse for a more dynamic labour market".[10] The Hartz plan, which consisted of four reform packages, implemented the Hartz I and II reforms in stages in 2003 and 2004, whereas the Hartz III and IV reforms were incorporated into the Annual Economic Reports 2004 and 2005. Firstly, Hartz I and II outlined how to make labour policy more concrete in relation to the needs of customers both in services and in benefits. Secondly, they introduced a wide range of measures to improve better job location and create new job centres across the country. As a result, the public employment service and the individual unemployed would find themselves faster.

Schröder's first government also set a commission to make suggestions for social policy improvement and to provide information on securing social services and social security in the future. The outcome was a report "The Financial Sustainability of the Social Security System" (*Nachhaltigkeit in der Finanzierung der Sozialen Sicherungssysteme*), the findings of which the government took as guidelines for social reforms in the Annual Economic Report 2003. The work of the Rürup Commission was one of the first thorough governmental efforts to develop the structure of the public finances for the impact of the ageing population on the national economy. The Rürup Commission proposed that the statutory pension insurance system (*Gesetzliche Rentenversicherung*), the statutory health insurance system (*Gesetzliche Krankenversicherung*) and the social long-term care insurance system (*Soziale Pflegeversicherung*) should be maintained but reformed to better cope with the financial impact of the ageing. It argued that the starting point for social reforms had to be ensuring that "the rising costs of social security in an ageing society are spread more evenly across all generations".[11] For example, it proposed that the statutory retirement age should be raised from 65 years to 67 years starting from 2011. The Commission was also aware of the fact that although the proposals would result in a total saving of as much as 1.5 percent of GDP, the reforms would "entail painful cuts in benefits and additional burden".[12]

The government also furthered national fiscal convergence in the German Stability Programme in December 2002. The government took into account the economic impact of the labour and social policy reforms and it believed that to achieve all the reforms the economy would require a strong economic growth or the deficit would exceed the 3.0 percent ceiling. It also acknowledged that the poor economic developments since 2000 had affected the deficit ratio more than was expected. The government was in particular concerned about the financial impact of the Tax Reform 2000, a tax shortfall, on the budget in the environment where the economy faced strong downward pressure. It admitted that the deficit in 2002 was "substantially higher than forecast in the Stability Programme of October 2000".[13] The deficit target of the Annual Economic Report 2003 of 2.8 percent was raised to more than 3.0 percent in the Stability Programme 2002. The government thus stated for the very first time that Germany might break the deficit rule and the deficit might increase up to 3.7 percent by the end of 2002.

Facing European economic monitoring II

Following the Commission's "early warning" to Germany in January 2002, the second phase of European economic monitoring took place in November 2002. The second recommendation of an early warning to the Ecofin Council became inevitable because the problems in the German economy had escalated after January 2002. Just before the second recommendation some leading politicians, that is Chancellor Schröder in Germany and President Chirac in France, had started to argue for more flexibility in national economic policy-making under the Stability Pact due to the rapidly declining European outlook. Both leaders agreed on developing further Franco-German cooperation in European fiscal policy in

October 2002.[14] Their main argument was that the Stability Pact should take more into account the existing economic circumstances in Member States. In addition, both Finance Ministers of these two countries, Hans Eichel and Francis Mer, increased their cooperation in economic policy. In Eichel's view, "we want to strengthen the cooperation of both Finance Ministries and we have a shared opinion on monetary and fiscal policy".[15] In practice, the uncertain developments in the European economy resulted in a political situation in which Member States or EU institutions did not have a clear vision or understanding of the coming trends or how to respond to them. For example, the EMU Finance Ministers within the Euro-12 group made a decision to reduce the deficit by 0.5 percent on a yearly basis in October 2002. However, Finance Minister Mer stated right after the meeting that "France has decided that we have other priorities", and thus France might not comply with the collective decision of the reduction of the deficit by 0.5 percent.[16]

Strikingly, the President of the Commission, Romano Prodi, called the political decisions of the EU institutions under the Stability Pact "stupid" in his interview in *Le Monde* on 18 October 2002. According to Prodi, "*Je sais très bien que le pacte de stabilité est stupide, comme toutes les décisions qui sont rigides*".[17] What should be noted here is that Prodi's opinion arose from the circumstances where the Ecofin Council had failed to implement the sanction procedure on Germany and France despite the Commission's recommendation in January 2002. His comment, however, caused a European-wide debate on the future of the Stability Pact. For example, French Prime Minister, Jean-Pierre Raffarin, considered that "it is not right that someone in the European Commission calls the Stability Pact stupid".[18] Despite his provocative statement, Prodi spoke for national fiscal discipline and fiscal policy coordination in EMU. In fact, the way in which Prodi would have reformed the Stability Pact would have involved the establishment of a harmonised institutional system for coordination within the EU. In his view, "it is impossible to coordinate and govern 12 economic policies in the single currency area without a single and powerful authority".[19]

In November 2002, the Commission reported to the Ecofin Council for the second time to issue an early warning to Germany for exceeding the deficit limit and approaching the debt rule rapidly. However, after political consideration allowed by the rules, the Ecofin Council decided not to issue a warning to Germany but it decided to recommend that Germany implement faster national reforms to ensure the stabilised budgetary policy with a new deadline of 21 May 2003. The Commission's disappointment at the decision can be seen in Prodi's statement: "In the Euro area, there is one clear identified problem, Germany."[20] Thus, ten months after the non-decision of the Ecofin Council in January 2002, fiscal policy coordination failed to implement the sanction procedure of the Stability Pact for the second time in succession. The decisions of the Ecofin Council in January and November 2002 not to apply the excessive deficit procedure on Germany (and France) resulted in the situation where the credibility of the Stability Pact together with its supranational sanction mechanism was at least partially lost.

Strengthening national fiscal policy coordination III

The Commission's recommendations increased the pressure and criticism towards the German government: not only was the economic trend against the government but also the opposition, the Bundesländer, the trade unions and the Commission. Schröder did not share the Commission's opinion but he asserted that "we do implement an anti-cyclical economic policy and in that way stabilise the impact of the economic cycle".[21] Schröder also pointed out that "this policy of the German government should be clear for all" but "still there are people who criticise us for pro-cyclical economic policy even though the government issues 15 billion Euros more public debt".[22] The failures in the implementation of the National Stability Pact in 2001 and 2002 also had an effect on national economic policy-making. As the National Stability Pact had not succeeded in ensuring stable budgetary policy or implementing the Stability Pact, the malfunctioning national economic coordination caused additional pressures on the government. What the National Stability Pact had specified in March 2002 was that all governmental levels, the federal government, the Bundesländer and the municipalities, had equal responsibility for implementing budgetary policy in line with the Stability Pact. However, the decision to adapt the National Stability Pact lacked a concrete strategy for stabilising the budgetary policy. Eichel thus wanted to hasten the implementation of the National Stability Pact so that instead of coming into force in January 2005, as was originally planned, it already came into force in July 2002. Due to the decision of the Ecofin Council in November 2002, the Financial Planning Council really started to tackle the increasing deficit and debt ratios by committing to the objective of zero net borrowing in 2006 in its meeting on 27 November 2002. It agreed to reduce deficit to less than three percent in 2003, and after that the Council would reduce the deficit by 0.5 percent of GDP annually.[23] This meant for the very first time that the Financial Planning Council fulfilled its responsibility for budgetary discipline under the National Stability Pact; the responsibility that was already specified in March 2002.[24]

In the Monthly Economic Report in January 2003, the Ministry of Finance focused on the functioning of the Financial Planning Council between the federal government, the Bundesländer and the municipalities. The main guideline for national economic coordination was the German Constitution, which defined the economic objectives of the federal government and those of the Bundesländer and the municipalities. Increasing economic policy coordination in EMU had, however, caused pressures to reform the system of national economic coordination. The Ministry of Finance was concerned about the practical role and meaning of Article 51a of the Law on Budgetary Procedures that set a binding responsibility for all the governmental levels to comply with the Stability Pact through the Financial Planning Council. It argued that to fully meet the fiscal rules it would be crucial that the Financial Planning Council "underlines a common and inter-coordinated consolidation policy".[25] Already in the following report in February 2003, the Ministry of Finance, however, reduced its political pressure and high expectations on the work of the Council because of its previous inability to reach a consensus about the required reforms and the timetable by stating that "the economic planning is a highly complex structure consisting of prognoses, varying standards in drawing up economic reports and different policy objectives".[26]

European guidelines for German national economic reforms III

In the Barcelona European Council of March 2002, the Member States renewed their commitment to making further progress in coordination between monetary and fiscal policies. In the wake of the non-decision of the Ecofin Council in January 2002, the European Council invited the Commission to present concrete "proposals to reinforce economic policy coordination in time for the 2003 Spring European Council".[27] Based on this invitation, the Commission introduced a crucial Communication "Strengthening the Coordination of Budgetary Policies" in November 2002 in which it outlined existing problems and potential solutions for the better implementation of the Stability Pact. The Communication was one of the first statements for reforming the Stability Pact to be more effective in coordinating fiscal polices and safeguarding stable budgetary policy over the economic cycle. Firstly, the Commission presented the clear division between the common monetary policy and national fiscal policies as the guiding principle in economic policy coordination: "A unique rule-based framework for the coordination of budgetary policies in EMU has been established to reflect the fact that the responsibility for the single monetary policy is entrusted to an independent European Central Bank whilst responsibility for budgetary policies remains decentralised in the hands of national authorities."[28] Secondly, it argued as the main difficulty that in some Member States national commitments to the common economic objectives had diminished and "there has been an unwillingness to acknowledge the implication of EMU on the conduct of fiscal policy at the national level".[29] Thirdly, it recognised that it had been very difficult to set a sound and applicable interpretation of the fiscal rules that could simultaneously take into account the existing general and country-specific economic developments. Fourthly, the Commission proposed that national policy-making and European economic surveillance should more thoroughly take into account the economic cycle thus avoiding pro-cyclical fiscal policies. Finally, it argued that fiscal discipline and stable budgetary policy should become the key national objectives not only in agreements but also in practice. The Commission thus urged that "Member States should reaffirm their political commitment to the Stability and Growth Pact".[30]

In the fourth Public Finances in EMU 2003 in May 2003, the Commission thought that economically, year 2002 and the beginning of 2003 were the most challenging period in national budgetary policies since the start of EMU. The Commission's argument was based on the fact that by 2003 only six EMU Member States had achieved budgetary positions that were in line with the requirement of close to balance or in surplus. The Commission was concerned in particular with the German economy. According to the Commission, "a deficit of 3.6 percent of GDP in 2002 has resulted in Germany being placed in an excessive deficit position: while the authorities are taking measures aimed at reducing the cyclically-adjusted budget deficit, only a very limited improvement in nominal terms is expected in 2003 as growth conditions deteriorate".[31] For the Commission, this dramatically declining trend "indicates a discretionary loosening of the fiscal stance by some Member States over the past two years, brought about by a combination of unfunded tax cuts, discretionary expenditure increases and failures as regards budgetary execution".[32] Regarding effective economic surveillance and policy coordination, the Commission emphasised as an essential requirement that Member States should provide reliable economic forecasts for policy-making and secondly, they should avoid raising taxes, and focus more on reducing the financial burden of population ageing and contribute more to growth and employment.

5.2 "Frozen" and "softened" European fiscal policy coordination

Tackling structural problems radically through Agenda 2010 in 2003

The German government faced an increasing need to strengthen its stabilisation policy but policy measures had mainly dealt with only short-term adjustments on the changes in the economic cycle until now. Now, after realising that the nature of the national problems had not only resulted from the economic cycle, the attention was directed to tackling the declining economy through more radical structural reforms. As the government was convinced that the problems in the economy, illustrated by stagnation, high unemployment and low productivity, existed because of structural problems, the Economic Plan 2003–2007 presented a new strategy for the modernisation of the public sector. Firstly, the structural reform plan, Agenda 2010, would improve the flexibility of the labour market, increase employment by reducing non-wage costs and stabilise the public finances by cutting public services. Secondly, the government focused on cutting the size of the public expenditure because it wanted to further fiscal stabilisation within the Stability Pact. Thirdly, it decided to finalise the implementation of the Tax Reform 2000, which would give an additional stimulus to national demand and growth. The government expected to have "reviving economic growth from 2004" and "a reduction in the unemployment rate between 2005 and 2007".[33] However, these actions were widely criticised because they did not eliminate public borrowing as the government borrowed 35 billion Euros in 2003 and 30.8 billion Euros in 2004. The Minister of Economics, Wolfgang Clement, however, argued that the government even in EMU had the right to issue new public debt "when the situation requires that".[34] Finance Minister Eichel also pointed out that "the focus only on net borrowing provides no final truth".[35]

The continually blackening outlook resulted in the situation where the government had to make radical decisions on public finance. It was politically ready to announce that unpopular reforms could not be avoided if the objective was to maintain public services and revive growth and employment. Schröder proposed a reform programme, Agenda 2010, officially in the policy statement in the *Bundestag* on 14 March 2003. The basis of the whole of the Annual Economic Report 2004 was built on Agenda 2010, which was one of the most significant reforms in the German history. The report, as its name *"Leistung, Innovation, Wachstum"* described, focused on ensuring public services, investing in innovation and supporting growth. Although the report set several new objectives for 2004, it was Agenda 2010 that would really decide whether the government could achieve its objectives in stabilisation and growth: Germany would experience "full employment by the end of this decade".[36] Now, the government expected to have a major improvement from the growth of –0.1 percent in 2003 to 1.7 percent in 2004 and a total of 100,000 less unemployed in 2004 (10.3%) than in 2003 (10.5%). The deficit would also recover from 4.0 in 2003 to 3.5 percent in 2004.

Agenda 2010 in terms of cuts went much deeper in welfare benefits than was proposed by the Hartz and Rürup Commissions. Based on the work of the Hartz Commission, the implementation of the third Hartz reform package (Hartz III) came into force in January 2004. The Hartz III replaced the Federal Labour Office and established a new Federal Employment Agency for improving employment services and management. This way the government expected to have more customer-focused employment services with better effectiveness and quality. In addition, Agenda 2010 relaxed job protection more than was proposed by the Hartz Commission. For example, by increasing local bargaining in companies, the government created more local flexibility to hire and fire employees, which implied that the role of trade unions in sector-wide and nationwide agreements would be less important. Agenda 2010 also contributed to the emergency of the so-called mini-jobs and midi-jobs. Mini-jobs with a monthly salary of less than 400 Euros and midi-jobs with a monthly salary up to 800 Euros were subjected to fewer taxes and other social security payments. Agenda 2010 introduced a new unemployment benefit I (*Arbeitslosengeld I*), which came into effect in 2004 and unemployment benefit II (*Arbeitslosengeld II*) to be adopted in 2005. Unemployment benefit I cut unemployment benefits so that the full duration of benefit for older people's unemployment was reduced from 32 months to 18 months, and for unemployed people under 55 years the benefit period was lowered to only 12 months.

Agenda 2010 also introduced major pension and health reforms based on the work of the Rürup Commission. Population ageing and its coming impact on public finance forced the government to cut pensions and encourage people to work longer, that is retiring later on in life. The driving force behind pension reforms was that coming generations could not carry the whole financial burden of ageing. The government thus decided to pass a law to ensure a stable contribution rate of pension of 19.5 percent (*Rentenversicherungsbeitrag*). Most significantly, from April 2004 the pensioners were obliged to pay long-term nursing care insurance (*Pflegeversicherungsbeitrag*) themselves. As the population ageing increases the use of public health services, according to Agenda 2010, people should pay more for their health care thus reducing the economic burden of the public sector. As the use of the health insurance funds (*gesetzliche Krankenkassen*) was also cut, the reform of the pension and health systems was estimated to save 10 billion Euros in 2004 and 26 billion Euros by 2006.[37]

Predictably, the massive cuts in public services and social and unemployment benefits planned and implemented by the SPD-led government, received a lot of criticism from the trade unions (IG Metall, OTV and HBV), whereas employers' associations (DIHK, BDI and BDA) were satisfied with the increasing flexibility in the national labour market, wages and employment. In this respect, Agenda 2010 introduced by the left-wing government was a major political risk for Schröder and the SPD. Despite the political resistance from the opposition (CDU/CSU), the trade unions and the German public, Schröder and Eichel achieved firm political acceptance for their extensive reform plan within their own SPD party. In fact, "at a special party conference in Berlin on June 1, Mr Schröder won an unexpectedly handsome vote of confidence, without having seriously to water down his plans".[38] The SPD Secretary, Olaf Scholz, took the view that "Agenda 2010 will be a success for it is broadly supported in the party".[39]

Facing European economic monitoring III

By mid-2003 it became apparent that Germany's budgetary position would not improve as the Commission and the Ecofin Council had required in November 2002 and that Germany would not fully comply with the Stability Pact. In addition, there were increasing internal problems in the government that cutting public expenditure so much together with the increasing European coordination was not the most optimal policy for the German economy. Schröder had to announce in June 2003 that regarding the government's economic policy "we have to clear a couple of fundamental questions".[40] Basically, Eichel had second thoughts according to which the existing economic circumstances should require "expansive national fiscal policy".[41] Eichel considered that the continual saving policy had not achieved the desired economic boost; rather, the national economy had to pay the price of the cuts in terms of unemployment. In his words, "we cannot save until we are dead".[42] The Greens also shared Eichel's opinion and the economic expert of the Greens, Oswald Metzger, criticised the government saying that it "should have seen what is coming".[43] By this he meant that the government should have responded earlier to the deterioration in the economic outlook after 2001 with more comprehensive measures than only the massive saving policy.

Before the decision of the Ecofin Council in November 2003, the ECB took a major role in the European debate on the importance of the Stability Pact. Although the ECB had chosen not to have any role in the fiscal problems of Member States before, it now decided to support the Commission's strict policy with strong political statements. The ECB realised that the declining developments in Germany and France could jeopardise the overall economic discipline in EMU. The Vice-President of the ECB, Lucas Papademos, argued that the fiscal rules were essential in EMU and therefore, the Commission should take a firm stand on the implementation of the rules of the Stability Pact. In his view, "the situation almost equals that of a potential alcoholic who has been given the key to the hotel minibar".[44] The President of the ECB, Wim Duisenberg, in turn urged Member States to implement effective reforms for public finances because they "are essential to increase the Euro area's growth potential and enhance its ability to better withstand external shocks".[45] He argued that the economic and structural reforms implemented in Germany had not been effective enough. Duisenberg criticised in particular the massive reduction in taxation because he did not support the kind of reforms that could jeopardise public finance as a whole. In his opinion, "countries should not reduce taxes but cut the public expenditure".[46] For Duisenberg, the deficit problems resulted from the fact that Member States that "had not achieved sound fiscal position in earlier years when the economic conditions were more favourable are now struggling to keep their budgets under control".[47]

On 8 October 2003, the Commission stated that France exceeded the debt and deficit criteria and it had not complied with the previous recommendations of the Commission and the Ecofin Council.[48] This meant that the Commission took the next step in the excessive deficit procedure against France. The Commission also declared that Germany had growing problems in fulfilling the fiscal rules, thus the Commission announced on

18 November 2003 that the next step in the excessive deficit procedure against Germany would also be taken.[49] Despite the recommendations, the Ecofin Council did not issue an early warning to Germany and France on 25 November 2003. If it had issued the warning, both countries would have been officially required to cut the deficit ratio below the criterion. Failure to comply with the warning would have resulted in the implementation of the final stage of the sanction procedure and a fine of billions of Euros. Now, Germany and France were only politically committed to bring debt and deficit ratios below the criteria by 2005. However, in response to this decision, the French government announced it would "respect the joint commitment", and the German government stated that it would "discharge its obligations".[50]

The Ecofin Council's decision was taken on 25 November 2003 when the Stability Pact was finally "frozen". The Ecofin Council allowed Germany to implement a national fiscal policy that had exceeded the deficit criterion for three consecutive years. What merits special attention here is that the vote of the Ecofin Council on 25 November 2003 was not about whether the excessive deficit existed in Germany but whether the Ecofin Council considered that the sanction mechanism should be applied to Germany for breaking the deficit rule. The Ecofin Council had already clearly stated on 21 January 2003 that the excessive deficit existed in Germany. Small Member States, Austria, Finland and the Netherlands, were very disappointed at the outcome of the vote in the Ecofin Council in which large Member States outvoted the small Member States to disregard the recommendations of the Commission. The Dutch Finance Minister, Gerrit Zalm, questioned whether this decision complied with the Maastricht Treaty and claimed after the decision that "all 12 members of the Euro would now pay the price of French and German fiscal incontinence".[51] As *The Economist* reported, the German and French "understanding of rules, goes a widespread feeling, is that they apply to everybody else".[52] As it was also argued: "This is not the end of the European Union's Stability and Growth Pact, but it is probably the beginning of the end."[53]

The Stability Pact, which was originally introduced to coordinate national fiscal policies in EMU, had failed dismally in its primary duty. Even the threat of financial sanctions for breaking the rules did not deter some Member States from running overly expansive fiscal policies for the final phase of the sanction mechanism was applied not once since its establishment in 1997. Apparently, without using the sanction procedure the objective of stable budgetary policy in EMU seems "toothless". Although Germany and France escaped the implementation of the sanction mechanism three times in succession in the Ecofin Council, other EU institutions and Member States should not have allowed them to run into major debt and have deficit stocks above the fiscal rules. In France, the deficit was 3.1 percent of GDP in 2002 and 4.1 percent in 2003, whereas Germany had a deficit of 3.5 percent in 2002 and 3.9 percent in 2003. The debt ratio of Germany also exceeded the 60.0 percent limit in 2002 (60.8%) and 2003 (64.2%), whereas France broke the debt rule for the first time in 2003 (63.0%). The flexibility allowed came as good news for Eichel and he argued that "the rules of the Stability Pact should not be implemented mechanically without any interpretation".[54] According to him, Germany had saved enough and thus, "the government has done everything to keep the budgetary deficit within the limit".[55] Germany also argued in the Stability Programme in December 2003 that the low-growth period, which had lasted three years, had had a critical impact on its ability to maintain a stable fiscal policy. Although Germany estimated the economy to have an upward trend with a high growth of 2.5 percent in 2004, it would break the rules (deficit 4.0% and debt 65.0%) again. The German government presented an Updated Stability Programme already in January 2004 in which it lowered the growth expectation from 2.5 to 1.5–2.0 percent for 2004. Despite the less favourable outlook, it kept the deficit and debt targets unchanged by announcing that it would adopt "additional measures to ensure its commitments" and that "the deficit develops at a faster pace in the direction of a close to balance position".[56]

European guidelines for German national economic reforms IV

In late 2003 there was a change in the presidency of the common monetary policy when the first President of the ECB, Wim Duisenberg, retired and the President of the French Central Bank, Jean-Claude Trichet, took over the single-currency area on 1 November. While Duisenberg had promoted the priority of price stability in 1999–2003, Trichet was believed to support a more overall growth approach, which would be based on his work in the French Central Bank; a change in the personal focus of the ECB President on the monetary policy was thus feasible. Although price stability remained as the first priority, it was still considered that the personal view of the new leader would support European policy mix for stronger stability and growth, the need of which was clearly stated in several recommendations of the European Council and the Commission. The main challenge of the ECB was still to cooperate with national fiscal authorities and strengthen economic stability in the Euro area in the circumstances where large Member States had not been successful in complying with the fiscal rules of the Stability Pact: a successful European policy mix could markedly improve stability and growth.

In economic conditions where prolonged low growth caused financial difficulties and slowed down the convergence process in the Euro area, the Commission introduced the broad economic policy guidelines for 2003–2005 to the Ecofin Council in April 2003. Firstly, the Commission made recommendations to achieve higher employment and for national employment policies to allow for a reasonable economic benefit for working by reforming the incentives of taxation and social benefits. Secondly, it was concerned about the high inflation rate and reminded the ECB that "monetary authorities should pursue price stability and, subjected to this being achieved, support the general economic policies".[57] Thirdly, it also argued that it was the macroeconomic policy-making in the Member States that would "play a key role in sustaining growth and employment and in preserving price stability".[58] Fourthly, it renewed its previous requirements that Member States should "maintain budgetary positions close to balance or in surplus throughout the economic cycle", "take all the necessary measures to ensure an annual improvement in the cyclically-adjusted budget position of at least 0.5 percent of GDP", and "avoid procyclical policies that counteract the full and symmetric play of the automatic stabilisers over the cycle".[59] In the proposal for the country-specific recommendations for Germany, the Commission was satisfied with Agenda 2010 and its far-reaching impact because it could "constitute important steps towards solving Germany's structural problems".[60] However, it urged Germany to continue the reforms of the Agenda 2010 to "reform the tax-benefit system", "ensure that wages reflect productivity", "improve job search assistance" and "encourage businesses to invest".[61] The Commission also urged Germany to reduce "the cyclically-adjusted deficit by at least one percentage point of GDP between the end of 2003 and 2005".[62]

In the fifth Public Finances in EMU 2004 in June 2004, the Commission considered that although Germany and France had produced "the most significant deficits", the enlarged EU had increased pressures for economic monitoring. The Commission expected that 2004 and 2005 would not be favourable for fiscal convergence and Germany and France would have deficits above the limit. Thus, in coming years it would be very challenging to reach a balanced fiscal position in EMU. However, it argued that "it is vital for Member States to reach budget positions which ensure that the automatic stabilisers work freely, and decrease the risk of unsustainable public finances in the light of ageing populations, and if the composition of the adjustment is right, would contribute to achieving over the next few years the Lisbon objectives of high growth and employment rates".[63] Most significantly, the Commission made three crucial findings in the wake of the latest fiscal surveillance on 25 November 2003. Firstly, it believed that "the processes underlying the coordination of economic policies in the EU had proven ineffective at times". Secondly, it argued that "the procedural and numerical rules which aim at ensuring fiscal discipline as an instrument for higher growth and stability have shown shortcomings".[64] Thirdly, it stated that "the authority and the instruments entrusted respectively to the Commission and to the Council" would require clarification and in this process, "the European Constitution is an important first step".[65] The Commission thus emphasised the concrete and immediate need for reforming institutional fiscal policy coordination under the Stability Pact on the one hand and the implementation of the fiscal rules in Member States on the other.

Institutional power struggle over European economic monitoring

In early January 2004 the Commission announced that it considered taking the failure of the Ecofin Council on 25 November 2003 to act under Article 232 of the Nice Treaty before the European Court of Justice. The Commission was disappointed at the politically-oriented decision not to apply the sanction mechanism to Germany and France, although they clearly broke the debt and deficit rules. The Commission submitted the appeal to the Court on 27 January 2004. In legal terms, the Commission claimed in the appeal that the Court should a) annul the decisions of the Ecofin Council not to adopt the recommendations of the Commission under Article 104(8) and Article 104(9) and b) annul the conclusions of the Ecofin Council insofar as they involved the excessive deficit procedure. The Ecofin Council rejoined that the Court should a) declare the action inadmissible or b) dismiss it. In simple terms, the case dealt with the procedure of the Stability Pact and with the question of whether the Ecofin Council had acted legally in deciding not to implement the Commission's recommendations on 25 November 2003. What has to be noted is that the Court was not asked to consider Germany and France as individual cases; the focus was on the legal dimension of the system of fiscal policy co-ordination. The Court was asked to give a ruling on the situation arising from the institutional power struggle between the Commission and the Ecofin Council. In Juncker's words, in this power struggle "it is impossible for normal people to understand what the fundamental basis of this issue is".[66]

The Commission argued that when the Ecofin Council did not adopt the Commission's recommendations, which argued that Germany and France had not taken effective national measures, it implied that both Member States had in fact taken effective measures. Although the Ecofin Council rejected the recommendations after the vote, it itself still simultaneously announced similar recommendations to Germany and France under Article 104(7). Procedurally, the Ecofin Council cannot adopt recommendations, amend or modify previously given recommendations unless the Commission first proposes them and in this case, the Commission did not propose new recommendations. Thus, the Commission believed that the Ecofin Council should have proceeded further under Article 104 and adopt Article 104(8) and Article 104(9) instead of deciding to hold the excessive deficit procedure in abeyance by issuing new recommendations. For the Commission, the Ecofin Council should have given notice to Germany and France with a specific deadline to put an end to their deficits under Article 104(9). However, the Ecofin Council argued that its decision on 25 November 2003 not to comply with the Commission's recommendations could not be considered any actionable decision. Thus, the Commission could not refer to Article 232 and its definition of failure to act. The Ecofin Council considered that its conclusions on the excessive deficit procedure were political and they did not create legal consequences and they did not prejudice the right and power of the Commission. The Ecofin Council also argued that it could hold the excessive deficit procedure in abeyance under Article 9(1) of Regulation 1467/97. Regarding the recommendations previously given under Article 104(7), the Ecofin Council claimed that the conditions in Germany and France had significantly changed by November 2003, and thus it was feasible to make new recommendations.

The Court started to resolve the issue by analysing Article 104 of the Maastricht Treaty and other Council Regulations. The Commission contended that the Ecofin Council had not fulfilled its duty under 104(8) and 104(9) of the Treaty. The former Article states that the Ecofin Council may make its recommendation public, and the latter specifies that the Ecofin Council may issue notice with a time limit to reduce the deficit ratio in a Member State. In addition, the Council Regulation on "Speeding up and Clarifying the Implementation of the Excessive Deficit Procedure" and its Article 9(1) states that there are only two situations when the procedure of the excessive deficit procedure can be held in abeyance: a) if the Member State acts in compliance with recommendations under Article 104(7) and b) if the Member State acts in compliance with notices under Article 104(9). In its twenty-page judgment on 13 July 2004, the Court stated that although the Ecofin Council had the responsibility for making final decision in the excessive deficit procedure, the procedure was a process in specific stages culminating in concrete sanctions under Article 104(11). The Court considered that the Ecofin Council on 25 November 2003, in reality, modified the recommendations that were previously issued under Article 104(7): a procedure that required a new proposal from the Commission. Thus, the decision of the Ecofin Council to adopt the modified recommendations under Article 104(7) instead of proceeding with Article 104(8) and Article 104(9) as proposed by the Commission was "unlawful". The Court thus stated that a) the action of the Commission was inadmissible insofar as it sought annulment of the failure of the Ecofin Council to adopt the recommendations of the Commission under Article 104(8) and Article 104(9), and b) the Court annulled the conclusions of the Ecofin Council's decision adopted on Germany and France under Article 104(7).[67]

Furthering structural reforms for a better national outlook in 2004

The major cuts in social benefits caused increasing political problems in the German government. Due to the domestic pressures, Schröder decided to step down from the leadership of the SPD. He considered that acting as a party leader together with pushing through politically painful reforms had taken too much time and power from the work of the Chancellor. Schröder left party politics to the new SPD party leader, Franz Müntefering, who took over the party on 21 March 2004. However, it was still Schröder who had to justify the reforms to the trade unions and to the left-wing of the SPD party. Agenda 2010 was heavily dependent on the political support from the trade unions and without Agenda 2010 the reforms would remain only superficial without any major impact on growth. Schröder and the Federation of German Trade Unions (*Deutscher Gewerkschaftsbund*), which represented the trade unions IG Metall and Verdi (*Vereinte Dienstleistungsgewerkschaft*), had a meeting (*SPD-Gewerkschaftsrat*) on 5 July 2004. The President of the Federation of German Trade Unions, Michael Sommer, the President of Verdi, Frank Bsirske, and the President of IG Metall, Jürgen Peters, wanted to discuss labour policy with Schröder because the government had undermined the position of the employed and unemployed persons too much.[68] The introduction of unemployment benefit II would, in the worst-case scenario, force more than 3 million people to reorganise their personal economic planning.[69] The trade unions were also concerned about the plan that would increase the working hours in a working week and introduce a working week with one free day less. The discussion of increasing flexibility on the labour market was started by the biggest German companies, General Motors and Karstadt Quelle, which argued that increasing the working week from 35 to 40 hours or even to 45 hours would increase productivity and competitiveness.[70] In Schröder's view, the discussion between 35 and 45 hours in a working week was an inadequate approach because working week should be decided according to the existing needs thus allowing more local flexibility to decide the working times.[71]

When formulating the objectives of the Economic Plan 2004–2008 and the Annual Economic Report 2005 Eichel acknowledged that there were some positive signs of a recovery in domestic demand and exports in the German economy, which could eventually start a new upswing in 2005.[72] The government would still require net borrowing over the whole period although the amount would diminish from 29.3 billion in 2004 to 19.5 billion Euros in 2008.[73] The Annual Economic Report 2005 continued to implement Agenda 2010 through which the government furthered reforms in public finances, unemployment and health benefits and pensions. The government also completed the final phase of the Tax Reform 2000, which had played a key role in financial reforms since 1999. The total impact of the tax reforms of the Schröder governments had been about 52 billion Euros from 1999. After four consecutive low-growth years 2001–2004, the German economy was expected to have a more positive growth rate of 2.0 percent in 2005. Based on Agenda 2010, the Hartz IV reform in 2005 was set to modernise services and benefits for the long-term unemployed. Hartz IV was one of the most crucial elements of the Hartz proposals because it created totally new nation-wide job centres to coordinate unemployment benefits and social security systems. Unemployment benefit

II, which combined previous unemployment benefits and social benefits into a single benefit, meant that the amount of benefits diminished on a monthly basis, thus increasing the economic incentives for finding work.

Of all the reforms of Schröder's second government, the labour policy met with the strongest resistance by far right from the introduction of the Hartz Report. The public did not understand why the government had to cut the size of the public sector to follow European fiscal rules strictly and without any exception although the national and regional economies had severe problems. In addition to the government's reforms, large companies promoted the idea of a longer working week. As a response, trade unions organised major demonstrations in Dresden and Leipzig in July and August 2004 that protested the Hartz IV reforms, the launch of unemployment benefit II, the creations of the mini- and midi-jobs and the so-called 2-Euro jobs.[74] Due to the mistrust in the public policy, Schröder's SPD party suffered major setbacks in regional elections in the New and the Old Länder in 2004 and 2005. The loss of the SPD party was 5.7 percentage points in North Rhein-Wesphalia, 13 percentage points in Saarland, 10 percentage points in Brandenburg and 4 percentage points in Thüringen.[75] The election results showed that the German public had rejected the "push-through" cuts in public services carried out by the present government. Schröder still responded to the results in September 2004 by saying that the support from the media and public had not been good although he "has tried to explain the rationale for the reforms for two years" but "the reform course has to continue".[76] However, due to the SPD's biggest defeat to the CDU for 50 years in the elections in North Rhein-Westphalia in May 2005, Schröder was forced to take a political risk and announce his intention to have premature parliamentary elections in September 2005 instead of September 2006. Declining economy, increasing unemployment and major cuts in public services did not provide the support required for Schröder's re-election but Angela Merkel and the CDU party took over the leadership in Germany in October 2005.

On the other hand, the associations of employers warned the government not to stop or postpone the economic and structural changes that they considered crucial for the growth and competitiveness of the economy. The President of the German Association of Chambers of Commerce and Industry (DIHK), Ludwig Georg Braun, argued that "we do not have money any more to maintain the existing unemployment benefit system".[77] Since the labour market had not contributed to the national competitiveness, but had only caused additional costs, the economic system required a thorough reform. Michael Rogowski, the President of the Federation of German Industries (BDI), also argued that regional elections in some Bundesländer should not have any influence on the reform policy chosen by the government. In his view, "the postponing of reforms would mean a downturn for Germany".[78] The labour market required new flexible instruments although the trade unions and the public were critical towards them.

The government thus faced harsh criticism both inside and outside Germany. The public, the trade unions and the opposition parties criticised the extent and speed of the reforms, whereas the Commission and German companies wanted to hasten national reforms. Due to the major criticism, Eichel announced that despite the cuts in public spending Germany exceeded the deficit criterion for the third time in a row in 2004. Eichel, however, was satisfied that tax reforms and other fiscal measures had been effective and the trend in the deficit had turned positive, declining from 3.9 percent in 2003 to 3.7 percent of GDP in 2004. In his view, the government should continue fiscal stabilisation but meeting the deficit rule through whatever actions and costs would be "unwise".[79] Eichel was convinced that there would be an upswing in 2005 and that the deficit would be below the limit. Although the government had run a strict fiscal policy, the net borrowing was still 40 billion in 2004 and 30 billion Euros in 2005; a high deficit even if compared to the period of Finance Minister Waigel in the mid-1990s.

Preparing for the "softening" of the European fiscal rules

At its 100th meeting on 16 June 2004, the Financial Planning Council expressed great concern over how to define effective German economic strategy and simultaneously take into account the policy guidelines of the EU when dealing with long-term stability problems. The Financial Planning Council made three significant decisions that were expected to support the government's effort to achieve stable budgetary policy in EMU. Firstly, the Financial Planning Council reconfirmed in the wake of the Ecofin Council meeting on 25 November 2003 that the federal government, the Bundesländer and the municipalities were responsible for implementing national budgetary policy under the Stability Pact. Secondly, the Financial Planning Council regarded the reduction of the deficit as an essential objective. It clearly stated that "the collective objective of the federal government, the Bundesländer and the municipalities is to bring the deficit below the three percent rule by 2005".[80] It also declared that all governmental levels have to respect the golden rule of public finance as defined in Article 115 of the German Constitution. Finally, the Financial Planning Council agreed that the increase in public expenditure would be maintained within 1.0 percent of GDP a year by 2006.

When fiscal problems escalated simultaneously in Germany and France the Commission started to think about the idea of reforming the Stability Pact. Prodi's Commission, whose term ended on 22 November 2004, thought that it could still seek a consensus on reforming the fiscal rules so that all Member States could make stronger commitment to them. The Commission held a special news conference on 3 September 2004 in which it presented a totally new Communication on how the Stability Pact should be improved. The Communication, which was the concrete start for reforming the rules, did not come as a surprise because in fact, the Commission already implied in its annual financial report Public Finances in EMU 2004 and the Communication of 24 June 2004 that the rules should be reformed towards better national implementation.[81] According to Prodi, "it is my firm belief that these proposals will provide for a stronger and more credible Pact".[82] Commissioner for Economic and Monetary Affairs, Joaquín Almunia, who was Solbes's successor in charge of fiscal affairs in the EU, introduced this new "Communication for Stronger Economic and Budgetary Coordination". Almunia believed that the proposal would "support macroeconomic stability, ensure sustainable public finances and contribute to the improvement of the EU's growth potential and the realisation of the Lisbon agenda".[83] The basis for the proposal was the fact that some Member States had been unable to comply with the collectively set rules because of the low-growth years and even stagnation in those Member States.

The suggestions in the Communication were based on four main objectives. Firstly, the Commission emphasised that Member States should focus more on the deficit and debt dynamics and the sustainability of public finances in national economic policy-making. Secondly, the Commission considered that the country-specific circumstances should be taken more into account when setting economic objectives for Member States. Thirdly, the country-specific circumstances should also be more thoroughly analysed when considering the implementation of the excessive deficit procedure under the Stability Pact. Finally, Member States should prepare more effectively for the coming financial burden of population ageing and a downturn in economically good times. All in all, the Commission believed that by reforming the interpretation of the fiscal rules, exceptional economic circumstances and medium-term economic objectives, the credibility of the Stability Pact could still be regained and strengthened. According to Almunia, "it is also clear that we cannot rely exclusively on one instrument, the Stability and Growth Pact, to coordinate our economic policies. We need to use more effectively the broad economic policy guidelines, an instrument that by nature is more flexible".[84]

In the informal meeting of the Ecofin Council in Scheveningen in the Netherlands on 10 and 11 September 2004 the EU Finance Ministers had an opportunity to give their first views on the Commission's suggestions. The Finance Ministers shared a relatively large consensus on the Communication and how the implementation of the Stability Pact should be strengthened. As a concrete result, the Ecofin Council outlined six key issues regarding the reform of the fiscal rules and the practical implementation of the Stability Pact in its meeting on 16 November 2004 that, according to the Ecofin Council, should be modified: a) the avoidance of pro-cyclical national fiscal policies, b) the definition of budgetary objectives, c) the definition of the debt and deficit criteria, d) the implementation of the excessive deficit procedure, e) the implementation of national structural reforms, and f) the improvement of European economic policy coordination.[85]

These reform plans came as good news for Germany and France, which had had the most problems with the Stability Pact. The German and French governments were delighted at the idea that the "one-size-fits-all" rules for deficit and debt had been questioned even by the Commission itself. According to the plans, major differences in economic trends would have an impact on how the Commission would interpret the medium-term economic objectives and the fiscal rules of the Stability Pact. However, in Eichel's opinion, the Commission's preliminary proposal for more flexible fiscal policy coordination meant "nothing at all for the time being".[86] On the other hand, other Member States (Finland and the Netherlands), which had succeeded in adjusting their national economies to European coordination, considered that their national economic sacrifices for common economic stability would become totally useless if the rules were relaxed. Furthermore, there might occur a major conflict of economic interests if the Commission allowed some Member States excessive deficits although the ECB had strictly spoken for fiscal discipline across the EMU area. According to Trichet, "the problem with the Stability Pact is not the Pact itself but that some Member States have not implemented the Pact adequately".[87] In addition, the relaxing of the fiscal rules could result in a situation where no one took the fiscal rules as the binding guidelines for national economic policy-making, and in a prolonged low-growth period, this new and flexible interpretation of the fiscal rules could allow a major and permanent increase in debt and deficit stock above the existing numerical criteria.

Regarding the Commission's plan of relaxing the original fiscal rules, Trichet made a strongly negative comment in December 2004 that the rules were still very much needed in EMU because EMU was more than a European monetary union. According to him, EMU should be regarded as a full economic and monetary union with consistent monetary and fiscal policies in European and national policy-making. In his view, "let us never forget that we cannot have a Monetary Union (M.U.) without Economic Union (E.U.), to make a coherent and economically rational E.M.U".[88] The Bundesbank shared this view in January 2005 that the fiscal rules are crucial and they should be fully respected in national economic policy-making. The Bundesbank also expressed grave concern that relaxing the original rules could in practical terms strengthen the credibility of the Stability Pact. The system of fiscal policy coordination was endangered by the critical economic developments under the Stability Pact and relaxing the rules, as proposed by the Commission, could finally lead to a dramatic situation where fiscal and monetary policies would face a major conflict of interest. For the Bundesbank, the primary problem of the Stability Pact does not relate to the formal fiscal rules but national implementation, "which will not be resolved by any proposed reforms".[89]

Unsurprisingly, Germany supported the Commission's suggestions by stating that "applying the rules merely to enforce compliance with quantitative prescriptions without precisely examining the individual case in no way makes these rules more credible, but will instead tend to make them less credible".[90] The government warned about the political and economic consequences to fiscal policy coordination of maintaining "the mechanical interpretation of the Stability Pact".[91] Schröder specified further Germany's policy on the eve of the meeting of the Ecofin Council on 18 January 2005 by arguing that the Commission should take into account in its assessment of fiscal developments in a Member State if the Member State had implemented major national economic and structural reforms, such as Agenda 2010 in Germany, and if those reforms had had an impact on the stability of public finances. According to Schröder, "a proper fiscal policy, defined by the Stability Pact, cannot be only assessed through the three percent deficit rule".[92] As Eichel still regarded the deficit and debt rules as "the core criteria of the Pact",[93] he was convinced that changes in the fiscal rules "would not mean the weakening of the Pact but its economically rational use".[94]

The rules were reformed in March 2005, long live the new rules!

To clarify fiscal policy coordination in EMU, the Ecofin Council finally decided to outline a proposal on 18 January 2005 on how to concretely improve the Stability Pact within the guidelines of the Communication of the Commission of September 2004 and the Ecofin Council decision of November 2004 by the Ecofin Council meeting on 8 March 2005.[95] However, the EU Finance Ministers wanted to secure an acceptable proposal by finalising the politically difficult question of the reform of the Stability Pact before the crucial Spring European Council in March. Despite the high hopes, the Ecofin Council could not reach a political consensus on the reform in its meetings on 17 February and 8 March.[96] These difficulties showed that a consensus among 25 EU Member States on the reform of the fiscal rules was very difficult to reach and that the possible changes could remain only minor and dealt only with clarifying some of the existing procedures. It also became obvious that where Germany and France as large Member States would have wanted to relax the strict interpretation of the rules, small Member States (Finland and the Netherlands) would have kept the rules as they were. According to Eichel, the sanction mechanism should be implemented only if national economic policy causes "gross policy errors" in EMU, meaning that if a Member State had pursued a consistent budgetary policy, even though it has resulted in exceeding the limits, the Member State could be left without penalties.[97] By contrast, the Finnish government argued that "the rules of the excessive deficit procedure under the Stability Pact should not be changed".[98] In Almunia's view, the main target of the reform should be to achieve "a very well balanced system of rules for budgetary discipline and at the same time room for manoeuvre for economic and political judgement".[99]

Eventually, the Ecofin Council in its additional 12-hour meeting in Brussels on 20 March 2005 reached agreement on a proposal for improving fiscal policy coordination within the Stability Pact. The Ecofin Council stated that the reform of the fiscal rules had become essential because the rules should be "applied across countries in a fair and consistent way", but "the aim is not to increase the rigidity or flexibility of current rules but rather to make them more effective".[100] As the full implementation of the Stability Pact had had major difficulties in some Member States, the Ecofin Council wanted to modify the rules of the Stability Pact to be more "simple", "transparent" and "enforceable" in both coordination and surveillance. The Ecofin Council reformed the original Stability Pact through three main coordination elements: a) improving European economic coordination between EU institutions and Member States, b) strengthening the preventive elements of the Stability Pact by urging Member States to attain their budgetary policies in balance, and c) clarifying the corrective arm of the Stability Pact by specifying the implementation of the excessive deficit procedure. The main difficulty in negotiations was the issue of whether to include a list of specific factors that would allow breaking the rules. Although the 3.0 percent deficit and 60.0 percent debt rules remained as the core criteria, the Ecofin Council approved a list of factors when the breaking of the rules would be possible but still not desirable. The Ecofin Council mentioned "structural reforms", "research and development", "systemic pension reforms", costs from "achieving European policy goals", costs from "the unification of Europe" and "all other relevant factors" as factors that would be taken into account in country-specific assessments under the excessive deficit procedure.

However, not to give an impression that any economic factors would automatically allow overly expansive budgetary policy the Ecofin Council wanted to clearly specify that "only major reforms, which have direct long-term cost-saving effects, including by raising potential growth, and therefore a verifiable positive impact in the long-term sustainability of public finances will be taken into account".[101] In addition, costs from achieving European policy goals and furthering the unification of Europe, such as German reunification, can only be considered "if it has a detrimental effect on the growth and fiscal burden of a Member State".[102] However, the Ecofin Council stated that these listed economic factors should not be taken into account when the Ecofin Council decided under Article 104(2) "whether a Member State has corrected its excessive deficit".[103] The factors can thus only be used as explanations for the emergence of an excessive deficit in a

Member State but not as explanatory factors when the Ecofin Council has required a Member State to correct its already existing excessive deficit. Despite the reformed rules, as before, if a Member State fails to meet the rules of the Stability Pact, the Ecofin Council "has the power to apply the available sanctions".[104] However, the Ecofin Council emphasised that the primary aim of the sanction mechanism is to "assist rather than to punish and therefore to provide incentives for Member States to pursue budgetary discipline".[105] The Spring European Council in Brussels approved the changes in the Stability Pact on 22–23 March 2005.[106]

Four main shortcomings of fiscal policy coordination still persisted. Firstly, fiscal policy coordination is only concerned about year-on-year deficit although this rule should be redefined as a medium-term target of 2–3 years. Secondly, European economic monitoring focuses only on budgetary deficits and not on public debts. Therefore, excessive debts should also be subjected to the excessive deficit procedure. Thirdly, the Ecofin Council will continue to possess final consideration in fiscal policy and thus, both the excessive deficit procedure and the early warning mechanism will be applied based on the political decision of the Ecofin Council and not on the agreement-based interpretation of the Commission. According to Artis and Corsetti's critical interpretation, "while the reform keeps the formal possibility of sanctions, events have already shown that sanctions are either not credible or subject to arbitrary political considerations which create a power divide within the Euro area".[107] Fourthly, some Member States have clearly been moving away from stable budgetary policy and sustainable public finances even under the strict original fiscal rules. Thus, it seems hard to believe that relaxing the fiscal rules alone could change the course of economic policy-making in EMU. For example, the relaxed deficit rule could result in a situation where national budgetary deficit ratios could permanently increase to a high level of 4.0–8.0 percent instead of the original 3.0 percent ratio.

As analysed in this research, the aim in European fiscal policy coordination has been to maintain a high degree of fiscal convergence and promote stability and growth throughout the EU and EMU areas; a rationale that is still valid and also recognised by the amended rules. However, the credibility of the reformed rules remains highly questionable unless Member States really commit to them. Contrary to the original strict view on breaking the rules, the changes made in the Stability Pact will now in practice allow national economic policy-making that breaks the fiscal rules as long as the deficit is minor, temporary and caused by a major downturn, major national economic and structural reforms or "other relevant factors". Eichel and Schröder can be considered the biggest winners of the new agreement because now, the fiscal rules finally and officially allow the same policy-making throughout EMU that has already been the practice in Germany since 2001. Eichel responded to this criticism of relaxing the fiscal rules by arguing that "the reform was not about allowing a license to issue more public debt".[108] The governments of the Benelux Countries also found that the reform has neither "weakened" nor "loosened" the Stability Pact. For them, the new rules "allow to take into account each country's specificities and to give to the time required for a return to a sustainable position".[109] On the other hand, the ECB raised its deep concern "about the proposed changes to the Stability and Growth Pact".[110] The ECB claimed that common economic agreements should be fully respected because "sound fiscal policy and a monetary policy geared to price stability are fundamental for the success of Economic and Monetary Union".[111] The statement clearly implies that relaxing national fiscal discipline could in reality raise fears of the possibly declining credibility of the common monetary policy, increasing interest rates and lower economic growth in EMU. Thus, the Vice-President of the ECB, Lucas Papademos, argued that "all parties to the Pact are expected to fulfil their responsibilities and implement the revised fiscal framework in a rigorous and credible manner.[112]

What is virtually certain is that excessive and increasing national debt and deficit stocks will not disappear in an instant, at least automatically. In the ECB's view, "in member countries with fiscal imbalances, the attainment of their medium-term fiscal objectives is not only contingent on the macroeconomic environment, but also requires the full and timely specification and implementation of consolidation measures".[113] The concrete reform process has clearly shown that large EMU Member States have more political and economic power and influence in the EU and EMU and they have in practice succeeded in relaxing the common criteria to better suit their own national circumstances (reuploading). As *Financial Times* ironically argued: "To the dismay again of smaller members of the Euro zone, France and Germany were also dealt a get-out-of-fiscal-jail card with the summit's relaxation of the Stability Pact's disciplines and widening of the excuses for avoiding them."[114] Now that large EMU Member States have softened the original fiscal rules of 1997 in March 2005 the question arises in what way, if at all, the new agreement will improve national economic policy-making in Germany and France and the national implementation of the Stability and Growth Pact elsewhere in EMU. *What will now happen to stability and growth in EMU?*

5.3 Economic developments and room for national fiscal flexibility

Recovering exports improving the German economic environment

Similarly to the developments during Schröder's first government in 1998–2002, the economic policy of the second government in 2003–2006 was also subjected to major uncertainties in the global and European environment. Internationally, the continual geopolitical crisis in the Middle

East, the prolonged military operation in Iraq, the high energy prices and the bird-flu epidemics in Asia made the chances of a fast recovery unlikely. In Germany, the catastrophic flood in East Germany and the threat of the expansion of the war in Iraq had a negative impact on the domestic market and the confidence of private consumption and investors over the national outlook. These unfavourable conditions were persistent and the economic activity was thus sluggish. When focusing on energy prices, the price of oil remained remarkably high since the major upturn in 2002 and continued to increase until 2005. Critical developments in Iraq and the financial and legal problems around Yukos, which is one of the world's biggest oil and gas producers, pushed the price of oil to a record high. On 17 June 2005, a barrel of crude oil in the US was at an all-time highest price of 58.60 USD. Due to the critical trends on the energy market, the ECB announced that it considered that risks of increasing inflation were stronger than so far, which could mean an increase in interest rates in the Euro area.[115] Although the economic outlook showed some positive signals for 2004 and 2005, the increasing price of oil and rapidly emerging inflation kept the pace of the recovery relatively slow in EMU.

The economic data on the components of the GDP growth shows that net exports and domestic demand developed positively in the Euro area on average in 2003 and 2004 (Figure 5.1). Domestic demand successfully compensated the decline in net exports, and the impact of net exports turned positive temporarily in early 2004. The fact that the contribution of net exports to GDP was negative for the whole of 2003 in the Euro area was an interesting finding. The fundamental factor behind diminishing net exports was the fast and strong appreciation of the Euro against the US dollar. The positive impact of domestic demand on GDP in the Euro area was primarily caused by private and public consumption in 2003 and 2004.[116] Due to the high exchange rate of the Euro, imports became favourable for EMU and thus, the Euro contributed to the domestic demand for imports. However, domestic demand did not manage to keep the output gap in balance but the gap was negative in the Euro area. The actual GDP was below the potential GDP by 1.1 percentage points in 2003 and 1.3 percentage points in 2004. According to the Commission's estimates, the output gap would also stay negative with 1.2 percentage points in 2005.[117] Given the high domestic demand, the possible recovery of net exports in 2005 could once again act as an awaited stimulus for the European economy, which has historically been dependent on export boost.

Common monetary policy and (in)stability

The economic problems in the Euro area since 2000 did not only cause fiscal problems but also the unanticipated developments challenged the common monetary policy. Surprisingly, the Euro appreciated against the US dollar from mid-2002 after declining dramatically from 1999 to 2002.

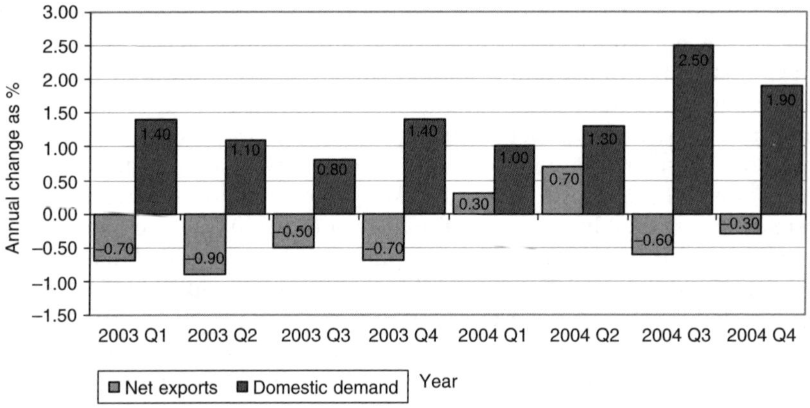

Figure 5.1 Contribution to real GDP in the Euro area 2003–2004.[118]

The Euro continued to appreciate although the economic growth in the US market was at a higher level than in the Euro area since 2001. In reality, the reasons for the appreciation of the Euro were not so much related to the Euro but to major downward pressures on the US dollar. The US dollar was falling because of a number of global and domestic uncertainties, such as the Iraq war, the potential impact of possible new terrorist attacks, the record-high price of oil, increasing current account deficit in the US budget and the expected increase in the interest rates. According to the ECB, the developments in the Euro "took place against the background of relatively high economic and geopolitical uncertainty".[119] If the US continued to run an increasing deficit in its current account, it would not be a major surprise in financial markets if the Euro-US dollar ratio would jump to a new record level in late 2005. On the other hand, an overly weak dollar and an overly strong Euro would endanger the exports of European countries outside the EMU area.

The Euro was quoted at 1.06 USD in January 2003 but after a dramatic rise, the Euro reached its highest rate of 1.3633 USD on 28 December 2004. Historically, the developments in the pound and the US dollar have been closely linked but the exchange rate trends in 2003 and 2004 did not support this historical connection at all. Although the Euro appreciated against the dollar since 2002 and most notably in 2003 and 2004, the pound did not experience the same trend. The Euro appreciated against the pound only slightly from January 2003 to May 2003 and thereafter, the Euro remained stable against the pound, whereas the Euro continued to appreciate against the dollar. The Euro depreciated against the pound from December 2003, although the Euro simultaneously reached its very high level against the dollar.

Figure 5.3 shows that although the risks for high inflation were low in the Euro area and Britain in 2003 and 2004, inflation in the Euro area

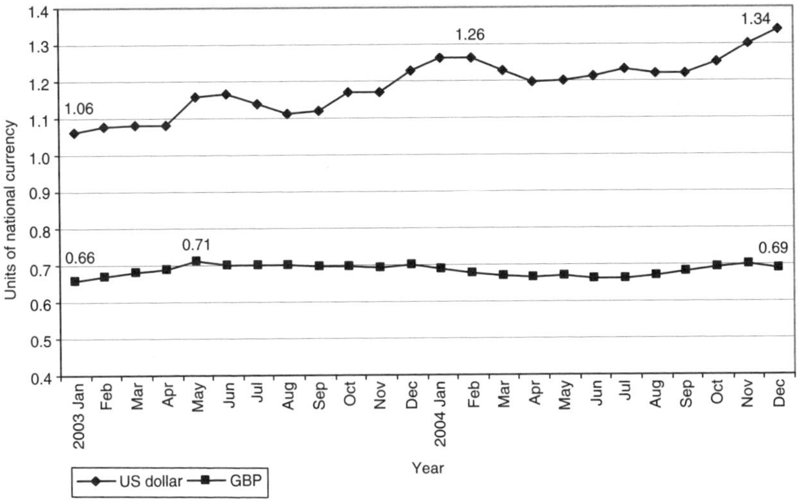

Figure 5.2 Exchange rate of the Euro 2003–2004.[120]

was still above the ultimate target of 2.0 percent. Inflation continuously exceeded the target rate of the ECB even though inflation was not lifted, for example, by high growth rates or the depreciated Euro. Duisenberg also acknowledged that "it will take inflation longer than originally expected to fall below the threshold of two percent".[121] On the other hand, the rapidly appreciated Euro, as shown in Figure 5.2, effectively eliminated the impact of the increased price of oil on the inflation. In fact, the appreciation should have reduced the pressures for a high inflation rate even more significantly, but this has not happened so far. In these circumstances, the ECB took the view that it was not only the common monetary policy but also national fiscal policies that had an essential role and the ability to "lower the likelihood of persistent inflation differentials in the Euro area".[122] In addition, the ECB released its strategy statement at the special press conference in Frankfurt on 8 May 2003 in which ECB officials confirmed that the monetary uncertainties were still under their control and being closely monitored. Duisenberg argued that "the current monetary policy stance remains consistent with the preservation of price stability over the medium term".[123] The ECB also renewed the price stability objective to be 2.0 percent or below over the medium term. According to Issing, "close to two percent is not a change, it is a clarification of what we have done so far".[124] Although the world market price of oil fell slightly by the end of 2002, the new and fast increase in the price of oil from 2003 kept inflation high.

Inflation was more favourable in Britain than in the Euro area in 2003 and 2004 although Britain had faster growth rates in the last few years. For example, the GDP rate in Britain grew 1.75 percent in 2002, 2.0 percent in 2003 and 3.25 percent in 2004. As a major policy shift, Britain changed one of its monetary fundamentals in 2003 that had a positive impact on the monetary policy. Chancellor Brown stated on 9 June 2003 that the British government and the Monetary Policy Committee had decided to replace the RPIX index (Retail Prices Index) by the CPI index (Consumer Prices Index) as the guideline for price stability in Britain. Brown also announced that the upper limit of inflation would simultaneously be dropped from 2.5 percent in terms of RPIX to 2.0 percent of CPI. This reduction in the inflation target stemmed from the fact that on average, RPIX gave some 0.5 percentage point higher inflation than CPI due to the differences in the definition of inflation components. Where the ECB uses HCPI as the measure of price stability in EMU, Britain will apply CPI from now on.

Figure 5.3 also shows that convergence in the long-term interest rates between the Euro area and Britain did not make further progress from 2003; rather, the gap in the interest rates widened in the last two years. Whereas the long-term interest rates reached the lowest level in 1999 for decades, they continuously increased from 2003 to mid-2004. The European and global economic uncertainties and the appreciated Euro pushed interest rates upwards. While the long-term interest rates in the Euro area on average were 3.69 percent in December 2004, the interest rates in Britain stood at 4.58 percent. In practice, due to the higher interest rates, debt interest payments were higher in Britain than the Euro area. On the other hand, Britain had much less debt interest to pay. The monetary envi-

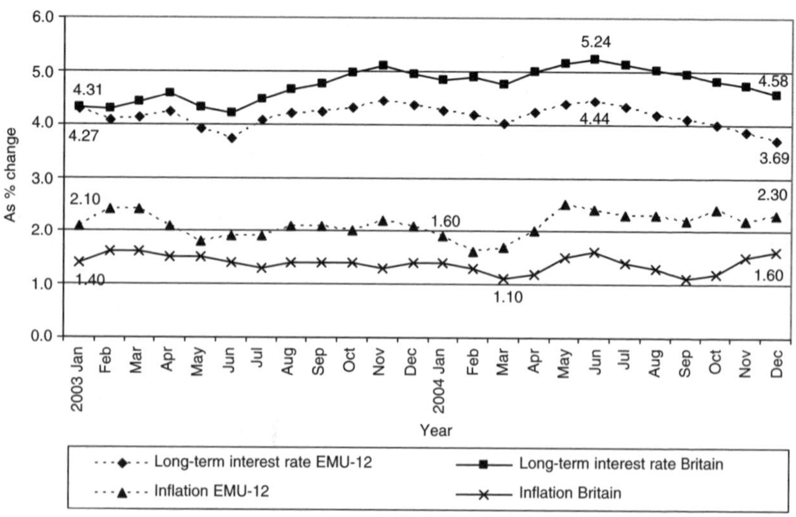

Figure 5.3 Long-term interest and inflation rates 2003–2004.[125]

ronment was exceptionally favourable with low inflation risks and low interest rates in the Euro area in 2003 and 2004 although the strong Euro counterbalanced the impact. What is worth noting is that although there have been economic shocks to the European economy, interest and inflation rates have been amazingly stable and favourable. In Duisenberg's words, "I cannot say for how long this trend remains, but I would believe that there is still a considerable timeframe".[126] The long-term interest rates are historically low, the Euro exchange rate against the US dollar is historically high and there is no immediate risk of major inflation in the Euro area although national fiscal discipline under the Stability Pact is highly questionable. Not even Issing could specifically explain this unique and complex relationship between monetary fundamentals and national fiscal policies. In his opinion, "the developments in inflation are not always dependent on the developments in fiscal policy".[127]

German budgetary policy on the edge

Compared to trends in 1998–2002, the outlook for the budgetary balance in EMU seems slightly more favourable for the end of the period 2003–2006 (Figures 5.4 and 5.5). Germany, France and the Euro area as a whole will exceed the 60.0 percent debt-to-GDP criterion during the whole four-year period. Of the three biggest economies, it is only Britain that will have no visible problems to stay within the upper limit of the debt rule, whereas Germany and France will continue to have debt difficulties under the Stability Pact at least until 2006. The public debt of Germany will stay at about 65.0 percent of GDP (65.5% in 2005 and 65.0% in 2006) although the German government has made a number of economic and structural reforms. Britain has had low debt ratios even though the debt ratio is expected to increase from 39.3 percent in 2003 to 41.1 percent in 2006.

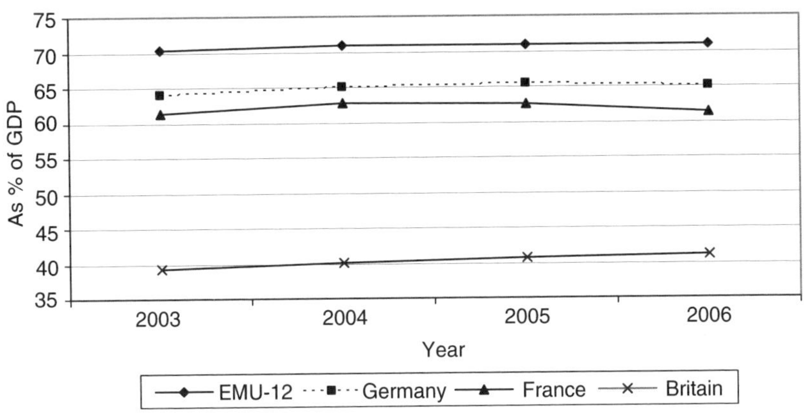

Figure 5.4 Public debt 2003–2006.[128]

The average debt in the Euro area has remained at a high level since the 1990s and the same trend will continue until 2006. Whereas the debt in the Euro area was 70.4 percent in 2003, the debt will remain at 70.9 percent until 2006. When breaking down the debt ratio in EMU, it is possible to see that for example, Belgium, Greece and Italy have no longer succeeded in cutting their debt stocks on any major scale. The debt-to-GDP ratio diminished from 100.5 percent in 2003 to 94.3 percent in 2005 in Belgium, from 103.0 percent in 2003 to 101.7 percent in 2005 in Greece and from 106.2 percent in 2003 to 106.0 percent in 2005 in Italy.

The budgetary deficit position has deteriorated in Germany, France, Britain and the Euro area as a whole from 2000 and this development has not helped these national governments to stabilise their budgetary policies in the low-growth circumstances. According to the IMF, "a public debt ration of about 60 percent and a relatively large structural budgetary deficit has restrained the use of active fiscal policy, which has been progressively tightened".[129] The ECB also urged Member States to contribute more effectively to the overall economic stability of the Euro area in national fiscal policies. In the wake of 25 November 2003, the ECB stated that "Germany and France now have to live up to their responsibilities and to honour their commitment to correct their excessive deficits as soon as possible and by 2005 at the latest".[130] Finally, the first clear signals of a more favourable economic outlook in Europe from late 2003 contributed to lowering national deficit ratios to some extent (Figure 5.5).

Although Germany reduced the deficit from 4.0 percent in 2003 to 3.5 percent in 2004, it still clearly exceeded the criterion. Germany, however, planned to reduce the deficit by 2005 to be in line with the recommendations of the Ecofin Council in November 2003. The deficit is

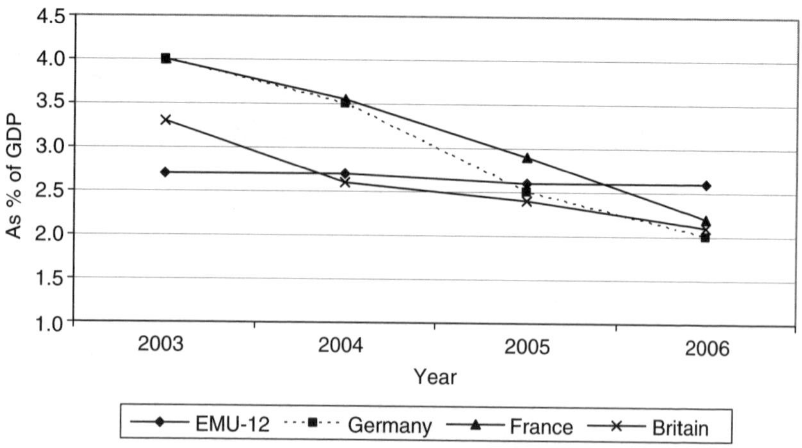

Figure 5.5 Budgetary deficit 2003–2006.[131]

expected to be 2.5 percent in 2005 and 2.0 percent in 2006: a policy target that was recently harshly criticised by the Commission's own economic forecasts.[132] Like Germany, France was also obliged to reduce the deficit under the limit by 2005 and it is expected to fall from 4.0 percent in 2003 to 2.2 percent in 2006. In Britain, the deficit will fall from 3.3 percent in 2003 to 2.1 percent in 2006. According to the British government, this positive trend in the British budgetary policy "illustrates that the government's performance against its fiscal rules, and shows that the government remains on track to meet its strict fiscal rules over the economic cycle".[133] Despite the relatively positive developments in all these three large EU Member States, the overall deficit in the Euro area will still remain high and without major reduction. While the deficit ratio in the Euro area was 2.7 percent in 2003 and 2004, the deficit will fall only slightly to 2.6 percent in 2005 and 2006. However, the Euro area on average is expected to stay within the 3.0 percent deficit limit at least until 2006.

Challenging trends in the public finances

Although Germany experienced unpredictable developments in public finance 1998–2002, the financial gap remained relatively stable apart from 2002. After 2002 the gap between expenditure and revenue, however, widened and the same trend will continue until 2006 (Figure 5.6). On the expenditure side, although the government planned to reduce public spending from 2003, the spending will not be reduced until 2006. Public spending will be reduced from 256.7 billion in 2003 to 253.6 billion Euros in 2006. Similarly, the revenue side experienced a boost from 218.1 billion in 2003 to 228.0 billion in 2004, 9.9 billion Euros up from 2003. Public revenue is first expected to increase to 236.3 billion in 2005 and then decline by 4.4 billion Euros to 231.9 billion in 2006. On the revenue side, the impact of the shortfall in tax income in 2002 and 2003 on the public finances has faded and the gap in the budget is expected to diminish by 2006. The second phase of the Tax Reform 2000 in 2003 improved domestic demand and thus the financial stability also experienced a positive trend (Figure 5.1). As an essential result, unlike in the period 1998–2002, the government will succeed in reducing the deficit from (38.6 billion) 2003 to (21.7 billion) 2006. This amount of deficit would be the lowest deficit for 14 years since 1992 (20.1 billion in 1992).

Contrary to the early years of the 21st century, the Euro area experienced positive growth trends from 2003. However, the growth did not recover from 2003 to 2004 as fast as it had weakened from 2000 to 2002. The main reason for the sluggish growth in Germany in 2003 was an unfavourable environment for exports, due largely to the appreciated Euro. The price of oil and the Euro remained high, which as key factors caused low growth rates in Germany and the Euro area. Given that the German economy grew only slightly or even negatively in 2001, 2002 and 2003, the current

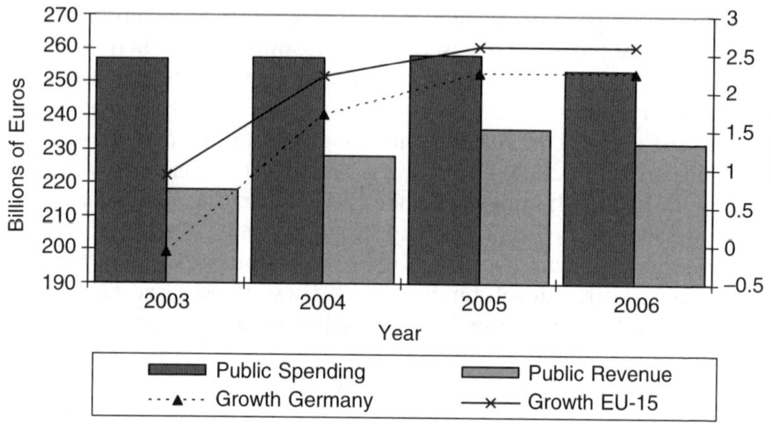

Figure 5.6 Public finance and annual growth 2003–2006.[134]

upward trend in Germany and the Euro area can be considered a good sign. Germany had a negative GDP growth rate of 0.1 percent in 2003, after which the growth rate was 1.7 percent in 2004. For 2005 and 2006, the German economy is expected to see a major boost of 2.25 percent of GDP in both years. Where the Euro area grew 0.9 percent in 2003 and 2.2 percent in 2004, the growth rate will reach 2.6 percent in 2005 and 2006. This highly positive prospect in the growth could act as a trigger for a more extensive European and German recovery after the prolonged downturn.

Figure 5.7 illustrates the trends in tax revenue and public expenditure from 2003 to 2006. The German government's plan was to reduce the GDP ratio of public expenditure and increase the public tax revenue. Duisenberg argued that the most difficult problem of the German government had been and still was to "find other supporting finance sources to compensate the tax cuts".[135] From 2000 to 2002, the government faced a situation in which the dwindling tax revenue caused major problems in public finance and the budgetary balance. For example, the Tax Reform 2000 cut the overall tax burden by 32 billion Euros in its various phases by 2003. Now, however, expectations show that the tax revenue could have a positive trend over this whole period 2003–2006 because the revenue is expected to increase from 196 billion in 2003 to as high as 221 billion Euros in 2006. Surprisingly, the overall tax burden in relation to GDP remained unchanged in 2003 and 2004 and will remain at a high level despite the government's measures. The overall tax burden was 40.7 percent in 2003, 40.4 percent in 2004 and 40.1 percent of GDP in 2005.[136] This result is a major disappointment for Schröder's governments, which have planned to stabilise the national budget primarily through tax reforms since 2000.

Contrary to the trends in the tax burden, the government has succeeded in reducing the GDP ratio of public expenditure. Whereas the expenditure

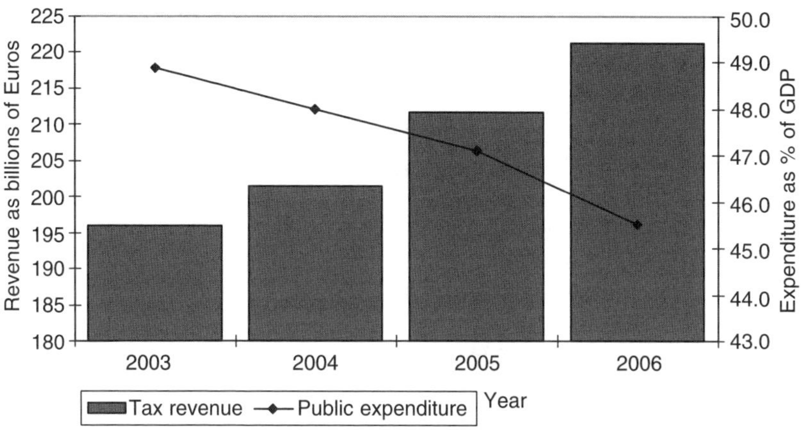

Figure 5.7 Tax revenue and public expenditure in Germany 2003–2006.[137]

was 48.9 percent of GDP in 2003 and 48.0 percent in 2004, it will drop to 45.5 percent in 2006. The major shortfall in the tax revenue in 2003, however, created political and economic pressures on Finance Minister Eichel to refocus the objectives and measures of his saving programmes. Due to the prolonged stagnation, the budget experienced a shortfall of 8.7 billion Euros in the tax revenue in 2003. In practice, the low economic activity in 2003 did not contribute to the public revenue side as much as was planned in the budget. This increased pressures to take more debt and widen the financial gap or raise taxes again. However, the President of the Federation of German Industries (BDI), Michael Rogowski, was strongly against a possible new increase in the tax rates to close the gap in the budget. According to him, "people who promote the idea of higher taxes should not be amazed by the totally lost economic growth".[138]

Improvements in the economy of the Bundesländer

Like Schröder's first government in 1998–2002, the second government also raised the political and economic need for the reconstruction of East Germany. What was notable for the New Länder was that the Solidarity Pact ensured major financial support from the federal government. The Solidarity Pact, which was agreed in the federal budget of 2002, allocated 159 billion Euros of public finance for the New Länder by 2019. Figure 5.8 shows the positive developments in the financial position of five New Länder and 11 Old Länder from 2003 to 2006. The biggest reduction in deficit in the New Länder will be in Saxony, where the deficit is expected to diminish from 391 million in 2003 to 100 million in 2006, a reduction in the deficit of a total of 74.4 percent in four years. The Old Länder will have an even more favourable trend than the New Länder. In fact, all the Old

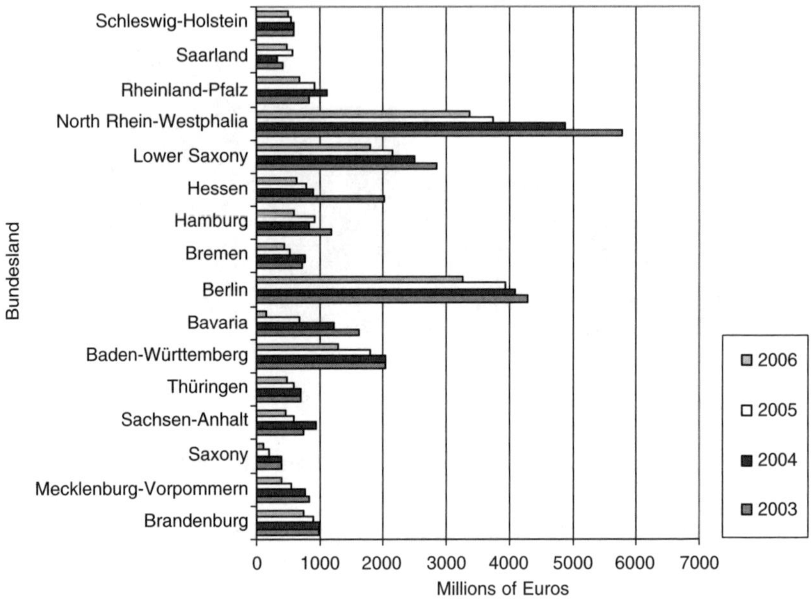

Figure 5.8 The financial position of Old and New Länder 2003–2006.[139]

Länder with large deficit stocks will succeed in reducing deficit from 2003 to 2006. For example, the deficit will fall from 5790 million in 2003 to 3370 million Euros in 2006 in North Rhein-Westphalia. As a whole, the financial position in the New Länder will improve from a deficit of 3671 million in 2003 to 2173 million in 2006. In the Old Länder, the deficit will fall from 22,300 million Euros in 2003 to 13,200 million in 2006, to almost the half of the existing overall deficit.

Stagnation on the national labour market

Table 5.2 summarises recent developments in labour market indicators in Germany and the Euro area from 2003 to 2004. In short, the national labour policy has not experienced any major improvement between Schröder's first government in 1998–2002 and his second government in 2003–2006 despite the governments' massive reform plans. On the one hand, sluggish economic growth has not helped create a declining trend in the unemployment rate in Germany. On the other hand, one of the main reasons for not having sizeable improvements in the unemployment rate in the Euro area owes much to the fact that many Member States have already reached a relatively low unemployment rate and thus, a major and fast decline in the overall unemployment rate is not likely. For example, according to the Bundesbank, "Ireland, Luxemburg, the Netherlands and Austria have virtually reached full employment".[140]

Table 5.2 Labour market indicators in Germany and EMU 2003–2004.[141]

	Labour productivity EMU-12	Real unit labour cost EMU-12	Unemployment rate EMU-12	Unemployment rate Germany
2003 Q1	0.6	1.8	8.7	11.2
2003 Q2	0.0	2.5	8.8	10.5
2003 Q3	0.2	2.4	8.8	10.3
2003 Q4	0.5	1.6	8.8	10.1
2004 Q1	1.1	1.0	8.9	11.0
2004 Q2	1.8	0.3	9.0	10.4
2004 Q3	1.4	0.1	8.9	10.5
2004 Q4	0.9	1.1	8.9	10.5

As illustrated in Figure 5.1 on improving trends in domestic demand and net exports in EMU, it could have been expected that there could also have been a cyclical upswing in employment in 2004. However, the most recent data on unemployment show that there will not be a fast and major turn in a positive direction on the labour market in Germany and the Euro area (Table 5.2). The unemployment rate in the Euro area increased from 8.7 percent in the first quarter of 2003 to 8.9 percent in the fourth quarter of 2004. The unemployment rate in Germany has varied between 11.0 and 10.0 percent in 2003–2004, but it experienced a fast and dramatic increase to 12.6 percent and 5.2 million unemployed in February 2005. However, in general terms, although the economic activity showed some signs of an economic recovery, which should have had an impact on employment, the unemployment rate remained unchanged in Germany in 2003 and 2004. In other words, the number of unemployed persons has not decreased as the German government would have hoped, but the fact is that the major reforms in the national labour policy require more time to be fully carried out.

If productivity continues to grow as the latest data shows, there could be a positive trend in employment in Germany and the Euro area. In the Euro area, on average, labour productivity has recovered from the fall prior to 2003. For example, labour productivity grew from 0.6 percent in the first quarter of 2003 to 1.8 percent in the second quarter of 2004, being the highest growth since the start of EMU (Figure 5.9). The impact of low economic growth and low growth in productivity on the labour policy is that these trends have kept the increase in wages relatively low. In the Euro area, real unit labour costs fell from 1.8 percent in the first quarter of 2003 to only 0.1 percent in the third quarter of 2004. Low and uncertain prospects in production and investment have forced the labour market to keep pay increases moderate, but rapid economic recovery would in turn increase salaries and real unit labour costs. Based on these empirical

- Major national economic and structural reforms
- National failure to comply with the European fiscal rules
- Institutional failure to coordinate national fiscal policies in EMU
- Large versus small E(M)U Member States
- National versus supranational economic interests
- First signals of improving economic outlook
- Reuploading national interests into the common fiscal policy-making
- Reinterpreting the fiscal rules of the Stability and Growth Pact

Figure 5.9 Summary: Reuploading German national "fits" 2003–2005.

findings it is possible to argue that the German labour market is in stagnation. Stagnation on the labour market, in practice, means that there is no need for additional labour force and investments due to the uncertainties in economic activity domestically and globally. The Research Institute for the World Economy in Kiel in Germany has estimated that the German economy will continue to experience low growth rates in the coming few years. The Institute has also estimated that the GDP growth would shrink from 1.9 percent in 2004 to only 1.2 percent in 2005.[142] This would be a major setback for the government and would cause increasing political and economic problems for Schröder and Eichel.

5.4 Reuploading German national "fits" 2003–2005

National economic realities in reuploading

Whereas the analysis of German fiscal policy-making in Sections 5.1 and 5.2 highlighted the importance of the timely effective policy actions under fiscal policy coordination, Section 5.3 made it clear that the economic trends were far from favourable to the reform policy of Schröder's second government in 2003–2005. On the one hand, it was Schröder's first government that failed to achieve stable fiscal policy during the last upswing in 1998–2000; a price that the economy now pays in terms of increasing fiscal problems and unemployment rates in EMU. On the other hand, three years of stagnation did not make it any easier for the government to maintain stable fiscal policy and comply with the Stability Pact at the same time. In the government's view, "the average annual increase in Gross Domestic Product in Germany since 1991 stands at only just under 1.5 percent", which "reflects a range of special factors, in particular economic adjustment in consequence of German reunification and the recent weakness of global growth".[143] In reality, the annual GDP growth in Germany has not been so low from the historical perspective after all. The average GDP growth rate in Germany was 1.8 percent between 1975 and 1984 and 2.7 percent between 1985 and 1995.[144] In the period 1996–2006, the economy grew 1.3 percent on average. Thus, Germany has experienced only few relatively low-growth years in EMU, not a major and prolonged recession. Although the low growth rates have created a need to issue more public debt and allow the deficit to grow in EMU, even German politicians have been aware of the fact that rapidly mounting debt and deficit stock are no long-term solution in the low-growth circumstances. In the short term, debt and deficit could increase economic activity but overly expansive fiscal policy in the long term would only result in worse developments. Now, the estimates show that the deficit ratio will decline, whereas the debt ratio will still stay at a high level of over 60.0 percent.

If national growth and fiscal developments were not favourable for the German economy in the EMU era, neither did the common monetary policy of the ECB manage to create an optimal environment for national growth and stability right from the start of EMU.[145] Firstly, despite the ultimate objective of the ECB, inflation in the Euro area exceeded the 2.0 percent target in 2000–2005, meaning that the ECB had clearly failed to attain the inflation within its own policy guidelines in EMU. Secondly, the ECB also made a serious miscalculation with the interest rate policy in the end of 2000. Interest rates did not then come down as rapidly as they should have after the upswing in 1998–2000 suddenly turned into a major and now prolonged downturn in the Euro area. This policy failure caused a more persistent decline in the European economy than would otherwise have been possible. Now the interest rates have come down and they have been at the lowest levels for decades, but the main damage to the European economy was already done in late 2000 and early 2001. Under the current economic conditions, according to the Vice-President of the Bundesbank, Jürgen Stark, any changes towards higher interest rates in EMU would "really challenge Member States".[146] Thirdly, the exchange rate problems that the Euro had right from the beginning of EMU completely turned around in 2002. A totally new problem in EMU was caused by the fact that the Euro appreciated so notably against the US dollar from 2002. However, Duisenberg was not concerned about the Euro because, according to him, "the speed at which it is strengthened is almost equal to the speed at which it declined two years ago".[147] Since the Euro reached its highest quote against the US dollar in December 2004, the Euro has depreciated slightly, but only slightly. In short, the most crucial finding is, however, that the Euro area has no longer had any traditional incredibility problems in its external monetary policy. Although the credibility for national fiscal discipline within the Stability Pact in EMU was in practice lost on 25 November 2003, the exchange rate of the Euro did not show any signs of lacking credibility: a fact that speaks for the increasing faith in the Euro and the common monetary policy of the ECB.

The way in which these critical national and European economic (fiscal and monetary) realities and developments relate to reuploading of fiscal policy coordination in EMU is that the reuploading process characterises the intimate relationship between the common economic objectives and national economic interests, commitments and policy-making in a unique way. By exceeding the fiscal limits of the Stability Pact in three consecutive years, intentionally or not, Germany as a politically and economically large and powerful EMU Member State believed that it could contribute to relaxing the strict fiscal rules by using the critical economic circumstances as the fundamental explanation and the Ecofin Council as the fundamental institutional body. Using the low-growth period 2001–2004 as the primary explanation for overly expansive national fiscal policy Germany assumed that the reinterpretation of the rules of the Stability Pact in the EU institutions would take place without any major difficulties, and the reinterpretation of the rules would also be transferred into a more flexible implementation of the Stability Pact than defined in the original agreement of 1997. Thus, as in the process of uploading the Stability Pact in 1995–1997, Germany tried once again to include its own national interests in the mechanisms of European fiscal policy coordination by reforming the common fiscal rules to better comply with its own reformulated national interests. In Dyson's words, "in effect, Germany is potentially the major standard-setter and policy broker in the Euro zone".[148] In agreement with Dyson, this reuploading process is the theoretical definition of the concrete policy-making process by which Germany, after breaking common standards and policies, has contributed to establishing new standards and policies within fiscal policy coordination in EMU (Figure 5.9). Now, this theoretical process of reuploading, introduced by Germany, has experienced the concrete process, for in March 2005 Member States eventually reformed the fiscal rules and the implementation of the Stability Pact to be more suitable for the current economic circumstances and more favourable for the national economies in a downturn.

Much at stake in Germany as the engine of the whole E(M)U economy

Regarding Germany's broad politico-economic environment, there are several factors that have a major impact on the performance of the German economy as an integral part of EMU in the immediate future. Firstly, economic growth has not yet recovered in Germany since the collapse in late 2000 although the monetary environment with low interest rates and stable inflation was favourable in the period 2003–2006, and although the EU Enlargement has opened up new market areas in particular for the biggest companies in Europe for German companies. As Germany, as the promoter and/or brake of the whole European economy, has experienced the state of stagnation, many other Member States have also had a low pace of growth in recent years. Although the growth in the whole Euro area was low in the period 2002–2006, European economies could benefit from the more favourable environment of 2007. Secondly, although the German government has focused on labour policy, unemployment has been high and in fact, it jumped to a record high level in 2005 and 2006. It seems that the national labour policy, as active as it has been, has remained ineffective and has not succeeded in supporting productivity and growth at all and *vice versa*.[149] Thirdly, public debt and budgetary deficit ratios have been high and have increased during Schröder's two governments. Although the deficit ratio is now expected to show a declining trend, furthering fiscal convergence is still a major challenge for the German government. To effectively pursue a stability-oriented and growth-supportive economic policy, the government should, for example, have used more public investments for employment in the downturn after 2000 but the deteriorated budgetary position did not allow any additional financial room for this: a fact that once again speaks for sustainable fiscal policy in the national economy in EMU.

Fourthly, most monetary policy instruments, price stability and interest rates have been favourable in EMU although the slowness of the ECB to respond to the downturn of 2000 exacerbated the decline. Interest rates are now favourable but the inflation persistently above 2.0 percent constitutes a risk to the economy and requires active monetary monitoring in EMU. Fifthly, the future of the exchange rate of the Euro remains unclear. Whereas the Euro was rated at 1.1789 USD on 1 January 1999, it sank to 0.8252 USD on 26 October 2000, but it rose abruptly to 1.3633 USD on 28 December 2004. Further appreciation of the Euro could freeze once and for all the economic recovery already achieved, but a sudden and strong depreciation of the Euro against the US dollar could, conversely, act as a long-waited economic stimulus for European and German exports, but it would in turn totally freeze the US economy and increase the major budgetary deficit in the US. Thus, the impact of the rapid depreciation of the Euro down to 1.00 USD or its fast appreciation up to 2.00 USD together with the continually rising price of oil would cause dramatic problems not only on both sides of the Atlantic but also throughout the world. Sixthly, one of the biggest threats to the German economy at the moment seems alongside the exchange rate policy to be the price of oil. The politico-economic developments suggest that the price of oil may remain at a record high for quite some time but a major reduction in political uncertainties and geopolitical tensions, for example in Iraq and the Middle East, could contribute to more favourable prospects in the world oil market.

Seventhly, the effectiveness of institutional fiscal policy coordination remains unclear although the judgment of the European Court of Justice in July 2004 finally ended the institutional power struggle between the Commission and the Ecofin Council over fiscal policy coordination, or did it? Although the Court considered that the decision of the Ecofin Council on 25 November 2003 was procedurally incorrect, it clearly emphasised that the Ecofin Council had flexibility in the excessive deficit procedure when it defined measures and deadlines for Member States. Surprisingly, although the judgment of the Court supported the Commission's view,

France and Germany and even the Ecofin Council were proclaimed political winners, and they all argued that the Court ruling had strengthened the implementation of the Stability Pact. Now, after the ruling, the responsibility to find a political solution to restore the credibility and effectiveness of institutional fiscal policy coordination between the Commission and the Ecofin Council is in the hands of Barroso's Commission and the EU presidency countries.

Finally, it is also an open question how and to what extent the reform of the fiscal rules of the Stability Pact will affect German economic policy-making. Although the state of stagnation is expected to disappear from the German economy in 2007, the German Council of Economic Experts argued in November 2004 that "the situation of public finances will still not improve noticeably".[150] In these circumstances, further constraining of the fiscal criteria could jeopardise not only the delicate balance of the German budgetary policy but also the whole institutional system of the Stability Pact. On the other hand, any relaxing could undermine the whole fiscal convergence process in EMU and the credibility of the single currency. Despite the reform of March 2005, it is still unclear how and in what way the fiscal rules will be interpreted in the future, given that the implementation of the Stability Pact is now a matter for the cooperation among 27 EU Member States. Based on the most recent assessment under the Stability Pact, the Commission was delighted to announce in Brussels on 14 December 2004 that Germany and France are "on track to correct their excessive budgetary deficits in 2005" although "the budgetary situation in the two countries remains vulnerable".[151] Thus, no further "steps" in the excessive deficit procedure against Germany are required for the time being, and the amended fiscal rules remain an integral part of fiscal policy coordination in EMU, at least for the time being.

Part III

Germany, the Stability and Growth Pact and Policy Coordination: Institutional Capacity for Effective Fiscal Policy Coordination in EMU

6
Reviewing the Institutional System of Fiscal Policy Coordination

6.1 Institutional system of the Stability and Growth Pact

Methodology of the review of the Stability Pact

Since Barre and Werner's plans in the 1960s and 1970s European countries have focused on designing the optimal relationship between European and national economic policy-making. Although the consensus on the common monetary policy was quickly reached following the start of the Internal Market programme in 1985, integration in fiscal policy did not receive such a determined and enthusiastic response in the 1980s and 1990s. In the EMU era, the desire to coordinate national fiscal policies has, nevertheless, arisen among Member States from the fact that fiscal spill-overs across the participating national economies in the monetary union could affect both positively and negatively the functioning of the monetary union and the achievement of a stabilised economic environment for long-term employment and growth. Member States have thus agreed on establishing additional coordination models and mechanisms for national fiscal policies in EMU. However, as the current situation between EU institutions and Member States in fiscal policy coordination implies, the immediate future of the relationship between fiscal policy coordination and national commitments will be crucial for achieving the fundamental aim – to have a successfully functioning EMU.

Reflecting the empirical lessons learned from the analysis of the formation (uploading), implementation (downloading) and reinterpretation (reuploading) of the fiscal rules of the Stability Pact, there are a number of essential policy elements with the potential to contribute to the success of European fiscal policy coordination. Firstly, this research has analysed how the establishment of institutional fiscal policy coordination has challenged national economic policy-making and increased national pressures for major adjustments in Germany (the uploading process 1995–1997). Secondly, this research has also analysed the extent to which the German economy has succeeded and failed in making national adjustments to comply with increased fiscal policy coordination in EMU (the downloading process 1998–2002). Thirdly, however, economic data or existing literature does not yet discuss, with up-to-date information, the current state and concrete prospects of fiscal policy coordination under the Stability Pact (the reuploading process 2003–2005): a fact that requires additional empirical data gathering.

Until now, the primary aim has been to evaluate the extent to which Germany has adjusted its national economic structures and policy-making processes to the post-Pact and post-EMU eras. Now, the focus moves towards impending challenges of fiscal policy coordination in EMU caused by the German implementation problems. This focus is justified by the fact that the present and looming challenges, which have primarily been created by the German economy, have not yet been thoroughly dealt with in the existing data or literature. Therefore, to have an extensive insight into and up-to-date knowledge of the current and coming state of the Stability Pact and fiscal policy coordination, a large number of key interviews have been conducted. These qualitative interviews should be regarded as a supporting research method and material when aiming at the foremost target of this research set in Chapter 1: how and to what extent has the formation of the Stability and Growth Pact affected the implementation of German national fiscal policy in EMU? In line with this main objective, the key focus of the interviews is to examine and analyse how the most recent experience from the performance of the German economy under the Stability Pact in 2002–2004 has affected the strengths and weaknesses of European fiscal policy coordination (a two-way relationship): *what has been the impact of the crisis in the German economy since 2002 on the implementation of the Stability and Growth Pact in EMU?*

Twenty leading officials and experts on the Stability Pact and fiscal policy coordination were interviewed in the Commission (supranational monitoring), the European Central Bank and the German Bundesbank (monetary authorities), the German Federal Ministry of Finance and the Bundesländer (national fiscal authorities) and leading German research institutes (academics).[1] The interviews were conducted in person, as a face-to-face interaction in June and July 2004, and the time spent on a single interview varied from one to two hours. The interviewer had a prepared list of main questions and topics that were based on the empirical analysis in previous chapters and the broad themes of the questions were given to the interviewees beforehand. All the interviews were semi-structured with open-ended questions. The time frame of the questions in the interview was set to be the implementation of the Stability Pact 1997–2004 and in particular the most recent critical developments under the Stability Pact 2002–2004. What has to be emphasised is that this research recognises the limitations of interviews as a method because even with long interviews not all possible themes, matters and comments presented can be included and therefore, some crucial points about the Stability Pact may be omitted from the interviews. However, in line with the primary objectives of this research, the topics analysed in detail in this chapter focus on institutional fiscal policy coordination, the role of the fiscal rules in EMU, German national commitments, national economic coordination and future fiscal challenges in the enlarged EU.

All interviews were recorded and the researcher simultaneously took precise notes of the key arguments of individual interviewees. All respondents were very willing to cooperate and gave in-detail and up-to-date answers in line with the previous findings of this research and the understanding of the researcher. These two dimensions mean that the answers have high reliability even though no answers or comments can be linked to any specific interviewees for the sake of confidentiality. Based on the case of the German economy under the Stability Pact, the most significant findings on institutional fiscal policy coordination, national commitments and coming fiscal challenges are presented and examined in this chapter as follows. Through nine core questions and answers, the chapter firstly presents the concrete findings of this research on fiscal policy coordination with detailed policy recommendations (practice), which is followed by analysis of the empirical interviews (empirics). Thus, the analytical result is an up-to-date political, economic, institutional and legal review of the system of fiscal policy coordination within the Stability Pact in EMU: both in practice and empirically.

Institutional system of the Stability Pact

Question 1:
How well is the institutional system of the Stability and Growth Pact functioning in Economic and Monetary Union at the moment?

Practice on institutional fiscal policy coordination

Although the original idea was to develop a simple and straightforward system of fiscal policy coordination, fiscal policy coordination in EMU has, however, developed into a highly complex construction of actors and mechanisms. Not only is the coordination system based on the authority of Member States but it also consists of four supranational elements: a) the convergence criteria in Articles 102a–109m of the Maastricht Treaty, b) the decision of the European Council on the Stability and Growth Pact in Amsterdam on 17 June 1997, c) Council Regulation 1466/97 on Multilateral Surveillance in line with the Broad Economic Policy Guidelines of Article 99 of the Maastricht Treaty, and d) Council Regulation 1467/97 on the Excessive Deficit Procedure in line with Article 104 of the Maastricht Treaty. Despite the formality of fiscal policy coordination, the system still allows national fiscal flexibility and the exceeding of the fiscal rules, for example if a Member State faces a severe temporary or exceptional recession. Although fiscal policy coordination has targeted economic objectives, for example macroeconomic stability, employment and growth in the Euro area, the system of fiscal policy coordination has also involved a lot of political and institutional interaction. The politics of fiscal policy coordination came into the European agenda at the latest when the sudden downturn in late 2000 caused substantial economic problems for some large Member States, that is Germany and France, to fully comply with the debt and deficit rules of the Stability Pact and the recommendations of the Commission and the Ecofin Council. As a result, the simple and straightforward system of fiscal policy coordination, which was established under a stable and predictable economic environment in the mid-1990s, was no longer functioning as planned under the changed and uncertain circumstances in EMU in the 21st century.

The guiding principle in fiscal policy coordination has been that to ensure monetary stability Member States have agreed not to run overly excessive (pro-cyclical) fiscal policies in EMU. For supporting active counter-cyclical fiscal policy, the Maastricht Treaty and the Stability Pact have defined debt and deficit rules, breaking of which may result in the sanction procedure and fines of up to billions of Euros. Burda and Wyplosz argue that theoretically, although both pro-cyclical and counter-cyclical fiscal policies have been applied in national policy-making, counter-cyclical fiscal policy by reducing the negative impact of the economic cycle results in a more stable economic environment in a monetary union in the long term than pro-cyclical fiscal policy. According to them, "counter-cyclical fiscal policy may be a corrective device to keep unemployment at its equilibrium level, and output near its trend growth path. Sustaining aggregate demand with public spending when private demand weakens, or directly boosting private demand with tax relief, could eliminate business cycles altogether."[2] To fully understand the full impact of EMU and the fiscal rules on national economic policy-making, it has to be emphasised that it is not only the monetary policy hand (the ECB) but also a major part of the fiscal hand (the Stability Pact) that are tightened in EMU.

Fiscal policy coordination worked well before the escalation of the present economic, political and institutional problems in 2002. Economically, the implementation problem with the Stability Pact in Germany raised two interrelated dimensions. Firstly, if the main cause of the German fiscal crisis was the economic cycle, then the adjustment process back to the fiscal balance should already have taken place within a few years; a development that has not occurred. Secondly, if the fiscal crisis was also caused by structural problems, as it apparently is, there should be more national flexibility in implementing the Stability Pact. It would be rational to assume that through the major measures taken by Schröder's two governments the downturn should have been tackled permanently if the question had only been about a normal downturn of the cycle. As the economy still continues to face a persistent downturn, the only rational explanation is that the crisis has been caused not only by the cycle but also by structural problems. If there were underlying structural problems in the economy, it would also be rational that Germany would be allowed more flexibility for national economic policy-making to support fast recovery because a very strict interpretation of the fiscal rules could slow down the pace of it significantly. In addition, the recovery from structural problems may not happen as fast as from cyclical problems because they usually require more extensive reforms. It is also noteworthy that the recovery of the German economy would have a major impact on the European economy as a whole.

Politically, if the perspective is too short-term and the fiscal rules are interpreted in a short-sighted (cyclical) way (the Commission), it would not allow the required economic and political room for the German government to tackle the persistent fiscal and structural problems, and it would not contribute to the fast recovery of the economy. As the IMF has pointed out, "long-diagnosed structural rigidities had not been confronted for many years, and this inaction lay at the heart of Germany's relatively poor economic performance and uncertain prospects".[3] Even though economic theory suggests there is a bias in a monetary union towards intentionally running excessive debt and deficit ratios, the empirical research presented here suggests that this has not been the case with the German economy between 1998 and 2006. By contrast, the German government has fought the increase in debt and deficit ratios. Institutionally, an essential reform would be that the economic trends in Member States should be taken into account more in the coordination procedures of the Stability Pact. EU institutions could thus apply country-specific policies depending on the national and European circumstances and thus improve the credibility and effectiveness of coordination. The guiding principle has to be in the future that all actions under European fiscal policy coordination should focus on preventing bad national economic policies, that is running expansive fiscal policy both in an upturn and downturn, that may cause an unfavourable economic environment to other Member States and the whole Euro area.

Empirics of institutional fiscal policy coordination

The interviews for this research showed that the monetary authorities of the European System of Central Banks were aware of the fact that the implementation of the Stability Pact had faced unanticipated difficulties in some large EMU Member States. Germany in particular was mentioned as one of the countries that had had the biggest problems with national fiscal stability in EMU. The interviews confirmed that fiscal policy coordination "is not dead although the behaviour of large EMU countries has partly undermined the fundamental objectives of the Stability Pact".[4] Although the Stability Pact was considered appropriate in EMU, the politics of the implementation process was the primary problem. Interviewees pointed out four main indicators that showed that the implementation of the Stability Pact was not working as planned. Firstly, Member States did not create the required fiscal room for the EMU era in the high-growth period 1998–2000. Secondly, Member States have had major problems with debt and deficit ratios even though the downturn in late 2000 has not been a major recession. Thirdly, Member States have issued more debt and deficit than ever before in the recent history despite the strict fiscal rules and agreements in EMU. Finally, every time a Member State has run a major deficit, European institutional policy coordination has not succeeded in finding a collective and lasting solution. For these reasons, "it is possible to state that the Stability Pact is not perfect because it is not working as planned".[5]

For those interviewees from the German government, the Stability Pact was a concrete system for sustainable budgetary policy and a stable economic environment. They had a clear opinion that the Stability Pact had worked very well from 1997 and thus, the European debate about "burying" the Stability Pact had been far too premature. However, the main problem with the fiscal rules related to national implementation that had "blurred" the picture. This blurring eventually escalated on 25 November 2003 when the Ecofin Council did not follow the Commission's recommendations. According to one fiscal authority, "this decision proved that the fiscal rules of the Stability Pact allow room for flexibility".[6] The decision of the Ecofin Council showed that the Stability Pact was a broad fiscal system with national economic flexibility. This meant that the interpretation of the fiscal rules was not done "automatically" and "mechanically", but "national economic circumstances had been taken into account".[7] The Stability Pact thus included flexibility, and flexibility should be an integral part in the future as well. Although the implementation has had some difficulties, Germany has closely cooperated with the peer pressure derived from the Commission and the Ecofin Council. On a point of criticism, fiscal interviewees believed that although the economic circumstances have been unfavourable for Germany during recent years, "this has not been sufficiently recognised by the coordination". Thus, criticism that Germany has been unwilling to cooperate and that Germany has voluntarily frozen the fiscal rules has been "dramatised and politicised too much": the reality is more complex than has been argued. Germany has "made commitments to fiscal coordination" and "executed economic and structural reforms" but macroeconomic trends and the financial impact of the national reforms should have a role in the interpretation of the fiscal rules.

The fiscal authorities of the Bundesländer interviewed identified the system of fiscal policy coordination as having two main dimensions – where the Stability Pact coordinated economic policies from the European perspective on the one hand, and where national implementation faced concrete challenges on the other. Although the deficit criterion had

European-wide difficulties, the Ecofin Council allowed notable flexibility for German policy-making through its flexible interpretation. Due to the fact that some Member States have exceeded the deficit limit, the main focus in coordination should be towards "the existing economic trends in Member States" within which the common rules and guidelines were implemented.[8] Interviewees also considered that the pressure deriving from EU institutions had not sufficiently contributed to the national effort of the federal government and the Bundesländer to reduce debt and deficit ratios. European formal expectations of national policy-making had been far too high. Although the original hopes in the Bundesländer about the Stability Pact were somewhat optimistic, achieving all the given recommendations in the given short time was unrealistic. The problems with the deficit had, however, given a good chance for a thorough national debate on the objectives of national economic policy and the system of national economic coordination. Interviewees believed that if the Stability Pact, the ECB and EMU would all have functioned in close and effective cooperation as planned, Germany would have had better growth, no problems with its budgetary policy and the general focus would have been turned from the macroeconomic preconditions to a more growth-supporting economic policy in EMU.

From the point of view of supranational monitoring, the institutional system of the Stability Pact had a critical setback in the meeting of the Ecofin Council on 25 November 2003. The basis of the setback was that Germany and France had not followed the previous European recommendations to stabilise their national budgetary policies and comply with the rules of the Stability Pact. After the decision not to apply the excessive deficit procedure to these Member States, the Commission decided to bring the case before the European Court of Justice. These economic, political, institutional and legal developments resulted in a conception that the Stability Pact had substantial difficulties and therefore, the implementation of the Stability Pact should be reformed. An interviewee confirmed that "the clarification and modification of the Stability Pact have been under review since November 2003".[9] Finally, Prodi's Commission produced a new Communication on how to reform the Stability Pact in September 2004. However, the responsibility for reviving the effectiveness of fiscal policy coordination under the Stability Pact transferred from Prodi's Commission to Jose Manuel Durao Barroso's new Commission on 22 November 2004.

Academics interviewed shared the opinion that fiscal policy coordination under the Stability Pact was not working effectively. The Stability Pact was seen "only as a set of rules" because large Member States had not made real commitments to the implementation of the common European guidelines.[10] For example, the commitments of the German government were not so strong that it could have fully respected the fiscal rules after the high-growth period 1998–2000. Interviewees identified four main periods in fiscal policy coordination. Firstly, there were sceptical views among those interviewed that coordination under the Stability Pact could economically work in the mid-1990s because fiscal convergence in Europe was just about to start. Secondly, once the Stability Pact was formed and incorporated into the European coordination system it was believed that the Stability Pact as a guiding institution could work. The Stability Pact with sound budgetary policy was a precondition for EMU and Member States that were committed to its implementation. Thirdly, the meaning of fiscal policy coordination radically changed in EMU and the national implementation problems jeopardised the whole coordination system. For example, Germany, which was not "the only guilty Member State in EMU", experienced "both short-term cyclical and long-term structural problems".[11] Finally, despite the problems, EMU continues to need institutionalised fiscal policy coordination for the deficit bias and furthering national economic and structural reforms. Thus, "the main future challenge is to maintain fiscal rules in EMU but how can this work because strict rules have not been successful in the first place"?[12]

Institutional duties in economic monitoring and implementation

Question 2:
What is the impact of the ruling of the European Court of Justice on 13 July 2004 on the implementation of the fiscal rules and coordination mechanisms of the Stability Pact?

Practice on institutional duties in economic monitoring and implementation

The economic monitoring under and the institutional implementation of the Stability Pact have been two of the key topics on the European political agenda since the decision of the Ecofin Council not to implement the sanction mechanism of the Stability Pact on 25 November 2003. The ruling of the European Court of Justice on 13 July 2004 legally defined the relationship between monitoring and implementation and thus, the ruling was a culmination of the present fiscal policy coordination. The whole legal issue of the relationship between monitoring and implementation stemmed from the fact that the Commission had done its duty in monitoring and reporting the existence of an excessive deficit in a Member State. The Ecofin Council had, however, allowed major national flexibility in the implementation of the Stability Pact through its political decisions. Although the Stability Pact clearly granted the ultimate right to the Ecofin Council to take existing circumstances into account in its considerations, the repeated decisions not to apply the sanction procedure to Germany and France created more room for national economic flexibility than was originally defined and intended. This dilemma between monitoring and implementation raised a fundamental question of who should have the power for determining when there was concrete and indisputable evidence on the breach of common agreements and decisions in fiscal policy in the EU and EMU, and when this information should lead to the implementation of the sanction procedure.

It can be economically, politically, institutionally and legally doubted whether the Stability Pact has any practical role in fiscal policy coordination if it is not implemented as agreed by Member States themselves. Economically, increasing debt and deficit ratios may negatively affect the credibility of the EMU area. The reason for this is that overly expansive national fiscal policies endanger the price stability target of the ECB and may result in tightening monetary policy in the already low-growth environment. Politically, implementation problems have raised a major debate on the responsibilities and role of large and small Member States in fiscal policy coordination. As the decisions of the Ecofin Council indicate, large Member States seem to have more political and economic power in fiscal policy coordination and they seem to get away with breaking the common agreements without facing any sanctions. Institutionally, it also seems that it has been much easier for the Commission and the Ecofin Council to find a long-lasting solution to economic problems in good times than in bad times. Institutional coordination and political decisions thus seem to be, at least partly, linked to good/bad national developments: the rules of the Stability Pact and the interpretation of the rules vary depending on Member States, given time and national circumstances.

Legally, the European Court of Justice, however, restored the formality of the common agreements in fiscal policy coordination. The fact that the sanction mechanism of the excessive deficit procedure was not implemented in the cases of Germany and France raised the institutional power struggle between the Commission and the Ecofin Council over supranational fiscal authority on 25 November 2003. In Issing's view, "there is a considerable doubt as to whether the decision of the Ecofin Council to allow the budgetary policy of Germany and France is in line with the Treaty".[13] The ruling of the Court on 13 July 2004 finally ended this debate on the formal institutional procedures of the Stability Pact. The judgement was as expected and it gave a final interpretation of the rules and institutional procedures and how they should be defined and implemented. The Court considered that the case, presented by the Commission, was essential and it supported the Commission's view on institutional duties and rights. Given the simple rules of the Stability Pact, the Court could have not made any other kind of a decision for the fiscal limits had been continually exceeded (January 2002, November 2002 and November 2003) and still the sanctions were not implemented.

The ruling was only a partial victory for the Commission however, since the Court stated that the appeal was justified, and it overturned the decision of the Ecofin Council in November 2003 but it sent the matter back to the consideration of the Ecofin Council. This ruling clarified the Treaty-based position of the Commission in monitoring and reporting and as a user of supranational economic authority. However, the Court did not deny the existence of the decision-making role of the Ecofin Council in fiscal policy. Thus, from now on, as before, the Ecofin Council has the right to political interpretation of the Stability Pact. The Ecofin Council, nevertheless, has to follow the formal institutional procedure of the Stability Pact more strictly than before. The qualified majority voting system may result in exactly the same kind of decision in the Ecofin Council as the decision that was the basis for this appeal to the Court in November 2003. Legally, however, even qualified majority decisions have to be in line with European law and common agreements, as defined by the Court. For small Member States, the ruling may have eliminated past trends by which large Member States had been able to interpret collective decisions depending on their existing circumstances rather than the existing agreements. What will follow from the ruling is not yet clear and it also remains to be seen whether the ruling makes the implementation of the Stability Pact any more effective in (large) EMU Member States.

Empirics of institutional duties in economic monitoring and implementation

For the monetary authorities interviewed the primary objective of the ruling of the Court was to make a legal interpretation of the institutional procedures under the Stability Pact and the ruling was expected to confirm how decisions should be made institutionally.[14] The ruling was also expected to discuss whether "the fiscal rules and their implementation should be reformed and improved".[15] Although European economic monitoring was already extensive, there was still a question of whether national governments were sufficiently committed to the common rules and agreements. Increasing political transparency in decision-making could be one practical method to improve the situation. If the Court had been in favour of the Ecofin Council's view, it was feared among the interviewees that it would have created a situation where there would have been great uncertainty regarding the binding nature of the fiscal rules. On the one hand, future decisions about the implementation could have greatly varied from one situation to another and on the other hand, allowing more and more national fiscal flexibility could have politically become more the rule than the exception. Now, after the ruling, the Stability Pact should be implemented formally and strictly, "even in the Ecofin Council". The Ecofin Council is no longer able to interpret the rules "in whatever way" it chooses claiming its right of political consideration.[16] However, according to one interviewee, "the future of the Stability Pact is not crystal clear yet".[17]

The fiscal authorities interviewed believed that the ruling would have a sizeable impact on European fiscal policy coordination. On the one hand, Member States have had to implement a number of common fiscal rules and economic policy guidelines in EMU. On the other hand, the introduction of common rules and policy guidelines has meant that some national economic authority has been transferred to common EU institutions. Although broad economic policy coordination has tightened the monetary hand and some parts of the fiscal hand, it is still, however, the Member States that retain fundamental power over fiscal policy. In this complex political environment, the Court clarified the relationship between institutional fiscal policy coordination and national policy implementation. The Court legally defined the institutional authority under the Stability Pact between the "flexibility"-inclined approach of the Ecofin Council and the more "mechanist" approach of the Commission.[18] Although the Court agreed with the Commission's agreement-based view, it still recognised the Ecofin Council's right to the political and flexible interpretation of the fiscal rules of the Stability Pact in EMU.

In the interviews with the representatives of the Bundesländer, it emerged that the ruling could also have an impact on national economic coordination. On the one hand, by ignoring the recommendations of the Commission the Ecofin Council did not fully follow the rules and objectives of the Stability Pact and for this reason the Court restored the strict and Treaty-based economic responsibilities. On the other hand, the Court allowed the political interpretation of the Ecofin Council as a result of exceptional circumstances in the German economy. Both impacts increased political and economic pressures on the German government for closer and more effective national economic coordination. It was domestically expected that the government would have to improve national economic coordination to better comply with the Stability Pact. In practice, the Court renewed the rule-based guidelines for national fiscal policies in EMU; a principle that has had major problems in German national policy-making. As one interviewee explained: "If there are no rules at all or no one executes them as planned, the future of cooperation is without any credible basis."[19]

The ruling did not change the fact that despite the active European monitoring and reporting, some Member States had continually broken the rules of the Stability Pact. Although Germany and France had not met the common criteria, it had not, according to the interviews with supranational officials, meant the end of the Stability Pact. By contrast, this fact had shown the full strength of European fiscal policy coordination. It was widely suggested in interviews that institutional duties in fiscal policy had become clearer because the Court reinforced the Commission's opinion on the Stability Pact. The Court confirmed that the Commission had the ultimate right of initiative and the Ecofin Council could not make any decision without an initiative from the Commission, which clarified the power of the Commission in its monitoring and initiative role. On the other hand, the Court did not deny the highest power of the Ecofin Council.

Thus, "there is still a sort of deadlock in the European Union".[20] Barroso's Commission has the key role in solving this institutional "deadlock" and continuing the challenging but crucial work of modifying the "institutional coordination under the Stability Pact".[21]

There was a clear understanding among academics that the ruling was essential and it had a major impact on fiscal policy coordination. Until the ruling, the Ecofin Council's decisions had supported the interpretation that the fiscal rules can be broken, such as in Germany. It was argued that "due to poor budget management, Germany had not managed to respect the fiscal rules because it had allowed the deficit ratio to grow far too much in good times."[22] It was regarded as a major surprise that this kind of national economic policy-making was allowed by the Ecofin Council. Now, the Court gave its legal view on the procedure and the politics of the implementation came to the final end. The Court had now stopped a pernicious development in institutional coordination where politics had taken over the common agreements. The ruling clearly stated that "the rules have to be followed and the monitoring of the Stability Pact cannot be prevented by institutional processes".[23] The Court in practice restored the meaning of common agreements and the need for full national commitments. Simultaneously, the decision strengthened the Commission's monitoring and reporting role because the Court formulated "the formal European perspective" to fiscal policy coordination.[24] One interviewee, however, raised a crucial point in saying that despite the ruling and the power struggle, fiscal policy coordination should continue to help national governments "to further economic consolidation for common stability and growth".[25]

Reinterpreting the fiscal rules of the Stability Pact

> **Question 3:**
> How could the existing knowledge of the Stability and Growth Pact in the EMU era reform the original definitions, interpretations and objectives of the fiscal rules?

Practice on reinterpreting the fiscal rules

One of the most essential outcomes of this whole research has been to examine how the rules and the implementation of the Stability Pact should be improved to better comply with developments in Member States. The practical need for the reform has stemmed from the economic developments due to which Germany and France as large EMU Member States have not achieved the common targets for national fiscal policies. The budgetary deficit rule has in particular caused most of the problems for these two national governments. For example, the Vice-President of the Bundesbank, Jürgen Stark, has been critical of the fact that these two large EMU Member States have managed national fiscal policies as if there were no single currency and common monetary policy in EMU. In his words, "there is a strong feeling in Europe that the great idea of European integration has been postponed", but the reality is that "the stability-oriented economic policy can only be dependent on political will".[26]

Firstly, the primary challenge for Member States is to decide how the rules and objectives of the Stability Pact could be reformed. The question also arises as to whether there should be more specific rules for stricter implementation, or whether the rules should allow more flexibility and a possibility for country-specific implementation depending on the existing economic circumstances, and which EU institutions should have the power to determine the nature of the existing circumstances (Figures 7.5 and 7.6). Politically, any tightening of the fiscal rules would be unlikely to occur in the EU of 25 Member States. Any loosening of the fiscal rules could, on the other hand, destroy the whole Stability Pact because, according to Buti and Pench, "greater flexibility carries the risk of greater scope for opportunistic behaviour".[27] An option that is still available is to maintain the institutional system of the Stability Pact as it is but to focus more on specifying the interpretation of the rules to better suit existing circumstances. Without opening the whole institutional system to question, those economic circumstances when the exceeding of the limits and the length of the exceeding could be possible (but still not desirable) should be specified. The Finance Minister of Austria, Karl-Heinz Grasser, was sceptical about reforming the rules and he ironically argued that "what Germany under Theo Waigel introduced, Germany also later buried". As an ultimate sanction mechanism for this "burying", Grasser suggested that a Member State that does not fully comply with the Stability Pact should "lose their right to vote".[28]

Secondly, there are also some other ideas to reform the rules of the Stability Pact in the European debate. The starting point for reforming the rules has to be the understanding that the current focus on short-term economic developments has supported neither long-term budgetary planning nor national policy implementation. Fiscal policy coordination requires a change in its focus from short-term to longer-term perspectives. Thus, the rules would no longer define debt and deficit ratios year-on-year (increase or reduction) but they should be achieved in the medium term from two to three years. The Commission would still monitor national economies but the rules would create more national flexibility in dealing with unanticipated developments and changes in the economic cycle.[29] This would be a major change in European fiscal strategy that has focused on fast fiscal stabilisation for and in EMU. The change in the focus from a short-term to a longer-term perspective would enable Member States to better tackle existing economic problems and prepare for coming economic challenges, such as population ageing. This policy change would not, however, eliminate the main objective that all Member States should target fiscal stabilisation in their national policy-making; rather, it would give them more flexibility and instruments to achieve this objective.

Thirdly, fiscal rules require an agreed institutional procedure when the economic circumstances in Member States are so exceptional that economic policy-making does not allow normal, counter-cyclical fiscal policy. The emergence of exceptional circumstances directly affects fiscal stability and economic growth, that is the two elements of the Stability and Growth Pact. Schröder has also pointed out this impact recently. According to Schröder, "in the current phase, on the basis of the Stability Pact, which is not just a Stability Pact but a Stability and Growth Pact, there is a need to strengthen the growth elements so that we will be able to comply with the criteria that are part of the Pact".[30] However, the main difficulty in the Stability Pact has related to the fact that the nature of exceptional circumstances has not been defined in the Stability Pact as accurately as the existing developments would have required. Although the Council Regulation on "Speeding up and Clarifying the Implementation of the Excessive Deficit Procedure" has specified the interpretation of the exceptional circumstances, the definition is still too general. According to the regulation, if the overall economic assessment shows "an annual fall of real GDP of at least 2 percent", the downturn is "exceptional".[31] The definition of "temporal" exceeding cannot be applied to the case of Germany because exceeding the deficit limit in three consecutive years is no longer temporal. The regulation allows exceeding the deficit limit if it is caused by "an unusual event outside the control of the Member State concerned and has a major impact on the financial position of the general government", or when it results from "a severe economic downturn". If, for example, unemployment is regarded as an indicator of "exceptional" or "unusual" or "severe" circumstances, it is possible to notice that unemployment in Germany has jumped from 7.8 percent in 2000 to 12.6 percent (5.2 million) in February 2005: a fact that shows the existence of somewhat "exceptional", "unusual" and "severe" circumstances. Or, should the unemployment rate have reached 20.0 percent and a total of about 8 million unemployed before the circumstances would have been defined as exceptional by the Commission and Germany could have exceeded the deficit criterion in its national economic policy-making?

Fourthly, the reform of the fiscal rules of the Stability Pact also raises the question of the importance of a good and informative deficit criterion. If the Stability Pact is to be revised, it should include a more rational interpretation of the deficit rule. It has been suggested that the real year-on-year deficit rule should be replaced by the cyclically-adjusted deficit criterion, showing thus the deficit over the economic cycle rather than temporally on a yearly basis. For example, where the deficit in real terms in Germany was 3.5 percent in 2002, 3.9 percent in 2003, 3.6 percent in 2004 and 2.8 percent in 2005, the cyclically-adjusted deficit showed figures of 3.5 percent in 2002, 3.2 percent in 2003, 2.9 percent in 2004 and 2.3 percent in 2005.[32] Thus, defining the deficit in real terms or in cyclically-adjusted figures results in different information. Based on macroeconomic theory, *it is the cyclically-adjusted budgetary deficit criterion that should be used in interpreting how and to what extent developments in budgetary policies comply with the existing economic cycle.* Focusing only on the real deficit ratio in the short term results in a partly blinkered understanding of developments in Member States, as the current state of the Stability Pact clearly illustrates. The cyclically-adjusted deficit defines the fiscal position without the impact of the economic cycle on the national economy. As Burda and Wyplosz define the practical usefulness of the cyclically-adjusted deficit criterion: "Countries where the cyclically-adjusted budget has improved are countries where fiscal policy has been exogenously tightened up".[33]

Finally, it has also been suggested that the golden rule of public finance could be incorporated into the Stability Pact. The main aim of the golden rule is to achieve sustainable public finances in national economic policy-making and it has been adopted for example in Britain and Germany, albeit with varying success. Firstly, the golden rule was put into action in Britain in 1998 when the "Code for Fiscal Stability" of the government was approved in December 1998. The British definition of the golden rule states that the government can borrow only for investments and not for funding normal public spending. In addition, the public debt level has to remain stable although there are public investments. The British government has officially defined the target debt to be "reduced to below 40 percent of GDP over the economic cycle" and the experience from the golden rule in budgetary policy has been positive.[34]

By contrast, Germany has had the golden rule in its Constitution since 1949 but it has not been successfully implemented and respected in national budgetary policy. Article 115 of the German Constitution defines that "revenue obtained by borrowing shall not exceed the total expenditures for investments provided for in the budget" but "exceptions shall be permissible only to avert a disturbance of the overall economic

Implementation of the Golden Rule under the Schröder Governments I and II 1998–2006

- 1998: deficit € 28.8 billion, investments € 29.2 billion
- 1999: deficit € 26.1 billion, investments € 28.6 billion
- 2000: deficit € 25.3 billion, investments € 29.4 billion
- 2001: deficit € 22.8 billion, investments € 27.3 billion
- **2002: deficit € 31.9 billion, investments € 24.1 billion**
- 2003: deficit € 18.9 billion, investments € 26.7 billion
- 2004: deficit € 24.6 billion, investments € 29.3 billion
- 2005: deficit € 22.0 billion, investments € 22.8 billion
- 2006: deficit € 21.7 billion, investments € 22.3 billion

Figure 6.1 The golden rule in German fiscal policy 1998–2006.[35]

equilibrium".[36] As Figure 6.1 shows, Schröder's government broke the golden rule of the public finance once in 2002. In 2002, the German government spent 24.1 billion Euros in public investments, whereas the deficit was 31.9 billion Euros. What is striking is that the budget of 2002 of Schröder's first government was thus not fully in line with the constitutional requirements of Article 115. Most recently, the golden rule of the Constitution was legally examined and defined in 2003. In a ruling with a wide domestic significance, the Constitutional Court of the Bundesland Berlin gave its constitutional interpretation of the golden rule in a case on 31 October 2003, which dealt with the question whether the public finances of the Bundesland Berlin had complied with the golden rule. The problem related to Article 115 because the public expenditure in the Berlin 2002–2003 budget was higher than investments: a fact that disrupted the stability of public finance. In its ruling, the Court renewed the crucial guideline in regional economic policy-making. As the primary principle, the Court stated that "the *Land* is responsible for managing its budget". Although the public finances would have experienced problems and there would have been ongoing saving and stabilisation programmes in the Bundesland, "the *Land* is still responsible for its expenditure".[37] Because of breaking the golden rule, the Berlin 2002–2003 budget was ruled as unconstitutional by the Berlin Constitutional Court. *Given this ruling, how would the Court have regarded the German federal budget of 2002?*

Empirics of reinterpreting the fiscal rules

Monetary authorities interviewed pointed out that "the fiscal rules have been active not more than five years and we should have more knowledge about the rules functioning over the cycle" because a possible and fast economic recovery in Member States could change the current understanding of the rules.[38] If Member States decided to specify the fiscal rules, the original objectives of the Stability Pact should be maintained. Originally, the Stability Pact protected monetary policy from unfavourable national fiscal policies in EMU: a rationale that is still essential. However, there is no return to Waigel's idea of automatic sanctions and a deficit rule of only 1.0 percent because the existing rules are tight and difficult enough to achieve and maintain in a downturn. The deficit bias, however, requires fiscal policy coordination and the rules have to be clear so that the enforcement can be secured. For monetary authorities, any new reinterpretation should safeguard "a balanced budgetary position in EMU" because overly expansive fiscal policies do not support the price stability objective.[39] Although the existing written rules were considered clear, the implementation proved different. To restore the respect towards fiscal discipline in EMU, it was seen that "Member States should really take more responsibility over the common rules".[40] In the short term, although the focus should be on furthering economic and structural reforms, the new reinterpretation could include some flexibility by allowing "some temporary fiscal relaxing during a temporary downturn".[41] In the long term, national economic planning, which was not satisfactory in the period 1998–2000, should target low debt and deficit ratios and growth-supporting activities more purposefully. Any reinterpretation requires "a common political will in Europe and a national commitment".[42]

For the German fiscal authorities, although the rules were introduced in 1995–1997, the rationale for having fiscal rules in EMU has remained. Those interviewed shared a clear opinion that under normal circumstances, Germany would not have had any major difficulties with the Stability Pact and there would have been more room for national automatic stabilisers to function in EMU, but the reduction in public revenue was not effectively compensated by other resources of income or cuts in public expenditure. It was thought that increasing fiscal policy coordination and loss of national monetary policy could have been successfully compensated by high growth. However, Germany did not have the required high-growth rates in EMU but rather a low-growth period undermining the government's economic objectives. These events led to the opinion of those interviewed that "exceptional economic circumstances" in a Member State should be "recognised and understood better and earlier by the EU institutions".[43] In practice, this understanding should result in redefining the medium-term objectives and the implementation of the rules within a realistic time frame automatically, not after formal and time-consuming negotiations. As one interviewee analysed the current coordination process: "Germany has known the circumstances for long, but common institutions have not".[44] What the existing rules need, according to those interviewed, is more clarification of institutional coordination and a more specific definition of exceptional circumstances: both cyclical and structural problems should be taken better into account when targeting a fast national recovery after a long low-growth period in EMU.

Interviewees in the Bundesländer pointed out that there were some apparent national problems derived from the fiscal rules of the Stability Pact. Those interviewed shared the belief that the primary problems of the Stability Pact did not relate to the institutional system but the concrete national policy measures under the strict fiscal policy coordination. As expressed in one interview, "it is not the Stability Pact that has caused low growth and unemployment. It has been the government."[45] It was considered that the implementation of any stricter European fiscal rules would require even more national adjustments and would thus be highly unrealistic: adjustments would cause additional federal and regional economic difficulties. The possibility for low growth should also be better taken into account in economic agenda-setting in EU institutions. Those interviewed were sceptical that the strict national implementation of the rules could bring any major benefits for the European economy under the unfavourable economic circumstances. The crucial point made in interviews was that constraining the federal budget more than it had been would also have a highly negative impact on the regional economy. If the common rules further constrain federal economic policy, the financial position of the Bundesländer weakens simultaneously and meeting the fiscal criteria becomes even harder to achieve in Germany.

The primary attention of supranational monitoring was directed to the clarification of the existing rules so that they could function better. It was believed that the best option would be to keep the institutional system and to have a renewed agreement on how the rules should be implemented from now on. For supranational monitoring, the Stability Pact was "as necessary as ever before in the enlarged Union".[46] It defines fiscal policy guidelines for Member States emphasising that the EMU era requires stable budgetary policy, and this fact has not changed. In one interviewee's opinion, "without the Pact, debt and deficit would have been much higher. Even those Member States with problems have understood this."[47] Although the Stability Pact had been criticised for eliminating all national budgetary flexibility, interviewees stated that the rules "should stay as they are" because "the Pact is flexible enough and this has been shown by the Ecofin Council".[48] However, the cyclically-adjusted deficit could still be taken more into account than before. Any reforms in the fiscal rules should try to ensure budgetary policies to be close to balance or in surplus. As also argued, "any reforms in the rules should also try to ensure that all Member States follow the rules, all of them".[49]

For academics, the reinterpretation of the fiscal rules was required because "we need more confidence on the single currency that has been put in jeopardy by fiscal problems".[50] The economics and politics of the Stability Pact should thus be thoroughly analysed. Economically, the spillovers still exist and have an impact on national economies. If there were no fiscal policy coordination at all, Member States could issue an unlimited amount of debt. Although financial markets could reduce the issuing by increasing interest rates, this may not stop them issuing more debt. European fiscal policy coordination failed to create an environment where national fiscal stability could have been ensured. In one interviewee's view, "the Ecofin has focused too much on politics under flexibility".[51] The Stability Pact was not working but what was working was coordination under the peer review of the broad economic policy guidelines. One interviewee thought that if peer pressure were any softer than today, it would mean softer coordination and softer commitments and thus, the policy results might become even more unclear. Instead, if peer pressure were any harder, it would mean harder coordination, but excessively hard coordination could cause a lack of commitments in turn and the objectives would fail. It was argued that it should also be clear by now that for large EMU Member States it is hard to fully commit themselves to strict European economic rules. As a solution, interviewees suggested that the power of interpretation should be taken away from the Ecofin Council to the Commission, which would thus have "a more powerful role in monitoring and identifying and governing budgetary deficits in Member States".[52] The unanimous and qualified majority voting systems of the Ecofin Council could also be replaced by the majority voting system. The Stability Pact should also include "better incentives for coordination" and active policy guidelines for "continual budgetary consolidation" and "achieving the sustainable public finances". In the long term, perhaps, low debt and deficits ratios could eventually allow the situation in European fiscal policy coordination, as raised in one interview, where there would be no further constraints on national fiscal policies in EMU.

6.2 National adjustments, political commitments and economic coordination

National adjustments and political commitments

Question 4:
To what extent have insufficient national adjustments and partial political commitments caused German problems in implementing the fiscal rules of the Stability Pact?

Practice on national adjustments and political commitments

The political and economic foundation of the Stability Pact, which was laid by the German government, was formulated in the wake of German reunification in the mid-1990s. Although the key argument for having fiscal policy coordination has remained solid from the mid-1990s (the deficit bias), the political and economic interests of Member States have changed. Where the Stability Pact originally acted more as a precondition for entering to EMU, it currently relates more to supporting growth and employment in EMU. In this respect, the implementation of the Stability Pact has faced a dilemma of changed national political and economic interests under the existing institutional system. It is thus arguable that, perhaps, the timing dimension plays a major role in understanding the current problems in European fiscal policy coordination, in particular in Germany, because the fiscal rules of the Stability Pact have not been implemented properly until the beginning of the 21st century, that is more than five years after its establishment. Has this timing dimension caused any problems for German national adjustments and political commitments?

National adjustments refer to changes in national policy strategies through which national economies have responded to increasing fiscal policy coordination and coming fiscal challenges. Firstly, the importance of national adjustments under the Stability Pact in EMU has stemmed from the fact that to obey the debt and deficit criteria national governments have had to improve national economic policy-making and make national economies function more effectively under increasing European coordination. Secondly, in addition to the common economic rules, national economies have had to prepare for the fact that the economic cycle may also cause some unpredictable changes for the need of national adjustments; a fact that emphasises the importance of effective economic planning and management. Thirdly, politically painful but economically rational adjustments may also cause additional costs for national governments in the short term when they reform their national economic policies; for example when governments cut public services to reduce the size of public spending and debt and deficit ratios. Despite the possible political cost in federal and regional elections, the German government has introduced major adjustments, such as the Tax Reform 2000, the Hartz reforms and Agenda 2010.

What links national adjustments to common policy objectives is national political and economic commitment; the full implementation of the required adjustments and policy reforms would be a clear indication of national commitment. In other words, sufficient national adjustments and full respect for common agreements can only be achieved through strong national commitments because major reforms may otherwise be politically and economically too painful to implement. Von Hagen, Hughes Hallett and Strauch have thus highlighted the significance of national consensus in policy reforms when saying that "the success of efforts to consolidate the government budget depends importantly on the quality of the budgetary adjustments undertaken".[53] The "quality" here refers to effective expenditure cuts, progressive stabilisation measures, a major reduction in debt and deficit without slowing down domestic demand and reducing economic growth simultaneously: these kinds of optimal adjustments would strengthen national commitments as well. However, the case of Germany under the fiscal constraints of the Stability Pact has illustrated that the German government's reform policy and commitments were not planned and implemented with full quality or optimality. Germany implemented sizeable reforms but the quality and timing of the measures were not optimal and, thus, the economy required increased flexibility for further adjustments under the strict fiscal rules. The additional pressure for the German economy also came from unanticipated economic shocks, such as the declining growth rate and the increasing oil price. The International Monetary Fund (IMF) has determined that Germany has also experienced major historically-developed structural problems. According to the IMF, "current problems stem from low growth trend, rooted in structural rigidities, reinforced by the global slowdown and reversal of the late 1990s surge in business investment".[54]

Chancellor Schröder's speech in Potsdam on 12 May 2004 was one of the most recent attempts to strike a better balance between national commitments and painful adjustments. In fact, the speech was also one of the most recent attempts to refocus German economic policy on the Stability Pact. Unsurprisingly, Schröder argued that fiscal policy coordination should focus more on the growth perspective than year-on-year fiscal discipline. According to Schröder, Germany continues to comply with the Stability Pact but "we need to respect the criteria without creating problems for the economy".[55] Due to the major problems in meeting the discipline-focused coordination in EMU, the government thus considered changing its policy and promoting a more growth-oriented perspective, which was originally included within the Stability Pact at the instigation of the French government and which was harshly criticised by the then German government in 1995–1997: a possible policy shift from stability to growth orientation. According to Schröder, "in the current situation and without giving up our consolidation course, do we need to make further cutbacks in the social welfare sector, as demanded by the conservatives, something I consider to be wrong for economic reasons and not just for social reasons? Or do we need to strengthen the economy, which is developing better than some descriptions would lead us to believe, so that growth potentials will be utilised and make it possible to comply with the criteria?"[56] As *The Economist* interpreted the German "partial-commitment" policy: "The idea that the German government may lose control of its national budget and be put under supervision by Brussels is, it seems, too humiliating to contemplate."[57] Given this knowledge, it would be extremely interesting to ask the former German (Kohl's) government *how differently it would have formulated the Stability Pact for EMU in the mid-1990s so that it would still suit Germany's interests in EMU in the 21st century*.[58]

Empirics of national adjustments and political commitments

The monetary authorities interviewed shared a strict opinion on fiscal discipline in EMU, believing that fulfilling the fiscal rules could only be achieved through strong national commitment and long-term reforms: a policy that had not been adopted and implemented in those Member States with the most problems. The fact that some Member States failed to reach the balanced fiscal position prior to EMU and not even during the first five years of EMU was considered an indication of a major policy failure. Fiscal convergence was not completed in the late 1990s, national adjustments were not timely correct, nor were the quality of the actions. In Germany, the government failed to create fiscal flexibility for bad times during the high-growth period 1998–2000. According to one interviewee, "low growth was partly caused by the unfavourable trends in the world, and partly because of the lack of growth-oriented economic reforms".[59] Germany did not manage to further national adjustments in a downturn but "under this stagnant situation, any country would have had similar or even worse problems".[60] For example, the Tax Reform 2000 had a major impact on the national economy but it was followed by a shortfall in tax revenue and thus, the budget experienced a lack of income causing a financial crisis. National reforms were sizeable but the focus should have been directed more to the reduction of public spending, and the scope and timing of adjustments should have been taken seriously earlier; these indicated ineffective national economic planning, management and commitment.

Fiscal authorities interviewed argued that the government had made a clear commitment to the Stability Pact and major adjustments had in practice strengthened this commitment. As the low-growth period was believed to be the main reason for fiscal stability problems in Germany, it was thus argued that the question of breaking the fiscal rules not only related to the lack of commitments and adjustments. Schröder's two governments implemented a wider range of reforms compared to the era of the CDU/CSU in the mid-1990s. In fact, "it has not been understood correctly how much Germany has done in the EMU era for 5–6 years".[61] Although the low-growth period did not allow any room for stabilisation in the short term, the government still implemented long-term economic reforms that had, according to one interviewee, a major impact on the fiscal balance. As interviewee pointed out, "despite the stagnation, the budgetary deficit has been only at 3.0–3.5 percent".[62] One interviewee also argued that "we have to realise that the impact of structural reforms comes late into macroeconomic realities".[63] For these reasons, those interviewed were convinced that the government's commitment to the Stability Pact was clear and strong and national adjustments, although they had faced unfavourable macroeconomic developments, could soon have an effect. One interviewee predicted, "if and when the macroeconomic situation turns for the better, the impact of the reforms will boost the national economy".[64]

In interviews with contacts in the Bundesländer, it arose that instead of lack of political commitments, Germany now pays the price for overly optimistic economic planning and thus, the implemented adjustments and compensations have been insignificant. Any rules cannot compensate for the erosion of planning and adjustments in the economic situation that emerged in Germany after 2000. When formulating the Stability Pact, the government and the Bundesländer did not have any major budgetary problems. In short, "the Pact was no problem at all".[65] Thus, failing to meet the fiscal criteria for three to four consecutive years was considered highly unlikely six or seven years ago. The fiscal rules suited the government but the Bundesländer had some doubts about implementation and possible cuts in public spending. Financial fears started to grow in the Bundesländer when the national economy experienced low growth rates, increasing unemployment rates and simultaneous public finance reforms. Despite the severe downturn after 2000, the first reforms were only "cosmetic" and effective reforms had to wait until 2003 and 2004. Before the politically painful but economically necessary reforms had not been implemented. Now, the focus should be on formulating an extensive reform strategy for the long term. Reflecting the economic experience, one interviewee summarised that "it was a fiscal rule against others but now it is the rule that is against Germany".[66]

From the point of view of supranational monitoring, the reasons for German national problems in meeting the fiscal rules become essential when EU institutions and Member States interpret economic developments and possible solutions. It was recognised that the low-growth period in Germany had complicated national fiscal convergence and adjustment processes. However, it was argued that low growth was not the key factor causing the fiscal rules to be broken in Germany. For supranational monitoring, the origin of the national budgetary problems lay in the high-growth era from 1998 to 2000. The main policy failure was that the German government did not prepare for economically bad times between 1998 and 2000. The national fiscal policy was then far too expansive, as noted by EU institutions: a policy failure that was the basis for the present fiscal indiscipline. Although the Stability Pact was meant to act as a catalyst for economic reforms, not all Member States reformed their economic policy to sufficiently stabilise budgetary policy in EMU. The rules should have guided Member States to implement cuts in public spending and contribute to fiscal convergence. However, "some countries have only planned and executed measures that secure economic balance in the short term instead of focusing on the sustainable future".[67] According to one interviewee, "this should not be the preferred national policy in EMU".[68]

For academics, the fiscal problems in Germany were a combination of a number of different factors from planning to low growth rates. Those interviewed believed that by implementing effective and timely optimal reforms the German government could have reduced the impact of fiscal policy coordination, the loss of monetary authority and the stagnation period. The belief of the government prior to the EMU era was that the economy could have success without any major adjustments despite the sizeable loss of national economic instruments in EMU. In one interviewee's opinion, the German government made a dramatic economic planning mistake when it thought that "the national economy could adjust to the EMU era without any preliminary economic reforms".[69] Some academics also argued that the stagnation period should not be seen as severe as suggested by the German government. In fact, growth rates were historically within a normal economic variation and therefore, the government should have managed to restore political commitments, implement effective national reforms and comply with the common fiscal rules. However, due to the declining growth rates, the government's political commitment started to decline as well.

National stability programmes in fiscal policy coordination

Question 5:
What has been the practical role of German Stability Programmes in fiscal policy coordination under the Stability Pact?

Practice and empirics of German Stability Programmes in coordination

The procedure of national stability programmes is based on Council Regulation 1466/97 on "The Strengthening of the Surveillance of Budgetary Positions" and also defines the objectives of national stability programmes.[70] Every Member State in EMU has to submit a stability programme to the Ecofin Council and the Commission and thus, the first stability programmes were submitted in 1999. To ensure national fiscal discipline and its European institutional monitoring, every stability programme, which has to be updated on a yearly basis, has to contain information about medium-term budgetary objectives, a budgetary position close to balance or in surplus, main anticipated macroeconomic developments and planned national economic reforms over three years. Originally, national stability programmes were expected to strengthen fiscal convergence by providing accurate information about national economic developments, and to ensure the compatibility of national economic policy-making and economic reforms with the broad economic policy guidelines and the Stability Pact.

Although the national governments are responsible for formulating the programmes, it is the Ecofin Council and the Commission that finally accept their content. However, recent developments under the national stability programmes have questioned the whole procedure in EMU because the programmes have not provided reliable and realistic information and they have not been implemented effectively. As discussed in Chapters 4 and 5, national stability programmes have in some cases been so politically-oriented that the economic information given has partly undermined the whole meaning of the procedure for the stable European economic environment. The political orientation in national stability programmes has been characterised by overly optimistic economic outlooks that have resulted in situations where the objectives of national governments have not been achieved. The Commission has also recognised this trend: "This has proved difficult in the absence of an agreed method to calculate cyclically-adjusted budget balances, and also because the nominal deficit targets in the programmes of Member States were sometimes based on optimistic growth assumptions and with adjustment efforts back-loaded towards the end of the time horizon of programmes".[71]

When empirically examining the stability programmes of the German government from the first programme of 1999 to the latest programme of December 2004, it is possible to notice the practical difficulty relating to budgetary planning (Table 6.1). The economic information given in the

Table 6.1 Comparison of the estimated economic factors to actual reported economic statistics 2000–2006.

	2000	2001	2002	2003	2004	2005	2006
Economic growth in % of GDP							
Stability Programme 1999a	2.7		2.5				
Stability Programme 1999b	2.5			2.0			
Stability Programme 2000	2.75	**2.75**			2.5		
Stability Programme 2001		2.0	3.0	**3.5**			
Stability Programme 2002			0.5	1.5	2.25	2.25	2.25
Stability Programme 2003				0.0	1.5	2.25	2.25
Stability Programme 2004a				0.1	1.5	2.25	2.25
Stability Programme 2004b					2.5	2.5	3.0
Actual economic growth	2.9	**0.8**	0.2	**–0.1**	1.5	–	–
Public debt in % of GDP							
Stability Programme 1999a	61.0	60.5	59.5				
Stability Programme 1999b	61.0	60.5	59.5	58.0			
Stability Programme 2000	61.0	60.5	59.5	58.5	**54.5**		
Stability Programme 2001		60.0	60.0	59.0	57.0	55.5	
Stability Programme 2002			61.0	61.5	60.5	59.5	57.5
Stability Programme 2003				64.0	65.0	65.5	65.0
Stability Programme 2004a					65.0	65.5	65.5
Stability Programme 2004b					65.5	66.0	66.0
Actual public debt	60.2	59.4	60.8	64.0	**65.0**	–	–
Budgetary deficit in % of GDP							
Stability Programme 1999a	2.0	1.5	1.0				
Stability Programme 1999b	1.25	1.0	1.0	0.5			
Stability Programme 2000	**1.0**	1.5	1.0	**0.5**	**0.0**		
Stability Programme 2001		2.5	2.0	1.0	0.0	0.0	
Stability Programme 2002			3.75	2.75	1.5	1.0	0.0
Stability Programme 2003				4.0	3.5	2.5	2.0
Stability Programme 2004a					3.25	2.5	2.0
Stability Programme 2004b					3.75	3.0	2.5
Actual budgetary deficit	**–1.3**	2.8	3.5	**4.0**	**3.5**	–	–

stability programmes has been inaccurate and thus, the information has not made economic monitoring and coordination any easier domestically or at the European level. What should be the foremost precondition for any economic policy-making are realistic growth objectives and growth scenarios for estimating other coming economic developments. Focusing on the economic growth section seen in Table 6.1 and the German Stability Programme 2000, the significance of the turnover in the German economic outlook in 2000 can be demonstrated by the fact that in 2000 the government still expected to have a growth rate of 2.75 percent in 2001, whereas the actual growth fell down to 0.8 percent in 2001. Similarly, where the Stability Programme 2001 estimated the growth to be as high as 3.5 percent in 2003, the actual growth was negative by 0.1 percent. These major errors in growth expectations were also reflected in other economic indicators although, for example estimates on public debt provided relatively more reliable results. However, whereas the Stability Programme 2000 estimated the debt to be 54.5 percent in 2004, the actual debt-to-GDP ratio broke the 60 percent rule by five percentage points in 2004.

The most unreliable data dealt with deficits. According to the Stability Programme 2000, the deficit of Germany would be 1.0 percent in 2000 although the revenue from the UMTS auction delivered a major surplus of 1.3 percent in 2000. In addition, the government estimated in the same programme that the deficit would be only 0.5 percent in 2003 and the budget would be free of any deficit in 2004. In reality, Germany had the highest deficit ratio of 4.0 percent of the EMU era in 2003 and 3.5 percent in 2004 and thus, Germany clearly broke the deficit rule of the Stability Pact in both years. These facts demonstrate how unpredictable economic developments were after 2000 and the uselessness of economic information provided by the German Stability Programmes. However, it is the duty of the Commission, the Economic and Financial Committee and the Ecofin Council to decide in EMU whether the economic objectives and other activities are "realistic", "sufficient", "consistent with the broad economic policy guidelines" and "ensure the avoidance of an excessive deficit".[72] In this respect, the question arises *whether all EU institutions have really fulfilled all their duties and responsibilities when assessing and accepting the objectives of the German Stability Programmes as defined by the Council Regulation 1466/97*.

On the other hand, it has to be emphasised that perfectly estimating the unpredicted economic developments after 2000 was impossible. The German fiscal authorities interviewed had also recognised the difficulties relating to stability programmes. They argued that the quality of the programmes should be improved by reforming the existing procedure so that they could be submitted every other year. This could improve the accuracy of the information because in reality, "there is no longer practical need for annual programmes in EMU".[73] It was considered that although programmes gave a good opportunity to present the coming economic trends and the policy actions of national governments, submitting stability programmes takes a lot of effort and the accuracy of the information in the long term cannot be guaranteed. The structure and content of the stability programmes should also be clarified to focus only on the fiscal trends in Member States: "In some countries programmes have become far too large to report and thus the message of them is blurring."[74] The possible refocus should be to go "back to fiscal policy, and only fiscal policy and what affects fiscal policy".[75]

National economic coordination under the Stability Pact

> **Question 6:**
> Could successfully functioning national economic coordination have contributed to the achievement of the stabilised budgetary policy in Germany under the Stability Pact?

Practice on German national economic coordination

According to Funk, it is German federalism that either allows or eliminates political and economic incentives for effective national policy co-ordination. In his opinion, "German federalism is notorious for the fact that the various levels of government try to influence each other's decisions, which often leads to harmful policy blockades".[76] In addition, Knott argues that "while managing the German economy must contend with the politics of budgeting, a second argument is that the budget process must also grapple with the uncertainties of macroeconomics".[77] The basis of German federalism consists of three governmental levels, the federal government, the Bundesländer and the municipalities, apart from which the Bundesbank and trade unions also play a major role. German federalism appears to be such a complex system that any major and rapid changes in economic and social policy are difficult to make and implement. Parliamentary elections every four years and regional elections in 16 Bundesländer mean that politically difficult but still economically crucial reforms cannot necessarily be introduced due to the political fear of the coming elections. In addition, the competition between the government party (SPD) and the opposition party (CDU/CSU), the government and the Bundesländer, and the Old and New Länder has not increased the effectiveness of national economic coordination. By contrast, although reviving growth would require major reforms that would directly affect the interests of all these actors, this large number of powerful veto players has slowed down national economic coordination.

In legal terms, according to Article 30 of the German Constitution, the Bundesländer are responsible for implementing governmental functions and Article 31 defines that "Federal law overrides Land law". On the other hand, Article 70 states that the Bundesländer have the competence and power to legislate insofar as the Constitution does not confer legislative powers on the federal level. In other words, the federal government has competence in policy areas where the competence is not given to the Bundesländer. In public finances, the Bundesländer have considerable autonomy because Article 104a stipulates that the federal government and the Bundesländer will "separately meet the expenditure" but the federal government "may grant the Länder financial assistance". Article 109 finally specifies that "the Federation and the Länder shall be autonomous and independent of each other in their budget management".[78] In practice, national economic coordination is based on multi-level planning, coordination and management. For example, the federal government introduces the federal budget, which imposes policy constraints on the whole national economy and within which the Bundesländer have their own economic planning, which both aim to provide updated information about economic developments for policy-making. Despite the multi-level economic planning and policy-making, Article 51a of the Law on Budgetary Procedures requires that the federal government, the Bundesländer and the municipalities have to comply with the Stability Pact in national economic policy-making as a whole.

The implementation of the economic plans requires effective national political and economic coordination in order to set realistic targets under the existing economic realities. This process has encountered the problem of incentives and commitments at every governmental level in Germany. Where the government has been obliged to respect the Stability Pact at the European level, coordination has, however, faced stiff competition from different politico-economic interests at the national level. The government has thus faced a political situation where the economic autonomy of the Bundesländer has not contributed to meeting the European fiscal rules. The government has in particular struggled with the deficit rule because the Bundesländer have not had political or economic incentive for taking part in overall deficit reduction. On the other hand, the main question for the Bundesländer has been why they should make economic sacrifices for the deficit that has been created by the government. For this reason, the government has tried to improve the functioning of the Financial Planning Council and the National Stability Pact in national economic coordination. Although the Financial Planning Council has allocated the overall deficit of Germany to the government and the Bundesländer with a ratio of 45 and 55 percentage points, it has not eliminated the main problem, the question of incentives and commitments. The question could also be asked as *why there should be any special and major incentives for national economic coordination for the common good in the Bundesländer*. It is in the common interest to stabilise the national economy so that in the long term both the government and the Bundesländer could have growth and in the existing circumstances, this cannot be achieved without effective national economic coordination.

In order to modernise and improve national coordination and the federal system of Germany the *Bundestag* and the *Bundesrat* established a new commission, the Federalism Commission in 2003. The Commission is set to focus on constitutional responsibilities, legislative power and financial relations and the main aim is to further develop the German national system of coordination and governance.[79] The importance of this modernisation stems from the fact that German federalism seems to suffer from its own multi-level structure, German federalism, in EMU in the 21st century.[80] The main challenge is whether Germany as a unified nation-state can find a solution to the question of the authority of different governmental levels and common objectives. It is hard to believe that the continual veto-game could result in any long-lasting political agreements in matters that are already difficult enough for the nation-state without any additional internal games. The only long-term solution would be that on the one hand, the government should give up some of its legislative rights in some policy areas and thus decentralise its power to the Bundesländer level and on the other hand, the Bundesländer should give up some of their constitutional rights and promote the introduction of a more cooperative national system with the government.

Empirics of German national economic coordination

Although monetary authorities regarded effective national economic coordination as an essential precondition for achieving stable budgetary policy in EMU, it was still pointed out that it belongs to national affairs and they as such did not affect monetary policy. The success in national planning and management could, however, contribute to stable national fiscal and monetary developments. For supranational monitoring, effective national coordination also had an important role in responding to fiscal policy coordination. In Germany, it was the Financial Planning Council that was introduced and developed as a "practical instrument for reforming and strengthening economic coordination".[81] However, what was criticised was that the decisions made in the Financial Planning Council were not implemented and monitored effectively at the national and regional levels. The lack of political and economic incentives and the lack of monitoring and sanction procedures "could undermine the potential work of the Council" and the whole meaning of national economic coordination in Germany.[82]

National economic coordination was a crucial mechanism for German fiscal authorities. Although critical economic developments should have acted as a major incentive for national economic coordination, this did not happen in Germany. It was believed that for the Bundesländer, more intensive coordination could jeopardise their constitutional autonomy and thus, there was some resistance to the required reforms. In one interviewee's words, "the government will always face the everlasting dilemma where tax reforms are welcome but a reduction of public expenditure is not".[83] As the German Constitution allows the Bundesländer considerable economic autonomy, they lack formal incentives for national economic coordination. According to one interviewee, "the Bundesländer seem to have no incentive for cutting the deficit ratio although Germany exceeds the European criterion for the third time".[84] For example, national economic coordination under Article 51a of the Law on Budgetary Procedures proved to be politically and economically weaker than was expected. The main reason was that after 2002 the Financial Planning Council had difficult problems to resolve but its formal mandate and political and economic power was not in accord with the problems. However, the Council has done "good work but still its role could be clarified".[85] It was argued that the Council should have more political and economic power and more peer pressure on the implementation of the national and regional debt and deficit targets.

The Bundesländer authorities interviewed had an opposite understanding of national economic coordination than the federal fiscal authorities. It was argued that the Bundesländer had coped well with the deficit criterion but it was the government that had caused the problems with the Stability Pact. It was considered that coordination under the National Stability Pact was a good instrument in the direction of flexible cooperation. Although the National Stability Pact was formulated in 1996–1997 for a national coordination framework, there was no incentive for close national economic coordination after the start of EMU. However, the government had an incentive again when economic problems escalated in 2001. Then, the National Stability Pact and the Financial Planning Council had too many difficult issues, which meant that achieving them all in a short time was unrealistic: "economically, the objectives have been easy to state but politically too hard to achieve".[86] Interviewees realised that the major reduction in the deficit ratio would also require a reduction in public spending but spending would be hard to reduce for political reasons. Based on the interviews, the Financial Planning Council should be developed from general discussions and meetings to an institution that would really tackle the increasing debt and deficit stocks. Interviewees believed that this would mean that the historic economic relationship between the government and the Bundesländer would face a new era, more flexibility from both sides: "Our fiscal system is so complicated that that I do not know if we really understand what we are doing. To simplify the system is the only way."[87]

In interviews with academics, the concrete nature of German federalism, which was no longer effectively working as an integral part of European integration, was considered the main cause of problems in national economic coordination. It was believed that in the best-case scenario, the Federalism Commission could propose new and radical changes in the system of national economic coordination. Those interviewed criticised the work of the Financial Planning Council because in German economic policy-making it "has no concrete meaning".[88] It was also argued that the National Stability Pact had failed in national economic coordination because "it has been a weak agreement with zero binding power".[89] Given the German coordination tradition, any definite deficit ratio given to the Bundesländer would be politically very difficult. What Germany would really require is a clear consensus on national economic strategy that would be predictable and based on a realistic vision and through which the government and the Bundesländer could be more committed to the achievement of the common objectives in EMU. However, "this does not mean that the Bundesländer should give up any part of their economic autonomy".[90] Collective actions beyond constitutional duties and power are required because the previous actions towards stabilising the economy have only resulted in a situation where public expenditure is increasing, tax cuts are causing a major shortfall in public revenue and Germany does not comply with the common rules.

6.3 Fiscal policy coordination under the coming fiscal challenges in Europe

The European Central Bank and European policy mix

Question 7:
How aligned could the common monetary policy of the European Central Bank and the objectives of national fiscal policies be in economic policy coordination in EMU?

Practice on the European Central Bank and European policy mix

European policy mix in European economic policy coordination seems to be a forgotten mechanism in the EMU era although it was the European policy mix that was thought to solve all possible problems in economic policy coordination in EMU. European economic policy coordination has not been successful if the focus is directed at the fiscal element of the economic policy coordination and the coordination between the common monetary policy and national fiscal policies. Although the present fiscal problems in EMU have had an impact on the common monetary policy and thus more effective coordination between these two core policy elements should have been an obvious outcome, no European policy mix has yet been developed any further in European economic policy coordination. In Commissioner for Economic Affairs Almunia's view, "the EU coordination framework has been perceived as focusing mainly on fiscal policy, and in particular on budgetary balances and fiscal discipline, rather than on the overall interaction of various policies. It is therefore clear that efforts need to be made to better interlink economic and budgetary policies."[91]

However, the President of the ECB, Wim Duisenberg, was against the idea of developing European policy mix further because it was believed to jeopardise monetary discipline. In Duisenberg's opinion, "there cannot be any scope for an active coordination of fiscal and monetary policies. Such active coordination is bound to be ineffective, given the inability of both fiscal and monetary policy-makers to fine tune economic developments. Commitments to *ex ante* coordination between fiscal and monetary policies may blur the responsibilities of monetary and fiscal authorities and ultimately reduce their incentives to pursue their objectives. The economic outcome of such coordination is likely to be worse than the conduct of policies within the existing institutional set-up as only the latter ensures genuine accountability."[92] The ECB's objection to European policy mix stems from the fact that the ECB's primary objective is to safeguard price stability in the Euro area, whereas national fiscal policies should ensure fiscal stability for the common monetary policy. However, despite the ECB's independence and the price stability objective, "monetary and fiscal policies are linked by the intertemporal budget constraints of the government", as recently pointed out by Stark and Remsperger.[93] Thus, the current fiscal problems in EMU Member States require an assessment of the potential benefits of closer coordination between monetary and fiscal policies to fully support the fast recovery of the Euro area.

The fundamental need for closer coordination derives from the fact that economic policy-making in national economies has been constrained by the lack of national monetary policy instruments and increasing fiscal policy coordination. As the fiscal developments in the EMU area show, policy coordination has not functioned as planned and fiscal problems in national economies have also started to threaten the monetary discipline and the independence of the ECB. If one still insists on the maximum independence of the ECB, one should question how credible in the long term the kind of monetary policy-making is that has no interaction and cooperation at all with other strongly related and powerful economic actors in a situation where some Member States are experiencing major fiscal difficulties in EMU. Optimal economic policy coordination would be a model within which the objectives of monetary, fiscal and labour policies could be integrated into a successfully functioning coordination framework for stability and growth without jeopardising the independence and monetary mandate of the ECB.[94] Improving growth and employment and strengthening fiscal discipline would also benefit the ECB's objectives in the long term.

Empirics of the European Central Bank and European policy mix

In the interviews, the question of coordinating monetary and fiscal policies in EMU raised a number of essential politico-economic perspectives. European policy mix was seen as a potential coordination mechanism that nevertheless had some disadvantages. Firstly, monetary authorities emphasised that the ECB should focus primarily on price stability. Secondly, academics agreed that the monetary discipline was crucial and it should be under the ECB's responsibility but this responsibility should not eliminate the option for effective coordination. Thirdly, for supranational monitoring, even though the ECB's mandate was very clear, economic policy coordination was still required for the credibility of the whole EMU system and for stability and growth. Finally, fiscal authorities considered that in some economic circumstances the monetary authority could play a broader role than only and strictly the price stability in the Euro area.

For the monetary authorities interviewed there was a clear division of labour in EMU so that the ECB and the ESCB were responsible for monetary policy and the fiscal authorities were responsible for stable fiscal policy under the Stability Pact. It was believed that the ECB should not be active in the kind of European policy mix that might jeopardise its primary objectives. In one interviewee's words, "the main rule is that each keeps its house in order".[95] In the present economic system, it is the fiscal authorities that have to stabilise national fiscal policies and create a safety distance for the monetary policy. However, critical developments in national fiscal policies have shown that fiscal authorities have failed to create this safety distance. Increasing national budgetary deficits affects price stability and thus, monetary authorities were concerned about the situation and the future of the Stability Pact. On the other hand, some interviewees were not convinced "why the monetary policy should jeopardise the price stability target of the Treaty for solving the fiscal problems in the Euro area that have been caused by ineffective budgetary policies".[96] According to one interviewee, "the starting point has to be that Member States first strengthen fiscal stability, which would also create room for the functioning of automatic stabilisers".[97] Thus, the first step in strengthening European policy mix should be "getting back to the situation where the Stability Pact is implemented strictly and formally".[98]

European policy mix, which had not worked as effectively as expected, was still regarded as a potential instrument in EMU among German fiscal authorities. Although the ECB should focus on monetary policy, European policy mix could still create new potential in reviving growth in the whole Euro area. For those interviewed, European policy mix was understood in broad terms from monetary and fiscal policy coordination to the work of the Euro-12 group. The developments in the Euro area had increased the concrete need for economic policy coordination in its full meaning. For example, when facing declining growth after 2000, the ECB was expected to operate a more active and growth-supportive monetary policy but interest rates were not reduced until early 2001. One interviewee believed that in those circumstances, "the Bundesbank would have preferred a significantly lower interest rate policy thus lowering the impact of the sharp decline on the economy".[99] It was also believed that better monetary and fiscal policy coordination would have contributed to better economic policy-making in the Euro area at that time. In practice, the Euro-12 group as an informal body could have the required potential in strengthening coordination under European policy mix and under circumstances such as those between 2000 and 2001.

Academics also recognised the importance of maintaining price stability in EMU. It was argued that "it would be a big mistake for monetary policy if the ECB started responding to existing and future fiscal problems".[100] Economic policy coordination should nevertheless continue and European policy mix could have an essential role in that process. It was argued that better European policy mix could have "prevented the fundamental error in the interest rate policy of the ECB in 2000".[101] The main institutional problem in European policy mix stems, according to one interviewee, from the political situation where "politicians speak for more active coordination, whereas monetary authorities resist that idea".[102] It also emerged in interviews that the ECB's official policy on fiscal discipline and fiscal policy coordination should be much clearer and the ECB should have a more active role in European debate than before. It was proposed that the ECB could be more outspoken and could state clearly how it would like to see national fiscal policies implemented in the coming years. This does not mean that the monetary policy should not focus on price stability in the future, too. For one interviewee, "the monetary hand is tightened and that causes problems for fiscal politicians. But, if the ECB is not guiding the monetary policy, who is?"[103]

Population ageing and sustainable public finances in EMU

Question 8:
How extensive will the impact of population ageing be on the public finances in EMU?

Practice and empirics of population ageing in the public finances

Population ageing relates to a critical question of the future of the public finances in EU and EMU Member States. On the one hand, the work force is expected to work more, to be more effective and work longer than before. On the other hand, the age structure in Europe shows that more and more people are retiring and contributors to the public finances in terms of taxpayers are diminishing. According to the ECB, the old-age dependency ratio, which means the population aged 65 years and older as a proportion of the population aged 15 to 64, will rise from 25 percent in 2000 to more than 50 percent in 2050 in EMU.[104] In Germany, the same ratio is expected to rise significantly faster and to a higher level than in the EMU area on average from 27.5 percent in 2001 to 56.4 percent in 2050.[105] The German government has also estimated that old age pension expenditure in relation to GDP will increase from 11.1 percent in 2010 to 14.9 percent in 2050.[106] These developments, which are defined as a demographic change, will have a major impact on fiscal stability in Germany and elsewhere in Europe. The demographic change has a number of different channels through which it has an indirect and direct impact on national budgets. Firstly, people live longer than ever before. Secondly, birth rates have fallen so that there will be fewer work force and taxpayers in a society than before. Thirdly, people choose to retire sooner and at a younger age than before and thus more retired people will use more public services. Fourthly, due to the baby boom after the Second World War, a large proportion of people will be retiring simultaneously in the near future. Finally, the level of living standards and costs has increased, meaning that personal health costs may increase further in the future. The result of population ageing is that there will be fewer taxpayers to meet the increased need for public services in the future. Everyone knows that ageing affects public finance but still no radical actions have been taken.

The main question for sustainable public finances is through which concrete measures it would be possible to ensure fiscal stability under the coming new challenges since the fiscal stability has not been achieved so far even without these problems? Obviously, the various costs of ageing for public finance require major flexibility for national fiscal policies to act in the long term. When national economies struggle with the fiscal rules for the "common European good", more and more fiscal discipline is also needed for the "national good". Simultaneously, when national economies are expected to respond effectively to population ageing they are also expected to comply with the common European rules and other common economic commitments: an economic environment that is likely to experience some further difficulties in the future. In these circumstances, the monetary authorities interviewed emphasised "the crucial need for sustainable public finances in the future", whereas fiscal authorities were concerned about how ageing affects already "fragile national fiscal stability".[107] In one interviewee's view in the Bundesländer, "in the near future, up to 50 percent of the German budget could be spent on social services and security benefits without any radical actions".[108] For one academic, "Germany should start preparing".[109]

The financial impact of the ageing scenario was already emphasised by the Helsinki European Council in December 1999. According to the Council, national economies should take into account the impact of ageing on their national economic policies and how it affects stable budgetary policy.[110] This recommendation was derived from the fact that ageing would have a negative impact on social services, public finance and growth. Simultaneously, two main factors, increasing life expectancy and decreasing birth rates, also cause a lack of new and skilled labour force. The only effective strategy would be to prepare for population ageing and its impact, and thus balance the economic burden between generations, that is intergenerational redistribution. If the present generation did not make adequate adjustments by cutting pensions and public services, then future generations would be forced to adjust themselves to the socio-economically weaker circumstances created by the present generation. A recent Commission study explains that the primary reason for the significance of population ageing stems from the fact that "when ageing-related expenditure increases, future generations would be obliged to bear the consequences".[111]

To ensure intergenerational fairness in public services and financial burden national economies should prepare for this major demographic change. Since all national developments and policy actions affect the extent of the ageing and thus, differences how and to what extent national economies should prepare for the change could vary across European countries. However, the study clearly states that "under current policies, even if optimistically interpreted, ageing-related expenditures are growing considerably in most countries".[112]

> **Question 9:**
> Did other EMU Member States implement significantly better national budgetary policy than the German government from 1998 to 2006?

Practice and empirics of budgetary developments in other EMU member states

It has been Germany and the German economy that have caused a major part of the problems in the Stability Pact. It is worth remembering that in 2001, German Finance Minister, Hans Eichel, literally still insisted that "no matter what, we will stay under the three percent fiscal rule".[113] On the other hand, budgetary developments outside the EMU area have not been so favourable after all. For example, the data shows that the developments in the budgetary deficit in Britain have not been so much better than in Germany. Even the British Chancellor, Gordon Brown, has had increasing difficulties in achieving his own golden rule and deficit targets (–3.3%) in 2005 and (–2.9%) 2006 although the economy has grown about 2.0 percent (1.9%) in 2005 and (2.2%) 2006. Britain will need more public net borrowing to close the larger-than-expected financial gap in the budget despite the optimistic growth expectation. The increasing deficit will have no immediate impact on the British economic stability because the debt-to-GDP ratio has been one of the lowest in the EU, but politically, it shows that even countries outside the single-currency area are also facing budgetary problems.

Figure 6.2 summarises developments in public debt in EMU Member States from 1998 to 2006. Based on the trends in the debt ratio in the EMU Member States, it is possible to identify three main groups of EMU Member States. Firstly, Belgium, Greece and Italy constitute Group One with debt ratios that have actually exceeded the whole national annual GDP. However, all these three countries have succeeded in cutting public debt. Belgium has had the biggest reduction in debt from 117.0 percent in 1998 to 89.4 percent in 2006. Group Two consists of Member States Austria, France, Germany and Portugal, whose debt ratios remained above the rule of 60.0 percent. Of these Member States, Germany had the highest (67.8%) and Austria the lowest (62.1%) debt ratio in 2006. Group Three states, that is Finland, Ireland, the Netherlands and Spain, have the lowest debt ratio in EMU. The most favourable debt trend has been in Ireland, where the

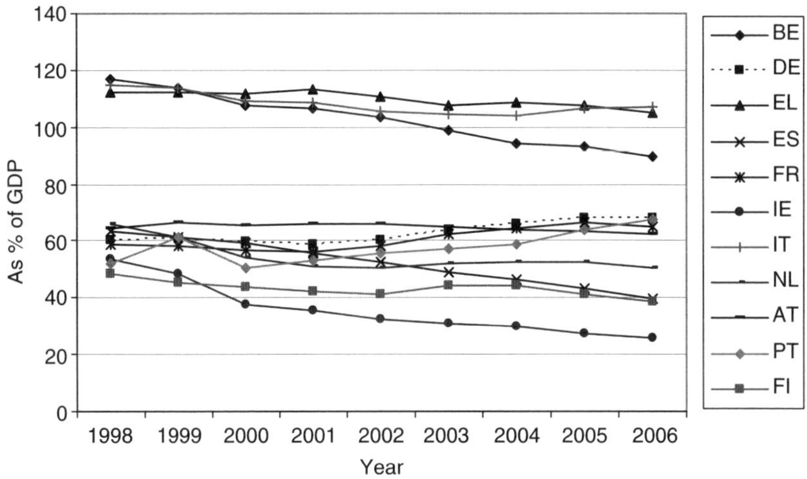

Figure 6.2 Public debt in the Euro area 1998–2006.[114]

debt ratio fell from 53.4 percent in 1998 to only 25.8 percent in 2006. Seven EMU Member States were thus above the public debt rule in 2006: Austria, Belgium, France, Germany, Greece, Italy and Portugal.

Figure 6.3 illustrates how the ratio of budgetary deficit of GDP has varied across EMU Member States from 1998 to 2006. Firstly, Finland has had the most favourable trend in budgetary position over the whole period. After peaking as high as 6.9 percent in 2000, the surplus of Finland decreased but

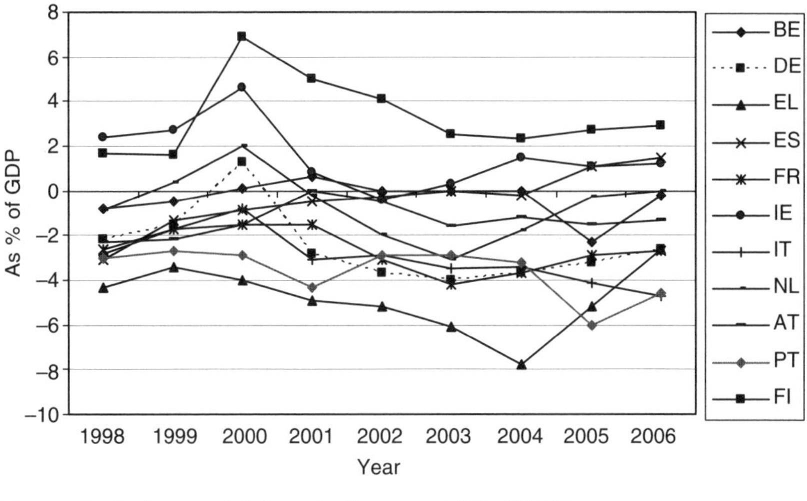

Figure 6.3 Budgetary deficit in the Euro area 1998–2006.[115]

it remained at a high level of 2.9 percent in 2006. Secondly, Belgium, Ireland, the Netherlands and Spain reached a balanced budgetary position or a surplus in 2006. For example, Spain had a major deficit of 3.1 percent in 1998 but in 2006 the economy experienced a surplus of 1.5 percent of GDP. Thirdly, there are many EMU Member States whose budgetary position was clearly negative in 2006. For example, the deficit of Germany diminished from 4.0 percent in 2003 to 2.6 percent in 2006. Similarly, France cut the deficit from the ratio of 4.2 in 2003 down to 2.7 percent in 2006. Fourthly, Italy and Portugal had the most unfavourable developments of all in their deficit position. The budgetary deficit of Italy was 4.7 percent and that of Portugal 4.6 percent in 2006. They were thus the only EMU Member States to break the deficit rule in 2006.

As shown through the interviews in this chapter, the institutional system of fiscal policy coordination has had clear strengths but it has also faced major political, economic, institutional and legal weaknesses in EMU. The interviewees represented different levels of economic policy-making processes but the answers were closely linked to the perceptions and interests of the institutions where they worked (Figure 7.5). Based on the clear and strong positions of the interviewees, it has been Germany that has caused the primary crisis in implementing the Stability Pact and the experience from the crisis of the German economy under European fiscal policy coordination has had a major impact on reforming the original rules of the Stability Pact of 1997. Interviewees also shared the view that the institutional system of the Stability Pact was still essential even though the rules and the implementation rules should be clarified. Although the main criticism in the interviews was directed towards Germany, economic trends show that Germany has not been the only Member State, or "bad student", to break the fiscal rules of the Stability Pact in EMU.

This fact can be confirmed by practical economic policy-making in some EMU Member States. For example, the case of Greece in 2004 created a new and critical debate on the institutional effectiveness of fiscal policy coordination. The explanation for the marked increase in the deficit of Greece stems from the fact that the economic information prior to the EMU era was false. According to the information of Prime Minister Karamanlis in September 2004, the Greek government expected a huge increase in the actual deficit ratio. After the correction of the figures from 1997 to 2000, Greece did not fulfil the deficit criterion of the Maastricht Treaty for EMU membership (–4.3% in 1998, –3.4% in 1999 and –4.0% in 2000) and thus, it joined EMU in 2001 on the basis of a false budgetary position. These critical developments in this already economically challenging and politically complex system of fiscal policy coordination provide great academic ammunition for the theoretical developments and interpretations of the present politico-economic circumstances in EMU as described by this research.

7
Challenging the Existing Understanding of Europeanisation in the Study of Germany, the Stability and Growth Pact and Policy Coordination

7.1 Uploading, downloading and reuploading of Europeanisation

Securing German adaptation "fits" in fiscal policy coordination

The key focus of this politico-economic research has been directed to European fiscal policy coordination, the implementation of the Stability and Growth Pact in Germany and German national adjustments in EMU. The primary objective has been to examine *how and to what extent the formation of the Stability and Growth Pact has affected the implementation of German national fiscal policy in EMU*. Europeanisation has been a useful and applicable concept in examining the extent to which EU institutions have mattered and affected German national economic policy-making as well as national policy responses in the EMU era. This research has clearly demonstrated that German national economic policy-making and national policy responses have also had a major impact on the role and functioning of EU institutions: the two-way relationship between EU institutions and Member States has been significant in fiscal policy coordination.

Europeanisation is one of the most topical issues in the current integration process but its practical role in and impact on fiscal policy coordination has remained partly unclear. Therefore, this research has put together an approach to analysing as well as theorising the concrete processes of Europeanisation in fiscal policy coordination through the case study of the German economy between 1998 and 2005. The adaptation position of the German economy, in practice, defined the extent to which Germany led the formation process of the Stability Pact for EMU (uploading) and the extent to which Germany had to adjust its own national politico-economic structures to secure the required national fiscal stability in EMU (downloading). This national adaptation position of Germany was analysed through the fundamental distinction between adaptation "fits" and "misfits" both in the uploading and downloading processes. According to Dyson, although Germany supported EMU and the Stability Pact on the basis of its own national objectives in the uploading process, the increased economic policy coordination still created "unanticipated consequences for powerful domestic actors" in the downloading process.[1] EMU (monetary policy) and the Stability Pact (fiscal policy) had a major impact on German economic policy-making despite the aim of securing a national adaptation "fit", German national politico-economic structures faced the unanticipated challenge of being labelled a "misfit" in the downloading phase of European fiscal policy coordination. In agreement with Dyson's view, "in the creation of EMU Germany was able to play the role of 'pace-setter' in a classic way, based on its capacity to 'upload' its own policy preferences and institutional practices to the EU level".[2]

Although Germany managed to upload its main national interests into the Stability Pact in 1995–1997, it still had political and economic challenges to solve, which threatened to become major adaptation "misfits" in EMU. In some policy areas (Figures 3.5, 3.6 and 3.7 on interest rate, exchange rate and inflation), Germany had adaptation "fits", which meant that in those areas Germany had to accomplish relatively fewer national adjustments to meet the pressure of economic policy coordination than in those policy areas where economic convergence had just started (Figures 3.1 and 3.2 on debt and deficit) as well as those other Member States that were more asymmetric (less converged) in terms of economic structures (for example Greece and Italy with large debts). If there had been major adaptation "misfits" in the formation process of economic policy coordination in a Member State, it would have been a question of the politico-economic role and power of the Member State to contribute to diminishing those national "misfits" through European cooperation and multi-level negotiations, as Germany as a large and powerful Member State did with fiscal policy in the case of the Stability Pact. Thus, the Stability Pact as a supranational coordination mechanism for the EMU era includes calculated and rational German political and economic interests, which could be understood as a clear pathway in institutional-building towards the making of a common European fiscal policy alongside the common monetary policy in EMU.

This politico-economic power of position also relates to the distinction between strong (large) and weak (small) Member States because Germany as an economically and politically strong Member State succeeded in effectively uploading its national interests into the system of European fiscal policy coordination. To reduce national "misfits" and increase national "fits" Germany took the leading role in the formation process of the Stability Pact to ensure fiscal discipline for the common monetary policy. However, Germany failed to some extent to take into account the timing element of fiscal policy coordination. This means that Germany focused primarily on solving its own and European fiscal problems in the short term, which had reached a critical point in the late 1990s, instead of thinking forward beyond the beginning of the third stage of EMU. The German government was convinced that national economic policy would remain stable and without any major difficulties in EMU and thus, the national economy would not require any major adjustments prior to the EMU era. However, the timing element of Europeanisation proved crucial when analysing why Germany had such severe national problems in implementing the Stability Pact in the 21st century even though it was Germany that shaped the content of the Stability Pact most in the period 1995–1997: why did not Germany manage to keep its national commitments to the full implementation of the fiscal rules of the Stability Pact in EMU?

The degree of national adaptation pressures also relates to the challenge of constraining and enabling in national economic policy-making under the Stability Pact. According to Dyson and Goetz, "when it comes to the effects of integration on Germany, perhaps the single most important theme in both political and academic discourse has been the interdependence between the enabling and the constraining dimensions of Germany's participation in integration".[3] As explained in this research, Germany's national targets in general terms were to reduce national "misfits" and increase national "fits" for the future economic, monetary and fiscal benefits in EMU. This way Germany planned to have fewer adaptation problems in EMU after 1999 than those Member States that did not succeed in promoting their national political and economic interests in the formation of EMU and the Stability Pact as effectively as Germany (Hypothesis One). This was the main reason why Germany took the "constraining-enabling" risk of increasing economic, monetary and fiscal policy coordination for EMU despite its likely political and economic threats in the future.[4] In practice, the monetary and fiscal preconditions for EMU, the convergence criteria, the more specific rules of the Stability Pact as well as the European processes have constrained the German fiscal policy more than they have enabled it in EMU so far, resulting in reforming and reinterpreting the original common fiscal rules (Hypothesis Two). Enabling in fiscal policy coordination implies that Member States may also achieve other national goals than what were planned and/or they may gain more political and economic power at the European level after the implementation of the common objectives of fiscal policy coordination. Constraining in fiscal policy coordination means in turn that Member States have to implement national fiscal policy under the common European fiscal rules and guidelines and breaking those rules could set in motion a supranational sanction procedure and fines amounting to billions of Euros. As Dyson and Goetz rightly claim: "While the notion of 'enabling constraints' discourages thinking in terms of trade-offs, enabling and constraining effects may also be seen as a matter of strategic calculation about the appropriate balance to be struck between the two".[5]

Three dimensions of Europeanisation in fiscal policy coordination

The first hypothesis argued in Chapter 1 that *the greater role a Member State has had in the formation (uploading) of the common institutional system for European fiscal policy coordination (the Stability Pact), the fewer national economic and other adaptation problems it has when implementing (downloading) the common fiscal objectives.*

Figure 7.1 summarises the three "-loading" phases of Europeanisation in fiscal policy coordination under the Stability Pact in EMU. Firstly, it was Chapter 3 that focused on the uploading dimension of Europeanisation in the formation of fiscal policy coordination. Uploading in fiscal policy coordination referred to a process by which a Member State, based on its

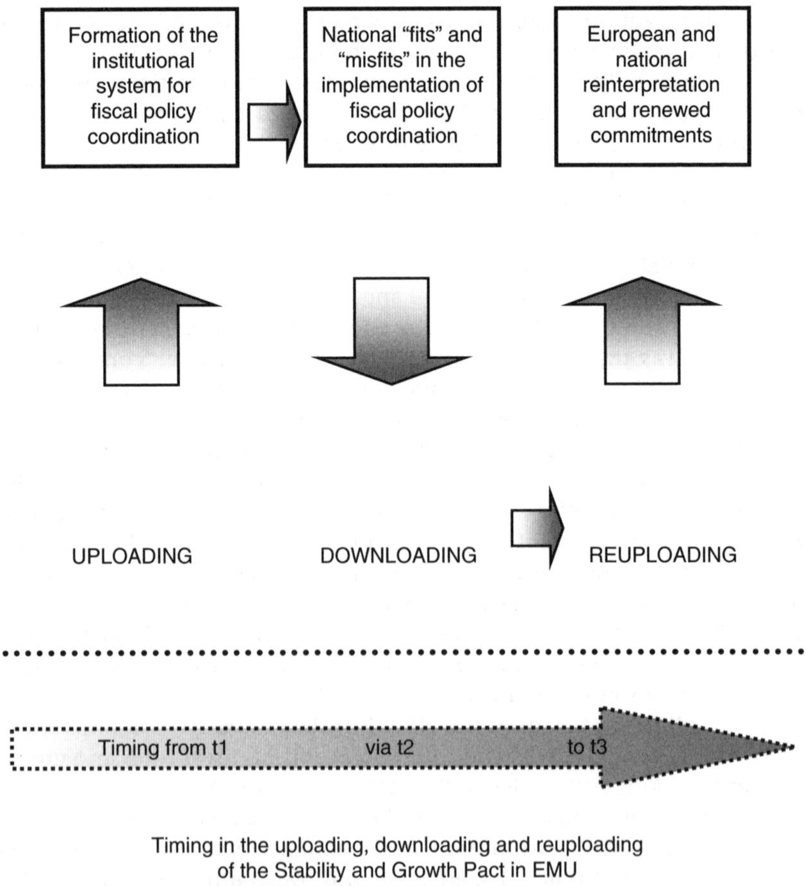

Figure 7.1 The three "-loading" phases of Europeanisation in fiscal policy coordination under the Stability Pact in EMU.

national politico-economic interests, tried to contribute to the institutional system and concrete objectives of the Stability Pact for the EMU era when it was negotiated, formulated and adopted 1995–1997 (t1). However, there was only one key uploader, Germany, in this uploading process, which, in practice, determined both the institutional system and the objectives for coordinating national fiscal policies in EMU. It was Germany's national political and economic interests on which the Stability Pact, together with its strict fiscal rules and supranational monitoring, was based. As the formation of European fiscal policy coordination was derived from German national interests and objectives, the uploading phase of European fiscal policy coordination was a clear bottom-up, nation-state-led process.

Although the German government introduced the content of the Stability Pact, fiscal policy coordination under the Stability Pact created not only national adaptation "fits" but also some major "misfits" for the German economy. Where adaptation "misfits" required active national reforms in economic, institutional, political and cooperational structures, adaptation "fits" meant that in those areas the scale and range of national adjustments could be much more limited. Whereas monetary policy was a major "fit" for the German economy, national economic policy-making under the strict rules of the Stability Pact in EMU turned out to be a significant "misfit". Although the German government itself promoted the idea of strict fiscal policy coordination, it still did not sufficiently prepare for the political and economic impact of the increasing coordination in EMU on its national structures; a major policy failure that is the primary reason for the present implementation problems in Germany. Although the uploading phase of Europeanisation refers only to the timely-specific formation process in which Member States themselves establish new common EU institutions and institutional coordination mechanisms, the uploading of the Stability Pact has had major long-term economic, institutional, political and cooperational implications, as the politico-economic circumstances in the downloading phase in the EMU era clearly indicate.

Secondly, where the uploading process acted as a starting point for the new and common system of the Stability Pact, the downloading phase 1998–2002 (t2) also appeared significant. Where uploading refers to a bottom-up process, downloading refers to a top-down implementation in which common objectives are put into practice in each Member State. The initial aim of the downloading phase was that the implementation of common fiscal objectives under the common EU institutions (the independent variable) should result in the same policy outcomes although practical implementation processes and adjustment measures may vary across Member States. Chapter 4 in particular focused on the downloading process of the Stability Pact in Germany and those national mechanisms through which the German government responded to the impact of fiscal policy coordination in EMU. Strikingly, the analysis discovered that the implementation did not result in the same kind of national policy outcomes; rather, it could be argued that there was no full implementation of the Stability Pact at all in Germany. Although the German government had believed, prior to the Stability Pact, that it would be mainly cost-free for Germany to adjust its national structures to the intensifying fiscal policy coordination in EMU, the analysis of German national economic policy doubtlessly showed that the adjustment process was far from cost-free. The German government has had to pay the price of not making the required, sufficient and timely-effective adjustments prior to EMU in increasing debt and deficit stocks, declining economic growth and increasing unemployment in EMU.

Due to its economic problems since 2000, Germany did not fully comply with the fiscal rules of the Stability Pact. In fact, it was the German economy that caused the most problems for the credibility of the whole system of fiscal policy coordination in EMU, as examined in Chapters 5 and 6. It is noteworthy that the economic problems in Germany resulted in a situation where the Commission and the Ecofin Council started to struggle over the institutional authority in fiscal policy coordination. The fact that Germany continually broke the fiscal rules and the fact that EU institutions did not find a mutual understanding of institutional duties and responsibilities in fiscal policy coordination meant that the whole Stability Pact was finally frozen on 25 November 2003. The Ecofin Council allowed Germany major fiscal flexibility in January 2002, November 2002 and November 2003 on which Germany increasingly insisted under the strict rules of the Stability Pact and the common monetary policy of the ECB. However, where small EMU Member States, for example Finland, easily succeeded in pursuing their fiscal policies while fully respecting the Stability Pact, Germany exceeded the deficit criterion from 2001. Thus, the policy outcome was not similar across the EMU area despite the same institutional system for fiscal policy coordination. As the strict fiscal policy coordination was no longer optimal and suitable for Germany's economic and political interests (from more "enabling" to more "constraining"), the German government contributed to reforming the original fiscal rules to better comply with its existing national circumstances from 2003 to 2005 (t3). In other words, once uploaded, German politico-economic interests between 1995 and 1997 turned out to be suboptimal in EMU in the 21st century (the timing element) and thus, the fiscal rules had to be reformed to be more suitable for Germany's new, changed interests; there had to be a reuploading process. This new nation-state-led process of reuploading was, in practice, characterised by the active and powerful role of the German government in politically reinterpreting the fiscal rules in the Ecofin Council. Although the Commission had monitored and reported the existence of the excessive deficit in Germany, the Ecofin Council, based on its right in the last resort to make a political and flexible interpretation of the fiscal rules of the

Stability Pact, persistently decided not to apply the excessive deficit procedure to Germany.

The timing element in the Europeanisation of fiscal policy coordination

The timing element played a major role in the path-dependent process from uploading via downloading to reuploading of the Stability Pact (Figure 7.1) and therefore, the timing element should be put into a more specific analysis. According to Ekengren, who is one of the pioneers in the temporal study of European integration, "every political organisation is grounded on a certain temporality, which historically is as unique and central to its constitution as its spatial definition".[6] In European fiscal policy co-ordination, as discovered in this research, this temporality or the timing dimension of Europeanisation has had a dual role in national economic policy-making under the common rules, guidelines and objectives. The timing element has primarily taken place at two highly interconnected governance levels: EU institutions and Member States. In order to have a profound understanding of the relationship between European and national economic policy-making this research analysed the relationship between these two main governance levels through the German economy. In Pierson's view, "placing politics in time, systematically situating particular moments (including the present) in a temporal sequence of events and processes, can greatly enrich our understanding of complex social dynamics".[7]

When tracing this "temporal sequence of events and processes" it was discovered that the role of the timing element, in practice, significantly varied from one economic policy area to another in the European Union. Figure 7.2 illustrates in general how the timing element and differences in national adaptation relates together in the common monetary policy and national fiscal policies, that is the two main elements of European economic policy. Monetary policy refers to exchange, credit and interest rate policies, whereas fiscal policy includes budgetary, taxation, labour and structural policies. The lower part of the figure focuses on the formation of the common monetary policy. In analysing the process of the start of the Euro area, three main adaptation phases in EMU Member States can be identified. Firstly, all EMU Member States had their own national currencies and national monetary policies (t1). The formation of the single European monetary policy, however, meant that all national monetary policies were replaced by a common monetary policy from 1999 and all national currencies in the monetary union were converted into the single currency, the Euro, from 2002 (t3). Despite the significance of the transformation from 12 different national monetary policies and currencies into a single currency and policy, the national adaptation of the policy change took place fast and without major problems in national implementation or

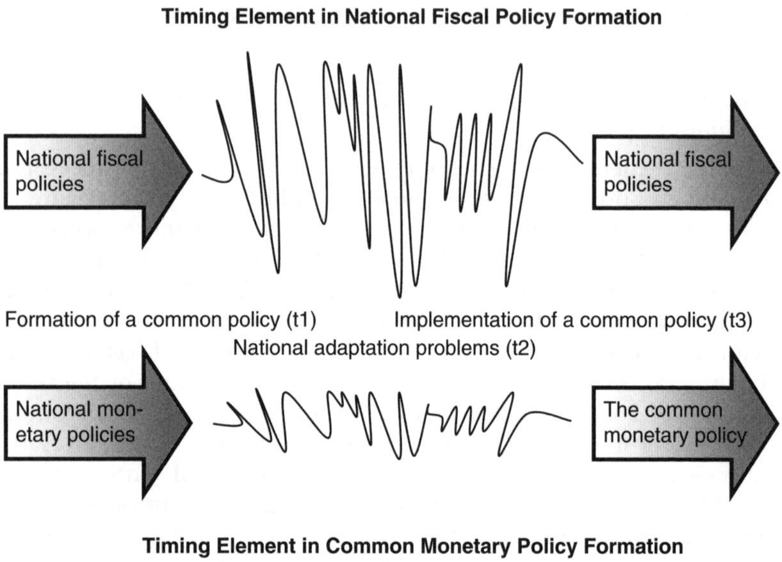

Figure 7.2 Timing element in the formation and implementation of common European fiscal and monetary policies.

with the time limit (t2). Although some EMU Member States initially had adaptation difficulties with the common monetary policy, difficulties in national adaptation were only minor fading in no time when the common monetary policy was implemented after 2002 (t3).

The upper part of the figure illustrates the making of a common European fiscal policy. Contrary to the developments in the common monetary policy, fiscal policy had dramatic difficulties ("misfits") in the implementation phase because, according to Hughes Hallett, Hutchison and Hougaard Jensen, "the fiscal issues related to the operation of EMU are in many ways more complex than the monetary issues".[8] Although all Member States in EMU have recognised and agreed on the main purpose of fiscal policy coordination, it is still noteworthy that some Member States have not yet succeeded in implementing the common fiscal policy objectives sufficiently and without major adaptation problems. Even though Member States have established the institutional system of the Stability Pact for coordinating and monitoring fiscal developments in Member States (t1), it is still not yet totally clear whether all Member States will really achieve the common fiscal policy objectives in EMU (t3). Although the implementation phase took place rapidly and without major adaptation problems in monetary policy, developments in the making of a common European fiscal policy have been the opposite, indicating the incompleteness of fiscal policy institutionalisation (t2).

The reason for this significant difference in national adaptation between monetary and fiscal policies can be derived, for example, from the political realist understanding of policy coordination and European cooperation.[9] Hoffmann has proposed the concepts of "low" and "high' politics, which can also be applied to European economic institutionalisation. Based on this original characterisation, economic integration is faster and easier to complete between national governments than political integration and thus, economic integration is defined as low politics, which now can be applied to monetary policy. From the standpoint of low politics, the benefits for national governments from the common monetary policy in EMU are assumed to be greater than the impact of the loss of national monetary authority and concrete monetary instruments on effective national economic policy-making. In other words, establishing the European Central Bank as the common monetary authority was expected to result in more net benefits to national governments than giving up the monetary authority would cause net economic and political difficulties at the national levels. In this respect, monetary policy as low politics has been politically and economically easy and fast to institutionalise (harmonise) in European economic integration.

By contrast, fiscal integration, if defined as high politics, affects the fundamental element of the other part of the national economy and therefore, similarly giving up fully and transforming national fiscal authority towards a common European fiscal policy in the environment of the common monetary policy is economically and politically less likely to happen. For example, budgetary, taxation, labour and structural policies belong to this definition of high politics in fiscal policy. If Member States had also totally given up the whole fiscal authority and all fiscal policy instruments along with the monetary authority in European economic integration, then the practical power to implement effective national economic policy would have been very limited. In these circumstances, there would no longer be national economic policy in EMU but highly institutionalised (harmonised) European fiscal federalism with common economic objectives, instruments and actions. Therefore, Member States have wanted to retain some of their authority in one of the most significant economic policy areas, that is they have treated fiscal policy as high politics. Although monetary integration has strictly and quickly proceeded through the three stages of the Delors Report, European economic institutionalisation in fiscal policy has not met with such enthusiasm as the establishment of the single-currency area: the difference between low and high politics.

The fundamental problems of the German economy with low growth, insufficient adjustments and ineffective national economic coordination resulted in six institutional procedures under fiscal policy coordination in 2002–2005. Until 2002, the downloading of Europeanisation had been successful in explaining the process of national implementation in fiscal policy coordination. However, the substantial "misfits" in national implementation after 2002 froze the whole downloading process of the Stability Pact in Germany, simultaneously freezing the explanatory capacity of the traditional two-way Europeanisation. After 2002, the process of Europeanisation in fiscal policy coordination has taken a totally new path, reuploading. Figure 7.3 summarises these six critical timing events in the process of reuploading from the point of view of the German economy. Firstly, as analysed in Chapter 4, Germany faced European economic monitoring under the Stability Pact for the very first time in January 2002 when the Commission made a recommendation of an early warning to the Ecofin Council that the debt and deficit ratios of Germany were dramatically increasing and threatening national economic stability. However, based on Germany's renewed commitments, the Ecofin Council only decided to closely monitor economic developments in Germany without putting the recommendation to a vote. Secondly, Germany was subjected to European economic monitoring for the second time in November 2002. As in the case of January 2002, the Commission made a recommendation of an early warning to the Ecofin Council but the Ecofin Council only decided to continue close monitoring over economic and financial developments in the German economy. This was the second time in succession when the excessive deficit procedure under the Stability Pact was not applied to Germany in the Ecofin Council.

Thirdly, the Commission made the third recommendation of an early warning against Germany in November 2003, which was the start for the most recent developments in European fiscal policy coordination; for reinterpreting the original rules of the Stability Pact. Although the Ecofin

Figure 7.3 Timing events in fiscal policy coordination 2002–2005.

Council this time put the recommendation to a vote on 25 November 2003, the decision was negative. Thus, the excessive deficit procedure was not applied for a third time in succession. The most significant result was that the Commission decided to bring the failure of the Ecofin Council to act before the European Court of Justice in January 2004. The fourth stage in fiscal policy coordination took place on 13 July 2004 when the European Court of Justice made its final ruling on whether the Ecofin Council had fully followed the decision-making rules and procedures of the Stability Pact on 25 November 2003. In its ruling, the Court took the view that the appeal of the Commission was correct and that the Ecofin Council had broken the institutional procedure of the excessive deficit procedure and thus the case was referred back to political consideration to the Ecofin Council.

Fifthly, the Commission introduced a new Communication in September 2004 in which it presented how the fiscal rules of the Stability Pact should be reformed to strengthen the implementation process in Member States. The Ecofin Council widely shared the opinion of the Commission and formulated a six-point list of concrete measures in November 2004 that should be taken into account in the reform of the Stability Pact. Sixthly and most recently, after extensive political debate and several Ecofin Council meetings in January, February and March, the Ecofin Council eventually reformed the fiscal rules and the interpretation of the fiscal rules of the Stability Pact to revive the credibility and effectiveness of fiscal policy coordination in EMU on 20 March 2005; a decision that was officially approved by the Brussels European Council on 22–23 March 2005. Thus, the historical process of forming an effective institutional system for fiscal policy coordination in EMU developed from articulating to coordinate national fiscal policies under the Stability Pact in 1995 via the continual failures to apply the sanction mechanism of the Stability Pact in 2002–2003 to the decision in which the original agreement on national fiscal policy-making in EMU was changed in 2005: from uploading (fit) via downloading (misfit) to reuploading (refit).

Which Europeanisation matters in fiscal policy coordination?

As demonstrated in this empirical research, Europeanisation, as presented in the existing academic literature, has too often been defined as a straightforward process in which the downloading phase just follows the uploading phase. Although the literature has acknowledged that Europeanisation should be interpreted as a two-way process, it still lacks a thorough understanding of what happens after the downloading phase in Europeanisation. In other words, there has been partial ignorance so far as to what really happens at the European level and domestically when the implementation of common policy objectives has significantly failed in a Member State.[10] It seems that the existing literature of Europeanisation has assumed that once the common policy objectives have been established and that although some national adaptation "misfits" may occur, there would not be any significant difficulties in the national implementation phase in the end; the full implementation has been expected to take place in Member States regardless of possible national adaptation problems.

However, as confirmed in this empirical research, this belief of the traditional Europeanisation literature has turned out to be questionable. Figure 7.4 summarises the new and reformed dynamics of Europeanisation in fiscal policy coordination. Europeanisation in intimate relation to economic integration has, in practice, developed in three different but interconnected phases in the post-Maastricht era. As a striking finding, as the case of Germany has clearly illustrated, the traditional logic of two-way Europeanisation (that is only the uploading and downloading processes) is not so effective and straightforward after all in European fiscal policy coordination. When major adaptation problems occur in the implementa-

Traditional "two-way" Europeanisation

PHASE I: UPLOADING 1995–1997	National political and economic interests launched the formation of new institutions for fiscal policy coordination in EMU
PHASE II: DOWNLOADING 1998–2002	Common institutions in fiscal policy started to function causing major changes and "misfits" in original national interests

New and reformed "three-way" Europeanisation

PHASE III: REUPLOADING 2003–2005

- Fading national commitments and malfunctioning institutional coordination
- Reforms in common policy objectives based on reformulated national interests
- Renewed national political commitments
- Changes in national interests launched the reform of common rules and agreements in European fiscal policy coordination
- Concrete policy outcome: refunctioning institutional fiscal policy coordination within reformed, relaxed fiscal rules in EMU

Figure 7.4 Reformed dynamics of Europeanisation in fiscal policy coordination.

tion phase (downloading) and the existing national interests no longer comply with those of the common policy objectives, then a Member State does not continue the implementation phase with whatever associated political and economic costs and measures. Instead, the Member State tries to contribute to reforming and reinterpreting the common objectives and the functioning of the common EU institutions to better suit changed national political and economic interests. This process of reuploading, which has been identified and extensively analysed through the case of the German economy from 2003 to 2005, provides a significant insight to the present study of the process of Europeanisation in EMU.[11]

Traditional Europeanisation has played a major role in the understanding of the logic of policy formation and policy implementation in the European political and economic integration process. Where uploading has really helped in analysing the formation of common coordination procedures in fiscal policy under the Stability Pact, the downloading phase has been useful in examining the national implementation of the common objectives in practice. However, the adaptation problems in the German economy were so severe that the downloading phase of fiscal policy coordination was not successful at all and it was partly frozen even though it was Germany that had uploaded its own national interests into the Stability Pact; a possible policy development that had not sufficiently been considered or taken into account by the traditional two-way Europeanisation. Due to the implementation problems after 2002, German national commitments towards fiscal policy coordination faded and Germany no longer fully respected the debt and deficit rules of the Stability Pact. Through the reinterpretation of the rules of the Stability Pact (reuploading national interests) Germany aimed at specifying common policy objectives to better comply with its changed and reformed national interests in EMU. Now that the fiscal rules have been reformulated (relaxed), the German government is able to renew its political and economic commitments to fiscal policy coordination. Therefore, the reuploading dimension can be defined as a new and concrete bottom-up process of Europeanisation: from national interests towards major changes in common institutional procedures and policy-making. The reuploading process has shown that national political and economic interests (of large and powerful Member States) have been brought back to the highest position in European politics and policy-making.

The key argument here is that the empirical evidence learned from the case of Germany is thus counter-intuitive on the traditional two-way understanding of Europeanisation. Germany has been the key actor (pace-setter) in uploading political and economic interests into European fiscal policy coordination. However, it has been Germany that has experienced the severest problems in downloading the fiscal rules of the Stability Pact in EMU; the rules that were created by Germany itself. Although Europeanisation still matters in the study of fiscal policy coordination, the first hypothesis has to be proved false and redefined, as follows: *Contrary to the traditional understanding of two-way Europeanisation, the greater role a Member State has had in the formation of the common institutional system for European fiscal policy coordination does not necessarily mean that the Member State has fewer adaptation problems, "misfits", in the national adjustment process when implementing the common fiscal objectives.* It should also be recognised that this lesson of the phases of Europeanisation is learned from the single case study of the German economy regarding the implementation of the Stability Pact in EMU and thus, it is not necessarily universally applicable to all EU and EMU Member States. However, the key theoretical and empirical argument of the research about reuploading national interests could also be applied to other large Member States' (for example France) policy areas other than only fiscal policy (for example environmental policy) even though the study of German economic policy has been country-specific; a major elaboration of this research that directly contributes to institutionalist theory-building.

7.2 Fiscal policy without a state in EMU?

National fiscal authority in practice in EMU

The second hypothesis argued in Chapter 1 that *the more institutionalised fiscal policy coordination is at the European level, the fewer adjustment problems will occur in fiscal policy implementation in a Member State and the less the Member State will try politically and economically to reform and reinterpret the common rules (reuploading).*

From the point view of national fiscal authority, there were widely shared political intentions among leading European economies to develop a common monetary union in Europe in the first phase of the historical pathway towards a common European economic policy; a pathway which paved the way from the Barre and Werner Plans through the European Monetary System to the Maastricht Treaty and EMU. In the second phase of this historical pathway, monetary integration was followed by strong coordination in fiscal policy to contribute to the stability and growth of the monetary union area; a pathway which was defined by the "hard" Maastricht convergence criteria, the fiscal rules of the Stability Pact as well as an increasing number of "soft" European coordination processes. In this way this European historical pathway from monetary integration to fiscal policy coordination has proceeded towards establishing a single and complete Economic and Monetary Union, in which not only the common monetary policy (the European Central Bank) but also fiscal policy (the Stability Pact) would be pursued independently from national governments at the European, supranational level. The Europeanisation of economic policy coordination in its broad meaning has had a wide range of politico-economic implications for national economic, monetary and fiscal, authority and concrete national economic policy-making processes.

In the post-Maastricht era, the role of national fiscal authority under the Stability Pact has, in practice, been characterised by the Franco-German alliance and the political competition between large and small EMU Member States. These two primary dichotomies in fiscal policy coordination have clearly illustrated how and to what extent national interests have been incorporated into common coordination mechanisms and objectives in EMU. Firstly, the Franco-German alliance and the politico-economic tensions between these two largest European economies have had a remarkable influence on European integration from as early as the Schuman Declaration of 9 May 1950. The creation of the EMU system in Maastricht in 1992 and the Stability and Growth Pact in Dublin in 1996 was further clear evidence of this political and economic bargaining between France and Germany. Dyson has thus defined the process of the establishment of EMU as a "child of the Franco-German couple".[12] The Franco-German bargaining as the driving force of monetary and fiscal integration has set several requirements for continual national economic convergence prior to EMU and common institutions for effective economic policy coordination in EMU. In Dyson's view, "the Euro zone created a new institutional context for the Franco-German relationship".[13]

Similarly to the establishment of the Stability and Growth Pact, the Franco-German alliance has continued to play the leading role in fiscal policy coordination in the EMU era because it has been France and Germany that have had the most serious problems with national fiscal policies under the fiscal rules of the Stability Pact. The fact that effective monetary policy instruments have no longer been at national governments' disposal has caused new and unforeseen difficulties in fiscal policy implementation in France and Germany when adjusting national economies to a downturn. Unforeseen fiscal difficulties have emerged in France and Germany although the objectives of the Stability and Growth Pact were formulated by the French and German governments themselves. Although the Ecofin Council has not applied the powerful sanction mechanism, the excessive deficit procedure, to France and Germany, fiscal developments in these two large national economies have shown that both national governments have not fully complied with the rules and objectives of the Stability Pact. The Ecofin Council has allowed France and Germany national fiscal leeway under the common rules more than was originally intended, although simultaneously, all other EMU Member States have been strictly and formally required to meet the fiscal rules.

This critical politico-economic situation has increased political pressures on France and Germany and other Member States to develop further fiscal policy coordination and its objectives and instruments. Finally, based on critical fiscal developments in France and Germany, the Ecofin Council and the European Council reformed the original rules of the Stability Pact in their meetings in March 2005. The fundamental reason for the reform was the fact that the common rules for national budgetary policy had not been applied fairly in EMU. The implementation of the Stability Pact had experienced major difficulties in France and Germany and thus, the rules had to be reconsidered. Although the Franco-German alliance has succeeded in redefining the deficit and debt rules in the Ecofin Council and the European Council, it is still questionable in what way this new agreement on the fiscal rules will improve the implementation of the Stability Pact. This situation has raised the question of why these two large Member States have not been required to respect the original rules, and why no sanctions have so far been imposed. Are there different fiscal rules for large Member States *vis-à-vis* small ones in EMU?

Secondly, the dichotomy between large and small EMU Member States has also played a major role in fiscal policy coordination. In particular, the differences in the roles have been most significant in the formation (uploading), implementation (downloading) and reform (reuploading) of the fiscal rules of the Stability Pact.[14] The dichotomy between large and small Member States in fiscal policy coordination stems from the fact that increasing political and economic interdependence has eroded the autonomous status of smaller Member States more than that of economically larger and politically more powerful countries. Although it is not claimed here that a smaller Member State is always politically and economically weaker or that a larger Member State is always politically and economically stronger, European economic integration has, in practice, shown that this relationship exists in the EU and EMU. Thus, it can be argued that the possibility of a Member State to run independent national economic policy and promote national economic interests is dependent on the national capacity for political and economic cooperation within the institutional systems of the EU and EMU. The guiding principle in European integration has been to link the common policy-making processes with the interests of both large and small Member States and thus replace national objectives with common objectives within common institutions. However, in fiscal policy coordination, as claimed in this research, Member States and common EU institutions have not yet succeeded in this fundamental aim. Fiscal policy coordination has not been led by common political and economic objectives but by the Franco-German bargaining and German and French national interests, that is large EMU Member States: the making of a common fiscal policy without a state in EMU is still clearly an unfinished process.

Although Germany has wanted to be at the heart of fiscal policy coordination as the economically and politically largest Member State, it has also been Germany that has had the severest problems with the common agreements, rules and objectives.[15] As a result of the implementation problems, Germany has continually broken the fiscal rules since 2002. Simultaneously, European institutional coordination has failed to apply the sanction mechanism of the excessive deficit procedure to Germany three times in a row. Due to the major problems with the fiscal rules, Germany has considered that the originally very strict rules of the Stability Pact should be reformed because of the existing unfavourable economic circumstances in Germany and the Euro area. Germany has argued that the strict rules should be reinterpreted in a way that would allow more national fiscal flexibility in a downturn, such as that from 2002 to 2005. In this process of reuploading, Germany as an economically and politically large Member State has tried once again to include its own national interests in the Stability Pact by asking for the reinterpretation and softening of the rules. By this process Germany has sought to modify the existing fiscal rules so that they would better serve the existing politico-economic interests of the German economy. As the Communication of the Commission in September 2004 and the decision of the European Council in Brussels in March 2005 have confirmed, the German government has succeeded very well in reuploading its interests into the new agreement on the Stability Pact. What defines national fiscal authority and fiscal policy coordination in EMU today is the development that France and Germany as economically and politically large Member States, in practice, seem to have the fundamental right to substantial leeway in national economic policy-making whenever their national interests so require, despite the commonly established agreements, rules and objectives. *Would the case be exactly the same, let us say, with Austria and Finland as small EMU Member States?*[16] In this respect, Buti and Pench make a clear, strong and timely crucial point: "For any reform of the Pact to be credible, Member States, especially the larger ones, need to exhibit greater willingness to subordinate short-term political gains to the long-term common good of protecting the monetary union from the risk of financial unsustainability."[17]

Supranational institutions in fiscal policy coordination

Figure 7.5 summarises the central issue of this research on EU institutions, policy coordination and national adjustments: *what is the current state of national fiscal authority in EMU?* Does national fiscal authority still exist under fiscal policy coordination in EMU? Could there be a common, effective and credible fiscal policy without a state in EMU? Primarily based on the interviews and other empirical findings of this research on the nature of institutional coordination in fiscal policy, the figure summarises the present roles of the main EU and EMU institutions in European fiscal policy coordination and their relationship towards participating EMU Member States. Competition between supranational authority and national control over economic, monetary and fiscal policy objectives has been a result of differences in economic interests and objectives (gaps), and it has taken place on different coordination levels, institutions and procedures. Although macroeconomic coordination between EU institutions and

Member States has in general been successful, it has involved a lot of dilemmas, bargaining and compromises over common objectives and national independence (joint-decision traps).

Firstly, bargaining over fiscal policy coordination in the Ecofin Council has mostly taken place between Germany and France in relation to the politico-economic influence of other Member States. The Ecofin Council has allowed Germany and France to implement fiscal policy above the common fiscal rules despite the view of small Member States (for example Austria, Finland and the Netherlands). Secondly, bargaining in fiscal policy among EU institutions has primary taken place between the Ecofin Council and the Commission. In this bargaining, the Ecofin Council has acted as a powerful intergovernmental institution with the strong nation-state emphasis, whereas the Commission with its agenda-setting, monitoring and reporting power has been the key federal actor in fiscal policy coordination. Thirdly, despite the independent role of the ECB in the common monetary policy in the Euro area since 1999, bargaining over the required economic stability in EMU between the Ecofin Council (responsible for fiscal policy) and the ECB (responsible for price stability) has also occurred. Fourthly and most recently, the European Court of Justice also took a view on the system of fiscal policy coordination.[18] Thus, it is justifiable to argue that the current state of European fiscal policy coordination does not only involve Member States but also powerful EU institutions: fiscal authority in the EU and EMU appears to be a highly complex and multi-level institutional system.[19]

Firstly, the Commission, together with its Directorate-General for Economic and Financial Affairs, has been the most active EU institution in fiscal policy coordination. The Commission's key role in fiscal policy coordination has been based on four main policy elements: the right of initiative, E(M)U-wide assessments, the formal interpretation of the fiscal rules, and strict economic monitoring and reporting. According to the Maastricht Treaty, the Commission's objective is "to ensure the proper functioning and development of the common market".[20] The Stability Pact specifies its duties in fiscal policy coordination to include the consideration of the existence of and the possible existence of an excessive budgetary deficit in a Member State. Thus, the fundamental basis of the Commission as a key European actor lies in its formal, Treaty-based institutional position. It has the ultimate right of initiative; it is responsible for monitoring and reporting over the fiscal developments in EU and EMU Member States; and, it has used its supranational power in fiscal policy coordination to a large extent. For example, the Commission presents country-specific economic objectives to be finally adopted by the Ecofin Council, and it has the duty to monitor the implementation of those objectives in EU and EMU Member States. In practice, it is this supranational and binding objective-setting and monitoring role of the Commission together with Treaty-based formal rules that constrains the traditional authority of Member States in fiscal policy. However, there is a major asymmetry in economic authority between the Commission and the Ecofin Council. Even though the Commission has a clear and strong Treaty-based mandate for monitoring and reporting, it is still the Ecofin Council that has the ultimate authority to set binding responsibilities in European fiscal policy.

Secondly, although the Commission's role relates to recommending, defining, monitoring and reporting broad guidelines for European economic policy together with the Ecofin Council and ensuring the required economic convergence between the EU and Member States, it is the European Central Bank and the European System of Central Banks that are the main institutions in the common monetary policy. According to Dyson, it is the ECB-centric Euro area that is "a factor in a process of redefining European states, their interests, policy agendas and who has authority over policy".[21] The ECB's role in European economic policy can be characterised by great autonomy, the price stability orientation and EMU-wide economic assessments for the successful implementation of the common monetary policy. To implement the common monetary policy with credibility in the financial market, the institutional system of the ECB is based on its independence from other supranational and national institutions. For this reason, the ECB has decided not to take an active role in solving the current fiscal problems with the Stability Pact in Member States.[22] However, this independence should not mean that monetary and fiscal policy coordination between the ECB, national central banks, national governments and EU institutions is completely unnecessary. By contrast, due to the persistently low growth and high unemployment rates in the Euro area, the ECB has increasingly been forced to cooperate more with EU institutions (the Commission and the Ecofin Council) as well as to coordinate more policy objectives between the common monetary policy and national fiscal policies for greater stability and better growth in EMU. It is the monetary and fiscal policy coordination (European policy mix) that could contribute to the overall effectiveness of European economic policy in strengthening stability and supporting growth. However, economic policy coordination should not challenge the ECB's independence in monetary policy but strengthen it. It would be a highly relevant question to ask *what it would mean for the overall monetary credibility on the financial market if the ECB was as isolated as possible from all other European and national economic and political processes*. As Winkler has observed: "The concern for EMU is that the independent ECB may live in (un)splendid isolation in the sense that it will lack the coordinated help of the European fiscal authorities and wage setters as well as support from the European public. Without a shared stability culture and political legitimacy the European Central Bank will make an ideal, because 'independent', scapegoat."[23]

Thirdly, fiscal policy coordination between the Commission, the ECB and the Ecofin Council has been questioned in the present political situation

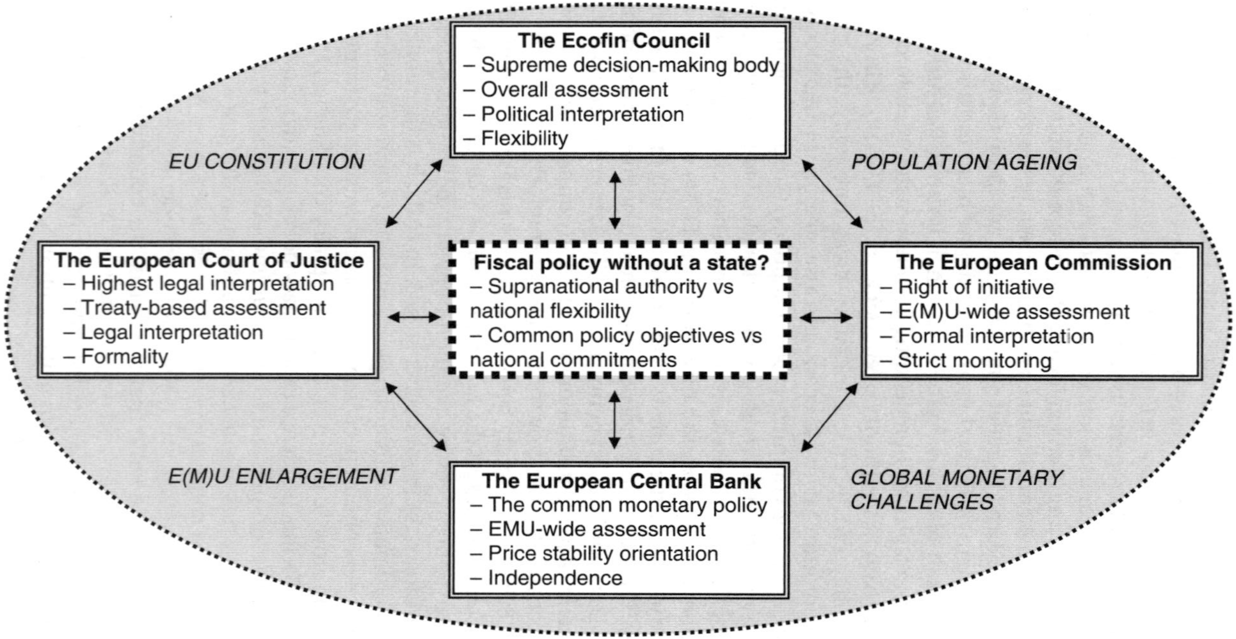

Figure 7.5 Multi-level authority in European fiscal policy coordination.

where some large EMU Member States have failed to comply with the Stability Pact. The institutional role of the Ecofin Council differs significantly from those of other EU institutions in fiscal policy coordination because firstly, it consists of the representatives of national governments and secondly, it has the supreme political authority over fiscal policy in the EU and EMU. The Ecofin Council has the responsibility to coordinate and stabilise national fiscal policies and contribute to economic growth, whereas the Commission monitors and reports the effectiveness of that coordination and the ECB works for price stability. According to Buti, Roeger and in't Veld, it is "the precise mission of the ECB to maintain price stability and guidelines for the conduct of national fiscal policies" that affect the interest "on the interplay between monetary and fiscal policies".[24] Due to this "interplay", there have been institutional coordination problems between monetary and fiscal actors in EMU. For example, the Ecofin Council has blamed the ECB for a far too tight monetary policy causing increasing pressures in national economies. On the other hand, the ECB has held the Ecofin Council and national governments responsible for the lack of required economic, structural and institutional reforms and adjustments for achieving national fiscal stability under the Stability Pact. In addition, the Ecofin Council has emphasised its right of political and flexible consideration over the fiscal rules of the Stability Pact, whereas the Commission has insisted on a strict and formal interpretation of the excessive deficit procedure of the Stability Pact in EMU.

The institutional crisis under the Stability Pact relates to the situation that the Ecofin Council did not apply the excessive deficit procedure to Germany and France in 2002 and 2003 despite their major deficits. The Ecofin Council has justified these decisions by its ultimate right of political interpretation of the Stability Pact and by allowing Member States more leeway due to economic circumstances. If the Ecofin Council continued to allow national economies to run excessive deficits, the positive economic expectations in the Euro area would depend entirely on the ECB and its monetary policy measures: *how could the ECB ensure overall economic stability through its exchange, credit and interest rate policies without having any fiscal discipline in the EMU Member States at all?* If the Ecofin Council allowed expansive fiscal policy to reduce the impact of a downturn, should the ECB also simultaneously run expansive monetary policy for the same purpose? If not, a tight and restrictive monetary policy would undo all national fiscal efforts. If so, expansive fiscal and monetary policies together would cause drastic inflation and interest rates and eventually a dramatic decrease in national output and a major increase in unemployment. It would be irrational to believe that it would be in the interests of the Ecofin Council that in the event of increasing debt and deficit stocks the ECB would be asked to implement expansionary credit and interest rate policies to reduce the national costs of the increasing stocks. However, such political compromises have historically been frequent between national finance ministers and national central banks in many European countries. As Huhne emphasises: "If the ECB were to become involved in any such horse-trading, its independence would be fatally compromised in the eyes of the financial markets."[25]

Fourthly and finally, major institutional problems in fiscal policy coordination between the Commission and the Ecofin Council finally resulted in a situation in which on 13 July 2004 even the European Court of Justice was asked to play a key role. The Court was asked by the Commission to give a legal interpretation of the correct institutional procedure under the excessive deficit procedure of the Stability Pact because the Court had the highest legal, Treaty-based authority over policy areas that were implemented in the European Union. In its ruling, the Court stated that the institutional procedure that resulted in the decision of the Ecofin Council on 25 November 2003 was not in line with the rules of the excessive deficit procedure. Therefore, the Court decided to overturn the decision and give the case back to the consideration of the Ecofin Council. Although the Court was not asked to issue an opinion on whether sanctions should have been imposed but only on the correctness of the institutional procedure, the ruling still strongly implied that the Ecofin Council could not allow infinite national leeway if and when the common rules had clearly and continually been broken; an implication that will have a major impact on national economic policy-making in the near future.

Reuploading as the first signal of too fast integration in fiscal policy?

The question of diminishing national fiscal authority and the need for reforming the institutional system of the Stability Pact in EMU can also be approached from the historical perspective of European fiscal policy evolution. Figure 7.6 illustrates the historical evolution process through which the critical relationship between European and national authority in fiscal policy coordination has come into being. Member States have created new formal and informal common institutions and procedures for fiscal policy coordination and EU institutions have thus received more and more duties and responsibilities that have previously been assigned to the exclusive competence of Member States.[26] It could be argued that there has been a calculated and systematic process to connect national fiscal authority with the common monetary policy in an almost irreversible way in the third stage of EMU; the making of a common European fiscal policy in EMU. As the main indications of this continual process, the convergence criteria have been set, along with the Stability Pact, the Luxemburg process, the Cardiff process, the Vienna strategy, the Cologne process and the Lisbon strategy, all highlighting the continual economic integration process in the EU and EMU.

In this respect, there are two dimensions in this question of fiscal integration, increasing European institutional coordination and the continual

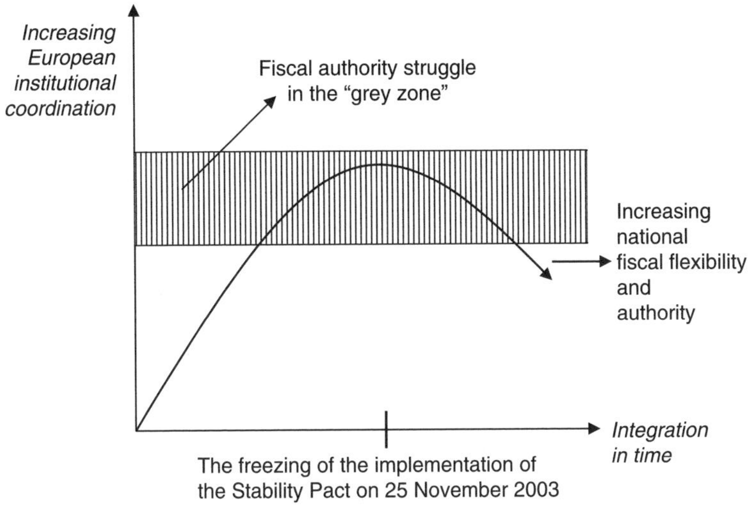

Figure 7.6 Evolution of the authority struggle in fiscal policy coordination.

integration process, as Figure 7.6 demonstrates. The starting point for the figure is the fact that when European institutional coordination has increased in the course of fiscal integration, national fiscal authority has simultaneously decreased in turn, that is a zero-sum authority game in terms of fiscal authority. The "grey zone" in the figure is the area where the fundamental fiscal authority struggle between EU institutions and Member States is finally played out.[27] In other words, it is the grey zone where Member States have started to consider that, perhaps, European fiscal policy coordination and fiscal constraints have gone too far and too fast to limit national fiscal policy-making, and they may decide to slow down the integration process and restore their fiscal authority to its previous condition.[28] This is the core question of whether Member States want to have more institutionalised European fiscal policy, or whether they want to retain the main parts of fiscal authority in national policy-making. Member States seem to have realised that they cannot have more institutional fiscal policy coordination and more national fiscal flexibility in EMU at the same time. According to the policy statement of the British government in December 2004, a high degree of national fiscal leeway continues to be crucial "when a country needs to adjust to country-specific shocks within a monetary union, since a country-specific monetary policy response is not an option".[29]

Currently, as German national developments before and after 25 November 2003 have shown, perhaps, strict and formal fiscal policy coordination has reached its ceiling so far. This argument claims that Germany, by not complying with common fiscal rules, has logically preferred national economic interests to more national fiscal flexibility over the common European objectives. On the other hand, it could be asked whether a great success in fiscal policy coordination and national implementation would in turn have implied that Germany would have wanted to further the making of a common European fiscal policy towards, perhaps, European fiscal federalism. Now, however, fiscal policy coordination faces its greatest challenge so far: *which way should fiscal policy coordination be developed in EMU from now on*? If coordination is further increased, then Member States will have less fiscal power and flexibility in their national policy-making and the achievement of common fiscal rules will become even more difficult. By contrast, if coordination goes backwards, the scope and range of coordination is reduced and the fiscal rules are relaxed to restore fiscal power and flexibility to Member States, then there will be less and less European coordination and monitoring and the idea of having a European-wide fiscal policy could collapse.[30] The current situation in fiscal policy coordination implies that increasing coordination and monitoring procedures have constrained some large EMU Member States too much because they have considered that their ability for effective national economic policy-making in a downturn has been significantly limited; a consideration that has resulted in relaxing the original fiscal rules of the Stability Pact. Thus, one might ask *whether reuploading is the very first signal of the development that European fiscal policy coordination under the Stability Pact in EMU has gone too far, too fast in terms of national fiscal authority and national fiscal flexibility*.[31]

In this reuploading process, the economically and politically larger a Member State is, the easier it is for that Member State to promote its own national interests at the European level, and the case of Germany is an excellent example. Germany, as the economically and politically most powerful European state, has had the fundamental privilege to forming (uploading), implementing (downloading) and reforming (reuploading) European-wide objectives and coordination systems in fiscal policy. European fiscal policy coordination has thus faced the dilemma between the objectives of common institutions (coordination) and the objectives of Member States (flexibility). At one level, this single coherent case study has clearly shown the extent to which Germany has succeeded and failed to comply with the fiscal rules of the Stability Pact in EMU finally resulting in reforming the original rules of 1997 in March 2005. At another level, the empirical study has also raised a much more critical question of the current relationship between common objectives and agreements and national objectives and commitments in European economic integration. The fiscal convergence process, coordinated and monitored by EU institutions, has not been entirely successful, partly because some Member States have no longer been committed to it, but more because some Member States have insisted on including more and more national fiscal leeway into the originally strict coordination procedures. Given the coordination and commitment failures under the increased amount of formal and informal fiscal policy coordination, the question should be posed as to whether there is still a commonly shared need and will for institutional fiscal policy coordination in Member States.

If there is still a need and will for European fiscal policy coordination, the institutional procedures and coordination models should be reformed and modified to better comply with the existing circumstances at once. If institutional coordination no longer matters and Member States want to reform the Stability Pact to allow more and more national fiscal flexibility, European institutional coordination has then reached its ceiling: the highest coordination level so far. In present circumstances, it is justifiable to arrive at the conclusion that national fiscal objectives have significantly overcome those of the EU and EMU and therefore, *there is not yet a common fiscal policy without a state in EMU*. The increasing amount of fiscal policy coordination has not eliminated the fundamental competition between European and national fiscal objectives and this has been illustrated by the lack of national commitment to the full implementation of the Stability Pact. Therefore, this research refutes and redefines the second hypothesis so that *the more institutionalised fiscal policy coordination is at the European level does not necessarily lead to a situation where there are fewer adjustment problems in fiscal policy implementation in a Member State but that the Member State with most adaptation problems would, in reality, try to reform and reinterpret the common rules based on its own changed national political and economic interests (reuploading)*. The case study on the German economy shows that the German government has actively tried to and succeeded in reforming the common fiscal rules because of major adaptation problems, "misfits", and the lack of national fiscal flexibility in a downturn.

How to get back to a win-win situation under the Stability Pact in EMU?

Both European fiscal policy coordination and national economic policy-making will have an important relationship in European economic integration in the future. The fundamental idea prior to EMU was to have effective EU institutions for coordinating and monitoring fiscal policies in EMU where Member States were expected to fully comply with the common economic rules for contributing to the establishment of a stable economic environment for growth, a win-win situation. However, most recent developments in European fiscal policy coordination have unfortunately created a win-lose situation, where EU institutions have coordinated and monitored, but the lack of national commitment and effective coordination procedures has resulted in increasing problems in implementing the Stability Pact in some large EMU Member States. In the worst-case scenario, if this critical tendency continues, the EMU area could already face a dramatic lose-lose situation in the immediate future where EU institutions would no longer coordinate and monitor and where Member States would no longer respect the common economic agreements and rules at all. Is there a way to move from a win-lose situation via a lose-lose situation back to a win-win situation in fiscal policy coordination under the Stability Pact?

An unanticipated success in finding a strong European political and economic will to develop an institutional system for more successful fiscal policy coordination could create a new process to turn the development back to the win-win situation, where Member States would again be fully committed to the common objectives under successfully functioning EU institutions. Vital research questions for this kind of successful coordination, which should be thoroughly analysed and developed further in the near future, are, for example, how fiscal rules, or any other kind of rules, could ensure fiscal stability in EMU; through which concrete measures the national implementation of common economic policy objectives could be improved; and what the impact of increasing European fiscal authority would be on national economic policy-making in EMU. These critical topics could point the way forward in the direction of further economic convergence and policy coordination in the Euro area, where effective coordination measures still continue to require active national economic policy-making. Although there may be a widely shared consensus over the current problems in fiscal policy coordination in Europe, agreeing on concrete, effective and fast solutions will be politically and economically very difficult. However, the making of the common European fiscal policy is in progress and the coming direction of this process is the core question of the current economic institutionalisation process in Europe. What is nearly certain is that in order to revive and strengthen the current state of fiscal policy coordination, this process requires reviving and strengthening political integration as well; political will is required for completing the content of the Stability and Growth Pact and for reviving national commitments to the common rules and objectives. Thus, the politics and economics of European fiscal policy coordination continue to go hand in hand: today's political achievements are tomorrow's economic prosperity.

Appendix
Eleven Years of the Stability Pact in the European Union 1995–2005

1995
- German Finance Minister, Theo Waigel, presented an idea of a Stability Pact in the Bundestag in Bonn in November.

1996
- The Dublin European Council in December formulated Waigel's original proposal for a Stability Pact to include two elements that would become the Stability and Growth Pact.

1997
- The Amsterdam European Council in June officially adopted the content of the Stability and Growth Pact and specified a) the debt and deficit rules of the Maastricht Treaty, b) the institutional procedure against a Member State that fails to comply with the fiscal rules and c) the sanction mechanism for imposing fines.

1998
- EU Member States for the final stage of EMU were selected.

1999
- Economic and Monetary Union started with 11 Member States.

2000
- The end of the high economic growth period 1998–2000.

2001
- Greece entered to Economic and Monetary Union.

2002
- Portugal was the first EMU Member State to break the deficit rule.
- Germany also broke the deficit rule.

2003
- As the Ecofin Council did not apply the sanction mechanism of the excessive deficit procedure to Germany and France on 25 November, the Stability Pact was in practice frozen.

2004
- In January, the Commission took the Ecofin Council to the European Court of Justice for its failure to act under the excessive deficit procedure on 25 November 2003.
- In July, the European Court of Justice shared the view of the Commission and returned the case back to the Ecofin Council.
- In September, the Commission introduced a new Communication for reforming the original Stability Pact of 1997.

2005
- On 20 March, the Ecofin Council reformed the fiscal rules and the interpretation of the rules in an additional meeting in Brussels.
- On 22–23 March, the new agreement on the fiscal rules of the Stability Pact was approved by the Brussels European Council.

Figure A.1 Eleven Years of the Stability Pact in the European Union 1995–2005.

Notes

1 The Europeanisation of Fiscal Policy Coordination

1 In this research, fiscal policy refers to the fiscal element of economic policy, including for example budgetary policy, public finances, labour policy, structural policy and taxation. The Stability and Growth Pact (or the Stability Pact) was officially adopted in the Amsterdam European Council in June 1997 for strengthening fiscal discipline in the third stage of EMU since 1999. The multi-level system of fiscal policy coordination is extensively analysed in Chapters 2–5 and through 20 key interviews in Chapter 6.

2 Buti and Sapir (2002), Brunila and Martinez-Mongay (2002), Allsopp and Artis (2003), Buiter (2003) and Commission (2004a), (2005a) and (2006a).

3 Although one could argue that the focus should be directed towards an aggregate fiscal position in EMU, the case of Germany clearly demonstrates in Chapters 3–6 that until 2006, although the aggregate deficit position in 12 EMU Member States has been satisfactory, national developments in German fiscal policy have still been severe after the beginning of the EMU era. Slovenia adopted the single currency, and Bulgaria and Romania joined the EU in 2007.

4 Since the late 1990s, European integration, Europeanisation and policy co-ordination have become interesting subjects among a number of scholars: in international relations, such as Moravcsik (1998) and Schimmelfennig and Sedelmeier (2002); in international political economy, such as Eichengreen and Frieden (1998b) and Mattli (1999); and also in comparative politics, such as Jachtenfuchs and Kohler-Koch (1995), Pierson (1996), Richardson (1996), Hix (1994) and (1999), Dyson (2000b), Marks and Hooghe (2001), Pollack (2001), Rhodes (2001), Schmidt (2002), and Dyson and Goetz (2003b).

5 The EU is an organisation which came into being after the Maastricht Treaty on 1 November 1993. The European Community (EC) refers to the former organisation, which was created by the Merged Treaty in 1965 combining the European Coal and Steel Community (ECSC), the European Economic Community (EEC) and the European Atomic Energy Community (Euratom) into a single European organisation.

6 For the changes in the role of the European nation-state within the integration process, see Keohane and Nye (1977), Wallace (1982), Keohane (1984) and Milward (1994).

7 Radaelli (2000, Vol. 4).

8 For Europeanisation, see Goetz (1995), Hix and Goetz (2000), George (2001) and Bache (2002).

9 Ladrech (1994, p. 71).

10 Rosamond (2000, p. 179).

11 Schmidt (2002, p. 2).

12 Ladrech (1994, p. 69).

13 Knill and Lehmkuhl (2002, p. 257). See Conzelmann (1998) and Knill and Lehmkuhl (1999). Similarly, Grabbe (2001) explores the mechanisms of Europeanisation in the context of the enlargement process towards Central and Eastern European countries.

14 Risse, Green Cowles and Caporaso (2001, p. 6).
15 *Ibid.*, p. 9.
16 Modified from Risse, Green Cowles and Caporaso (2001, p. 6). For the empirical specification of this model for the study of fiscal policy coordination, see Chapter 7. See Bulmer and Lequesne (2002), Schmidt (2002) and Bulmer, Dolowitz, Humphreys and Padgett (2003).
17 Bache (2002, p. 7) separates the third dimension (the Type 3 Europeanisation) of this relationship that involves "interconnections and transfer mechanisms between European states". This research also identifies the importance of this dimension, and the interaction (and a variation in interaction) between Member States is empirically analysed within the bottom-up and top-down processes (Chapters 3–5).
18 Buller and Gamble (2002, p. 13).
19 Anderson (2003, p. 44).
20 Börzel (2002, p. 193).
21 Theoretically, new institutionalism has had a major impact on the understanding of European institutionalisation and the formation of common European institutions since the seminal work of March and Olsen (1989). Since the late 1980s, new institutionalism has been divided into three main approaches: rationalist, constructivist and historical institutionalisms. On rationalist institutionalism, see Scharpf (1988) and (1997), Garrett and Tsebelis (1996) and Moravcsik (1993) and (1998); on constructivist institutionalism, see Christiansen, Jorgensen and Wiener (1999), Schimmelfennig (2001), Schimmelfennig and Sedelmeier (2002) and Bache and Marshall (2004); and on historical institutionalism, see Steinmo, Thelen and Longstreth (1992), Pierson (1996) and Armstrong and Bulmer (1998).
22 In political science, Ekengren (1997) and (2002) and Pierson (1996) and (2004) were among first scholars to highlight the study of the temporal dimension in policy-making in the European Union. On time, timing and tempo in policy change, see Dyson (2000c), (2002), (2003a), Dyson and Goetz (2003b) and Schmidt and Radaelli (2004). In economics, the optimality of the chosen monetary and fiscal policy, in t1 compared to t3 in Figure 1.2, has been analysed through the concept of time inconsistency. See Kydland and Prescott (1977) and Barro and Gordon (1983).
23 For timing in the downloading of European policy guidelines in telecommunications, see Bulmer, Dolowitz, Humphreys and Padgett (2003).
24 Buller and Gamble (2002, p. 24).
25 *Ibid.*, p. 21.
26 *Ibid.*, p. 21.
27 Bache (2002, p. 5). See Bache and Flinders (2004b).
28 Economic and other policy adjustments at the national level were already required during the first implications of globalisation; see Hall (1986) and (1992) and Schmidt (2001) and (2002).
29 Jupille and Caporaso (1999, p. 438).
30 Dyson (2000a, p. 661).
31 Smith (1996, p. 13) argues that for this reason the economic and political interests of each Member State have become a part of the interests of all other Member States and those of the common EU institutions.
32 On the role of Britain in the formation of European monetary policy, see Buller (2003).
33 The role of German national interests in the formation of the Stability Pact (uploading) will be analysed in Chapter 3.

34 The implementation of the Stability Pact (downloading) in Germany in the EMU era will be analysed in Chapter 4.
35 The reform of the original fiscal rules of the Stability Pact (reuploading) will be analysed through the problems in the German economy in Chapter 5 and through 20 key interviews in Chapter 6.
36 Austria, Belgium, Finland, France, Germany, Ireland, Italy, Luxemburg, the Netherlands, Portugal and Spain constituted the third and final stage of EMU in 1999. Greece joined EMU in 2001.
37 Issing (2002, p. 345). Germany and France had a different view on the future of European economic policy. Whereas France highlighted the key role of national governments (*gouvernement économique*), Germany spoke for ensuring economic stability (*Stabilitätsgemeinschaft*) in the EMU era. See Chapter 4.1.
38 Buti, Roeger and in't Veld (2001, p. 822).
39 Fiscal policy coordination has been proved and verified in economics, by Buiter and Marston (1985); Canzoneri and Gray (1985); Rogoff (1985); Bryson (1994); Beetsma and Bovenberg (1995); and Demertzis, Hallett and Viegi (1999), to be more efficient than its total decentralisation in a monetary union.
40 European Council (1996).
41 The need for strict fiscal rules for EMU was based not only on eliminating counter-cyclical fiscal policies, for example in Mediterranean countries, but also on the aim of securing economic stability in EMU.
42 Currently, economic theory does not consider EMU an optimal currency area; see Chapter 2.1.
43 European Central Bank (2001b, p. 48).
44 Council of Ministers (2005f) and European Council (2005). See Chapters 6–7.
45 Council of Ministers (2002b), (2002c) and (2003e).
46 European Central Bank (2001b, p. 49).
47 The Euro-12 group consists of the Finance Ministers of the EMU Member States but it is still without an official decision-making role in the EU and EMU. However, Mr Juncker, who has been named Mr Euro, has acted as the first President of the Euro-12 group since January 2005.
48 Virén (2000, p. 5).
49 One macroeconomic implication of the increase in the economic and political effectiveness of EMU is the fact that the exchange rate of the Euro has achieved its highest level compared to the US dollar (1 € = 1.3633 USD) on 28 December 2004 since its establishment in January 1999. For the first year of EMU, see Allsopp and Vines (1998), von Hagen (2000), Brunila and Martinez-Mongay (2002) and Allsopp and Artis (2003).
50 There are several policy measures which serve to increase national fiscal stability in the EMU era, such as minimising the seigniorage dilemma and the free-rider problem and implementing the no-bail-out principle. See Chapters 2, 5 and 6.
51 State has a different meaning depending on whether integration is based on a federalist, confederalist or nation-state-led process; see Burgess (2000), Coudenhove-Kalergi (1923), Forsyth (1981) and Milward (1994).
52 The system of fiscal policy coordination, which is analysed in Chapter 2, consists of the Maastricht Treaty, the procedure of the broad economic policy guidelines, the Stability and Growth Pact, the procedure of stability and convergence programmes and the excessive deficit procedure.
53 Maastricht Treaty (1992) and European Council (1996), (1997c), (1998a), (1998b), (1999b) and (2000b).

2 The Institutional System of Fiscal Policy Coordination

1 Artis and Winkler (1997, p. 2).

2 In extensive economic literature, for example, Dyson (1994) gives five reasons why monetary and fiscal policies should be coordinated in EMU. Further, Virén (2000) and (2001) identifies eight requirements that should be fulfilled before fiscal policy coordination could effectively take place in EMU.

3 On the optimal currency area theory in EMU, see Mundell (1961), McKinnon (1963), Kenen (1969), Eichengreen (1991), Bayoumi and Eichengreen (1992) and Alesina and Wacziarg (1999).

4 Breuss and Weber (1999, p. 5). On monetary union, see Balassa (1961) and (1973) and Molle (1990) and (2001).

5 *Ibid.*, p. 32.

6 Robson (1998, p. 214).

7 Gros and Thygesen (1998, p. 323).

8 *Ibid.*

9 Eichengreen (1998, p. 28).

10 See Begg *et al.* (1991), Allsopp and Vines (1996), Eichengreen (1998), Eichengreen and Wyplosz (1998), Buti and Martinot (2000), De Grauwe (2000), Beetsma (2001), Korkman (2001), Brunila (2002) and Buti, Eijffinger and Franco (2003b).

11 Begg *et al.* (1991, p. 32).

12 Buti (2001, p. 99).

13 De Grauwe (2000, p. 197) empirically demonstrates how and to what extent centralised fiscal policy affects national welfare in two monetary union countries in the case of a negative demand shock. In his view, if national budgets are not centralised in a monetary union, then "national fiscal policies should be used in a flexible way". This means that if and when participating economies in a monetary union are hit by a negative shock, "they should be allowed to let the budgetary deficit increase through the built-in (or automatic) budgetary stabilisers (declining government revenues, increasing social layouts)". Member States would otherwise have to deal with economic problems without national fiscal stabilisers and effective national adjustments and policy instruments.

14 Begg *et al.* (1991, p. 32).

15 Chari and Kehoe (1998, p. 22).

16 *Ibid.*, p. 1.

17 Eichengreen (1998, p. 28).

18 Beetsma, Debrun and Klaassen (2001, p. 4).

19 Beetsma, Debrun and Klaassen (2001, p. 9).

20 *Ibid.*

21 Eichengreen (1998, p. 27).

22 Buti and Sapir (1998, p. 32).

23 Winkler (1996, p. 18).

24 Gros and Thygesen (1998, p. 346).

25 *Ibid.*, p. 347.

26 For the European processes in economic policy coordination, see Table 2.1.

27 Beetsma, Debrun and Klaassen (2001, p. 8). For models of fiscal policy coordination, see Chapter 2.2.

28 For the golden rule of public finance, see Chapters 2.4 and 6.1.

29 For differences in monetary and fiscal convergence in EMU, see Chapters 4–5 and Figure 7.2.
30 Virén (2000, p. 5).
31 Cobham (1989, p. 215).
32 Buti, Franco and Ongena (1998, p. 95).
33 Buti and Sapir (1998, p. 17).
34 Commission (2002f, p. 4).
35 Commission (2002b).
36 Commission (2002f, p. 4).
37 Protocol on the Excessive Deficit Procedure (1992, Article 1).
38 Maastricht Treaty (1992, Article 104c).
39 *Ibid.*
40 Protocol on the Excessive Deficit Procedure (1992, Article 1).
41 Maastricht Treaty (1992, Article 104c).
42 *Ibid.*, Article 109j.
43 Protocol on the Convergence Criteria Referred to in Article 109j of the Treaty Establishing the European Community (1992, Article 1).
44 Maastricht Treaty (1992, Article 109j).
45 Protocol on the Convergence Criteria Referred to in Article 109j of the Treaty Establishing the European Community (1992, Article 4).
46 Maastricht Treaty (1992, Article 109j).
47 Protocol on the Convergence Criteria Referred to in Article 109j of the Treaty Establishing the European Community (1992, Article 3).
48 Maastricht Treaty (1992, Article 99).
49 See European Council (1996), Amsterdam Treaty (1997) and Figure A.1 in Appendix.
50 European Council (1997a).
51 *Ibid.* On the politics of the Stability Pact in EMU, see Dyson and Featherstone (1999), Brunila, Buti and Franco (2001a) and Heipertz and Verdun (2003a).
52 European Council (1997a).
53 Council of Ministers (2002a).
54 Council of Ministers (1997a, Articles 1, 3 and 7).
55 *Ibid.*, Articles 3 and 7.
56 *Ibid.* For the "economic data crisis" of Greece in 2004, see Chapter 6.3.
57 Council of Ministers (1993, Article 1).
58 *Ibid.*, Article 4.
59 Council of Ministers (1997b, Article 2).
60 *Ibid.*
61 *Ibid.*, Articles 12 and 15. Public debt is not subjected to the sanctions of the excessive deficit procedure.
62 European Council (1997b).
63 Cangiano and Mottu (1998, p. 26).
64 On the institutional power struggle under the Stability Pact, see Chapters 3–7.
65 Scharrer (2000, p. 206).
66 The system of European economic policy coordination is defined by coordination between the common monetary policy, the broad economic policy guidelines, the Stability and Growth Pact, and the European processes (Luxemburg, Cardiff and Cologne) and the common strategies (Vienna and Lisbon); and the close relationship of all of them at the national and European levels is analysed in Chapters 4–7.
67 Nice (2002, Article 4).

68 Maastricht Treaty (1992, Article 103). For the procedural steps, see Council of Ministers (2003a). In order to guarantee the functioning of effective decision-making in the EU and to allow an equal entry for the new Member States to the EU, the reforms of committee structures took place in preparation for the EU Enlargement in 2004. For example, the weighting of votes was changed in the Council, and the number of national representatives in the European Parliament was reformed.
69 Nice (2002, Article 114). For the EFC, see the Council of Ministers (1998c) and (1998d).
70 Council of Ministers (2003b, Article 1).
71 *Ibid.*
72 For the timetable the excessive deficit procedure, see Cabral (2001) and Commission (2002f).
73 On setting medium-term fiscal targets in EMU, see Artis and Buti (2001).
74 Council of Ministers (1997a, Article 5).
75 Council of Ministers (1997a, Articles 5 and 6). For the procedural steps, see Commission (2002f).
76 *Ibid.*, Article 5.
77 *Ibid.*, Article 6.
78 *Ibid.*, Articles 6 and 10. For the practice in the early warning mechanism, see Chapters 2.4, 5 and 6.
79 Nice (2002, Article 104).
80 Stark (2001, p. 81).
81 Nice (2002, Article 104).
82 *Ibid.*
83 For the case of Germany under the Stability Pact, the institutional power struggle between the Commission and the Ecofin Council, and the legal action of the Commission to take the failure of the Ecofin Council to act to the European Court of Justice after the Ecofin Council decided not to execute the sanction procedure against Germany and France on 25 November 2003, see Chapters 2.4, 5, 6 and 7.
84 Nice (2002, Article 104). For the procedural steps, see European Central Bank (1999b).
85 Cabral (2001, p. 147).
86 For the legal responsibilities of EU institutions, see the Treaty of Nice and its Article 230 on annulment, Article 232 on failure to act and Article 235 on damage; and for the verdict of the European Court of Justice on the implementation of the excessive deficit procedure in July 2004, see Chapters 5–7.
87 Issing (2002, p. 345).
88 For an analysis of the developments in fiscal policy coordination since 2001, see Chapters 4–6.
89 Council of Ministers (2001, annex II).
90 Commission (2002c).
91 Council of Ministers (2002b).
92 Commission (2002d).
93 Council of Ministers (2002c).
94 Council of Ministers (2002d).
95 Council of Ministers (2002b).
96 Commission (2002e) and Commission (2003a).
97 Council of Ministers (2003c, Article 1). The adjustments of the German government and the impact of the measures on the German economy are analysed in detail in Chapters 3–6.

98 Commission (2003e).
99 Council of Ministers (2003e).
100 *Ibid.* This decision of the Ecofin Council on 25 November 2003 and the politico-economic impact of the decision on European fiscal policy coordination are analysed in Chapters 5–6.
101 Commission (2003b).
102 Council of Ministers (2003d).
103 Commission (2003c).
104 Commission (2003d).
105 Council of Ministers (2003e).
106 From 2002 until December 2004, the early warning mechanism had been applied to four countries (Portugal, Germany, France and Italy), and the excessive deficit procedure altogether to 12 countries.
107 On the German economic interests in the formation of the Stability Pact, see Chapter 3.
108 Schuknecht (2002, p. 103).
109 *Financial Times*, 25.7.2002.
110 See *The Economist* (29.11.2003a), Süddeutsche Zeitung (14.1.2004) and Chapters 5–6.
111 Jonung (2002, p. 419). On power struggle between EU institutions, see Chapters 4–7.
112 Gros and Thygesen (1998, p. 337).
113 Buti, Franco and Ongena (1998, p. 82).
114 Artis (2002b, p. 111). See Artis and Corsetti (2005).
115 Buiter (2003, p. 96).
116 El-Agraa (2001, p. 143).
117 *Financial Times*, 25.7.2002.
118 *Ibid.*
119 Brunila, Buti and in't Veld (2003, p. 1).
120 Willett (1999, p. 37).
121 Artis and Winkler (1997, p. 7).
122 Allsopp (2002a, p. 88).
123 Buti, Eijffinger and Franco (2003a, p. 10). On economic stabilisers, see Hughes Hallett and Piscitelli (2002).
124 Beetsma (2001, p. 36).
125 Artis and Winkler (1997, p. 19).
126 Bibow (2001, p. 246).
127 Issing (2002, p. 347).
128 Buti and Giudice (2002a, p. 844).
129 Gros and Thygesen (1998, p. 333).
130 Buiter (1999, pp. 7 and 29).
131 HM Treasury (1998, p. 16). On the golden rule in Britain and Germany, see Chapter 6.
132 Balassone and Franco (2001, p. 381).
133 Willett (1999, p. 55).
134 Artis and Winkler (1999, p. 183).

3 The German Dynamics of Uploading the Stability Pact

1 Tsoukalis (1993, p. 208).
2 Therefore, the German Council of Economic Experts (Sachverständigenrat, 1990, p. 15) was convinced in 1990 that the "fiscal stabilisation of unified

Germany to be very difficult in the coming years". On the developments in the German economy (fiscal and monetary policy) prior to EMU, the collapse of the East German economy and the creation of the German currency union, see Stolper (1940), Hardach (1976), Braun (1992), Giersch, Paqué and Schmieding (1992), Owen Smith (1994), Schwinn (1997), Seibel (1998), Zohlnhöfer (1999), Harding and Paterson (2000a), Zohlnhöfer (2001) and Wiesenthal (2004).

3 Streeck and Trampusch (2005).

4 The term "Old Länder" after 1990 refers to those Länder (governmental regions) that were part of West Germany before reunification in 1990 and "New Länder" refers to Länder previously in East Germany. It would also be possible to define New and Old Länder as New and Old federal states in Germany.

5 Scharpf (2000a, p. 68).

6 Eichengreen and Wyplosz (1998, p. 98).

7 OECD (2003) and Commission (2003g).

8 The liabilities of East Germany were taken over by, for example the Debt-Processing Fund, the German Unity Fund, the Treuhand Agency, the ERP Special Fund, and the Indemnification Fund and the Redemption Fund for Inherited Liabilities. See Bundesministerium der Finanzen (1995) and Bundesbank (1997).

9 Owen Smith (1994, p. 132).

10 British Convergence Programme (2003), French Stability Programme (2003), Commission (2003g) and German Stability Programme (2004a). A minus indicates an annual budgetary surplus.

11 Barrell and Weale (2003, p. 133).

12 Current coordination challenges arise from the fact that the Länder play a major political role together with the federal government in economic affairs in the Upper House of German Parliament (*Bundesrat*). As an example of this major political power (*Financial Times*, 16.12.2004), the Länder can currently veto about 60 percent of all bills against the 10 percent originally considered in the German Constitution. On German economic policy-making, see Bundesministerium der Finanzen (2000a).

13 Bundesministerium der Finanzen (2003a).

14 Bundesministerium der Finanzen (2002a) and (2002b) and Commission (2003g).

15 Scharpf (2000a, p. 50).

16 Ardy (2000, p. 13).

17 Stern (1999, p. 152). On the constitutional, political and economic role of the Bundesbank in the German national politics, see Bundesbank (1999).

18 Heisenberg (1999, p. 21).

19 Giersch, Paqué and Schmieding (1992, p. 262). In reality, the ratio of 1:1 was only applied to savings in East Germany up to certain limits. Most assets were converted at a rate of 2 East German Marks to 1 West German Mark. On the one hand, the high rate of conversion was expected to discourage migration from East to West. On the other hand, the dramatic increase in prices and the massive revaluation of about 300 percent had a decidedly negative impact on the competitiveness of industry in East Germany.

20 For the crisis of the EMS and the policy actions of the Bundesbank, see Streit (1998), Weimer (1998), Baltensperger (1999) and Kitterer (1999).

21 IMF (1997).

22 Frenkel and Goldstein (1999, p. 696).

23 IMF (1997). GBP is expressed in the USD per the pound. A downward (upward) movement denotes an appreciation (depreciation) of the D-Mark.
24 IMF (1997). Consumer Price Index (CPI) for EU-15, Germany and France; Retail Price Index (RPI) excluding mortgage interest payments for Britain.
25 For the Bundesbank in the EMU negotiations and its strong position on fiscal discipline in the Delors Committee and the EC Monetary Policy Committee, see Dyson and Featherstone (1999).
26 Commission (2003g).
27 Süddeutsche Zeitung (23.11.1995) and Süddeutsche Zeitung (8.12.1995).
28 Heipertz and Verdun (2003b, p. 7).
29 von Hagen, Hughes Hallett and Strauch (2002b, p. 103).
30 The political coalition of Kohl's governments in the 1990s, which was based on CDU (Christian Democratic Union, *Christlich Demokratische Union Deutschlands*), CSU (Christian Social Union, *Christlich Soziale Union*) and FDP (Free Democratic Party, *Freie Demokratische Partei*), guaranteed the political support for the implementation of EMU in three stages as well as the introduction of the Stability Pact: for example Finance Minister, Theo Waigel (CSU), Minister of Economics, Günter Rexrodt (FDP) and Minister for Labour Affairs, Norbert Blüm (CDU). See *Die Zeit*, 17.11.1995 and 28.3.1997.
31 *Süddeutsche Zeitung*, 18.9.1996.
32 *Die Zeit*, 17.11.1995; SPD (Social Democratic Party, *Sozialdemokratische Partei Deutschlands*).
33 Allensbacher Jahrbuch (2002).
34 To try to convince the highly sceptic German public of the political and economic advantages of EMU, the German government considered it crucial that the EMU project would receive the Bundesbank's full political, institutional and economic support. See Dyson and Featherstone (1999).
35 *Die Zeit*, 15.11.1996.
36 *Süddeutsche Zeitung*, 11.9.1995.
37 *Süddeutsche Zeitung*, 11.11.1995.
38 European Council (1996).
39 *Die Zeit*, 22.11.1996. On the political role of "*das Paar Delors/Pöhl*" in the EMU negotiations, see *Die Zeit*, 7.5.1998.
40 *Die Zeit*, 20.12.1996. See Figures 3.1 and 3.2.
41 Bundesministerium der Finanzen (2002a).
42 Heisenberg (1999), Brunila, Buti and Franco (2001a) and Collignon and Schwarzer (2003).
43 Scharpf (2000a, p. 85).
44 The Industrial Union of Metalworkers (IG Metall, *Industriegewerkschaft Metall*), the Public Services, Transport and Traffic Union (ÖTV, *Gewerkschaft Öffentliche Dienste, Transport und Verkehr*) and the Trade, Banks and Insurances Union (HBV, *Gewerkschaft Handel, Banken und Versicherungen*) have been the most influential trade unions in Germany. The Confederation of German Employers' Associations (BDA, *Bundesvereinigung der Deutschen Arbeitgeberverbände*), the Federation of German Industries (BDI, *Bundesverband der Deutschen Industrie*), the German Association of Chambers of Commerce and Industry (DIHK, *Deutscher Industrie- und Handelskammertag*) and the National Federation of German Skilled Crafts and Trades (ZDH, *Zentralverband des Deutschen Handwerks*) have in turn been the most influential associations of employers.
45 *Die Zeit*, 20.12.1996.

46 For the definition of different forms of Euroscepticism and "hard" and "soft" Eurosceptics, see Taggart (1998), Szczerbiak and Taggart (2000) and Taggart and Szczerbiak (2004).
47 Huffschmid (1998, p. 102).
48 On the economic impact of reunification on national labour policy, see von Hagen and Strauch (1999).
49 Allensbacher Jahrbuch (2002).
50 International Statistical Yearbook (2002) and Commission (2003g).
51 Streeck (1997, p. 33).
52 Hemerijck and Schludi (2000, p. 127).
53 For labour policy in Germany, see Culpepper (2001), Kitschelt and Streeck (2004), Leibfried and Obinger (2004) and Streeck and Hassel (2004). For productivity, wage policy and unemployment in the Euro area, see Calmfors (1996), Buti and Nava (2003), Commission (2003h) and Herrmann (2003).
54 Streeck (1997, p. 47).
55 Streeck and Hassel (2004, p. 107).
56 Streeck (1997, p. 47).
57 Manow and Seils (2000, p. 265).
58 The Saving Programme 1996, which consisted of three national economic plans, was also named as "*das Sparpaket*", "*das Krisenprogramm Kohls*" and "*das Notprogramm*" in the German political debate.
59 Sachverständigenrat (1995, Articles 1 and 4).
60 Political cooperation and actual policy-making between the federal government and the Länder plays a key role in Germany when targeting economic objectives and reforms. The Länder have their own political and economic power, and the functioning of their own regional institutions and electoral rules and electoral cycles can either improve or slow down coordination with the federal government.
61 Haushaltsgrundsätzegesetz (1969, Articles 1 and 2).
62 *Ibid.*, Article 50.
63 The very first meeting of the Financial Planning Council was held on 14 March 1968.
64 Haushaltsgrundsätzegesetz (1969, Article 51). Due to the national and European economic pressures in the early 1990s, the government reformed the existing Law on Budgetary Procedures to make it more effective for the planning, implementation and monitoring of national budgetary policy. When Kohl reformed the Law on Budgetary Procedures in 1993, the main objective was to make the law compatible with the EC law on public finances and budgetary policy. However, the law upheld German national jurisdiction, the decentralisation of economic power, in public finances between the federal government and the Länder. The government reformed the law again in December 1997 by including more flexibility in the national budgetary process and strengthening further the requirements for annual budgets. See Haushaltsgrundsätzegesetz (1993) and Bundesministerium der Finanzen (2000a).
65 *Süddeutsche Zeitung*, 13.3.1996 and 13.6.1996 and *Die Zeit*, 14.6.1996.
66 *Süddeutsche Zeitung*, 27.4.1996b.
67 *Süddeutsche Zeitung*, 14.9.1996, 12.6.1996a, 27.4.1996b and 12.6.1996b. On the alternative plan of the main opposition party SPD for public reforms, see *Süddeutsche Zeitung*, 27.4.1996c.
68 Sachverständigenrat (1996, p. 17).

69 Bundesministerium für Wirtschaft (1996), *Süddeutsche Zeitung*, 9.2.1996, 27.4.1996a and 27.4.1996d and Bundesministerium für Wirtschaft (1997). Further, retirement pay was significantly reduced from 70 percent to 64 percent of take-home pay (*Nettolohn*). The government's plan also included some other social reforms in providing child allowance (*Kindergeld*), public services and counselling (*öffentlicher Dienst*), social security (*Krankenversicherung*) and public administration (*öffentliche Verwaltung*).

70 *Süddeutsche Zeitung*, 14.6.1996 and *Die Zeit*, 20.12.1996.

71 Bundesministerium für Wirtschaft (1996, p. 26) and *Süddeutsche Zeitung*, 25.1.1996.

72 *Süddeutsche Zeitung*, 1.2.1996.

73 Schmidt (2002, p. 170).

74 Bundesministerium für Wirtschaft (1996, p. 27) and *Süddeutsche Zeitung*, 29.1.1996.

75 Although the government executed the pension reform simultaneously, it did not achieve as much publicity and criticism as cutting unemployment benefits. The main reason for this was that the pension reform was directed to only a small group of people, elderly people, instead of the powerful working class and trade unions. According to Hinrichs (1998, p. 27), "in Germany there are no large and influential organizations representing the interests of the elderly".

76 *Süddeutsche Zeitung*, 7.6.1996 and 2.10.1996. The other big German car manufacturers Audi, Opel, Porsche and BMW as well as Siemens continued to apply the old 100 percent level at this point so as not to cause protest among their workers.

77 Streeck and Hassel (2004, p. 108).

78 See Table 3.1.

79 European Council (1997c).

80 European Council (1998a).

81 European Council (1998b). See European Council (1998b, annex II).

82 Dierx, Ilzkovitz and Sekkat (2003, p. 8).

83 Bundesministerium für Wirtschaft (1997, p. 2).

84 *Ibid.*, pp. 121 and 138.

85 *Ibid.*, p. 10. See *Frankfurter Allgemeine Zeitung*, 17.1.1997 and 20.1.1997 and *Süddeutsche Zeitung*, 22.1.1997.

86 See Sachverständigenrat (1998).

87 Bundesministerium für Wirtschaft (1998, p. 10).

88 For the political impact of the supply-side policy reforms, see Sachverständigenrat (1997, pp. 5–7).

89 Bundesministerium für Wirtschaft (1998, pp. 17–18). There were also new actions in labour policy that created occupational training opportunities and extended responsibility for the unemployed to find work, invested in research and technology, developed structural reforms in East Germany, improved the national capital market, and set an Action Plan for the Service Sector. For policy reforms, see Schmähl (1992), Schmidt (1998), Wewer (1998), Schmidt (1999a), Schmähl (2002) and Seeleib-Kaiser (2003).

90 Dyson and Featherstone (1999, p. 371).

91 von Hagen and Strauch (1999, p. 20).

92 Heipertz and Verdun (2003b, p. 7).

93 Bundesministerium für Wirtschaft (1996, p. 55).

94 *Süddeutsche Zeitung*, 11.9.1995.

95 As *Süddeutsche Zeitung*, 18.12.1995 reported: "While politicians want to introduce a strict saving strategy, the public become more and more frustrated." German public opinion was clearly against cuts in public services and social policy but at the same time, it favoured fiscal soundness: a perennial dilemma for democratic governments obliged to reconcile the conflicting preferences of their citizens.
96 Bundesministerium für Wirtschaft (1995, p. 10).
97 Bundesministerium der Finanzen (1998, p. 3).
98 Bundesministerium der Finanzen (1995), (1996), (1997) and (1998).
99 Manow and Seils (2000, p. 292).
100 Schmidt (2000a, p. 233).
101 Dyson and Featherstone (1999, p. 374).
102 Bundesministerium der Finanzen (2000a, p. 19).
103 von Hagen and Strauch (1999, p. 1).
104 *Die Zeit*, 19.1.1996.
105 Bundesministerium für Wirtschaft (1996, p. 23).
106 Dyson (2003a, p. 229).

4 Downloading the Stability Pact in Germany

1 Buti and Sapir (1998, p. 83).
2 There were also changes elsewhere in German politics when the CDU had a new chairman, Wolfgang Schäuble, after Helmut Kohl retired being in CDU power from 1973. Theo Waigel also stepped down from the leader's position of the Christian Social Union and Edmund Stoiber took over the CSU party.
3 For the SPD's campaign manifesto, see SPD Programme (1998) and Lees (1999).
4 In concrete policy-making, fiscal policy is the product of two interconnected factors: first, policy interests in the national party system and whether there is support for policy actions for fiscal stability in the system; and second, national budgetary institutions and whether they can coordinate these interests.
5 The coalition programme (Coalition Agreement 1998) for 1998–2002 focused on: a) reducing debt and deficit and strengthening economic growth, b) improving employment, c) reducing the tax burden on companies and employees, and d) reforming the social policy of the German welfare state.
6 Bundesministerium der Finanzen (1999a, p. 5).
7 Sachverständigenrat (1999, p. 1).
8 For an academic debate on the Alliance for Jobs, see Streeck and Heinze (1999).
9 See *Süddeutsche Zeitung*, 5.10.1998 and 20.10.1998.
10 Bundesministerium der Finanzen (1999a, p. 54) and Coalition Agreement (1998). The government set a new electricity tax and mineral oil tax, which resulted in an increase in costs, 4.1 billion Euros, for private and industrial consumption.
11 The Ecofin Council required that national governments submit their stability and convergence programmes by the end of 1998. See Council of Ministers (1997a).
12 German Stability Programme (1999a, p. 22).
13 *Ibid.*, p. 20.

14 European Central Bank (1999a).
15 European Central Bank (1999b, p. 59).
16 *Ibid.*, p. 61.
17 Süddeutsche Zeitung, 17.2.1999.
18 *Süddeutsche Zeitung*, 8.2.1999 and 11.2.1999.
19 *Süddeutsche Zeitung*, 8.2.1999.
20 *Süddeutsche Zeitung*, 11.2.1999.
21 *Süddeutsche Zeitung*, 13.3.1999 and 15.3.1999.
22 Similarly to the characterisation of *Die Zeit* of *"das Paar Delors/Pöhl"* and *"das Duo Kohl/Waigel"*, *Süddeutsche Zeitung* (10.9.1999) dubbed Finance Minister Hans Eichel as *"der Arnold Schwarzenegger der Bundesregierung"*, and *The Economist* (17.5.2003) "Iron Hans".
23 As *Süddeutsche Zeitung* (26.6.1999) reported: "The success or the failure in the fight against public debt is, in Finance Minister Eichel's view, a question of life or death for the red-green government."
24 *Die Zeit*, 21.2.1997 and 24.1.1997.
25 On gouvernement économique, see Dyson and Featherstone (1999) and Maes and Quaglia (2003).
26 *Die Zeit*, 13.12.1996 and 14.3.1997.
27 Officially, Duisenberg took over the European Monetary Institute (EMI) and replaced the EMI President, Alexandre Lamfalussy, when the ECB was formed on the basis of the EMI in January 1999. On French policy-making and objectives on the election of the President of the ECB, see Howarth (2001).
28 European Council (1999a).
29 Commission (1999, p. 14).
30 *Ibid.*, pp. 25–6.
31 *Ibid.*, p. 44.
32 European Council (1999b).
33 *Ibid.*
34 European Council (1999c).
35 European Council (2000b). The Lisbon Council introduced an open method of coordination between EU institutions and Member States. For the revised Lisbon strategy, see European Council (2005).
36 Bundesministerium der Finanzen (2000d).
37 German Stability Programme (1999b, p. 12).
38 Sachverständigenrat (2000, p. 94).
39 *Süddeutsche Zeitung*, 13.11.1999.
40 *Süddeutsche Zeitung*, 29.5.1999.
41 Bundesministerium der Finanzen (2000b, p. 23).
42 *Ibid.*, p. 18. The objective of the tax reforms was to succeed better in tax competition, competitiveness and employment. Although the Tax Reform 2000 cut public spending by as much as 37.2 billion Euros, the government simultaneously aimed at securing its financial position without net borrowing in 2006. These massive cuts in the public finances though caused a lot of criticism. The need for economic reforms was also recognised by the opposition parties and trade unions, but the concrete measures to achieve the financial balance were largely criticised by Edmund Stoiber (CSU), Wolfgang Schäuble (CDU), Wolfgang Gerhardt (FDP) and Herbert Mai (ÖTV).
43 *Ibid.*, p. 26.

44 *Ibid.*, p. 15. The government included the fiscal principles in its five-year economic plan, Economic Plan 2001–2005 in 2001. The government (Bundesministerium der Finanzen, 2001b, pp. 6 and 7) believed that "the increasing fiscal manoeuvre makes it possible to introduce crucial future investments in the long term and make a significant contribution to the growth potential in the national economy". The government was also convinced that "Germany will fulfil its responsibilities under the European Stability and Growth Pact and under the broad economic policy guidelines".
45 *Süddeutsche Zeitung*, 12.7.1999.
46 *Süddeutsche Zeitung*, 16.7.1999, 28.7.1999 and 29.12.1999.
47 *Süddeutsche Zeitung*, 1.9.1999.
48 *Süddeutsche Zeitung*, 6.9.1999.
49 *Süddeutsche Zeitung*, 3.9.1999.
50 Commission (2000b, p. 70).
51 Commission (2000a, p. 1).
52 *Ibid.*
53 Commission (2000a, p. 99).
54 German Stability Programme (2000, p. 11).
55 See *Süddeutsche Zeitung*, 2.5.2000, 18.2.2000a and 18.2.2000b. Due to the increase in exports, the falling Euro temporarily relieved pressure for structural reforms.
56 Sachverständigenrat (2001, p. 9). See Bundesministerium der Finanzen (2001a).
57 *Süddeutsche Zeitung*, 23.3.2000 and 13.9.2000.
58 *Ibid.*, p. 41. The government justified the reduction in the pension from 69 to 67 percent of salary by saying that more public spending on services for elderly people and other citizens could thus be provided.
59 Commission (2001c, p. 31).
60 *Ibid.*
61 *Ibid.*, p. 83.
62 Commission (2001d, p. 1).
63 *Ibid.*, p. 125.
64 *Ibid.*, p. 126.
65 See Solidarpaktfortführungsgesetz (2001).
66 Haushaltsgrundsätzegesetz (2001, Article 51a).
67 Bundesministerium der Finanzen (2001a, p. 32).
68 German Stability Programme (2001, p. 6).
69 *Süddeutsche Zeitung*, 6.2.2001.
70 German Stability Programme (2001, p. 9).
71 *Süddeutsche Zeitung*, 26.6.2001.
72 *Süddeutsche Zeitung*, 19.9.2001, 5.11.2001 and 28.11.2001.
73 Sachverständigenrat (2002, p. 138).
74 *Süddeutsche Zeitung*, 4.9.2001.
75 For these purposes, the government set a new law, the Job-AQTIV Law. For policy developments and challenges in the Alliance for Jobs, see Streeck and Heinze (1999), Timmins (2000) and Dyson (2005a).
76 Bundesministerium der Finanzen (2002c, p. 34).
77 *Süddeutsche Zeitung*, 29.1.2002.
78 *Süddeutsche Zeitung*, 13.2.2002b.
79 *Süddeutsche Zeitung*, 2.2.2002.
80 *Süddeutsche Zeitung*, 9.2.2002.

81 *Süddeutsche Zeitung*, 31.1.2002.
82 Commission (2002i, p. 169).
83 *Ibid.*, p. 170.
84 *Süddeutsche Zeitung*, 18.3.2002.
85 The National Stability Pact in Germany was introduced for the first time in 1996–1997.
86 For the criticism of the National Stability Pact, see the key interviews in Chapter 6.
87 Commission (2002h, p. 90).
88 *Ibid.*
89 Bundesministerium der Finanzen (2002e, p. 8).
90 See Buti, Franco and Ongena (1998) and Gros and Thygesen (1998).
91 Commission (2003g).
92 Output gap refers to two different states of an economy. First, if a positive output gap occurs in the economy, actual output is more than the full capacity output. Second, a negative output gap means that the actual output of the economy is less than full capacity output. Economic theory believes that where positive output gap can cause inflation, negative output gap is also a result of inefficient use of resources.
93 Commission (2003g).
94 European Central Bank (1999a, p. 71). See Bundesbank (2000) and (2002).
95 *Süddeutsche Zeitung*, 4.6.1999.
96 European Central Bank (2001a, 2002, and 2003a).
97 British Convergence Programme (2000).
98 European Central Bank (2001b, p. 27).
99 European Central Bank (2004b).
100 European Central Bank (2001b, p. 32).
101 European Central Bank (2001a) and (2003a). Inflation as HICP.
102 See *The Economist*, 5.4.2003.
103 For other essential factors why Britain had such a low inflation level compared to the EMU area, see British Convergence Programme (1998), European Central Bank (1999a) and (2000b).
104 European Central Bank (1998, p. 35).
105 In their economic programmes, Britain, France and Germany estimated the debt ratios with relative accuracy in 1998–2002 despite the uncertain economic prospects in the period. For example, Britain was estimated to have the debt ratio of 38.2 percent in 1999 (the debt was 45.0% in 1999), 40.1 percent in 2000 (42.1% in 2000) and 38.1 percent in 2001 (38.9% in 2001). France was estimated to have the debt ratio of 60.3 in 1999 (58.5%), 57.0 in 2000 (57.2%) and 57.1 in 2001 (56.8%). Germany was estimated to have the debt ratio of 61.0 in 1999 (61.2%), 60.0 in 2000 (60.2%) and 60.0 in 2001 (59.4%).
106 In their economic programmes 1999–2001, Britain was estimated to have the deficit at 0.4 percent of GDP in 1999, 1.1 percent in 2000 and 0.2 percent in 2001. France was estimated to have the deficit at 2.1 percent in 1999, 1.7 percent in 2000 and 1.3 percent in 2001. Germany was estimated to have the deficit at 2.0 percent in 1999, 1.0 percent in 2000 and 2.5 percent in 2001.
107 On the golden rule of the public finance, see Chapters 3 and 7.
108 Commission (2003g).
109 German Stability Programme (2000, p. 26).
110 German Stability Programme (2001).

111 For 1998, Bundesministerium der Finanzen (2003a), French Stability Programme (2003) and British Convergence Programme (2003). For 1999–2002, European Central Bank (2004a). A minus indicates an annual budgetary surplus.
112 European Central Bank (2001b, p. 48).
113 European Central Bank (2000b, p. 47). However, it has to be noted that the debt and deficit ratios consist of different economic factors to some extent. For example, developments in interest rates play a major role in the debt stock, but they do not significantly affect the deficit level. The modernisation of the public financial structure and the privatisation process of the state-owned companies also contributed to the debt level more. On the other hand, modernising and cutting public spending massively, as done in Germany, should have had a more positive impact on both the debt and deficit ratios.
114 Bundesministerium der Finanzen (2002a) and Commission (2003g).
115 Commission (2002i).
116 Commission (2004a). See Schmidt (1999b) and Schmidt (2000b). Social transfers are regarded as somewhat fixed costs in society, and changing their financial structure requires time.
117 Bundesministerium der Finanzen (2002a) and Commission (2003g).
118 *The Economist*, 4.10.2003b.
119 Bundesministerium der Finanzen (2003a).
120 However, active investment policy could still be implemented as an instrument of an active national fiscal policy in EMU. According to Neumann (*Die Zeit*, 12.11.1998), "Our economic growth is on the long-term cycle. Some people want to have the boost effect of Keynesianism. As the central bank cannot accelerate the growth, we need for more investments."
121 Bundesbank (2001) and Bundesbank (2003).
122 Commission (2003g).
123 European Central Bank (1999a, p. 30).
124 Commission (2003g).
125 Bundesbank (2001, p. 66).
126 *The Economist*, 7.6.2003a.
127 Bundesministerium der Finanzen (2000b, p. 19).
128 Bundesbank (2001, p. 24).
129 The President of the Bundesbank, Ernst Welteke, considered that the very beginning of the Euro had been successful to the common monetary policy because national economic reforms had contributed to the growth in the Euro area, which had in turn strengthened the Euro area. Welteke stated his belief in *Süddeutsche Zeitung* (30.8.2000) that "when this growth potential of Europe is realised, then the Euro becomes significantly stronger".
130 British Convergence Programme (2002, p. 7).
131 IMF (1997), Bundesbank (1998) and IMF (1999).
132 Commission (2004a).
133 European Central Bank (2002, p. 49).
134 It should also be noted that the threat of an early warning was launched in the state election year of Germany and thus, it was used as a political pressure on Chancellor Schröder and Finance Minister Eichel.
135 *Süddeutsche Zeitung*, 13.2.2002a.
136 von Hagen and Strauch (1999, p. 20).
137 Allsopp (2002b, p. 23).

138 Although this chapter has focused on the critical political and economic problems in Germany in the implementation phase of the Stability Pact, further research work in the future could also be directed towards the analysis of policy processes in the party and election politics when planning and introducing economic reforms in Germany in the EMU era. For most recent analysis on the German economy, see Deeg (2005), Dyson (2005b), Smith (2005) and Streeck and Trampusch (2005). Germany's political and economic system has also recently been studied and revisited from the semi-sovereign state thesis perspective, which was originally presented by Katzenstein. The semi-sovereign state thesis emphasises that German national politics is based on multi-level, multi-actor and consensus-seeking policy-making, in which both formal and informal power plays the key role.
139 Bundesministerium der Finanzen (2000b, p. 19).
140 *Ibid.*, p. 20.
141 German Stability Programme (2002, p. 14).

5 Reuploading Fiscal Policy Coordination in EMU

1 German Finance Minister, Hans Eichel, in *Der Spiegel*, 29.12.2001.
2 Coalition Agreement (2002).
3 Bundesministerium für Wirtschaft und Arbeit (2003, p. 6).
4 Waigel argued that even worse times could occur because the UMTS revenue of 50.7 billion Euros had gone without any results for fiscal stability. In his words (*Süddeutsche Zeitung*, 20.11.2002), "then Hans Eichel had a piece of gold in his hands, now he carries a millstone on his shoulders".
5 Sachverständigenrat (2003, p. 2).
6 *Ibid.*, p. 13.
7 Bundesministerium für Wirtschaft und Arbeit (2003, p. 30).
8 *Süddeutsche Zeitung*, 21.10.2002a.
9 *Ibid.*
10 Bundesministerium für Wirtschaft und Arbeit (2003, p. 20).
11 Bundesministerium für Gesundheit und Soziale Sicherung (2002, p. 3).
12 *Ibid.*, p. 4.
13 German Stability Programme (2002, p. 21).
14 *Süddeutsche Zeitung*, 18.10.2002.
15 *Süddeutsche Zeitung*, 5.11.2002.
16 *Süddeutsche Zeitung*, 9.10.2002.
17 *Le Monde*, 18.10.2002. Similarly, the Chief Economist of the Bundesbank, Norbert Walter, argued in *Süddeutsche Zeitung* (6.9.2002) that the whole deficit criterion should be abolished in a couple of years.
18 *Süddeutsche Zeitung*, 19.10.2002.
19 *Süddeutsche Zeitung*, 21.10.2002b.
20 *Süddeutsche Zeitung*, 20.11.2002. In Waigel's words (*Süddeutsche Zeitung*, 20.11.2002): "If someone wants to find a role model in economic policy, then we have to look at Finland."
21 *Süddeutsche Zeitung*, 24.12.2002.
22 *Ibid.* As a critical response to Schröder, the Bavarian Finance Minister, Kurt Faltlhauser (CSU), argued in *Süddeutsche Zeitung*, 27.12.2002: "We simply do not have the money. The public finance of today is in a more critical condition than ever before since 1949. We have an income crisis without a doubt.

And still the European Stability Pact increasingly constrains the national budgetary policy."

23 German Stability Programme (2002, p. 6).
24 In line with the decisions of the Financial Planning Council and the Annual Economic Report 2003, the government finalised the German National Stability Programme 2002 on 18 December 2002.
25 Bundesministerium der Finanzen (2003c, p. 46).
26 Bundesministerium der Finanzen (2003d, p. 67).
27 European Council (2002).
28 Commission (2002g, p. 3).
29 *Ibid.*, p. 5.
30 *Ibid.*, p. 8.
31 Commission (2003f, p. 1).
32 *Ibid.*, p. 1.
33 Bundesministerium der Finanzen (2003f, p. 8).
34 *Süddeutsche Zeitung*, 14.1.2003.
35 *Ibid.*
36 Bundesministerium für Wirtschaft und Arbeit (2004, p. 10).
37 Agenda 2010 also launched a further reduction in the tax ratio. As *Mittelstand*-companies, which refer to small- and medium-sized companies, constituted the micro basis of the whole economic growth, they were allowed to carry a reduced tax burden and easier book-keeping systems than bigger companies.
38 *The Economist*, 7.6.2003b.
39 *The Economist*, 19.4.2003.
40 *Süddeutsche Zeitung*, 16.6.2003.
41 *Ibid.*
42 *Der Spiegel*, 23.6.2003.
43 *Süddeutsche Zeitung*, 24.6.2003.
44 *Süddeutsche Zeitung*, 5.5.2003.
45 European Central Bank (2003b).
46 *Süddeutsche Zeitung*, 11.7.2003.
47 European Central Bank (2003b).
48 Commission (2003c).
49 Commission (2003e).
50 French Stability Programme (2003, p. 2) and German Stability Programme (2003, p. 6).
51 *The Economist*, 29.11.2003b.
52 *The Economist*, 4.10.2003a.
53 *The Economist*, 11.10.2003.
54 *Süddeutsche Zeitung*, 15.11.2003.
55 *Ibid.*
56 German Stability Programme (2004a, p. 3).
57 Commission (2003i, p. 5).
58 *Ibid.*, p. 4.
59 *Ibid.*, p. 5.
60 *Ibid.*, p. 24.
61 *Ibid.*, p. 27.
62 *Ibid.*, p. 28.
63 Commission (2004b, p. 3).
64 *Ibid.*, p. 8.
65 *Ibid.*, p. 9.

66 *Süddeutsche Zeitung*, 2.2.2004.
67 European Court of Justice (2004).
68 *Financial Times Deutschland*, 5.7.2004a and 5.7.2004b.
69 IG Metall (2004).
70 *Süddeutsche Zeitung*, 19.5.2004.
71 *Süddeutsche Zeitung*, 5.7.2004b. On 23 July, Daimler Chrysler made a decision with its employees that the working week would be partly extended up to 40 hours and the number of daily breaks would also be reduced. This way Daimler Chrysler would annually save 500 million Euros. To compensate these changes to the work force, Daimler Chrysler promised that no reduction in the labour force would be planned or implemented before 2007. In order to secure jobs in the national factories the employees of Daimler Chrysler were thus willing to reduce their benefits and increase working hours.
72 Bundesministerium der Finanzen (2004d, p. 37).
73 Bundesministerium der Finanzen (2004c).
74 The 2-Euro jobs meant low-paid jobs that paid workers only one or two Euros per hour. The employees of the auto manufacturer, General Motors, also protested against the job cuts by walking out for a day on 19 October 2004, whereas the employees of Opel in Bochum suspended their work for the whole week.
75 The right-wing party, the CDU, and the far-right parties, the NPD and PDS, were winners. For the regional elections, see *Frankfurter Allgemeine Zeitung*, 7.9.2004, 20.9.2004 and 21.9.2004 and *Die Zeit*, 23.5.2005.
76 *Frankfurter Allgemeine Zeitung*, 23.9.2004c.
77 *Frankfurter Allgemeine Zeitung*, 9.8.2004.
78 *Frankfurter Allgemeine Zeitung*, 1.9.2004a.
79 *Frankfurter Allgemeine Zeitung*, 1.9.2004b and 10.9.2004.
80 Financial Planning Council (2004).
81 See Commission (2004a) and (2004b).
82 Commission (2004c).
83 *Ibid.*
84 Commission (2004d).
85 Council of Ministers (2004).
86 *Frankfurter Allgemeine Zeitung*, 4.9.2004a.
87 *Frankfurter Allgemeine Zeitung*, 11.9.2004.
88 European Central Bank (2004g).
89 Bundesbank (2005, p. 42).
90 German Stability Programme (2004b, p. 34).
91 Bundesministerium der Finanzen (2004f, p. 42).
92 *Financial Times Deutschland*, 17.1.2005b.
93 *Financial Times Deutschland*, 17.1.2005a.
94 *Financial Times Deutschland*, 18.1.2005.
95 Council of Ministers (2005b). The Ecofin Council established a new position of Semi-permanent President of the Group of EMU Finance Ministers in September 2004, who would chair the monthly meetings of EMU Finance Ministers. The Prime Minister of Luxemburg, Jean-Claude Juncker, who was appointed to this two-year position starting from January 2005 and who was also proclaimed Mr Euro, was expected to act as a coordinator between the monetary policy of the ECB and the fiscal objectives of EMU Member States, the so-called Euro policy. The idea behind this new actor was that the President could act as the common spokesman with a single and collectively

shared opinion on all questions related to the Euro; an actor would have been needed right from the beginning of the third stage of EMU in 1999.

96 Council of Ministers (2005c) and (2005d).

97 *Financial Times*, 18.2.2005.

98 Finnish government (2005).

99 *International Herald Tribune*, 18.2.2005. As an implication of difficulties in negotiations, Juncker raised the possibility after the nine-hour Ecofin Council meeting on 8 March that the rules would not be reformed after all. For him (Council of Ministers, 2005e), "we have the option of not reforming the Pact and I would not rule that out".

100 Council of Ministers (2005f, p. 3).

101 *Ibid.*, p. 11.

102 *Ibid.*, p. 15.

103 *Ibid.*

104 *Ibid.*, p. 12.

105 *Ibid.*

106 European Council (2005).

107 Artis and Corsetti (2005).

108 *Süddeutsche Zeitung*, 21.3.2005.

109 Council of Ministers (2005h).

110 European Central Bank (2005d).

111 *Ibid.*

112 European Central Bank (2005f).

113 European Central Bank (2005c, p. 73).

114 *Financial Times*, 24.3.2005c.

115 *Frankfurter Allgemeine Zeitung*, 3.9.2004.

116 European Central Bank (2004b, p. 49). According to the Commission (2005d, p. 48), the main economic risks in Germany are "a continuing stagnation of private consumption translating into tax shortfalls and the labour market developing more unfavourably than projected".

117 Commission (2004j).

118 European Central Bank (2004d), (2004e) and (2005c).

119 European Central Bank (2004b, p. 61).

120 European Central Bank (2004a), (2004e), (2004f) and (2005a).

121 European Central Bank (2003b).

122 European Central Bank (2004b, p. 46).

123 European Central Bank (2003b).

124 European Central Bank (2003c).

125 European Central Bank (2003a), (2004a), (2004d), (2004e), (2004f) and (2005b). Inflation as HICP.

126 *Süddeutsche Zeitung*, 11.7.2003.

127 *Süddeutsche Zeitung*, 16.6.2003.

128 British Convergence Programme (2003), French Stability Programme (2003), German Stability Programme (2003) and Commission (2004b).

129 IMF (2003, p. 11).

130 European Central Bank (2004b, pp. 56–7).

131 British Convergence Programme (2003), French Stability Programme (2003), German Stability Programme (2003) and Commission (2004b). A minus indicates an annual budgetary surplus.

132 Commission (2005c) and (2005d).

133 British Convergence Programme (2003, p. 13).

134 Bundesministerium der Finanzen (2004c) and Commission (2004a).
135 *Süddeutsche Zeitung*, 19.8.2003.
136 Commission (2004a).
137 Bundesministerium der Finanzen (2003f) and Commission (2004a).
138 *Süddeutsche Zeitung*, 16.5.2003. On taxation policy in Germany, see Ganghof (2004).
139 Berlin (2003), Brandenburg (2003), Bremen 2003, Hamburg (2003), Hessen (2003), Mecklenburg-Vorpommern (2003), Niedersachsen 2003, Nordrhein-Westfalen (2003), Rheinland-Pfalz (2003), Saarland 2003, Sachsen (2003), Sachsen-Anhalt (2003), Schlewig-Holstein (2003), Thüringen (2003), Baden-Württemberg (2004) and Bayern (2004).
140 Bundesbank (2001, p. 21).
141 European Central Bank (2004d) and (2004e) and Bundesbank (2004a), (2004b), (2004d) and (2005) and European Central Bank (2005e).
142 *Frankfurter Allgemeine Zeitung*, 14.9.2004.
143 German Stability Programme (2003, p. 11).
144 IMF (1993) and (2004).
145 For a summary of the main economic trends in Germany in 1998–2006, see Figure A.1 in Appendix. It should also be noted that the start of the EMU era had an asymmetrical impact on the German economy and the rest of the national economies of EMU. Where lowering interests rates reduced public debt costs outside Germany notably relieving their national fiscal positions and room for manoeuvre, Germany lacked these benefits at the beginning of the EMU era.
146 *Süddeutsche Zeitung*, 5.7.2004a.
147 European Central Bank (2003b).
148 Dyson (2000b, p. 254).
149 The major decline in the labour market, not only in Germany but also throughout the Euro area, speaks for the fast and active implementation of the structural measures of the Lisbon Strategy of 2000.
150 Sachverständigenrat (2004, p. 16).
151 Commission (2004l).

6 Reviewing the Institutional System of Fiscal Policy Coordination

1 The choice of experts for interviews was based on four main criteria: first, they were experts in the Stability Pact and EMU; second, they had been involved with the German economy and fiscal policy coordination at the national and European levels; third, they represent the key actors in fiscal policy coordination; and fourth, academics were the heads of main research institutes in Germany thus possessing up-to-date knowledge of the German economy as a part of the Euro area. Due to the political, economic, institutional and legal sensitivity of the topic and for the absolute granting of confidentiality to the interviewees, the list of individual interviewees cannot be provided here.
2 Burda and Wyplosz (1997, p. 394). See Eichengreen and Frieden (1998b), Bordo and Jonung (2000), Boyer (2002) and Brunila, Buti and in't Veld (2002).
3 IMF (2003, p. 14).
4 Monetary official, 2004, with the author.

5 *Ibid.* For the budgetary deficit in EMU in 1998–2006, see Figure 6.3.
6 Fiscal official, 2004, with the author.
7 *Ibid.*
8 Fiscal official of a Bundesland, 2004, with the author.
9 Supranational official, 2004, with the author.
10 Academic, 2004, with the author.
11 *Ibid.*
12 *Ibid.*
13 *Süddeutsche Zeitung*, 10.2.2004.
14 The question of the ruling was very topical. Whereas the first half of the interviews were conducted in June 2004 before the decision, the decision was already publicly available for the interviewees in the second half in July. Thus, where the first half presented their views on how the ruling could be formulated, the second half were able to take a more specific view. This fact and its impact on the answers have been taken into account in the analysis. However, all interviewees shared the opinion that ideally, the ruling could act as a culmination point for clarifying the relationship between institutional authority and responsibilities on the one hand and national commitments and binding rules on the other.
15 Monetary official, 2004, with the author.
16 *Ibid.*
17 *Ibid.*
18 Fiscal official, 2004, with the author.
19 Fiscal official of a Bundesland, 2004, with the author.
20 Supranational official, 2004, with the author.
21 *Ibid.*
22 Academic, 2004, with the author.
23 *Ibid.*
24 *Ibid.*
25 *Ibid.*
26 *Süddeutsche Zeitung*, 2.12.2002.
27 Buti and Pench (2004, p. 1032).
28 *Süddeutsche Zeitung*, 27.5.2004. As another idea, there could a new rule in the EU laying down that if a Member State exceeded the budgetary deficit criterion, let us say, by one percentage point a year, the national net payments to the EU would be in turn increased by two percentage points.
29 For differences in the economic cycle in EMU Member States, see Altavilla (2004).
30 Bundesregierung (2004b).
31 Council of Ministers (1997b, Article 2). A GDP fall between 0.75 and 2.0 percent may also be considered exceptional but a fall less than 0.75 percent may not. See European Parliament (1996) and Chapter 2.
32 Commission (2004a, p. 17).
33 Burda and Wyplosz (1997, p. 397).
34 British Convergence Programme (1998, p. 22).
35 Bundesministerium der Finanzen (1999b), (2000e), (2001b), (2002e), (2003f) and (2004c).
36 German Constitution (1949, Article 115).
37 Verfassungsgerichtshof (2003).
38 Monetary official, 2004, with the author.
39 *Ibid.*

40 *Ibid.*
41 *Ibid.*
42 *Ibid.*
43 Fiscal official, 2004, with the author.
44 *Ibid.*
45 Fiscal official of a Bundesland, 2004, with the author.
46 Supranational official, 2004, with the author.
47 *Ibid.*
48 *Ibid.*
49 *Ibid.*
50 Academic, 2004, with the author.
51 *Ibid.*
52 *Ibid.*
53 von Hagen, Hughes Hallett and Strauch (2002a, p. 17).
54 IMF (2003, p. 7).
55 Bundesregierung (2004b).
56 *Ibid.*
57 *The Economist*, 8.11.2003.
58 Milton Friedman (*Süddeutsche Zeitung*, 27.11.2002) took the view when referring to EMU that "I do not know how it would be possible to allow more flexibility and if that is possible in the first place".
59 Monetary official, 2004, with the author.
60 *Ibid.*
61 Fiscal official, 2004, with the author.
62 *Ibid.*
63 *Ibid.*
64 *Ibid.*
65 Fiscal official of a Bundesland, 2004, with the author.
66 *Ibid.*
67 Supranational official, 2004, with the author.
68 *Ibid.*
69 Academic, 2004, with the author.
70 See Council of Ministers (1997a) and Chapter 4.
71 Commission (2002g, p. 5).
72 Council of Ministers (1997a).
73 Fiscal official, 2004, with the author.
74 *Ibid.*
75 *Ibid.*
76 Funk (2000, p. 28).
77 Knott (1981, p. 2)
78 German Constitution (1949).
79 On the reform of German federalism, see Scharpf (2004) and *Financial Times*, 16.12.2004.
80 On the problems and challenges of German federalism in the process of establishing the first European Constitution, see Fischer (2003), Margedant (2003) and Thaysen (2003).
81 Supranational official, 2004, with the author.
82 Supranational official, 2004, with the author.
83 Fiscal official, 2004, with the author.
84 *Ibid.*
85 *Ibid.*

86 Fiscal official of a Bundesland, 2004, with the author.
87 *Ibid.*
88 Academic, 2004, with the author.
89 *Ibid.*
90 *Ibid.*
91 Commission (2004e).
92 European Central Bank (2003d).
93 Stark and Remsperger (2004, p. 3).
94 The appointment of Jean-Claude Juncker as the first President of the Euro-12 group from January 2005 has increased the actual role of the Euro-12 group in economic policy coordination.
95 Monetary official, 2004, with the author.
96 *Ibid.*
97 *Ibid.*
98 *Ibid.*
99 Fiscal official, 2004, with the author.
100 Academic, 2004, with the author.
101 *Ibid.*
102 *Ibid.*
103 *Ibid.*
104 European Central Bank (2004b, p. 58).
105 German Stability Programme (2003, p. 40).
106 German Stability Programme (2002, p. 37). The British government set up a specific commission, the Pensions Commission, which submitted an official report on 12 October 2004. The shocking conclusion drawn in the report was that Britain would face a major financial gap of 83 billion Euros in the future if the current saving pace was not changed. See *The Guardian*, 12.10.2004 and *The Independent*, 17.10.2004.
107 Monetary and fiscal official, 2004, with the author.
108 Fiscal official of a Bundesland, 2004, with the author.
109 Academic, 2004, with the author.
110 European Council (1999c).
111 Commission (2003j, p. 11).
112 *Ibid.*, p. 24.
113 German Finance Minister, Hans Eichel, in *Der Spiegel*, 29.12.2001.
114 Commission (2006c). The debt of Luxemburg remained at 7.4 percent in 1998–2006.
115 Commission (2006d). Luxemburg had a surplus of 3.4 percent in 1998 that however transformed into a net borrowing of 1.5 percent of GDP in 2006.

7 Challenging the Existing Understanding of Europeanisation in the Study of Germany, the Stability and Growth Pact and Policy Coordination

1 Dyson (2003a, p. 207).
2 *Ibid.*, p. 201.
3 Dyson and Goetz (2003a, p. 10).
4 See Harding and Paterson (2000b).
5 Dyson and Goetz (2003a, p. 11).
6 Ekengren (1997, p. 69).

7 Pierson (2000b, p. 72).
8 Hughes Hallett, Hutchison and Hougaard Jensen (1999, p. 1).
9 It is also worth pointing out that although the fundamental objective of European economic, monetary and fiscal policy coordination has been to maintain a high degree of economic convergence, the case of Germany has shown that continual and successful convergence is very difficult to maintain, and there may also occur disintegration in some policy questions in the integration process.
10 For the traditional two-way Europeanisation, see Chapter 1 and Figures 1.1 and 1.2.
11 This research does not claim that reuploading presents a totally unique and unprecedented idea of changing interests and ongoing cyclical and dynamic European cooperation, because it is already widely known that policy-making processes in the EU are based on multi-level interaction. For example, Dyson (2003a), Jeffery (2003) and Lodge (2003), when studying German economic policy, German national policy-making and competition policy have understood and defined Europeanisation as a two-way process. However, the significance of the argument of reuploading in fiscal policy coordination in EMU is that it captures a concrete, fast and direct process by which Germany changed common European fiscal policy objectives: a process that has not taken place before in any policy area in the EU on this large scale. In short, the single case study of the German economy produced surprising counter-intuitive results from those predicted by the uploading and downloading concepts of Europeanisation.
12 Dyson (2000b, p. 67).
13 *Ibid.*, p. 85.
14 On the historical dichotomy between large and small countries in international and European cooperation, see Cameron (1978), Gourevitch (1978), Katzenstein (1984) and (1985), Krasner (1988), Cerny (1995) and Keohane and Milner (1996).
15 From the perspective of economics, Buti and Pench (2004) summarise four main reasons why large EMU Member States have not complied with the fiscal rules: a) the economic cost of fiscal convergence is larger for large countries, b) fiscal convergence requires growth, c) economic size and power reduce the likelihood of sanctions on fiscal misbehaviour, and d) national differences in budgetary institutions.
16 Austria, Finland and Ireland as small EMU Member States, succeeded in meeting the fiscal rules of the Stability Pact because of various reasons, for example from better growth, better employment to more timely-effective adjustments and economic reforms in their national economies.
17 Buti and Pench (2004, p. 1032).
18 On other EU institutions in policy coordination, see Nugent (1999), Dinan (2003) and Lord (2003).
19 It is also worth noting that there are three key principles to define authority and objectives between EU institutions and Member States (national sovereignty) in the EU: a) (positive and negative) loyalty stating that the Member States have to be totally loyal to the EU in all actions and that national actions may not threaten or postpone the fulfilment of common objectives, b) subsidiarity declaring the objective that the decisions in the EU should be made as close to the administrative levels of the Member States as possible, and c) flexibility (hardcore) meaning that it is no longer a precondition for integration in the new fields that all Member States have to join collectively and simultaneously.

20 Nice (2002, Article 211).
21 Dyson (2000b, p. 121).
22 Despite the dire financial problems in EMU Member States, Wim Duisenberg has claimed that any more coordination between monetary and fiscal policies would undermine the institutional autonomy of the ECB. See European Central Bank (2003d).
23 Winkler (1996, p. 16).
24 Buti, Roeger and in't Veld (2002, p. 241). See Buti and Giudice (2002b).
25 Huhne (2002, pp. 116–17).
26 On divided authority and competence in fiscal policy coordination, see Chapter 2 and Table 2.1. On the role of the soft and hard rules of economic policy coordination in constraining national economic authority in the EU and EMU, see Enderlein (2004).
27 Based on Scharpf's understanding (1996, pp. 25–37), there are three primary ways to solve the problem of increasing authority conflicts in the European Union: a) to reform existing institutions, b) to develop new procedures for institutional cooperation, or c) to increase national control and authority.
28 Member States' great concern about the pace and direction of European integration was reflected in the total rejection of the European Constitution in France and the Netherlands in May and June 2005. The European Constitution and the whole European political and economic integration process experienced a dramatic setback as the French and Dutch voters rejected the Constitution on 29 May and 1 June 2005. As a result, the Brussels European Council decided to freeze the ratification process of the European Constitution on 16 June 2005.
29 British Convergence Programme (2004, p. 64).
30 For the fusion theory of European integration, see Wessels (1997) and Wessels and Linsenmann (2002). An alternative scenario is a scenario in which the convergence of national budgetary institutions in objectives and processes, such as in independent forecasting, independent professional national statistics and fiscal policy rules and procedures. See Eichengreen and Wyplosz (1998) and Buti, von Hagen and Martinez-Mongay (2002a).
31 The claim that reuploading is a signal of a wider systemic failure in the EU raises the question of trade-off between the size and relative resources of Member States and the size of the potential systemic failure. Future research should examine and analyse whether Member States have the political and economic ability to fast and effectively solve the problems of institutional fiscal policy coordination in EMU.

Bibliography

Alesina, Alberto and **Wacziarg**, Romain (1999) "Is Europe Going Too Far?", National Bureau of Economic Research, Working Paper Series, Working Paper No. 6883, Massachusetts.

Allensbacher Jahrbuch (2002) Allensbacher Jahrbuch der Demoskopie 1998–2002. Band 11.

Allsopp, Christopher (2002a) "The Co-ordination of Monetary, Fiscal and Labour Market Policies in the Euro Area", in Iain Begg (ed.), *Europe: Government and Money. Running EMU: Challenges of Policy Co-operation*, The Federal Trust, 83–100.

Allsopp, Christopher (2002b) "The Future of Macroeconomic Policy in the European Union", Bank of England, External Unit Discussion Paper, No. 7, February.

Allsopp, Christopher and **Artis**, Michael J. (2003) "The Assessment: EMU, Four Years On", *Oxford Review of Economic Policy*, Vol. 19, No. 1, 1–29.

Allsopp, Christopher and **Vines**, David (1996) "Fiscal Policy and EMU", *National Institute Economic Review*, No. 158, 91–107.

Allsopp, Christopher and **Vines**, David (1998) "The Assessment: Macroeconomic Policy after EMU", *Oxford Review of Economic Policy*, Vol. 14, No. 3, 1–23.

Altavilla, Carlo (2004) "Do EMU Members Share the Same Business Cycle?", *Journal of Common Market Studies*, Vol. 42, No. 5, 869–96.

Amsterdam Treaty (1997) "Treaty of Amsterdam Amending the Treaty on European Union, the Treaties Establishing the European Communities and Related Acts", *Official Journal C 340*, 10 November.

Anderson, Jeffrey J. (2003) "Europeanization in Context: Concept and Theory", in Kenneth Dyson and Klaus H. Goetz (eds), *Germany, Europe and the Politics of Constraint*. Proceedings of the British Academy, No. 119, Oxford: Oxford University Press, 37–53.

Ardy, Brian (2000) "A Question of Fit for EMU: Process and Policy in the Fiscal Domain", *Working Paper 13/2000*, European Institute, South Bank University, London.

Armstrong, Kenneth A. and **Bulmer**, Simon J. (1998) *The Governance of the Single European Market* (Manchester: Manchester University Press).

Artis, Michael J. (2002a) "The Performance of the European Central Bank", *International Review of Applied Economics*, Vol. 16, No. 1, 19–29.

Artis, Michael J. (2002b) "The Stability and Growth Pact. Fiscal Policy in EMU", in Fritz Breuss, Gerhard Fink and Stefan Griller (eds), *Institutional, Legal and Economic Aspects of the EMU* (Wien: SpringerWienNewYork), 101–15.

Artis, Michael J. and **Buti**, Marco (2001) "Setting Medium-Term Fiscal Targets in EMU", in Anne Brunila, Marco Buti and Daniele Franco (eds), *The Stability and Growth Pact. The Architecture of Fiscal Policy in EMU* (Basingstoke: Palgrave), 185–203.

Artis, Michael J. and **Corsetti**, Giancarlo (2005) "Market Sanctions Will Replace Pact", *Financial Times*, 24.3.2005.

Artis, Michael J. and **Winkler**, Bernhard (1997) "The Stability Pact: Safeguarding the Credibility of the European Central Bank", European University Institute, Robert Schuman Centre, *EUI Working Paper RSC No. 97/54*, Florence, Italy.

Artis, Michael J. and **Winkler**, Bernhard (1999) "The Stability Pact: Trading off Flexibility for Credibility", in Andrew Hughes Hallett, Michael M. Hutchison and Jensen Svend E. Hougaard (eds), *Fiscal Aspects of European Monetary Integration* (Cambridge: Cambridge University Press), 157–87.

Bache, Ian (2002) "Europeanization: A Governance Approach", *ESRC Seminar Series*, UACES Study Group on the Europeanisation of British Politics and Policy-Making, Paper presented on 29 September, University of Sheffield, UK.

Bache, Ian and **Flinders**, Matthew (eds) (2004a) *Perspectives on Multi-Level Governance* (Oxford: Oxford University Press).

Bache, Ian and **Flinders**, Matthew (2004b) "Conclusions", in Ian Bache and Matthew Flinders (eds), *Perspectives on Multi-Level Governance* (Oxford: Oxford University Press), 195–206.

Bache, Ian and **Marshall**, Adam (2004) "Europeanisation and Domestic Change. A Governance Approach to Institutional Adaptation in Britain", *Queen's Papers on Europeanisation*, Queen's University, Belfast.

Baden-Württemberg (2004) Finanzplan 2003–2007, Finanzministerium, Stuttgart.

Balassa, Bela (1961) *The Theory of Economic Integration* (Homewood: Richard Irwin).

Balassa, Bela (1973) "Monetary Integration in the European Common Market", in Alexander K. Swoboda (ed.), *Europe and the Evolution of the International Monetary System*, Proceedings of the First Conference of the International Center for Monetary and Banking Studies (Geneva: Sijthoff), 93–128.

Balassone, Fabrizio and **Franco**, Daniele (2001) "The SGP and the 'Golden Rule'", in Anne Brunila, Marco Buti and Daniele Franco (eds), *The Stability and Growth Pact. The Architecture of Fiscal Policy in EMU* (Basingstoke: Palgrave), 371–93.

Baltensperger, Ernst (1999), in the Bundesbank (ed.), *Fifty Years of the Deutsche Mark* (Oxford: Oxford University Press), 439–523.

Barro, Robert, J. and **Gordon**, David (1983) "A Positive Theory of Monetary Policy in a Natural Rate Model", *Journal of Political Economy*, Vol. 91, 589–610.

Bayern (2004) "Finanzplan des Freistaats Bayern 2003–2007", January.

Bayoumi, Tamim and **Eichengreen**, Barry (1992) "Shocking Aspects of European Monetary Unification", National Bureau of Economic Research, Working Paper Series, *Working Paper No. 3949*, Massachusetts.

Beetsma, Roel M. (2001) "Does EMU Need a Stability Pact?", in Anne Brunila, Marco Buti and Daniele Franco (eds), *The Stability and Growth Pact. The Architecture of Fiscal Policy in EMU* (Basingstoke: Palgrave), 23–52.

Beetsma, Roel M. and **Bovenberg**, A.L. (1995) "The Interaction of Fiscal and Monetary Policy in a Monetary Union: Balancing Credibility and Flexibility", Tilburg University Center for Economic Research, *Discussion Paper No. 95101*.

Beetsma, Roel, **Debrun**, Xavier and **Klaassen**, Franc (2001) "Is Fiscal Policy Coordination in EMU Desirable?", The Graduate Institute of International Studies, *HEI Working Paper No. 04/2001*, Geneva.

Begg, David, **Giavazza**, Francesco, **Spaventa**, Luigi and **Wyplosz**, Charles (1991) "European Monetary Union: The Macro Issues. In The Making of Monetary Union. Monitoring European Integration", *CEPR Annual Report*, 3–66.

Berlin (2003) Finanzplannung von Berlin 2003 bis 2007, Berlin.

Bibow, Jörg (2001) "Making EMU Work: Some Lessons from the 1990s", *International Review of Applied Economics*, Vol. 15, No. 1, 233–59.

Bordo, Michael and **Jonung**, Lars (2000) "Lessons for EMU from the History of Monetary Unions", The Institute of Economic Affairs, *IEA Readings 50* (West Essex: Hartington).

Boyer, Robert (2002) "Co-ordination of Economic Policies in Europe: From Uncertainty to Apprenticeship", in Iain Begg (ed.), *Europe: Government and Money. Running EMU: Challenges of Policy Co-operation*, The Federal Trust, Sachsen-Anhalt, 39–54.

Brandenburg (2003) Finanzplan 2003–2007, Ministerium der Finanzen, Brandenburg.

Braun, Hans-Joachim (1992) *The German Economy in the Twentieth Century. Contemporary economic history of Europe series* (London: Routledge).

Bremen (2003) Finanzplan 2003–2007, Der Senator für Finanzen, Bremen.

Breuss, Fritz and **Weber**, Andrea (1999) "Economic Policy Coordination in the EMU: Implications for the Stability and Growth Pact?", European University Institute, Robert Schuman Centre for Advanced Studies, *EUI Working Papers, RSC No. 99/26*, Italy.

British Convergence Programme (1998) December 1998, HM Treasury.

British Convergence Programme (1999) December 1999, HM Treasury.

British Convergence Programme (2000) December 2000, HM Treasury.

British Convergence Programme (2001) December 2001, HM Treasury.

British Convergence Programme (2002) December 2002, HM Treasury.

British Convergence Programme (2003) December 2003, HM Treasury.

British Convergence Programme (2004) December 2004, HM Treasury.

Brunila, Anne (2002) "Fiscal Policy: Coordination, Discipline and Stabilisation", Bank of Finland, *Discussion Papers, 7/2002*. Helsinki.

Brunila, Anne, **Buti**, Marco and **Franco**, Daniele (eds) (2001a) *The Stability and Growth Pact. The Architecture of Fiscal Policy in EMU* (Basingstoke: Palgrave).

Brunila, Anne, **Buti**, Marco and **Franco**, Daniele (2001b) "Introduction", in Anne Brunila, Marco Buti and Daniele Franco (eds), *The Stability and Growth Pact. The Architecture of Fiscal Policy in EMU* (Basingstoke: Palgrave), 1–20.

Brunila, Anne, **Buti**, Marco and **in't Veld** (Jan 2002) "Cyclical Stabilisation under the Stability and Growth Pact: How Effective Are Automatic Stabilisers?", Bank of Finland, *Discussion Papers, 6/2002*, Helsinki.

Brunila, Anne, **Buti**, Marco and **in't Veld** (Jan 2003) "Fiscal Policy in Europe. How Effective Are Automatic Stabilisers?", *Empirica*, Vol. 30, 1–24.

Brunila, Anne and **Martinez-Mongay**, Carlos (2002) "Fiscal Policy in the Early Years of EMU", in Marco Buti and André Sapir (eds), *EMU and Economic Policy in Europe. The Challenge of the Early Years*, European Commission (Cheltenham: Edward Elgar), 150–69.

Bryson, J.H. (1994) "Fiscal Policy Coordination and Flexibility under European Monetary Union: Implications for Macroeconomic Stabilization", *Journal of Policy Modelling*, Vol. 16, No. 6, 541–57.

Buiter, Willem H. (1999) "Notes on 'A Code for Fiscal Stability'", 30 September.

Buiter, Willem H. (2003) "Ten Commandments for a Fiscal Rule in the E(M)U", *Oxford Review of Economic Policy*, Vol. 19, No. 1, 84–99.

Buiter, Willem H. and **Marston**, R. (1985) *International Economic Policy Coordination* (Cambridge: Cambridge University Press).

Buller, Jim (2003) "The Disadvantage of Tying One's Hands: The Rise and Fall of the Europeanisation of British Monetary Policy", *ESRC Seminar Series*, UACES Study Group on the Europeanisation of British Politics and Policy-Making, Paper presented 19 September, University of Sheffield, UK.

Buller, Jim and **Gamble**, Andrew (2002) "Conceptualising Europeanisation", *ESRC Seminar Series*, UACES Study Group on the Europeanisation of British Politics and Policy-Making, Paper presented on 29 November, University of Sheffield, UK.

Bulmer, Simon, **Dolowitz**, David, **Humphreys**, Peter and **Padgett**, Stephen (2003) "Electricity and Telecommunications: Fit for the European Union", in Kenneth Dyson and Klaus H. Goetz (eds), *Germany, Europe and the Politics of Constraint*, Proceedings of the British Academy, No. 119 (Oxford: Oxford University Press), 251–69.

Bulmer, Simon and **Lequesne**, Christian (2002) "New Perspectives on EU-Member State Relationships", *Research in Question*, No. 4, January, Centre d'etudes et de recherché internationals, Sciences Po.

Bundesbank (1997) *Monthly Report, March 1997*, Deutsche Bundesbank.

Bundesbank (1998) *Annual Report, 1998*, Deutsche Bundesbank.

Bundesbank (ed.) (1999) *Fifty Years of the Deutsche Mark. Central Bank and the Currency in Germany since 1948* (Oxford: Oxford University Press).

Bundesbank (2000) *Annual Report 1999*, Deutsche Bundesbank.

Bundesbank (2001) *Annual Report 2000*, Deutsche Bundesbank.

Bundesbank (2002) *Annual Report 2001*, Deutsche Bundesbank.

Bundesbank (2003) *Annual Report 2002*, Deutsche Bundesbank.

Bundesbank (2004a) *Monthly Report*, February 2004, Deutsche Bundesbank.

Bundesbank (2004b) *Monthly Report*, June 2004, Deutsche Bundesbank.

Bundesbank (2004c) *Monthly Report*, May 2004, Deutsche Bundesbank.

Bundesbank (2004d) *Monthly Report*, September 2004, Deutsche Bundesbank.

Bundesbank (2005) *Monthly Report*, January 2005, Deutsche Bundesbank.

Bundesministerium der Finanzen (1995) Der Finanzplan des Bundes 1995 bis 1999, August, Bonn.

Bundesministerium der Finanzen (1996) Der Finanzplan des Bundes 1996 bis 2000, August, Bonn.

Bundesministerium der Finanzen (1997) Der Finanzplan des Bundes 1997 bis 2001, August, Bonn.

Bundesministerium der Finanzen (1998) Der Finanzplan des Bundes 1998 bis 2002, August, Bonn.

Bundesministerium der Finanzen (1999a) Jahreswirtschaftsbericht der Bundesregierung 1999, Neue Wege zu mehr Beschäftigung.

Bundesministerium der Finanzen (1999b) Finanzplan des Bundes 1999 bis 2003, Berlin.

Bundesministerium der Finanzen (2000a) Das Haushaltssystem der Bundesrepublik Deutschland, Oktober.

Bundesministerium der Finanzen (2000b) Jahreswirtschaftsbericht 2000 der Bundesregierung, Arbeitsplätze schaffen – Zukunftsfähigkeit gewinnen.

Bundesministerium der Finanzen (2000c) Finanzpolitische Leitplanken, Sieben Wegweiser für eine zukunftsfähige, gerechte und europataugliche Finanzpolitik, Volks- und Finanzwirtschaftliche Berichte, November.

Bundesministerium der Finanzen (2000d) Hans Eichel: "Finanzpolitik für das nächste Jahrzehnt" an der Humboldt-Universität am 9, November, Berlin.

Bundesministerium der Finanzen (2000e) Finanzplan des Bundes 2000 bis 2004.

Bundesministerium der Finanzen (2001a) Jahreswirtschaftsbericht 2001 der Bundesregierung, Reformkursen fortsetzen – Wachstumsdynamik stärken.

Bundesministerium der Finanzen (2001b) Finanzplan des Bundes 2001 bis 2005, Fachblick, Haushalt, Berlin.

Bundesministerium der Finanzen (2002a) Bundeshaushalt 2003, Tabellen und Übersichten, Fachblick, Finanz- und Wirtschaftspolitik, November.

Bundesministerium der Finanzen (2002b) Schuldenbericht, Fachblick, Haushalt.

Bundesministerium der Finanzen (2002c) Jahreswirtschaftsbericht 2002 der Bundesregierung, Vor einem neuen Aufschwung – verlässliche Wirtschafts- und Finanzpolitik.

Bundesministerium der Finanzen (2002d) Finanzplanungsrat befürwortet Nationalen Stabilitätspakt, Beschluss, Finanzplanungsrat 21.3.2002.

Bundesministerium der Finanzen (2002e) Finanzplan des Bundes 2002 bis 2006, Fachblick, Haushalt.

Bundesministerium der Finanzen (2003a) Entwicklung der Einnahmen des Verwaltungshaushalts der Gemeinden und Gemeindeverbände 1993 bis 2002, Bundesministerium der Finanzen, Referat V A 3. 24. 09. 2003.

Bundesministerium der Finanzen (2003b) Bund – Länder Finanzbeziehungen auf der Grundlage der geltenden Finanzverfassungsordnung, Referat V A 1, Oktober.

Bundesministerium der Finanzen (2003c) Monatsbericht, Januar, Berlin.

Bundesministerium der Finanzen (2003d) Monatsbericht, Februar, Berlin.

Bundesministerium der Finanzen (2003e. Monatsbericht, Juli, Berlin.

Bundesministerium der Finanzen (2003f) Finanzplan des Bundes 2003 bis 2007, Fachblick, Haushalt.

Bundesministerium der Finanzen (2004a) Monatsbericht, Februar, Berlin.

Bundesministerium der Finanzen (2004b) Monatsbericht, Mai, Berlin.

Bundesministerium der Finanzen (2004c) Finanzplan des Bundes 2004 bis 2008, Fachblick, Haushalt.

Bundesministerium der Finanzen (2004d) Monatsbericht, Juli, Berlin.

Bundesministerium der Finanzen (2004e) Monatsbericht, Juni, Berlin.

Bundesministerium der Finanzen (2004f) Monatsbericht, Dezember, Berlin.

Bundesministerium für Gesundheit und Soziale Sicherung (2002) "Nachhaltigkeit in der Finanzierung der Sozialen Sicherungssysteme", Der Bericht der Rürup Kommission, Berlin.

Bundesministerium für Wirtschaft (1995) Jahreswirtschaftsbericht 1995, Bundesministerium, Bonn.

Bundesministerium für Wirtschaft (1996) Jahreswirtschaftsbericht 1996, Bundesministerium, Bonn.

Bundesministerium für Wirtschaft (1997) Jahreswirtschaftsbericht 1997, Reformen für Beschäftigung, Bundesministerium für Wirtschaft, Bonn.

Bundesministerium für Wirtschaft (1998) Jahreswirtschaftsbericht 1998, Den Aufschwung voranbringen – Arbeitsplätze schaffen, Bundesministerium für Wirtschaft, Bonn.

Bundesministerium für Wirtschaft und Arbeit (2003) "Jahreswirtschaftsbericht 2003, Allianz für Erneuerung – Reformen gemeinsam voranbringen", Berlin.

Bundesministerium für Wirtschaft und Arbeit (2004) "Jahreswirtschaftsbericht 2004 der Bundesregierung", Leistung, Innovation, Wachstum, Berlin.

Bundesregierung (2004b) "Schröder: Stability Pact Needs to Be Interpreted in Growth-Oriented Sense", http://www.bundesregierung.de, 13.5.2004.

Burda, Michael and **Wyplosz**, Charles (1997) *Macroeconomics: A European Context*, 2nd Edition (Oxford: Oxford University Press).

Burgess, Michael (2000) *Federalism and European Union: The Building of Europe 1950–2000* (London: Routledge).

Buti, Marco (2001) "Comment on Beetsma, Debrun and Klaassen: Is Fiscal Policy Coordination in EMU Desirable?", *Swedish Economic Policy Review*, 99–105.

Buti, Marco (2003) *Monetary and Fiscal Policies in EMU. Interactions and Coordination* (Cambridge: Cambridge University Press).

Buti, Marco and **Giudice**, Gabriele (2002a) "Maastricht's Fiscal Rule at Ten. An Assessment", *Journal of Common Market Studies*, Vol. 40, No. 5, 823–48.

Buti, Marco and **Giudice**, Gabriele (2002b) "EMU's Fiscal Rules: What Can and Cannot Be Exported", *European Commission*, 30 April.

Buti, Marco, **Eijffinger**, Sylvester C. and **Franco**, Daniele (2003a) "Revisiting the Stability and Growth Pact: Grand Design or Internal Adjustment?", CEPR, *Discussion Papers, No. 3692*, London.

Buti, Marco, **Eijffinger**, Sylvester C. and **Franco**, Daniele (2003b) "Revisiting EMU's Stability Pact: A Pragmatic Way Forward", *Oxford Review of Economic Policy*, Vol. 19, No. 1, 100–11.

Buti, Marco, **Franco**, Daniele and **Ongena**, Hedwig (1998) "Fiscal Discipline and Flexibility in EMU: The Implementation of the Stability and Growth Pact", *Oxford Review of Economic Policy*, Vol. 14, No. 3, 81–97.

Buti, Marco, **von Hagen**, Jürgen and **Martinez-Mongay**, Carlos (eds) (2002a) *The Behaviour of Fiscal Authorities. Stabilization, Growth and Institutions* (Palgrave).

Buti, Marco, **von Hagen**, Jürgen and **Martinez-Mongay**, Carlos (2002b) "The Behaviour of Fiscal Authorities: An Overview", in Marco Buti, Jürgen von Hagen and Carlos Martinez-Mongay (eds), *The Behaviour of Fiscal Authorities, Stabilization, Growth and Institutions* (Palgrave), 1–14.

Buti, Marco and **Martinot**, Bertrand (2000) "Open Issues on the Implementation of the Stability and Growth Pact", *National Institute Economic Review*, No. 174, October, 92–104.

Buti, Marco and **Nava**, Mario (2003) "Towards a European Budgetary System", *EUI Working Papers, RSC No 2003/8*, Florence, Italy.

Buti, Marco and **Pench**, Lucio R. (2004) "Why Do Large Countries Flout the Stability Pact? And What Can Be Done About It?", *Journal of Common Market Studies*, Vol. 42, No. 5, 1025–32.

Buti, Marco and **Sapir**, André (eds) (1998) *Economic Policy in EMU. A Study by the European Commission Services* (Oxford: Clarendon Press).

Buti, Marco and **Sapir**, André (eds) (2002) *EMU and Economic Policy in Europe. The Challenge of the Early Years*, European Commission (Cheltenham: Edward Elgar).

Buti, Marco, **Roeger**, Werner and **in't Veld** (Jan 2001) "Stabilizing Output and Inflation: Policy Conflicts and Co-operation under a Stability Pact", *Journal of Common Market Studies*, Vol. 39, No. 5, 801–28.

Buti, Marco, **Roeger**, Werner and **in't Veld**, (Jan 2002) "Monetary and Fiscal Policy Interactions under a Stability Pact", in Marco Buti, Jürgen von Hagen and Carlos Martinez-Mongay (eds), *The Behaviour of Fiscal Authorities. Stabilization, Growth and Institutions*. (Palgrave), 241–67.

Börzel, Tanja A. (2002) "Pace-Setting, Foot-Dragging and Fence-Sitting: Member State Responses to Europeanization", *Journal of Common Market Studies*, Vol. 40, No. 2, 193–214.

Börzel, Tanja and **Sedelmeier**, Ulrich (2006) "The EU Dimension in European Politics", in Paul Heywood, Erik Jones, Martin Rhodes and Ulrich Sedelmeier (eds), *Developments in European Politics* (Basingstoke: Palgrave), 54–70.

Cabral, Antonio J. (2001) "Main Aspects of the Working of the SGP", in Anne Brunila, Marco Buti and Daniele Franco (eds), *The Stability and Growth Pact. The Architecture of Fiscal Policy in EMU* (Basingstoke: Palgrave), 139–57.

Calmfors, Lars (1996) EMU-utredningen, SOU 1996:158, Oktober, Stockholm.

Cameron, David R. (1978) "The Expansion of Public Economy. A Comparative Analysis", *American Political Science Review*, Vol. 72, 1243–61.

Cangiano, Marco and **Mottu**, Eric (1998) "Will Fiscal Policy Be Effective Under EMU?", International Monetary Fund, *IMF Working Paper, WP/98/176.*

Canzoneri, M. and **Gray**, J. (1985) "Monetary Policy Games and the Consequences of Noncooperative Behavior", *International Economic Review*, 547–63.

Cerny, Philipp (1995) "Globalization and the Changing Logic of Collective Action", *International Organization*, Vol. 49, No. 4, 595–625.

Chari, V.V. and **Kehoe**, Patrick J. (1998) "On the Need for Fiscal Constraints in a Monetary Union", *Working Paper 589*, Federal Reserve Bank of Minneapolis.

Christiansen, Thomas, **Jorgensen**, Knud Erik and **Wiener**, Antje (1999) "The Social Construction of Europe", *Journal of European Public Policy*, Vol. 6, No. 4, 528–44.

Coalition Agreement (1998) "Coalition Agreement between the SPD and Alliance 90/The Greens", October, Bonn, Germany.

Coalition Agreement (2002) "Coalition Agreement 2002–2006 between the SPD and Alliance 90/The Greens", October, Germany.

Cobham, David (1989) "Strategies for Monetary Integration Revisited", *Journal of Common Market Studies*, Vol. 27, No. 3, 203–18.

Collignon, Stefan and **Schwarzer**, Daniela (2003) *Private Sector Involvement in the Euro. The Power of Ideas* (London: Routledge).

Commission (1999) "Broad Economic Policy Guidelines", *European Economy, No. 68*, European Commission.

Commission (2000a) "Public Finances in EMU 2000", *European Economy, Reports and Studies*, No. 3, Luxemburg.

Commission (2000b) "Broad Economic Policy Guidelines", *European Economy*, No. 70, European Commission.

Commission (2001a) "European Governance", A White Paper, Commission of the European Communities, Brussels 25.7.2001, COM (2001), 428.

Commission (2001b) "Amended Proposal for a Decision of the European Parliament and of the Council on Community Incentive Measures in the Field of Employment", Commission of the European Communities, Brussels 27.2.2001, COM (2001), 124.

Commission (2001c) "Broad Economic Policy Guidelines", *European Economy*, No. 72, European Commission.

Commission (2001d) "Public Finances in EMU 2001", *European Economy, Reports and Studies*, No. 3, Luxemburg.

Commission (2002a) "Commission Regulation (EC) No. 351/2002 of 25 February 2002 Amending Council Regulation (EC) No. 3605/93 as Regards References to ESA 95", *Official Journal L 055*, 26.2.2002.

Commission (2002b) "Communication from the Commission on Streamlining the Annual Economic and Employment Policy Co-ordination Cycles", COM (2002) 487.

Commission (2002c) "Commission Adopts Report on Government Finances in Portugal as a First Step of the Excessive Deficit Procedure", IP/02/1360, Brussels, 24.9.2002.

Commission (2002d) "Commission Considers that an Excessive Government Deficit Exists in Portugal", IP/02/1476, Brussels, 16.10.2002.

Commission (2002e) "Commission Adopts Report on Government Finances in Germany as a First Step of the Excessive Deficit Procedure", IP/02/1705, Brussels, 19.11.2002.

Commission (2002f) "Co-ordination of Economic Policies in the EU: A Presentation of Key Features of the Main Procedures", The European Commission, Directorate-General for Economic and Financial Affairs, *Euro Papers*, No. 45, July.

Commission (2002g) "Strengthening the Co-ordination of Budgetary Policies", Communication from the Commission to the Council and the European Parliament, COM (2002) 668, Brussels, 27.11.2002.

Commission (2002h) "Broad Economic Policy Guidelines, European Economy", No. 4, European Commission.

Commission (2002i) "Public Finances in EMU 2002", European Economy, *Reports and Studies*, No. 3, Luxemburg.

Commission (2003a) "Commission Considers that an Excessive Government Deficit Exists in Germany", IP/03/12, Brussels, 8.1.2003.

Commission (2003b) "Commission Considers that an Excessive Government Deficit Exists in France", IP/03/640, Brussels, 7.5.2003.

Commission (2003c) "Commission Proceeds with Excessive Deficit Procedure for France", IP/03/1353, Brussels, 8.10.2003.

Commission (2003d) "Commission Asks France to Take New Measures to Reduce the Budget Deficit in 2004", IP/03/1420, Brussels, 21.10.2003.

Commission (2003e) "Commission Proceeds with Excessive Deficit Procedure for Germany", IP/03/1560, Brussels, 18.11.2003.

Commission (2003f) "Public Finances in EMU 2003", European Economy, *Reports and Studies*, No. 3, Luxemburg.

Commission (2003g) "Statistical Annex of European Economy", European Commission, Economic and Financial Affairs, ECFIN/156/2003, Autumn, Luxemburg.

Commission (2003h) "The EU Economy: 2003 Review", European Commission, ECFIN/391/03, 26.11.2003, Brussels.

Commission (2003i) "Broad Economic Policy Guidelines for the 2003–2005 Period", Commission Recommendation, European Commission, 24.4.2003.

Commission (2003j) "Population Ageing and Public Finance Targets", by Heikki Oksanen, European Economy, No. 196, European Commission, December.

Commission (2004a) "Public Finances in EMU 2004", European Economy, *Reports and Studies*, No. 3, Luxemburg.

Commission (2004b) "Public Finances in EMU 2004", Communication from the Commission to the Council and the European Parliament, COM (2004) 425 final, 24.6.2004, Brussels.

Commission (2004c) "Communication for Stronger Economic and Budgetary Coordination", IP/04/1062, 3.9.2004, Brussels.

Commission (2004d) "Strengthening Economic Governance and Improving the Stability and Growth Pact", Commissioner Joaquín Almunia, Press Conference, Speech/04/387, 3.9.2004, Brussels.

Commission (2004e) "Economic Governance in a European Union of 25 Member States", Commissioner Joaquín Almunia, Conference on EMU and Economic Governance, Speech/04/424, 28.9.2004, Brussels.

Commission (2004f) "Conference on EMU and Economic Governance: Closing Address", The President of the European Commission Romano Prodi, Conference on EMU and Economic Governance, Speech/04/427, 28.9.2004, Brussels.

Commission (2004g) "Convergence Report 2004", European Economy, No. 6/2004, Luxemburg.

Commission (2004h) "Communication from the Commission to the Council and the European Parliament. Building Our Common Future. Policy Challenges and Budgetary Means of the Enlarged Union 2007–2013". 10.2.2004, Brussels.

Commission (2004i) "Communication from the Commission to the Council and the European Parliament, Financial Perspectives 2007–2013". 14.7.2004, Brussels.

Commission (2004j) "Statistical Annex of European Economy, European Commission, Economic and Financial Affairs", ECFIN/174/2004, Spring, Luxemburg.

Commission (2004k) "Commission Reports on Greek Statistics, Starts Infringement Procedure", European Commission, IP/04/1431, 1.12.2004.

Commission (2004l) Kommission sieht Deutschland und Frankreich auf richtigem Weg zur Korrektur des übermässigen Haushaltsdefizits im Jahr 2005. Kommission, IP/04/1471, 14.12.2004.

Commission (2004m) "Commission Proceeds with Excessive Deficit Procedure for Greece", IP/04/1527, Brussels, 22.12.2004.

Commission (2005a) "Improving the Stability and Growth Pact: the Commission's Three Pillar Approach", European Economy, *Occasional Papers,* No. 15, February.

Commission (2005b) "March 2005: Economic Sentiment Declined in Both the EU and the Euro Area", IP/05/372, Brussels, 31.3.2005.

Commission (2005c) "Commission Spring Economic Forecast 2005–2006", IP/05/384, Brussels, 4.4.2005.

Commission (2005d) "The Economy for the Euro Area, the European Union and Candidate Countries in 2004–2006", European Economy, *Economic Forecasts,* No. 2, Spring.

Commission (2006a) "Economic Forecasts Autumn 2006", *European Economy,* No. 5.

Commission (2006b) "Public Finances in EMU 2006", *European Economy,* No. 3.

Commission (2006c) "Statistical Annex to European Economy".

Commission (2006d) "General Government Data", Part II, Autumn.

Conzelmann, Thomas (1998) "'Europeanization' of Regional Development Policies? Linking the Multi-Level Governance Approach with Theories of Policy Learning and Policy Change", *European Integration Online Papers* (EIoP), Vol. 5, No. 6. http://eiop.or.at/eiop/texte/1998-006a.htm.

Coudenhove-Kalergi, Richard N. (1923) *Pan-Europa.*

Council of Ministers (1993) Council Regulation (EC) No. 3605/93 of 22 November 1993 on the "Application of the Protocol on the Excessive Deficit Procedure Annexed to the Treaty Establishing the European Community", *Official Journal L 332*, 31.12.1993.

Council of Ministers (1997a) Council Regulation No. 1466/97 of 7 July 1997 on the "Strengthening of the Surveillance of Budgetary Positions and the Surveillance and Coordination of Economic Policies", *Official Journal L 209*, 2.8.1997.

Council of Ministers (1997b) Council Regulation No. 1467/97 of 7 July 1997 on "Speeding up and Clarifying the Implementation of the Excessive Deficit Procedure", *Official Journal L 209*, 2.8.1997.

Council of Ministers (1998a) "The Council of the European Union", Council Regulation (EC) No. 974/98 on the Introduction of the Euro, 3.5.1998.

Council of Ministers (1998b) "The Council of the European Union. Council Regulation (EC), No. 2866/98 on the Conversion Rates between the Euro and the Currencies of the Member States Adopting the Euro", 31.12.1998.

Council of Ministers (1998c) "Council Decision 98/743/EC of 21 December 1998 on the Detailed Provisions Concerning the Composition of the Economic and Financial Committee", *Official Journal L 358*, 31.12.1998.

Council of Ministers (1998d) "Council Decision 1999/8/EC of 31 December 1998 on Adopting the Statutes of the Economic and Financial Committee", *Official Journal L 5*, 9.1.1999.

Council of Ministers (2001) "The 2329th Meeting of the Council (Economic and Financial Questions)" held in Brussels on 12 February 2001, 6168/2001, 5.4.2001.

Council of Ministers (2002a) "Council Recommendation of 21 June 2002 on the Broad Guidelines of the Economic Policies of the Member States and the Community", *Official Journal L 182*, 11.7.2002.

Council of Ministers (2002b) "The 2407th Meeting of the Council (Economic and Financial Questions)", held in Brussels on 12 February 2002, 6196/02, 25.2.2002.

Council of Ministers (2002c) "The 2460th Meeting of the Council (Economic and Financial Affairs)", held in Brussels on 5 November 2002, 13770/2002, 6.12.2002.

Council of Ministers (2002d) "Council Recommendation to Portugal", Ecofin Council Meeting, Brussels, 5.11.2002.

Council of Ministers (2003a) "Broad Guidelines of the Economic Policies 2003", The Council of the European Union, Office for Official Publications of the European Communities, Luxembourg.

Council of Ministers (2003b) "Council Decision Amending Council Decision 2000/604/EC on the Composition and the Statutes of the Economic Policy Committee", 2003/0814, 6.6.2003.

Council of Ministers (2003c) "Council Decision of 21 January 2003 on the Existence of an Excessive Deficit in Germany. Application of Article 104(6) of the Treaty Establishing the European Community", *Official Journal L 034*, 11.2.2003.

Council of Ministers (2003d) "Council Decision of 3 June 2003 on the Existence of an Excessive Deficit in France. Application of Article 104(6) of the Treaty Establishing the European Community", *Official Journal L 165*, 3.7.2003.

Council of Ministers (2003e) "The 2546th Meeting of the Council (Economic and Financial Affairs)", held in Brussels on 25 November, 14492/2003, 25.11.2003.

Council of Ministers (2004) "The 2617th Meeting of the Council (Economic and Financial Affairs)", held in Brussels on 16 November, 14429/04, 16.11.2004.

Council of Ministers (2005a) Preparation of Eurogroup and Council of Economics and Finance Ministers in Brussels on 17 and 18 January, MEMO/05/12, 14.1.2005.

Council of Ministers (2005b) "The 2634th Meeting of the Council (Economic and Financial Affairs)", held in Brussels on 18 January, 5283/05, 18.1.2005.

Council of Ministers (2005c) "The 2638th Meeting of the Council (Economic and Financial Affairs)", held in Brussels on 17 February, 6141/05, 17.2.2005.

Council of Ministers (2005d) "The 2646th Meeting of the Council (Economic and Financial Affairs)", held in Brussels on 8 March, 6873/05, 8.3.2005.

Council of Ministers (2005e) "Meetings of the Eurogroup and the Economic and Financial Affairs Council: No Agreement on the Reform of the Stability and Growth Pact", Press Release, Brussels, 8.3.2005.

Council of Ministers (2005f) "Improving the Implementation of the Stability and Growth Pact", Ecofin Council Report 7423/05, Brussels, 21.3.2005.

Council of Ministers (2005g) "The 2651st Meeting of the Council (Economic and Financial Affairs)", held in Brussels on 12 April, 7754/05, 12.4.2005.

Council of Ministers (2005h) "Statement by the Governments of the Benelux Countries on the Stability and Growth Pact", Working Document, 22.3.2005.

Culpepper, Pepper C. (2001) "Employers, Public Policy and the Politics of Decentralized Cooperation in Germany and France", in Peter A. Hall and David Soskice (eds), *Varieties of Capitalism. The Institutional Foundations of Comparative Advantage* (Oxford: Oxford University Press), 275–304.

Deeg, Richard (2005) "The Comeback of Modell Deutschland? The New German Political Economy in the EU", *German Politics*, Vol. 14, No. 3, 332–53.

Demertzis, M., **Hallett**, Hughes and **Viegi**, N. (1999) "Can the ECB be Truly Independent? Should It Be?", *Empirica*, Vol. 26, No. 2, 217–40.

Dierx, Adriaan, **Ilzkovitz**, Fabienne and **Sekkat**, Khalid (2003) "Structural Reforms on European Product Markets: The Cardiff Process", 13.8.2003.

Dinan, Desmond (2003) "Governance and Institutions: Anticipating the Impact of Enlargement", *Journal of Common Market Studies*, Vol. 41, No. 2, 27–43.

Dyson, Kenneth (1994) *Elusive Union. The Process of Economic and Monetary Union in Europe* (London: Longman).

Dyson, Kenneth (2000a) "EMU as Europeanization: Convergence, Diversity and Contingency", *Journal of Common Market Studies*, Vol. 38, No. 4, 645–66.

Dyson, Kenneth (2000b) *The Politics of the Euro-Zone. Stability or Breakdown?* (Oxford: Oxford University Press).

Dyson, Kenneth (2000c) "EMU as Europeanisation: Convergence, Diversity and Contingency", in Amy Verdun (ed.), *The Euro. European Integration Theory and Economic and Monetary Union* (Lanham: Rowman & Littlefield), 91–108.

Dyson, Kenneth (2002) *European States and the Euro: Europeanization, Variation, and Convergence* (Oxford: Oxford University Press).

Dyson, Kenneth (2003a) "Economic Policies: From Pace-Setter to Beleaguered Player", in Kenneth Dyson and Klaus H. Goetz (eds), *Germany, Europe and the Politics of Constraint. Proceedings of the British Academy*. No. 119 (Oxford: Oxford University Press), 201–29.

Dyson, Kenneth (2003b) "Die Wirtschafts- und Währungsunion als Prozess der Europäisierung: Konvergenz, Unterschiede und Unvorhersehbarkeit", in Markus Jachtenfuchs and Beate Kohler-Koch (Hrsg.) *Europäische Integration*, 2, Auflage (Opladen: Laske & Budrich), 449–78.

Dyson, Kenneth (2005a) "The Politics of Economic Reform in Germany: Global, Rhineland or Hybrid Capitalism?", in Kenneth Dyson and Stephen Padgett (eds), *The Politics of Economic Reform in Germany* (Oxford: Routledge), Forthcoming.

Dyson, Kenneth (2005b) "Economic Policy Management: Catastrophic Equilibrium, Tipping Points and Crisis", in Simon Green and William E. Paterson (eds), *Governance in Contemporary Germany. The Semi-Sovereign State Revisited* (Cambridge: Cambridge University Press), 115–37.

Dyson, Kenneth and **Featherstone**, Kevin (1999) *The Road to Maastricht. Negotiating Economic and Monetary Union* (Oxford: Oxford University Press).

Dyson, Kenneth and **Goetz**, Klaus H. (2003a) "Living with Europe: Power, Constraint and Contestation", in Kenneth Dyson and Klaus H. Goetz (eds), *Germany, Europe and the Politics of Constraint. Proceedings of the British Academy*, No. 119 (Oxford: Oxford University Press), 3–35.

Dyson, Kenneth and **Goetz**, Klaus H. (eds) (2003b) *Germany, Europe and the Politics of Constraint. Proceedings of the British Academy*, No. 119 (Oxford: Oxford University Press).

Dyson, Kenneth and **Padgett**, Stephen (eds) (2005) *The Politics of Economic Reform in Germany* (Oxford: Routledge).

The Economist (5.4.2003) "Brown at the Edges", 33–4.

The Economist (19.4.2003) "A Mutinous Rumble in the Ranks", 36–7.

The Economist (17.5.2003) "Germany's Finance Minister under the Gun", 38.

The Economist (7.6.2003a) "Don't Give In", 12–13.

The Economist (7.6.2003b) "The Chancellor Gets His Way, So Far", 35–6.

The Economist (4.10.2003a) "The Rise of the Eurosceptiques", 38–9.

The Economist (4.10.2003b) "Let's Slash Together", 41.

The Economist (11.10.2003) "Europe's Stability Pact Stabbed", 44–5.

The Economist (8.11.2003) "Stability of Instability", 48.

The Economist (29.11.2003a) "Unstable and Incredible", 12–13.

The Economist (29.11.2003b) "The Death of the Stability Pact", 45–6.

Eichengreen, Barry (1991) "Is Europe an Optimum Currency Area?", National Bureau of Economic Research, *Working Paper Series, Working Paper No. 3579*, Massachusetts.

Eichengreen, Barry (1998) "European Monetary Unification: A Tour D'Horizon", *Oxford Review of Economic Policy*, Vol. 14, No. 3, 24–40.

Eichengreen, Barry and **Frieden**, Jeffry (1998a) "Introduction", in Barry Eichengreen and Jeffry Frieden (eds), *Forging an Integrated Europe*, Michigan University, 1–17.

Eichengreen, Barry and **Frieden**, Jeffry (eds) (1998b) *Forging an Integrated Europe* (Michigan: Michigan University).

Eichengreen, Barry and **Wyplosz**, Charles (1998) "Stability Pact. More than a Minor Nuisance?", *Economic Policy*, Vol. 13, No. 26, 67–113.

Ekengren, Magnus (1997) "The Temporality of European Governance", in Knud Erik Jorgensen (ed.), *Reflective Approaches to European Governance* (Basingstoke: Macmillan), 69–86.

Ekengren, Magnus (2002) *The Time of European Governance* (Manchester: Manchester University Press).

El-Agraa, Ali M. (2001) *The European Union. Economics & Policies*, 6th Edition (Essex: Prentice Hall).

Enderlein, Henrik (2004) "Break it, Don't Fix It!", *Journal of Common Market Studies*, Vol. 42, No. 5, 1039–46.

European Central Bank (1998) "European Central Bank Agreement of 1 September 1998 between the European Central Bank and the national central banks of the Member States outside the Euro area laying down the operating procedures for an exchange rate mechanism in stage three of Economic and Monetary Union", C 345/6, *Official Journal of the European Communities*, 13.11.1998.

European Central Bank (1999a) *ECB Annual Report 1999.*

European Central Bank (1999b) *ECB Monthly Bulletin*, May 1999.

European Central Bank (2000a) *ECB Monthly Bulletin*, June 2000.

European Central Bank (2000b) *ECB Annual Report 2000.*

European Central Bank (2001a) *ECB Monthly Bulletin*, May 2001.

European Central Bank (2001b) *ECB Annual Report 2001.*

European Central Bank (2002) *ECB Annual Report 2002.*

European Central Bank (2003a) *ECB Monthly Bulletin*, October 2003.

European Central Bank (2003b) "Introductory Statement", Willem F. Duisenberg, President of the European Central Bank and Lucas Papademos, Vice-President of the European Central Bank, Frankfurt, 8 May 2003.

European Central Bank (2003c) "Press Seminar on the Evaluation of the ECB's Monetary Policy Strategy", Willem F. Duisenberg, President of the European Central Bank and Lucas Papademos, Vice-President of the European Central Bank and Otmar Issing, Member of the Executive Board of the ECB, Frankfurt, 8 May 2003.

European Central Bank (2003d) "Monetary and Fiscal Policy in the Euro Area", Introduction by Dr Willem F. Duisenberg, President of the European Central Bank, The International Monetary Conference, Berlin, 3 June 2003.

European Central Bank (2004a) *ECB Monthly Bulletin*, March 2004.

European Central Bank (2004b) *ECB Annual Report 2003.*

European Central Bank (2004c) *ECB Monthly Bulletin*, February 2004.

European Central Bank (2004d) *ECB Monthly Bulletin*, July 2004.

European Central Bank (2004e) *ECB Monthly Bulletin*, October 2004.

European Central Bank (2004f) *ECB Monthly Bulletin*, November 2004.

European Central Bank (2004g) "A Stability-Oriented Monetary Policy as a Necessary Condition for Long-Term Growth", Speech by Jean-Claude Triechet, President of the European Central Bank, Brussels, 9 December 2004.

European Central Bank (2005a) *ECB Monthly Bulletin*, January 2005.

European Central Bank (2005b) *ECB Monthly Bulletin*, February 2005.

European Central Bank (2005c) *ECB Monthly Bulletin*, March 2005.

European Central Bank (2005d) "Statement of the Governing Council on the Ecofin Council's Report on Improving the Implementation of the Stability and Growth Pact", Press Release, 21.3.2005.

European Central Bank (2005e) *ECB Monthly Bulletin*, May 2005.

European Central Bank (2005f) Interview with Lucas Papademos, Vice-President of the European Central Bank, 31.3.2005.

European Court of Justice (2004) "Judgement of the Court. The Commission of the European Communities versus the Council of the European Union", Case C-27/04, 13 July.

European Council (1996) "Dublin European Council", 13–14 December, Presidency Conclusions, Ireland.

European Council (1997a) "Resolution of the European Council on the Stability and Growth Pact", Amsterdam, 17 June, *Official Journal C 236*, 2.8.1997.

European Council (1997b) Resolution of the European Council of 13 December 1997 on Economic Policy Coordination in Stage 3 of Economic and Monetary Union and on Articles 111 and 113 of the EC Treaty, *Official Journal C 35*, 2.2.1998.

European Council (1997c) "Luxembourg European Council", 20–21 November. *Presidency Conclusions on Meeting on Employment.*

European Council (1998a) Presidency Conclusions, "Cardiff European Council", 15–16 June, *Presidency Conclusions*, Britain.

European Council (1998b) Presidency Conclusions, "Vienna European Council", 11–12 December, Italy.

European Council (1999a) Presidency Conclusions, "Berlin European Council", 24–25 March, Germany.

European Council (1999b) Presidency Conclusions, "Cologne European Council", 3–4 June, Germany.

European Council (1999c) Presidency Conclusions, "Helsinki European Council", 10–11 December, Finland.

European Council (2000a) Presidency Conclusions, "Santa Maria da Feira European Council", 19–20 June, Portugal.

European Council (2000b) Presidency Conclusions, "Lisbon European Council", 23–24 March, Portugal.

European Council (2001) Presidency Conclusions, "Göteborg European Council", 15–16 June, Sweden.

European Council (2002) Presidency Conclusions, "Barcelona European Council", 15–16 March, Spain.

European Council (2003) Presidency Conclusions, "Brussels European Council", 20–21 March, Belgium.

European Council (2005) Presidency Conclusions, "Brussels European Council", 22–23 March, Belgium.

European Parliament (1996) "The Coordination of National Fiscal Policies in the Context of Monetary Union", Directorate General for Research, *Working Paper E 6*, Economic Affairs Series.

Financial Planning Council (2004) Einvernehmlicher Beschluss der 100, Sitzung des Finanzplanungsrates, 16 Juni.
Financial Times (25.7.2002) "Europe's Instability Pact".
Financial Times (16.12.2004) "Germany Seeks to Fix Its Flawed Federal Constitution".
Financial Times (18.2.2005) "Small EU States Oppose Moves to Relax Fiscal Pact".
Financial Times (24.3.2005a) "Easing of Euro Rules Pleases Central Europe".
Financial Times (24.3.2005b) "German Business Confidence Declines".
Financial Times (24.3.2005c) "EU's Big Boys Behaving Badly".
Financial Times Deutschland (5.7.2004a) "Betriebsräte kritisieren Gewerkschaftsspitze".
Financial Times Deutschland (5.7.2004b) "Pflegereform beschert Rot-Grün Prügel von allen Seiten".
Financial Times Deutschland (17.1.2005a) "Eichel unterstützt Änderungen am Stabilitätspakt".
Financial Times Deutschland (17.1.2005b) "Exklusiv: Schröder weicht Defizitgrenze auf".
Financial Times Deutschland (18.1.2005) "Hardliner schwenken auf Schröder-Kurs ein".
Finnish government (2005) Ecofin-neuvosto 17.2.2005 lopputiedote, Tiedote 18/2005.
Fischer, Thomas (2003) "Deutscher Föderalismus vor der Herausforderung einer europäischen Verfassung", Das Parliament, B 29-30/2003, 14.7.2003, 3–5.
Forsyth, Murray (1981) *Union of States: The Theory and Practice of Confederation* (New York: Leicester University Press).
Frankfurter Allgemeine Zeitung (17.1.1997) "Rexrodt erwartet für 1997 4,2 Millionen Arbeitslose".
Frankfurter Allgemeine Zeitung (20.1.1997) "Die SPD fordert einen Nachtragshaushalt für 1997".
Frankfurter Allgemeine Zeitung (9.8.2004) "Braun verteidigt Clement gegen Hartz-Kritik".
Frankfurter Allgemeine Zeitung (1.9.2004a) "Wirtschaft warnt vor Reformpause".
Frankfurter Allgemeine Zeitung (1.9.2004b) "Eichel meldet 3,7 Prozent Staatsdefizit".
Frankfurter Allgemeine Zeitung (3.9.2004) "Die Europäische Zentralbank nimmt Inflatiosrisiken ernster".
Frankfurter Allgemeine Zeitung (4.9.2004a) "Zukunft der Defizitverfahren gegen Deutschland und Frankreich offen".
Frankfurter Allgemeine Zeitung (4.9.2004b) "Hartz IV mit ordnungspolitischem Kompass".
Frankfurter Allgemeine Zeitung (7.9.2004) "Ein Erfolg mit Mängeln".
Frankfurter Allgemeine Zeitung (10.9.2004) "Gemeinsam zu mehr Wachstum in Europa".
Frankfurter Allgemeine Zeitung (11.9.2004) "Eichel verbietet der Bundesbank den Mund".
Frankfurter Allgemeine Zeitung (14.9.2004) "Deutschlands Wachstumspotential schrumpft".
Frankfurter Allgemeine Zeitung (20.9.2004) "CDU und SPD geschwächt".
Frankfurter Allgemeine Zeitung (21.9.2004) "Die Landtagswahlen – Die Ergbnisse in den Wahlkreisen".
Frankfurter Allgemeine Zeitung (23.9.2004a) "Frankreich begrenzt die Staatsausgaben und baut die Neuverschuldung ab".
Frankfurter Allgemeine Zeitung (23.9.2004b) "Griechenland gesteht Verletzung des Stabilitätspakts im Jahr 2000".

Frankfurter Allgemeine Zeitung (23.9.2004c) "Wir brauchen andere Mentalitäten in Deutschland".

French Stability Programme (2003) The Stability Programme, Annexes to the 2005–2007, December 2003.

Frenkel, Jacob A. and **Goldstein**, Morris (1999) "The International Role of the Deutsche Mark", in the Bundesbank (ed.), *Fifty Years of the Deutsche Mark* (Oxford: Oxford University Press), 685–729.

Funk, Lothar (2000) "Economic Reform and Model Deutschland", in Rebecca Harding, and William E. Paterson (eds), *The future of the German Economy: An End to the Miracle?* (Manchester: Manchester University Press), 16–35.

Ganghof, Steffen (2004) *Wer regiert in der Steuerpolitik? Einkommensteuerreform zwischen internationalem Wettbewerb und national Verteilungskonflikten* (Frankfurt: Campus Verlag).

Garrett, Geoffrey and **Tsebelis**, George (1996) "An Institutional Critique of Intergovernmentalism", *International Organization*, Vol. 50, No. 2, 269–99.

George, Stephen (2001) "The Europeanization of UK Politics and Policy-Making: The Effects of European Integration on the UK", *Queen's Online Papers on Europeanisation*, Queen's University, Belfast.

German Constitution (1949) "Grundgesetz (Basic Law)", *German Constitution*, 23 May 1949, Last amended 31 August 1990.

German Stability Programme (1999a) "German Stability Programme", *Economic and Financial Reports*, January, Federal Ministry of Finance.

German Stability Programme (1999b) "German Stability Programme", *Economic and Financial Reports*, Updated December 1999, Federal Ministry of Finance.

German Stability Programme (2000) "German Stability Programme", *Economic and Financial Reports*, October, Federal Ministry of Finance.

German Stability Programme (2001) "German Stability Programme", *Economic and Financial Reports*, December, Federal Ministry of Finance.

German Stability Programme (2002) "German Stability Programme", *Economic and Financial Reports*, December, Federal Ministry of Finance.

German Stability Programme (2003) "The Update of the German Stability Programme", December, Federal Ministry of Finance.

German Stability Programme (2004a) "The Update of the German Stability Programme", January, Federal Ministry of Finance.

German Stability Programme (2004b) "German Stability Programme", December, Federal Ministry of Finance.

Giersch, Herbert, **Paqué**, Karl-Heinz and **Schmieding**, Holger (1992) *The Fading Miracle. Four Decades of Market Economy in Germany* (Cambridge: Cambridge University Press).

Goetz, Klaus H. (1995) "National Governance and European Integration: Intergovernmental Relations in Germany", *Journal of Common Market Studies*, Vol. 33, No. 1, 91–116.

Gourevitch, Peter (1978) "The Second Image Reversed. The International Sources of Domestic Politics", *International Organization*, Vol. 32, No. 4, 881–912.

Grabbe, Heather (2001) "How Does Europeanization Affect CEE Governance? Conditionality, Diffusion and Diversity", *Journal of European Public Policy*, Vol. 8, No. 6, 1013–31.

De Grauwe, Paul (2000) *Economics of Monetary Union*, 4th Edition (Oxford: Oxford University Press).

Gros, Daniel and **Thygesen**, Niels (1998) *European Monetary Integration. From the European Monetary System to Economic and Monetary Union*, 2nd Edition (Essex: Longman).

The Guardian (12.10.2004) "Minister Hints at Switch in Pensions Policy".

von Hagen, Jürgen (2000) "The First Year of EMU. In EMU and Economic Growth in Europe", University of Bonn, Center for European Integration Studies, *Policy Paper B7/2000*, Bonn, 3–16.

von Hagen, Jürgen, **Hughes Hallett**, Andrew and **Strauch**, Rolf (2002a) "Quality and Success of Budgetary Consolidations", in Marco Buti, Jürgen von Hagen and Carlos Martinez-Mongay (eds), *The Behaviour of Fiscal Authorities. Stabilization, Growth and Institutions* (Palgrave), 17–38.

von Hagen, Jürgen, **Hughes Hallett**, Andrew and **Strauch**, Rolf (2002b) "Budgetary Institutions for Sustainable Public Finance", in Marco Buti, Jürgen von Hagen and Carlos Martinez-Mongay (eds), *The Behaviour of Fiscal Authorities. Stabilization, Growth and Institutions* (Palgrave), 94–112.

von Hagen, Jürgen and **Strauch**, Rolf (1999) "Tumbling Giant: Germany's Experience with the Maastricht Fiscal Criteria", University of Bonn, Center for European Integration Studies, *Working Paper B5/1999*, Bonn.

Hall, Peter A. (1986) "Governing the Economy", *The Politics of State Intervention in Britain and France* (Cambridge: Polity Press).

Hall, Peter A. (ed.) (1989) *The Political Power of Economic Ideas: Keynesianism across Nations* (Princeton, N.J.: Princeton University Press).

Hall, Peter A. (1992) "The Movement from Keynesianism to Monetarism: Institutional Analysis and British Economic Policy in the 1970s", in Sven Steinmo, Kathleen Thelen and Frank Longstreth (eds), *Structuring Politics. Historical Institutionalism in Comparative Analysis* (Cambridge: Cambridge University Press), 90–113.

Hamburg (2003) Finanzplan 2002–2006, Freie und Hansestadt Hamburg.

Hardach, Karl (1976) Wirtschaftsgeschichte Deutschlands im 20, Jahrhundert (Goettingen: Vandenhoeck & Ruprecht).

Harding, Rebecca and **Paterson**, William E. (eds) (2000a) *The Future of the German Economy: An End to the Miracle?* (Manchester: Manchester University Press).

Harding, Rebecca and **Paterson**, William E. (2000b) "Germany in a Global Era", in Rebecca Harding, and William E. Paterson (eds), *The Future of the German Economy: An End to the Miracle?* (Manchester: Manchester University Press), 1–15.

Haushaltsgrundsätzegesetz (1969) Gesetz über die Grundsätze des Haushaltsrechts des Bundes und der Länder, BGB1, I 1969, S 1273, 19.8.1969.

Haushaltsgrundsätzegesetz (1993) Zweites Gesetz zur Änderung des Haushaltsgrundsätzegesetzes, Bundesgesetzblatt 1993 Teil I, S 1928, 26.11.1993.

Haushaltsgrundsätzegesetz (2001) Gesetz über die Grundsätze des Haushaltsrechts des Bundes und der Länder, Bundesgesetzblatt 2001 Teil I, S 1273, 20.12.2001.

Heipertz, Martin and **Verdun**, Amy (2003a) "Ruling Europe. Theory and Politics of the Stability and Growth Pact", MPIfG Research Report, Max Planck Institute, Cologne, Germany.

Heipertz, Martin and **Verdun**, Amy (2003b) "The Dog that Would Never Bite? The Past and Future of the Stability and Growth Pact", *MPIfG Working Paper 03/12*, November, Max Planck Institute, Cologne, Germany.

Heisenberg, Dorothee (1999) *The Mark of the Bundesbank. Germany's Role in European Monetary Cooperation* (Boulder: Lynne Rienner Publishers).

Hemerijck, Anton and **Schludi**, Martin (2000) "Sequences of Policy Failures and Effective Policy Responses", in Fritz W. Scharpf and Vivien A. Schmidt (eds), *Welfare and Work in the Open Economy*, Vol. I, *From Vulnerability to Competitiveness* (Oxford: Oxford University Press), 125–228.

Herrmann, Andrea (2003) "From the EMS to EMU: How Economic and Monetary Union Changes the Structure of Wage-Bargaining Throughout the Euro-Zone", *EUI Working Papers, SPS No 2003/4*, Florence, Italy.

Hessen (2003) Finanzplan des Lnades Hessen 2003–2007, Hessisches Ministerium der Finanzen, Oktober, Wiesbaden.

Hinrichs, Karl (1998) "Reforming the Public Pension Scheme in Germany: The End of the Traditional Consensus?", Arbeitspapier Nummer 11/1998, Zentrum für Sozialpolitik, Universität Bremen.

Hix, Simon (1994) "The Study of the European Community. The Challenge to Comparative Politics", *West European Politics*, Vol. 17, No. 1, 1–30.

Hix, Simon (1999) *The Political System of the European Union*, Macmillan Press.

Hix, Simon and **Goetz**, Klaus (2000) "Introduction: European Integration and National Political Systems", *West European Politics*, Vol. 23, No. 4, 1–26.

HM Treasury (1998) "The Code for Fiscal Stability", March.

Howarth, David J. (2001) *The French Road to European Monetary Union* (Basingstoke: Palgrave).

Howell, Kerry (2002) "Developing Conceptualizations of Europeanization and European Integration: Mixing Methodologies", ESRC Seminar Series, UACES Study Group on the Europeanisation of British Politics and Policy-Making, Paper presented on 29 November 2002, University of Sheffield, UK.

Huffschmid, Jörg (1998) "Hoist with Its Own Petard: Consequences of the Single Currency for Germany", in Bernard H. Moss and Jonathan Michie (eds), *The Single European Currency in National Perspective. A Community in Crisis?* (Basingstoke: Macmillan), 87–104.

Hughes Hallett, Andrew and **Piscitelli**, Laura (2002) "Does One Size Fit All? A Currency Union with Asymmetric Transmissions and a Stability Pact", *International Review of Applied Economics*, Vol. 16, No. 1, 71–96.

Hughes Hallett, Andrew, **Hutchison**, Michael M. and **Hougaard Jensen**, Svend E. (1999) "Fiscal Aspects of European Monetary Integration: An Introduction", in Andrew Hughes Hallett, Michael M. Hutchison and Svend E. Hougaard Jensen (eds), *Fiscal Aspects of European Monetary Integration* (Cambridge: Cambridge University Press) 1–11.

Huhne, Christopher (2002) "Is Euro Area Economic Policy Co-ordinated Enough?", in Iain Begg (ed.), *Europe: Government and Money. Running EMU: Challenges of Policy Co-operation. The Federal Trust*, 113–26.

IG Metall (2004) Arbeitslosengeld II führt Millionen in die Armutsfalle, http://igmetall.de, 30.6.2004.

IMF (1993) World Economic Outlook, World Economic and Financial Surveys, May, International Monetary Fund.

IMF (1997) World Economic Outlook, World Economic and Financial Surveys, October, International Monetary Fund.

IMF (1999) World Economic Outlook, World Economic and Financial Surveys, May, International Monetary Fund.

IMF (2003) Germany – 2003 Article IV Consultation, Staff Report, November, International Monetary Fund.

IMF (2004) World Economic Outlook, World Economic and Financial Surveys, April, International Monetary Fund.

The Independent (17.10.2004) "Don't Panic, Just Step Up Your Savings".

International Herald Tribune (18.2.2005) "Changes to Budget Rules in Euro Zone Will Only Be 'Minor'", 15.

International Statistical Yearbook (2002).

Irish Stability Programme (2003) Stability Programme, December.

Issing, Otmar (2002) "On Macroeconomic Policy Coordination in EMU", *Journal of Common Market Studies*, Vol. 40, No. 2, 345–58.

Jachtenfuchs, Markus and **Kohler-Koch**, Beate (eds) (1995) *Europäische Integration* (Opladen: Leske und Budrich).

Jeffery, Charlie (2003) "The German Länder: From Milieu-Shaping to Territorial Politics", in Kenneth Dyson and Klaus H. Goetz (eds), *Germany, Europe and the Politics of Constraint. Proceedings of the British Academy*, No. 119 (Oxford: Oxford University Press), 97–108.

Jonung, Lars (2002) "EMU – the First 10 Years: Challenges to the Sustainability and Price Stability of the Euro Area – What Does History Tell Us?", in Marco Buti and André Sapir (eds), *EMU and Economic Policy in Europe. The Challenge of the Early Years*, European Commission (Cheltenham: Edward Elgar), 409–48.

Jupille, Joseph and **Caporaso**, James A. (1999) "Institutionalism and the European Union: Beyond International Relations and Comparative Politics", *Annual Review of Political Science 2*, 429–44.

Katzenstein, Peter (1984) *Corporatism and Change. Austria, Switzerland and the Politics of Change* (Ithaca: Cornwell University Press).

Katzenstein, Peter (1985) *Small States in World Markets. Industrial Policy in Europe* (Ithaca: Cornwell University Press).

Kenen, Peter B. (1969) "The Theory of Optimum Currency Areas: An Eclectic View", in Robert A. Mundell and Alexander K. Swoboda (eds), *Monetary Problems of the International Economy* (Chicago: University of Chicago), 41–60.

Keohane, Robert O. (1984) *After Hegemony. Cooperation and Discord in the World Political Economy* (Princeton, N.J.: Princeton University Press).

Keohane, Robert O. and **Milner**, Helen (eds) (1996) *Internationalization and Domestic Politics* (Cambridge: Cambridge University Press).

Keohane, Robert O. and **Nye**, Joseph N. (1977) *Power and Interdependence. World Politics in Transition* (Boston, MA: Little, Brown and Co).

Kitschelt, Herbert and **Streeck**, Wolfgang (2004) "From Stability to Stagnation: Germany at the Beginning of the Twenty-First Century", in Herbert Kitschelt and Wolfgang Streeck (eds), *Germany. Beyond the Stable State* (London: Frank Cass), 1–34.

Kitterer, Wolfgang (1999) "Public Finance and the Central Bank", in the Bundesbank (ed.), *Fifty Years of the Deutsche Mark* (Oxford: Oxford University Press), 165–217.

Knill, Christoph and **Lehmkuhl**, Dirk (1999) "How Europe Matters. Different Mechanisms of Europeanization", *European Integration Online Papers (EIoP)*, Vol. 3, No. 7, http://eiop.or.at/eiop/texte/1999-007a.htm.

Knill, Christoph and **Lehmkuhl**, Dirk (2002) "The National Impact of European Union Regulatory Policy: Three Europeanization Mechanisms", *European Journal of Political Research*, Vol. 41, No. 2, 255–80.

Knott, Jack H. (1981) *Managing the German Economy. Budgetary Politics in a Federal State* (Toronto: Lexington Books).

Korkman, Sixten (2001) "Fiscal Policy Coordination in EMU: Should It Go Beyond the SGP?", in Anne Brunila, Marco Buti and Daniele Franco (eds), *The Stability and Growth Pact. The Architecture of Fiscal Policy in EMU* (Basingstoke: Palgrave), 287–310.

Krasner, Stephen D. (1988) "Sovereignty: An Institutional Perspective", *Comparative Political Studies*, Vol. 26, 66–94.

Kydland, Finn E. and **Prescott**, Edward (1977) "Rules Rather Than Discretion: The Inconsistency of Optimal Plans", *Journal of Political Economy*, Vol. 85, No. 3, 473–91.

Ladrech, Robert (1994) "Europeanization of Domestic Politics and Institutions: The Case of France", *Journal of Common Market Studies*, Vol. 32, No. 1, 69–88.

Lees, Charles (1999) "The Red-Green Coalition", *German Politics*, Vol. 8, No. 2, 174–94.

Lees, Charles (2005) "The Law of Diminishing Returns? Environmental Policy in the Federal Republic of Germany", in Simon Green and William E. Paterson (eds), *Governance in Contemporary Germany. The Semi-Sovereign State Revisited* (Cambridge: Cambridge University Press), 212–38.

Leibfried, Stephan and **Obinger**, Herbert (2004) "The State of the Welfare State: German Social Policy between Macroeconomic Retrenchment and Microeconomic Recalibration", in Herbert Kitschelt and Wolfgang Streeck (eds), *Germany. Beyond the Stable State* (London: Frank Cass), 199–218.

Lodge, Martin (2003) "Competition Policy: From Centrality to Muddling Through?", in Kenneth Dyson and Klaus H. Goetz (eds), *Germany, Europe and the Politics of Constraint. Proceedings of the British Academy*, No. 119 (Oxford: Oxford University Press), 231–50.

Lord, Christopher (2003) "The European Parliament in the Economic Governance of the European Union", *Journal of Common Market Studies*, Vol. 41, No. 2, 249–67.

Maastricht Treaty (1992) "The Treaty of the European Union", *Official Journal C 191*, 29 July.

Maes, Ivo and **Quaglia**, Lucia (2003) "France and Italy's Policies on European Monetary Integration: A Comparison of 'Strong' and 'Weak' States", *EUI Working Papers, RSC No 2003/10*, Florence, Italy.

Manow, Philip and **Seils**, Eric (2000) "Adjusting Badly. The German Welfare State, Structural Change and the Open Economy", in Fritz W. Scharpf and Vivien A. Schmidt (eds), *Welfare and Work in the Open Economy. Diverse Responses to Common Challenges*, Vol. II (Oxford: Oxford University Press), 264–307.

March, James G. and **Olsen**, Johan P. (1984) "The New Institutionalism: Organizational Factors in Political Life", *American Political Science Review*, Vol. 78, 734–49.

March, James G. and **Olsen**, Johan P. (1989) *Rediscovering Institutions. The Organizational Basis of Politics* (New York: Macmillan).

Margedant, Udo (2003) "Die Föderalismusdiskussion in Deutschland", Das Parliament, B 29-30/2003, 14.7.2003, 6–13.

Marks, Gary and **Hooghe**, Liesbet (2001) *Multi-Level Governance and European Integration* (Lanham: Rowman & Littlefield).

Mattli, Walter (1999) *The Logic of Regional Integration. Europe and Beyond* (Cambridge: Cambridge University Press).

McKinnon, Ronald I. (1963) "Optimum Currency Area", *The American Economic Review*, Vol. LIII, September, No. 4, 717–25.

Mecklenburg-Vorpommern (2003) Finanzplan 2003–2007, Finanzministerium.

Milward, Alan S. (1994) *The European Rescue of the Nation-State* (London: Routledge).

Molle, Willem (1990) *The Economics of European Integration: Theory, Practice, Policy* (Aldershot: Dartmouth).

Molle, Willem (2001) *The Economics of European Integration: Theory, Practice, Policy*, 4th Edition (Aldershot: Dartmouth).

Le Monde (18.10.2002) "La France sera en minorité si elle n'est pas le levain de l'Europe: Dans un entretien au Monde, M. Prodi souligne qu'il n'y a pas de futur de l'Europe sans une alliance forte entre Paris et Berlin".

Moravcsik, Andrew (1993) "Preferences and Power in the European Community: A Liberal Intergovernmentalist Approach", *Journal of Common Market Studies*, Vol. 31, No. 4, 473–524.

Moravcsik, Andrew (1998) *The Choice for Europe: Social Purpose and State Power from Messina to Maastricht* (Ithaca, NY: Cornell University).

Mundell, Robert A. (1961) "A Theory of Optimum Currency Areas", *The American Economic Review*, Vol. LI. September, No. 4, 657–65.

Nice (2002) "The European Union Consolidated Versions of the Treaty on the European Union and of the Treaty Establishing the European Community", *Official Journal of the European Communities*, C 325/01, 24.12.2002.

Niedersachsen (2003) Finanzplan 2003 bis 2007, Niedersachsen.

Nordrhein-Westfalen (2003) Finanzplan 2003–2007 mit Finanzbericht 2004/2005, Nordrhein-Westfalen.

Nugent, Neill (1999) *The Government and Politics of the European Union*, 4th Edition, (Hampshire: Macmillan).

OECD (2003) *OECD Statistical Compendium 2003/02.*

Owen Smith, Eric (1994) *The German Economy* (London: Routledge).

Pierson, Paul (1996) "The Path to European Integration: A Historical Institutionalist Analysis", *Comparative Political Studies*, Vol. 29, No. 2, 123–62.

Pierson, Paul (2000a) "Increasing Returns, Path Dependence, and the Study of Politics", *American Political Science Review*, Vol. 94, No. 2, 215–67.

Pierson, Paul (2000b) "Not Just What, But When: Timing and Sequence in Political Processes", *Studies in American Political Development*, Vol. 14, 72–92.

Pierson, Paul (2004) *Politics in Time: History, Institutions and Social Analysis* (Princeton, N.J.: Princeton University Press).

Pollack, Mark A. (2001) "International Relations Theory and European Integration", *Journal of Common Market Studies*, Vol. 39, No. 2, 221–44.

Protocol on the Convergence Criteria Referred to in Article 109j of the Treaty Establishing the European Community (1992) Maastricht Treaty, Protocol No. 6, 7 February.

Protocol on the Excessive Deficit Procedurel (1992) Maastricht Treaty, Protocol No. 5, 7 February.

Protocol on the Statue of the European System of Central Banks and of the European Central Bank (1992) Maastricht Treaty, Protocol No. 3, 7 February.

Radaelli, Claudio M. (2000) "Whither Europeanization? Concept Stretching and Substantive Change", *European Integration Online Papers (EIoP)*, Vol. 4, No. 8, http://eiop.or.at/eiop/texte/2000-008a.htm.

Rheinland-Pfalz (2003) Finanzplan 2003–2007, Ministerium der Finanzen, Mainz.

Rhodes, R.A.W. (2001) *Understanding Governance. Policy Networks, Governance, Reflexivity and Accountability* (Buckingham: Open University).

Richardson, Jeremy (1996) "Actor-based Models of National and EU Policy Making: Policy Networks, Epistemic Communities and Advocacy Coalitions", in H. Kassim and A. Menon (eds), *The European Union and National Industrial Policy* (London: Routledge), 26–51.

Risse, Thomas, **Green Cowles**, Maria and **Caporaso**, James (2001) "Europeanization and Domestic Change: Introduction", in Maria Green Cowles, James Caporaso and Thomas Risse (eds), *Transforming Europe. Europeanization and Domestic Change* (Cornell University Press), 1–20.

Robson, Peter (1998) *The Economics of International Integration*, 4th Edition (London: Routledge).

Rogoff, Kenneth (1985) "Can International Monetary Policy Cooperation Be Counterproductive", *Journal of International Economics*, Vol. 18, 199–217.

Rosamond, Ben (2000) *Theories of European Integration* (Basingstoke: Macmillan).

Saarland (2003) Finanzplan (2003–2007), Ministerium für Finanzen.

Sachsen (2003) Finanzplan (2003–2007), Staatsministerium der Finanzen, Freistaat Sachsen.

Sachsen-Anhalt (2003) Finanzplan 2003–2007, Ministerium der Finanzen, Sachsen-Anhalt.

Sachverständigenrat (1990) Sachverständigenrat zur Begutachtung der gesamtwirtschaftlichen Entwicklung, Jahresgutachten 1990/91, Stuttgart.

Sachverständigenrat (1991) Sachverständigenrat zur Begutachtung der gesamtwirtschaftlichen Entwicklung, Jahresgutachten 1991/92, Stuttgart.

Sachverständigenrat (1995) Sachverständigenrat zur Begutachtung der gesamtwirtschaftlichen Entwicklung, Jahresgutachten 1995/96, Stuttgart.

Sachverständigenrat (1996) Sachverständigenrat zur Begutachtung der gesamtwirtschaftlichen Entwicklung, Jahresgutachten 1996/97, Stuttgart.

Sachverständigenrat (1997) Sachverständigenrat zur Begutachtung der gesamtwirtschaftlichen Entwicklung, Jahresgutachten 1997/98, Stuttgart.

Sachverständigenrat (1998) Sachverständigenrat zur Begutachtung der gesamtwirtschaftlichen Entwicklung, Jahresgutachten 1998/99, Stuttgart.

Sachverständigenrat (1999) Sachverständigenrat zur Begutachtung der gesamtwirtschaftlichen Entwicklung, Jahresgutachten 1999/00, Stuttgart.

Sachverständigenrat (2000) Sachverständigenrat zur Begutachtung der gesamtwirtschaftlichen Entwicklung, Jahresgutachten 2000/01, Stuttgart.

Sachverständigenrat (2001) Sachverständigenrat zur Begutachtung der gesamtwirtschaftlichen Entwicklung, Jahresgutachten 2001/02, Stuttgart.

Sachverständigenrat (2002) Sachverständigenrat zur Begutachtung der gesamtwirtschaftlichen Entwicklung, Jahresgutachten 2002/03, Stuttgart.

Sachverständigenrat (2003) Sachverständigenrat zur Begutachtung der gesamtwirtschaftlichen Entwicklung, Jahresgutachten 2003/04, Wiesbaden.

Sachverständigenrat (2004) Sachverständigenrat zur Begutachtung der gesamtwirtschaftlichen Entwicklung, Jahresgutachten 2004/05, Wiesbaden.

Scharpf, Fritz W. (1988) "The Joint-Decision Trap: Lessons from German Federalism and European Integration", *Public Administration*, Vol. 66, No. 3, 239–78.

Scharpf, Fritz W. (1996) "Negative and Positive Integration in the Political Economy of European Welfare State", in Gary Marks, Fritz W. Scharpf, Philippe C. Schmitter and Wolfgang Streeck (eds), *Governance in the European Union* (London: Sage), 15–39.

Scharpf, Fritz W. (1997) *Games Real Actors Play: Actor-Centered Institutionalism in Policy Research* (Boulder: Westview Press).

Scharpf, Fritz W. (2000a) "Economic Changes, Vulnerabilities and Institutional Capabilities", in Fritz W. Scharpf and Vivien A. Schmidt (eds), *Welfare and Work in the Open Economy. From Vulnerability to Competitiveness*, Vol. I (Oxford: Oxford University Press), 21–124.

Scharpf, Fritz W. (2000b) "Notes Towards a Theory of Multilevel Governing in Europe", The Max-Planck Institute, *MPIfG Discussion Paper 00/5*, Cologne, Germany.

Scharpf, Fritz W. (2004) "Der deutsche Föderalismus – reformbedürfig under reformierbar?", The Max-Planck Institute, *MPIfG Working Paper 04/2*, Cologne, Germany.

Scharrer, Hans-Eckart (2000) "Reasons for the Weak Euro", *Intereconomics*, Vol. 35, No. 5, September/October, 205–6.

Schimmelfennig, Frank (2001) "The Community Trap: Liberal Norms, Rhetorical Action, and the Eastern Enlargement of the European Union", *International Organization*, Vol. 55, No. 1, 47–80.

Schimmelfennig, Frank and **Sedelmeier**, Ulrich (2002) "Theorizing EU Enlargement: Research Focus, Hypotheses, and the State of Research", *Journal of European Public Policy*, Vol. 9, No. 4, 500–28.

Schlewig-Holstein (2003) Finanzplan 2003–2007, Finanzministerium.

Schmidt, Manfred G. (1998) "Sozialstaatliche Politik in der Ära Kohl", in Göttrik Wewer (hrsg.), *Bilanz der Ära Kohl. Christlich-liberale Politik in Deutschland 1982–1998* (Opladen: Leske + Budrich), 59–87.

Schmidt, Manfred G. (1999a) "Grundzüge der Sozialpolitik in der DDR", *Arbeitspapier Nummer 18/1999*, Zentrum für Sozialpolitik, Universität Bremen.

Schmidt, Manfred G. (1999b) Immer noch auf dem "mittleren Weg", Deutschlands Politische Ökonomie am Ende des 20, Jahrhunderts, Arbeitspapier Nummer 7/1999, Zentrum für Sozialpolitik, Universität Bremen.

Schmidt, Manfred G. (2000b) Thesen zur Reformpolitik im Föderalismus der Bundesrepublik Deutschland, Arbeitspapier Nummer 4/2000, Zentrum für Sozialpolitik, Universität Bremen.

Schmidt, Vivien A. (2000a) "Values and Discourse in the Politics of Adjustment", in Fritz W. Scharpf and Vivien A. Schmidt (eds), *Welfare and Work in the Open Economy. From Vulnerability to Competitiveness*, Vol. I (Oxford: Oxford University Press), 229–309.

Schmidt, Vivien A. (2001) "Europeanization and the Mechanics of Economic Policy Adjustment", *European Integration Online Papers (EIoP)*, Vol. 5, No. 6, http://eiop.or.at/eiop/texte/2001-006a.htm.

Schmidt, Vivien A. (2002) *The Futures of European Capitalism* (Oxford: Oxford University Press).

Schmidt, Vivien A. and **Radaelli**, Claudio M. (2004) "Policy Change and Discourse in Europe: Conceptual and Methodological Issues", *West European Politics*, Vol. 27, No. 2, 183–210.

Schmähl, Winfried (ed.) (1992) Sozialpolitik im Prozess der deutschen Vereinigung (Campus: Frankfurt).

Schmähl, Winfried (2002) "The '2001 Pension Reform' in Germany. A Paradigm Shift and Its Effects", Arbeitspapier Nummer 11/2002, Zentrum für Sozialpolitik, Bremen.

Schuknecht, Ludger (2002) "The Implementation of the Stability and Growth Pact", *OECD Journal of Budgeting*, Vol. 1, No. 3, 81–116.

Schwinn, Oliver (1997) Die Finanzierung der Deutschen Einheit, Ein Untersuchung aus institutionalistischer Perspektive (Opladen: Leske+Budrich).

Seeleib-Kaiser, Martin (2003) "Continuity or Change? Red-Green Social Policy after 16 Years of Christian-Democratic Rule", *Arbeitspapier Nummer 3/2003*, Zentrum für Sozialpolitik, Universität Bremen.

Seibel, Wolfgang (1998) "An Unavoidable Disaster? The German Currency Union of 1990", in Pat Gary and Paul 't Hart (eds), *Public Policy Disasters in Western Europe* (London: Routledge), 96–111.

Smith, Michael (1996) "The European Union and a Changing Europe: Establishing the Boundaries of Order", *Journal of Common Market Studies*, Vol. 34, No. 1, 5–28.

Smith, Mitchell P. (2005) "Introduction – From Modell Deutschland to Model Europa: Europe in Germany and Germany in Europe", *German Politics*, Vol. 14, No. 3, 275–82.

Solidarpaktfortführungsgesetz (2001) Gesetz zur Fortführung des Solidarpaktes, zur Neuordnung des bundesstaatlichen Finanzausgleichs und zur Abwicklung des Fonds "Deutsche Einheit", Solidarpaktfortführungsgesetz – SFG, Bundesgesetzblatt 2001 Teil I. S 3921, 20.12.2001.

SPD Programme (1998) "Arbeit, Innovation und Gerechtigkeit", SPD-Programm für die Bundestagswahl 1998, 17.4.1998, Leipzig, Germany.

Der Spiegel (29.12.2001) "Angst vor dem Neuen", 41–3.

Der Spiegel (23.6.2003) "Optimismus auf Pump", 28–9.

Stark, Jürgen (2001) "Genesis of a Pact", in Anne Brunila, Marco Buti and Daniele Franco (eds), *The Stability and Growth Pact. The Architecture of Fiscal Policy in EMU* (Basingstoke: Palgrave), 77–105.

Stark, Jürgen and **Remsperger**, Hermann (2004) "Budgetary Policy Rules. A Response to Criticism of the Stability Pact", Unpublished Working Paper, Bundesbank.

Steinmo, Sven, **Thelen**, Kathleen and **Longstreth**, Frank (eds) (1992) *Structuring Politics. Historical Institutionalism in Comparative Analysis* (Cambridge: Cambridge University Press).

Stern, Klaus (1999) "The Note-Issuing Bank within the State Structure", in the Bundesbank (ed.), *Fifty Years of the Deutsche Mark* (Oxford: Oxford University Press), 103–64.

Stolper, Gustav (1940) *German Economy 1870–1940* (New York: Reynal & Hitchcock).

Streeck, Wolfgang (1997) "German Capitalism: Does It Exist? Can It Survive?", in Colin Crouch and Wolfgang Streeck (eds), *Political Economy of Modern Capitalism. Mapping Convergence and Diversity* (London: Sage), 33–54.

Streeck, Wolfgang and **Hassel**, Anke (2004) "The Crumbling Pillars of Social Partnership", in Herbert Kitschelt and Wolfgang Streeck (eds), *Germany. Beyond the Stable State* (London: Frank Cass) 101–24.

Streeck, Wolfgang and **Heinze**, Rolf G. (1999) "Runderneuerung des deutschen Modells", in Hans-Jürgen Arlt and Sabine Nehls (eds), *Bündnis für Arbeit. Konstruktion, Kritik und Karriere.* (Opladen: Westdeutscher Verlag).

Streeck, Wolfgang and **Trampusch**, Christine (2005) "Economic Reform and the Political Economy of the German Welfare State", in Kenneth Dyson and Stephen Padgett (eds), *The Politics of Economic Reform in Germany* (Oxford: Routledge).

Streit, Manfred E. (1998) "Die deutsche Währungsunion", in Deutsche Bundesbank (ed.), *Fünfzig Jahre Deutsche Mark.* Notenbank und Währung in Deutschland seit 1948. C. H. Beck, 675–719.

Süddeutsche Zeitung (11.9.1995) "Waigel will Haushaltsdiszipline in der Währungsunion sichern".

Süddeutsche Zeitung (11.11.1995) "Zur Wahrung der Stabilität des künftigen Euro-Geldes: Waigel schlägt Strafen für Verstösse vor".

Süddeutsche Zeitung (23.11.1995) "Tietmeyer hofft auf raschen Stabilitätspakt".

Süddeutsche Zeitung (8.12.1995) "Tietmeyer ebenfalls für Maastricht-Ergänzung".

Süddeutsche Zeitung (18.12.1995) "Schöne Worte und geheime Ängste."

Süddeutsche Zeitung (25.1.1996) "Bündnis für Arbeit nimmt Gestalt an".

Süddeutsche Zeitung (29.1.1996) "Bericht über, Notprogramm' der Bundesregierung".

Süddeutsche Zeitung (1.2.1996) "Eine echte Steuerreform – wer's glaubt".

Süddeutsche Zeitung (9.2.1996) "Kohl umwirbt SPD für Kampf gegen Arbeitslosigkeit".

Süddeutsche Zeitung (13.3.1996) "Deutschland muss sich selbts noch qualifizieren".

Süddeutsche Zeitung (27.4.1996a) "Regierungserklärung und Bundestagsdebatte zum Sparprogramm".

Süddeutsche Zeitung (27.4.1996b) "Reaktionen auf das Sparprogramm der Bundesregierung".

Süddeutsche Zeitung (27.4.1996c) "SPD legt Alternativpapier vor".

Süddeutsche Zeitung (27.4.1996d) "Die umstrittenen Pläne der Bundesregierung".

Süddeutsche Zeitung (7.6.1996) "Mehr als 80000 Menschen gehen auf die Strasse. Protest gegen Sparpläne wächst".

Süddeutsche Zeitung (12.6.1996a) "Beim Treffen der Ministerpräsidented mit Kohl Länder legen kein eigenes Sparkonzept vor".

Süddeutsche Zeitung (12.6.1996b) "DGB kritisiert erneut Bonner Vorhaben, Sparpaket teils verfassungswidrig".

Süddeutsche Zeitung (13.6.1996) "Waigel: Stabilitätskriterien des Maastrichter Vertrages müssen erfüllt werden".

Süddeutsche Zeitung (14.6.1996) "Ministerpräsidenten bei Bundekanzler Kohl".

Süddeutsche Zeitung (14.9.1996) "Gesetze über Sozialkürzungen können in Kraft treten. Kanzlermerhheit setzt das Sparpaket durch".

Süddeutsche Zeitung (18.9.1996) "Deutsch-französischer Rat erörtert Probleme der geplanten Währungsunion".

Süddeutsche Zeitung (2.10.1996) "Massiver Protest gegen Lohnkürzung bei Krankheit".

Süddeutsche Zeitung (22.1.1997) "Rexrodts Prognose für 1997. Mehr Wacstum und noch mehr Arbeitslose".

Süddeutsche Zeitung (5.10.1998) "Schwierige Koalitionsverhandlungen erwartet".

Süddeutsche Zeitung (20.10.1998) "Koalitionsvertrag von SPD und Grünen".

Süddeutsche Zeitung (8.2.1999) "Lafontaine: Stabilitätspakt für Euro-Länder revidieren".

Süddeutsche Zeitung (11.2.1999) "Europa aus der Welt der Träume in die Realität führen".

Süddeutsche Zeitung (17.2.1999) "EU-Kommission kritisiert deutsches Stabilitätsprogramm".

Süddeutsche Zeitung (13.3.1999) "Lieber Sorgfalt als Tempo".

Süddeutsche Zeitung (15.3.1999) "Ich bin der Herr, dein Kanzler".

Süddeutsche Zeitung (19.5.1999) "EZB warnt Finanzpolitiker im Euro-Raum".

Süddeutsche Zeitung (29.5.1999) "Nach Eichels Konzept zur Ausgaben-Kürzung".

Süddeutsche Zeitung (4.6.1999) "Duisenberg sieht Potential für Kursanstieg".

Süddeutsche Zeitung (26.6.1999) "SZ-Interview mit Bundesfinanzminister Hans Eichel. Überlebensfrage für die Rot-Grün".

Süddeutsche Zeitung (12.7.1999) "Minister hält an Sparprogramm fest. Eichel sieht Kommunen nicht belastet".

Süddeutsche Zeitung (16.7.1999) "Städtetages Präsident trifft Bundesregierung. Sparpaket geht zu Lasten der Kommunen".

Süddeutsche Zeitung (28.7.1999) "Bündnis für Finanzverantwortung vorgeschlagen. Kommunen verlangen Mitspracherecht bei Sparplänen".

Süddeutsche Zeitung (1.9.1999) "Bundesfinanzminister setzt sich durch. Widerstand in der SPD gegen Eichel schwindet".

Süddeutsche Zeitung (3.9.1999) "Diskussion über Sparpaket".

Süddeutsche Zeitung (6.9.1999) "Streit um das Sparpaket. Finanzminister Eichel attackiert die Union".

Süddeutsche Zeitung (13.11.1999) "Ernst Welteke zur Haushalt- und Finanzpolitik".

Süddeutsche Zeitung (29.12.1999) "Fraktion steht hinter Eichles Steuerplänen".

Süddeutsche Zeitung (18.2.2000a) "Opposition kritisiert, verheerende Bilanz".

Süddeutsche Zeitung (18.2.2000b) "'Mitschuld and Euro-Schwäche'. Opposition kritisiert den Jahreswirtschaftsbericht der Regierung".

Süddeutsche Zeitung (23.3.2000) "SZ-Interview mit Bundesfinanzminister Hans Eichel über die künftige Haushaltspolitik".

Süddeutsche Zeitung (2.5.2000) "Wirtschaftsdaten glanzvoll wie lange nicht".
Süddeutsche Zeitung (30.8.2000) "SZ-Interview mit Bundesbankpräsident Ernst Welteke".
Süddeutsche Zeitung (13.9.2000) "Auftakt der viertätigen Haushaltsberatungen im Bundestag".
Süddeutsche Zeitung (6.2.2001) "Interview mit Pedro Solber über die Euro-Einführung".
Süddeutsche Zeitung (26.6.2001) "Schröder schließt Konjunkturprogramm aus".
Süddeutsche Zeitung (4.9.2001) "Bund soll 2002 weniger ausgeben als geplant".
Süddeutsche Zeitung (19.9.2001) "Bundesfinanzminister Eichel gegen Hektik in der Steuerpolitik".
Süddeutsche Zeitung (5.11.2001) "Eichel fehlen 15 Milliarden DM".
Süddeutsche Zeitung (7.11.2001) "EU-Finanzminister beraten über Wachstumsschwäche".
Süddeutsche Zeitung (28.11.2001) "Opposition weist Regierung Schuld an der Wirtschafskrise an".
Süddeutsche Zeitung (11.1.2002) "SZ-Interview mit Otmar Issing".
Süddeutsche Zeitung (29.1.2002) "EU-Kommission will Deutschland wegen Neuverschuldung verwarnen".
Süddeutsche Zeitung (31.1.2002) "EU-Kommission verwarnt Berlin".
Süddeutsche Zeitung (2.2.2002) "Schreyer: EU-Warnung für Defizit akzeptieren".
Süddeutsche Zeitung (9.2.2002) "Frühwarnung strittig bis zur letzten Minute".
Süddeutsche Zeitung (13.2.2002a) "Solbes verlorene Schlacht".
Süddeutsche Zeitung (13.2.2002b) "Blauer Brief abgewendet".
Süddeutsche Zeitung (18.3.2002) "Eichel will Ländern Sparen verordnen".
Süddeutsche Zeitung (6.9.2002) "Reparieren, ohne zu zerstören".
Süddeutsche Zeitung. (9.10.2002) "Treffen der Finanzminister. Euro-Staaten rügen Frankreich".
Süddeutsche Zeitung (18.10.2002) "Wegen mangelnder Flexibilität".
Süddeutsche Zeitung (19.10.2002) "Kommissionspräsident nennt Stabilitätspakt dumm".
Süddeutsche Zeitung (21.10.2002a) "Eichel und Fischer für flexibleren Stabilitätspakt".
Süddeutsche Zeitung (21.10.2002b) "Wirtschaftspolitik zentral koordinieren".
Süddeutsche Zeitung (5.11.2002) "Finanzminister beraten über Stabilitätspakt".
Süddeutsche Zeitung (20.11.2002) "Schulden und Sühne. EU-Kommission leitet Defizit-Strafverfahren gegen Deutschland ein".
Süddeutsche Zeitung (27.11.2002) "SZ-Interview mit Wirtschafts-Nobelpreisträger Milton Friedman. Deutschland braucht eine Dosis Deflation".
Süddeutsche Zeitung (2.12.2002) "SZ-Gespräch zur Haushaltspolitik. Bundesbank-Vize Stark kritisiert Regierung".
Süddeutsche Zeitung (24.12.2002) "Ich bin Kanzler, kein Philosoph, ich rede lieber konkret".
Süddeutsche Zeitung (27.12.2002) "Interview mit Bayerns Finanzminister Kurt Faltlhauser (CSU) über den Tarifstreit im Öffentlichen Dienst".
Süddeutsche Zeitung (14.1.2003) "Wirtschaft verurteilt Abkehr vom Sparkurs".
Süddeutsche Zeitung (19.4.2003) "Eichel gibt Risiken für Etatplan zu".
Süddeutsche Zeitung (5.5.2003) "Stabilitätspakt unter Obhut der EU-Kommission".
Süddeutsche Zeitung (16.5.2003) "Wir leben über unsere Verhältnisse".
Süddeutsche Zeitung (30.5.2003) "Keine Lobby will sparen, alle wolle nur ein Kuchenstück".

Süddeutsche Zeitung (16.6.2003) "Koalition in Klausur".
Süddeutsche Zeitung (24.6.2003) "Metzger: Weder Lüger noch Wahrheit".
Süddeutsche Zeitung (11.7.2003) "Duisenberg fordert Neuordnung der Finanzen".
Süddeutsche Zeitung (19.8.2003) "Bundesbank dämpft Konjunktur-Optimismus".
Süddeutsche Zeitung (15.11.2003) "Eichel attackiert EU-Kommission".
Süddeutsche Zeitung (14.1.2004) "EU-Kommission verklagt die Finanzminister".
Süddeutsche Zeitung (2.2.2004) "Bessere Zahlen".
Süddeutsche Zeitung (10.2.2004) "SZ-Interview mit Otmar Issing".
Süddeutsche Zeitung (19.5.2004) "Deutsche Bahn will zurück zur 40-Stunden-Woche".
Süddeutsche Zeitung (27.5.2004) "Deutschland soll EU-Stimmrecht verlieren".
Süddeutsche Zeitung (5.7.2004a) "Höhere Zinsen stellen Staat vor Herausforderung".
Süddeutsche Zeitung (5.7.2004b) "Kanzler für flexible Lösung".
Süddeutsche Zeitung. 21.3.2005) "Ökonomischer, rationaler, wachstumsorientierter".
Szczerbiak, Aleks and **Taggart**, Paul (2000) "Opposing Europe: Party Systems and Opposition to the Union, the Euro and Europeanisation", Sussex European Institute, *Working Paper No. 36* (Brighton: University of Sussex).
Taggart, Paul (1998) "A Touchstone of Dissent: Euroscepticism in Contemporary Western European Party Systems", *European Journal of Political Research*, Vol. 33, 363–88.
Taggart, Paul and **Szczerbiak**, Aleks (2004) "Contemporary Euroscepticism in the Party Systems of the EU Candidate States of Central and Eastern Europe", *European Journal of Political Research*, Vol. 43, No. 1.
Thaysen, Uwe (2003) "Der deutsche Föderalismus zwischen zwei Konventen", Das Parliament, B 29-30/2003, 14.7.2003, 14–23.
Thüringen (2003) Mittelfristiger Finanzplan für die Jahre 2003 bis 2007, Thüringen.
Timmins, Graham (2000) "Alliance for Jobs: Labour Market Policy and Industrial Relations after the 1998 Elections", in Rebecca Harding and William E. Paterson (eds), *The future of the German Economy: An End to the Miracle?* (Manchester: Manchester University Press), 36–53.
Tsoukalis, Loukas (1993) *The New European Economy. The Politics and Economics of Integration*, 2nd Revised Edition (Oxford: Oxford University Press).
Verfassungsgerichtshof (2003) "Urteil des Verfassungsgerichtshof des Landes Berlin", *VerfGH 125/02*, 31.10.2003.
Virén, Matti (2000) "Fiscal Policy, Automatic Stabilisers and Policy Coordination in EMU", The Research Institute of the Finnish Economy, *Discussion Papers*, No. 744, Helsinki.
Virén, Matti (2001) "Fiscal Policy, Automatic Stabilisers and Coordination", in Anne Brunila, Marco Buti and Daniele Franco (eds), *The Stability and Growth Pact. The Architecture of Fiscal Policy in EMU* (Basingstoke: Palgrave), 259–86.
Wallace, William (1982) "Europe as a Confederation: The Community and the Nation-State", *Journal of Common Market Studies*, Vol. 21, No. 1 & 2, 57–68.
Weimer, Wolfram (1998) Deutsche Wirtschaftsgeschichte, Von der Währungsreform bis zum Euro, Hoffmann & Campe.
Wessels, Wolfgang (1997) "An Ever Closer Fusion? A Dynamic Macropolitical View on Integration Processes", *Journal of Common Market Studies*, No. 2, 267–99.
Wessels, Wolfgang and **Linsenmann**, Ingo (2002) "EMU's Impact on National Institutions. Fusion towards a 'gouvernance economique' or fragmentation?", in Kenneth Dyson (ed.), *European States and the Euro. Europeanisatio, Variation and Convergence* (Oxford: Oxford University Press), 53–77.

Wewer, Göttrik (ed.) (1998) *Bilanz der Ära Kohl. Christlich-liberale Politik in Deutschland 1982–1998* (Opladen: Leske + Budrich).

Wiesenthal, Helmut (2004) "German Unification and 'Model Germany': An Adventure in Institutional Conservatism", in Herbert Kitschelt and Wolfgang Streeck (eds), *Germany. Beyond the Stable State* (London: Frank Cass), 37–58.

Willett, Thomas D. (1999) "A Political Economy Analysis of the Maastricht and Stability Pact Fiscal Criteria", in Andrew Hughes Hallett, Michael M. Hutchison and Jensen Svend E. Hougaard (eds), *Fiscal Aspects of European Monetary Integration* (Cambridge: Cambridge University Press), 37–66.

Winkler, Bernhard (1996) "Towards a Strategic View on EMU: A Critical Survey", *Journal of Public Policy*, Vol. 16, No. 1, 1–28.

Die Zeit (17.11.1995) "Kulturkampf der Geldhüter".

Die Zeit (19.1.1996) "Maastricht auf der Kippe".

Die Zeit (14.6.1996) "Bonner Kulisse".

Die Zeit (15.11.1996) "Die Märkte zittern".

Die Zeit (22.11.1996) "Stabilität ohne Wachstum".

Die Zeit (13.12.1996) "Frank und fröhlich".

Die Zeit (20.12.1996) "Der Stabilitätspakt wird Bonn noch viel Ärger mit den Bundesländern einbringen".

Die Zeit (24.1.1997) "Der Präsident der Bundesbank is die zentrale Figur in einem deutsch-französischen Drama".

Die Zeit (21.2.1997) "Im Clinch mit dem Club Med".

Die Zeit (14.3.1997) "Die Macht am Main".

Die Zeit (28.3.1997) "Das Nullsummenspiel".

Die Zeit (7.5.1998) "Die Dolchstosslegende".

Die Zeit (12.11.1998) "Zankapfel Bundesbank".

Die Zeit (23.5.2005) "Schröder will Neuwahlen im Bund".

Zohlnhöfer, Reimut (1999) "Der lange Schatten der schönen Illusion: Finanzpolitik nach der deutschen Einheit", *Leviathan*, Vol. 28, 14–28.

Zohlnhöfer, Reimut (2001) *Die Wirtschaftspolitik der Ära Kohl* (Opladen: Leske+Budrich).

Index